T0320231

MULTIMEDIA AND REGIONAL ECONOMIC RESTRUCTURING

Since the explosion of multimedia, the creation and promotion of multimedia clusters has become a target for regional development strategies across the globe. This work offers the first inter-regional comparision of the multimedia industry.

Analysing thirteen American, European and Asian regions, leading academics examine factors which drive the emergence of multimedia clusters and processes by which they are formed. Each case is considered in the context of the globalizing industry, and issues discussed include:

- spatial distribution
- human resource supply and development
- networks, globalization and strategies of innovation
- institutional support structures
- new media policies and the role of the state
- regional embeddedness (organic or artificial)
- industrial restructuring
- uneven urban and regional development
- governance and sociotechnical constituencies
- regional companies in national projects.

The regional comparative approach taken by the authors will ensure that *Multimedia and Regional Economic Restructuring* holds a place of particular importance in the literature of this field. This ground-breaking work will be of value to researchers in business, technology, economics and industrial sociology.

Hans-Joachim Braczyk, Gerhard Fuchs and **Hans-Georg Wolf** are all based at the Center of Technology Assessment in Baden-Württemberg, Stuttgart, Germany. Hans-Joachim Braczyk also holds a chair of industrial sociology at the University of Stuttgart.

ROUTLEDGE STUDIES IN THE MODERN WORLD ECONOMY

ROUTLEDGE STUDIES IN THE WORLD ECONOMY

MULTIMEDIA AND REGIONAL ECONOMIC RESTRUCTURING

Edited by
Hans-Joachim Braczyk,
Gerhard Fuchs
and Hans-Georg Wolf

London and New York

First published 1999
by Routledge
2 Park Square, Milton Park, Abingdon, Oxon, OX14 4RN

Simultaneously published in the USA and Canada
by Routledge
270 Madison Ave, New York NY 10016

Routledge is an imprint of the Taylor & Francis Group

Transferred to Digital Printing 2005

Typeset in Garamond
by Curran Publishing Services

British Library Cataloguing in Publication Data
A catalogue record for this book is available from the
British Library

Library of Congress Cataloguing in Publication Data
Multimedia and regional economic restructuring / edited by Hans-
Joachim Braczyk, Gerhrd Fuchs and Hans-Georg Wolf
448 p. 15.6 x 23.4 cm
Includes bibliographical references and index.
1. Multimedia systems industry – Case studies. 2. Regional eco-
nomics – Case studies. I. Braczyk, Hans-Joachim, 1942–
II. Fuchs, Gerhard, 1958– . III. Wolf, Hans-Georg, 1964–
HD9696.M842M85   1999   98–51215
338.4'70067—dc21   CIP

ISBN 0–415–19857–7

CONTENTS

CONTENTS

CONTENTS

FIGURES

MAPS

TABLES

CONTRIBUTORS

Hans-Joachim Braczyk worked at the Freie Universität of Berlin, at the Technological University of Berlin, at the Institute of Social Research in Dortmund, at the University of Bielefeld and as Director of the ASIF Institute of Bielefeld which he founded. Since 1992 he has been a member of the board of the Center of Technology Assessment in Baden-Württemberg and head of the department 'Technology, Organization, Work'. His work focuses on changes in industry and the transformation to a service and information society. He holds a Chair of Industrial Sociology at the University of Stuttgart.

Shauna Brail recently completed her PhD in Economic Geography at the University of Toronto. Her dissertation explored the emergence and evolution of the multimedia industry in Toronto and compared the regional economic geography of Toronto's multimedia industry to multimedia clusters in New York and San Francisco. She is currently working in the Commerce Practice Area at The Boston Consulting Group.

Philip Cooke is Professor of Regional Development and Director, Centre for Advanced Studies, Cardiff University, Wales (UK). He is editor of *European Planning Studies*, a journal of spatial theory, empirics and policy. He recently co-authored *The Associational Economy* (Oxford University Press 1998) and co-edited *Regional Innovation Systems* (UCL Press 1998). As coordinator of the major EU-DG12-TSER project on 'Regional Innovation Systems: Designing for the Future, he is co-author with P. Boekholt and F. Toedtling of the forthcoming book *The Governance of Innovation in Europe: Regional Perspectives on Global Competitiveness* (Pinter).

Edmund Egan is a Senior Associate with the Economic Strategy Group of ICF Kaiser International, Inc., which specializes in cluster-based regional development strategy. In 1997 he earned his Ph.D. in City and Regional Planning from the University of California at Berkeley. His doctoral dissertation, entitled *The Spatial Dynamics of the US Computer Software Industry*, was the first statistical analysis of spatial trends in the US software industry. Since joining ICF Kaiser in 1996, he has continued his research interests in information technology and structural economic change, and has managed research projects into the determinants of US regional economic competitiveness, and the locational strategies and economic impacts of global companies.

Gerhard Fuchs studied economics, political science and sociology at the Ludwig Maximilians University, Munich. He has held teaching and research positions at the Ludwig Maximilians University, Northwestern University, Evanston/Il., and the Max Planck Institute for the Study of Societies. Since 1994 he has worked at the Center of Technology Assessment in Baden-Württemberg. He has published in the fields of technology policy, information and communication technologies and international political economy.

Meric Gertler is Professor of Geography and Planning at the University of Toronto, where he is also Co-Director of the Program on Globalization and Regional Innovation Systems in the Centre for International Studies. His current research focuses on the role of culture and institutions in local and regional economic change. He has served recently as a consultant to the European Commission and the OECD on topics related to innovation, technology transfer, learning and regional development.

Wolf Heydebrand is Professor of Sociology at New York University. He received his M.A. (1961) and Ph.D. (1965) in sociology from the University of Chicago. His current research interests include the theory of social networks, the processes of innovation in large-scale organizations, and the impact of economic globalization on the rule of law in Europe and the United States.

Josef Hilbert is head of the Service Sector Department at the Institute of Work and Technology (Science Center North Rhine-Westphalia), Gelsenkirchen (Germany). His research activities focus on innovation and re-engineering in social services.

Hing Ai Yun teaches at the Department of Sociology, National University of Singapore. She is currently researching new work forms, emerging social forms and family policies.

Gwawr Hughes is a researcher and Ph.D. candidate at the Centre for Advanced Studies, Cardiff University, Wales (UK). Specializing in the investigation of business networking among SMEs and the role of enterprise support policies, her research involves comparative evaluations of networking programs in Scandinavia and the UK. Winner of the Saunders Lewis Memorial Prize in 1996, she is the author of a number of research reports and articles in journals such as *Firm Connections*.

Mika Kautonen is a researcher at the Work Research Centre at the University of Tampere, Finland.

Tony Kinder is Chair of the Strategic Service Committee of the West Lothian Council in Scotland, overseeing economic development in 'Silicon Glen.' He is director of a venture capital company and an industrial property development company, and is active in training initiatives. His research interests include economic clustering, national systems of innovation, and diffusion of lean production.

Alfonso Molina is Reader in Innovation and Management of Technology and Director of the Technology Management and Policy Programme (TechMaPP) at the University of Edinburgh. Research interests focus on theoretical approaches to the understanding of technological development and innovation, with particular application to a wide range of information and communications technologies. He has written extensively on these themes and worked on numerous occasions for various directorates of the European Community.

Richard Naylor works at the Centre for Urban and Regional Development Studies (CURDS) in Newcastle upon Tyne, UK. He is a Junior Research Associate whose interests lie in the urban and regional development implications of new information and communication technologies. His current work focuses on the Internet and electronic commerce in particular.

Jürgen Nordhause-Janz is a social scientist and senior researcher at the Industrial Development Department at the Institute of Work and Technology (Science Center North Rhine-Westphalia), Gelsenkirchen (Germany). His research activities focus on innovation and structural change.

John V. Pavlik is the Executive Director of the Center for New Media at Columbia University's Graduate School of Journalism, where he is also a professor, and senior fellow at the San Diego Supercomputer Center. His publications include *Video on Demand Systems: Technology, Interoperability and Trials* (co-edited by Shih-Fu Chang, Dimitris Anastassious and Alexandros Eleftheriadis) (Kluwer 1997), *New Media Technology: Cultural and Commercial Perspectives*, (Allyn and Bacon, Simon and Schuster Education Group, 2nd edn. 1998), *The People's Right to Know: Media, Democracy and the Information Highway* (with Frederick Williams; translated into Japanese by Sangyo-Tosho), *Demystifying Media Technology* (with Everette E. Dennis) and *Public Relations: What Research Tells Us*. He has also authored more than a dozen computer software packages for education in journalism and communication. He is a Faculty Research Fellow, Columbia Institute for Tele-Information (CITI), Columbia University School of Business, and a Faculty Associate,

Institute for Learning Technologies, Teachers College. He chairs the Columbia University Web Advisory Committee.

Henrik Räsänen is presently serving as a Research Fellow at the Tampere University of Technology, Finland. Prior to this he was the Director of the IT-Centre of Expertise, which is an IT-related virtual science park. He has solid industrial international executive experience in the high-technology field.

Dieter Rehfeld is a senior researcher at the Industrial Development Department at the Institute of Work and Technology (Science Center North Rhine-Westphalia), Gelsenkirchen (Germany). His research activities focus on production clusters and regional change.

Åke Sandberg is an associate professor at the Arbetslivsinstitutet (the National Institute for Working Life) in the field of work organization and information technology. He is presently engaged in studies of production and employment in the new media industry in Sweden.

AnnaLee Saxenian is an internationally-recognized scholar of regional development. Her research on technology regions such as California's Silicon Valley, Boston's Route 128, and Cambridge, England has been published in the *California Management Review, Technology Review, Inc.*, and a wide range of academic and trade journals. Her book *Regional Advantage: Culture and Competition in Silicon Valley and Route 128* (Harvard University Press, 1994) received the Association of American Publishers award for best professional and scholarly book of 1994 in the category of business and management. She is a professor in the Department of City and Regional Planning at the University of California at Berkeley. She has held teaching positions at the Massachusetts Institute of Technology (MIT), Harvard, and the Chinese University of Hong Kong. She holds a doctorate in Political Science from MIT, a master's degree in City and Regional Planning from the University of California at Berkeley, and a bachelor's degree in economics from Williams College in Massachusetts.

Gerd Schienstock is currently working as a research professor at the Work Research Centre at the University of Tampere, Finland. His research focuses on regional innovation systems, work organization and management systems, technology assessment, and the information society.

Allen J. Scott is professor in the Department of Public Policy and the Department of Geography at the University of California – Los Angeles. He has published widely on issues of urban and regional development and related policy questions. His latest book is *Regions and the World Economy* (Oxford University Press 1998).

Rolf Sternberg is Professor of Economic Geography and Head of the Department of Economic and Social Geography, Faculty of Economics and Social Sciences, University of Cologne. He studied Geography and received his first degree and PhD. from the University of Hannover. He has also taught in the Department of Geography at the Technical University of Munich. His research focuses on the consequences of technological change and the implications of technology policies for regional development. He has authored (1988) and co-authored (1996/7) two books on German science parks, and a book on the impact of national technology policies on the development of high-tech regions in the US, UK, Germany, Japan, and France. Currently he is involved in a EU Fourth Framework 'Targeted socio-economic research' project on 'Networks, collective learning and RTD in regionally-clustered high-technology SMEs'.

Detlev Sträter studied sociology, political science, finance and public law in Marburg as well as regional and urban planning in Karlsruhe. Dr. Sträter is senior research Fellow at the IMU-Institute for Media Research and Urban Studies in Munich. He focuses on the development of regional industry, labour markets and regional economic structure, media and telecommunications research.

Puay Tang is a political scientist with a Ph.D in International Relations from the Johns Hopkins University. She is a Research Fellow at the Science Policy Research University (SPRU), University of Sussex, UK, focusing on the management of intellectual property rights and the application and development of new information and communication technologies. She also works on electronic commerce and its implications for regulatory issues and business activities, and on the evaluation of science and technology policy. She is on the editorial board of the journal *ICS* and has advised the UK Parliamentary Office on Science and Technology on 'electronic government.'

Hans-Georg Wolf studied public administration and received a doctorate in sociology. As a researcher in the Center of Technology Assessment in Stuttgart, he works on information and communications technologies and regional economies. He has published in the fields of sociology of science, technology and organizations.

ACKNOWLEDGEMENTS

The chapters in this book are based on papers prepared for the International Conference on Multimedia and Regional Economic Restructuring, held at the Center of Technology Assessment in Baden-Württemberg, Stuttgart, 8–11 October 1997. Authors and editors have profited from the discussion and the contributions of participants in the workshop, which gathered researchers from a variety of disciplines.

The contributors have substantially revised and, as far as possible, updated their papers in the light of the discussion at the Conference, and we are grateful to them for the attention they have given to this task, and to the discussants at the conference as well as the referees which provided detailed comments.

We would like to thank especially the following reviewers for their time and efforts: Edgar Grande, Technical University Munich; Åke Sandberg, National Institute for Working Life Solna; Allen J. Scott, University of California Los Angeles.

Special thanks are also owed to a number of people who have given us valuable support at various times during the preparation of this book. Monika Baumunk read carefully all the manuscripts and provided logistical support, Larry Martinez helped with checking language problems, Christine Ehrhardt organized the communication with the authors and urged them to stick to the deadlines, Sandra Wassermann gave valuable research support, Simone Grünig was responsible for formatting and harmonizing the texts and Raphael Menez did the final editing of the book and was in charge of all issues related to maps, tables and figures. Without the help of all these people the book could not have been produced.

In addition we would like to thank Routledge and its editorial staff, namely Elizabeth Brown, for their good cooperation in producing the book.

The editors

ACRONYMS

ASP	Amsterdam Science Park
ATM	asynchronous transfer mode
BAMP	Bay Area Multimedia Partnership
CAPTAIN	Character and Pattern Telephone Access Information Network System (Japan)
CATV	Cable TV
CBDC	Cardiff Bay Development Corporation
CBT	computer based training
CEO	chief executive officer
CIM	computer integrated manufacturing
CMA	Census Metropolitan Area (Toronto)
CorpTech	Corporate Technology Information Services, US
CWI	Centrum voor Wiskunde en Informatica, Amsterdam
DCS	digital cellular system
DMI	Digital Media Institute, research unit of Tampere University of Technology
DTI	Department of Trade and Industry (UK)
DVDs	digital video disks
EDB	Economic Development Board (Singapore)
EDI	electronic data interchange
EDP	electronic data processing
ERC	Engineering Research Center (New York)
FDI	Foreign Direct Investment/Investors
FIRE	financial (banking), insurance, and real estate
FTE	full time employee
GSM	global system for mobile communications
GTA	Greater Toronto Area
HBO	Hoger Beroepsonderwijs
HTML	Hypertext Markup Language
IAT	Institut für Arbeit und Technik (Germany)
IC2	Institute at the University of Texas at Austin
I-commerce	Internet commerce
ICT	information and communication technologies
IHK	Chamber of Industry and Commerce (Munich and Upper Bavaria)
IICS	International Interactive Communications Society

IMAS	Interactive Media Association of Scotland
IMAT	Interactive Multimedia Arts and Technologies Association (Canada)
IMU	Institut für Medienforschung und Urbanistik
I-Networks	innovation networks
INS	Information Network System (Japan)
ISDN	integrated services digital network
ISP	Internet service provider
ITP	Interactive Telecommunications Programme (NYU)
ITT	International Telephone and Telegraph
iTV	interactive TV
IVSS	Interactive Video Services Stuttgart
LMDS	local multipoint distribution system
MDA	Multimedia Development Association
MFG	Medien- und Filmgesellschaft Baden-Württemberg
MILIA	annual multimedia conference, Cannes, France
MITI	Ministry of International Trade and Industry (Japan)
MM	Multimedia
MOC	Ministry of Construction (Japan)
MPEG	Motion Pictures Experts Group (develops global standards for compressed digital video)
NCB	National Computer Board (Singapore)
NII	national information infrastructure (Singapore)
NRW	North Rhine-Westphalia
NTT	Nippon Telegraph and Telephone
NYITC	New York Information Technology Center
NYNMA	New York New Media Association
NYU	New York University
PCS	personal communications services
PMR	PMR Group, Inc.
PoP	Point of Presence
PTO	public telecommunications operators
SIC	Standard Industrial Classification
SICS	Swedish Institute of Computer Science Intelligent Systems Lab
SIGGRAPH	Association of Computing Machinery's Special Interest Group on Computer Graphics
SISU	Swedish Institute for Systems Development
SME	small or medium enterprise
STC	sociotechnical constituencies analysis
TCI	Tele-Communications Inc.
TIME	telecommunication, information technologies, media industry and electronics
TUT	Tampere University of Technology
UNIX	AT&T Bell Laboratories operating system
USENET	user's network
WDA	Welsh Development Agency
WWW	World Wide Web

1

INTRODUCTION

Hans-Joachim Braczyk, Gerhard Fuchs
and Hans-Georg Wolf

In recent years, the emergence of an information society on a global scale has been heralded as one of the most promising developments for spurring technology, economic growth, job creation, and socio-political change in virtually all advanced industrialized countries (see Castells 1996). Countries, regions, and localities are eager to transform themselves into digital societies. Better than any other configuration, the Internet represents the three main points of reference that show quite clearly the specificity and enormous potential of the information society:

1   The electronic inter-connectivity of almost any place of the globe.
2   An interactive electronic communication allowing almost anybody to contact anybody else.
3   Devices for integrated access, processing and display of different types of data and media such as audio, video, images, graphics and texts.

These three properties provide communicative opportunities that have never existed before in the history of mankind. Not surprisingly, advocates of the information society are enthusiastically drawing a picture of a utopian digital future which for the first time could mean the end of inequalities and imbalances in social life, and of unequal opportunity for economic, political and social participation. Literature in this tradition contains an impressive collection of ideas, concepts, dreams and visions, along with some useful information. In most cases, however, such books consist of questionable forecasts and normative descriptions of how the world would or should look, if developments take the direction the authors favour. However, as long as the story of the future is presented in the light of what is technically possible, or might be possible the next time around, it will never be an adequate representation of events to come.

Leaving aside what might happen in a more or less distant future, the present volume, in its core, focuses on empirical observations of the most recent evolution of an important segment of a global information society.

1

This segment, whose contours admittedly cannot yet be sharply drawn, is termed multimedia. Irrespective of the definition provided (see below), multimedia comprises both an opulent bundle of wishes, expectations and hopes with respect to a range of advantages claimed for the information society and measurable relations with respect to the interconnectivity, interactivity and integration of different media.

The chapters of this book highlight fifteen urban centres, regions and countries in the USA, Canada, South East Asia, and Europe. They analyse, describe and critically assess the very recent emergence of a multimedia industry in the areas under investigation. Before we unfold the book's concept it is necessary to reflect on the phenomenon of globalization. This is strongly associated with the idea of an information society. It is also the victim of some unnecessarily misleading interpretations about what is going on in the world we are living in.

The economic structure, the technological capabilities and the political shape of modern industrialized countries have been exposed, it is said, to the regime of a process which spans the globe, blurring the boundaries of nations and continents, and penetrating institutional limitations. There is rivalry among obviously distinct types of capitalism. Scholars and intellectuals distinguish between a shareholder-value economy and a consensus-driven economy attributing the former to the USA and the United Kingdom, the latter to Japan, Germany and most of the other Western European countries. The latter are faced with continuing or even increasing discrepancies between their labour market figures and those of the former, with the USA taking the lead with an impressive job growth and an equally impressive low rate of unemployment during the recent decade. The consensus-oriented countries thus continue to face considerable pressure to change and are undergoing a more or less far-reaching transition of their economies as well as of several of their most basic societal institutions.

At first glance, this process of transition could be characterized as a process of mutual adaptation which might well result in one single pattern of capitalist economy predominating worldwide. The dynamics towards global interdependence and integration of each national economy have become considerably stronger. This seems in fact to justify the view that economic globalization will induce a process that will make the institutional patterns of each country more uniform.

However, normative and analytical concepts of a world society have now been under discussion for a couple of years. Irrespective of different meanings implied by the debaters involved, the idea of a world society appears partly to describe and partly to anticipate one single society on a global level. This consists of several 'sub-societies' which are progressively losing first their national economic integrity and then political sovereignty in favour of one world administration. The recent formation of supranational economic and political – or at least regulatory – entities through and within the triad may illustrate that such an evolution is no mere fantasy.

In academic and political debate this putative development is associated with globalization. Irrespective of its ambivalent meaning, 'globalization' often appears in such debates to indicate exactly this growing uniformity.

If we subscribe to the idea of a growing uniformity, a question arises for actors in a given local constellation. They may perceive their own institutions to be tightly bound up with global trends in economy, technology and social affairs, but also as in some ways defective. What kinds of action, then, should they take to adjust to globalization? The actors concerned are most likely to imitate what they observe in the most advanced regions in the world and try to speed up local adjustment.

At the same time, however, from a different perspective – the current confrontation of seemingly different institutional shapes of modern capitalism – uniformity does not appear as an opportunity but as a risk. Uniformity in this sense does not mean equality but a reduction in structural and institutional differences among and between different localities, regions and countries and an increase in shared structural and institutional properties. It predominantly refers to the needs of the free flow of capital, free trade, jurisdictional and tax regulation. Diversity, however, is connected with specifically endowed national, regional and local infrastructures, knowledge bases, labour forces and, not least, production structures. In this latter respect the deeper implications of globalization lie in a tighter interconnection of regions, which implies growing uniformity as well as exploitation of regional diversity by distant actors (see Giddens 1990: 64). Thus, from the point of view of a certain locale, if the actors concerned are aware of this ambiguity of globalization, they are likely not only to be aware of, but even to advance, the specificity of their endowments as compared to other locales and thus treat diversity as a valuable asset.

What kind of role do the information and communication technologies (ICT) play in the process of globalization? Several advances in economic and technological globalization could not have happened without a dramatic development in and diffusion of information and communication technologies. This has given rise to the widespread idea that globalization came into existence *only* with the help of such technologies or that globalization has been caused by the information and communication technologies. This would be a gross oversimplification. There are manifold interdependencies, however, between globalization and ICT. Some interesting similarities must be taken into consideration. Obviously, there is the global reach as such, the growing interaction due to network arrangements (electronic or organizational), the implicit tendency towards uniformity, and, perhaps surprising, the necessity for local specificity which means at least articulating diversity.

Whether and how the emergence of multimedia clusters in the selected regions contributes to global uniformity and at the same time enhances the range of diversity is of particular interest for the following discussion. From the point of view of regional actors, we argue that diversity is a decisive factor. It allows regional actors to create the most suitable conditions for cultivating the formation of a multimedia industry by thorough deployment of their locale's resources, generated by entrepreneurial enterprises, public and private educational and service institutions, and, especially, the labour force.

The more regional actors believe they must adapt their economic infrastructure, technology base, and institutional settings to the dictates of an overarching global information society, the less their influence on the process of shaping their own emerging multimedia industry, and vice versa. With that hypothesis in mind, we see that a perceived requirement for uniformity greatly restricts the policy space for innovative local programmes. Conversely, a perception that diversity is the key to multimedia sector development opens up the policy space and innovative focus. It is not, however, an either/or situation. Globalization will be a factor promoting both uniformity and diversity. The process of the formation of a multimedia industry will be examined in the following dimensions:

Economic sector/industrial branch Because of its typically hybrid origins, the multimedia industry cannot be attributed to one or even a few identifiable branches. As we know from Scott's (1996, 1998) analysis of the Californian multimedia sector, this industry may consist of enterprises of very mixed background. Telecommunications, hardware and software, computer graphics and design, production of cultural products, database management, financial services and advertising agencies are just some of the industrial sectors contributing to today's multimedia industry. This remarkable variety raises the question of whether the regions under investigation are going to form similar production structures or whether they are likely to create very specific ones tied to the specific location.

Spatial distribution The process of globalization and the ongoing expansion of an information society in advanced industrialized countries lead to an assumption that spatial considerations will become increasingly obsolete. The 'death of distance' (Cairncross 1997) and an increasing irrelevance of geography are widely postulated. In particular, the capability of ICTs to allow interconnectivity and interactivity will contribute, it is said, to bridging all parts of the globe. It is assumed that globalization based on ICT will replace the earlier driving forces towards industrial agglomerations. If this is true, a more balanced spatial distribution of multimedia production structures is to be expected. It is possible, however, that a further concentration and cluster formation perhaps even in urban agglomerations may occur. In that case, the expectation of a more equal spatial distribution in favour of areas that have until now benefited less from globalization and from the advantages of ICT is obviously misleading.

Education and professional skills The concept of the information society overlaps those of a knowledge society and knowledge-based industries. Obviously, knowledge and knowledge acquisition assume a growing weight as far as the preconditions for a dynamic and vivid information society are concerned. In this respect multimedia obtains a strategic importance. On the one hand, a wide range and a high level of knowledge and skills are needed to bring multimedia production into existence, and to operate and maintain that industry. On the other hand, multimedia configurations and products represent an effective instrument with almost unlimited potential for flexible, cheap and rapid access to a growing extent of different knowledge sources. The importance of educational institutions as well as of digital knowledge bases in an emerging information society can hardly be overestimated. The following chapters will look at the regions under investigation and discuss the role of education systems in the operation of multimedia firms and of knowledge bases for the tailoring of multimedia products.

Professional expertise Professional expertise is built upon the foundation of education and training and also develops through occupational experience. A region's wealth and variety of different professional and occupational groups thus reflect its structure in terms of the internal differentiation of its industries and is, to a certain extent, an expression of the regional educational system. In the context of the axis of uniformity and diversity, it is interesting to consider specific regional professional expertise and its strategic role within the multimedia industry. Are there places of excellence and expertise in multimedia which cannot simply be copied by others?

Product/content For several reasons, content is the key variable determining success within the multimedia business. Compared to the entire range of elements, components and processes involved with multimedia production, it is the actual content of the product that most determines quality and price. Apart from simple replications of content that is already otherwise available in such forms as film, texts or audio files, multimedia products can be specifically tailored to particular production processes as well as to the characteristics of integrated processing, mediating and displaying its elements. Further, content is in a variety of ways interwoven with cultural and social contexts. Think, first of all, of language. English already represents a *sine qua non* in the world of the information society – as it does in a knowledge society – and in particular with respect to worldwide communication via Internet, e-mail or the World Wide Web. But it is often the regional language, part of its habit, custom and knowledge base, which is inextricably connected with content. Given this situation, content seems to be the kind of asset which regions could best shield against competitors and imitators from outside. Presumably, from the point of view of content, the multimedia product allows the largest space to accentuate regional specificity. It still remains to be seen which regions can make best use of this potential.

Industrial organization Will the information society, with multimedia as a Trojan horse, introduce entirely new forms of industrial organization? There is already extensive literature on network phenomena and virtual organizations connected with multimedia and associated industries. It indicates that the actors in this field apparently prefer very flexible, loosely coupled and temporary relations with their contractors, partners, and employees. Furthermore, at least until now, there has been hardly any organizational integration of the various professional 'species' that participate in the multimedia production. The well known example of the entertainment and film industry suggests what is likely to occur in the multimedia industry. A constellation of a few dominating, large corporations on the one hand and, on the other, a large number of highly specialized firms, individual experts and freelancers on the other hand is very likely to come into existence. Project organization seems to prevail. Bearing in mind this kind of industrial organization, the authors of this volume explore how the actors involved apply the electronic and distance-bridging network potential of multimedia to their own organizations. The experience and preferences of multimedia producers will reveal whether they can really forgo face-to-face communication and fully rely on electronic interaction.

Labour market Almost all industrialized countries are suffering to a greater or lesser degree from a considerable loss of jobs in their well-established, so-called 'mature' industries. With these uncomfortable but often unavoidable consequences of economic structural change in mind, politicians, unions and participants in the labour market tend to expect compensation from an incubating information society and in particular from an emerging multimedia industry. To provide proper empirical evidence, the impact of multimedia production on the labour market should be assessed with respect to quality and quantity. What is the extent of job creation in multimedia production? What kind of skills are required to find employment in that industry? Are new jobs and job descriptions being developed that require a special education?

Organic versus artificial embedding From the viewpoint of regional actors, one of the most interesting as well as challenging issues is the range of driving forces that are spurring the development of multimedia sectors. It is important to learn from empirical evidence precisely which kinds of local action are likely to succeed. Confronted with the consequences of economic change and faced with the requirements of globalization, political and economic actors are eager to promote, or even to create, new economic sectors and production structures including multimedia.

The fact is that the emergence of multimedia production is of very recent origin. At the moment this is sometimes paralleled by enormous efforts by politicians, administration-related agencies and intermediaries, to establish such an industry in their jurisdiction. However, this coincidence cannot be considered as constituting a causal relationship between political action and the emergence of the new industry. It is necessary to study more thoroughly the factors that generate multimedia operations. Only thorough analysis can reveal whether and to what extent further preconditions and driving forces have to be taken into account, particularly in the very premature and incubating period of development. In the light of empirical results from different regions of the world, the profile of truly influential local action will become clearer. Is it possible for regional (predominantly political) actors deliberately to create new production structures? What are the areas in which regional actions seem to be feasible and what instruments should be applied?

What is multimedia?

At the moment multimedia is a widely used catchword. It is difficult to assign it a precise definition or a concept on which there is agreement across disciplinary boundaries. The technical artifact 'multimedia' is usually described as a combination of several digital media, which are partly time-sensitive (e.g. sound or moving pictures) and partly time-insensitive (e.g. graphics or text) and which can be used interactively and in an integrative manner. Multimedia products can be used locally (off-line, e.g. CD-ROM) or by using telecommunications networks (on-line). In the latter case they build upon an existing or developing telecommunications infrastructure.

In more general terms multimedia is used to describe the present state in the development of ICT. Important actors in this field are content developers, program and service providers, network operators, new suppliers of network transmission capacities, and software and hardware producers from the areas of the computer, telecommunications and consumer electronics industries.

This broad characterization is useful in order to identify the actors in the 'multimedia' value chain. There will be few exclusively multimedia actors or multimedia corporations, but many will be in a position to contribute something to multimedia.

The research presented in this book focuses particularly on one group of participants in the multimedia value chain: the producers of multimedia-content. We are in fact talking about a very small group of companies that concentrates exclusively on such activities. There is a larger number of firms which develop part of their business in the direction of multimedia. These are sectors with a high affinity to multimedia such as publishing, broadcasting or advertising. Multimedia as such does not represent a sector in its own right – even if for the sake of brevity we talk in the following chapters of a multimedia sector – but media is a cross-sectoral productive and service activity.

The lack of clear-cut sector boundaries makes it difficult to analyse the emerging multimedia industry. Adding to this, the rapid development of multimedia as a new industry implies that multimedia production is very inadequately registered in most official statistics. Thus, the contributors to this book had to perform much exploratory work, carry out case studies and qualitative interviews, organize their own surveys among multimedia producers and draw on a variety of heterogeneous statistical sources. Inevitably, therefore, an inter-regional comparison of the observations given in the following chapters is not always feasible. Even so, the richness of data on the very young and fast-changing multimedia industry in different regions is, in our opinion, a particular strength of this book.

Industrial clusters

The research question that initially gave rise to this book was: 'Based on what prerequisites and requirements will regional clusters in the multimedia industry emerge and how can the emergence of such clusters be supported?' Central to this question is the idea of clusters.

The clustering of industries is, according to Porter (1990), an important source of competitive advantage. Enright, referring to Porter, defines an industrial cluster as a 'set of industries related through buyer-supplier and supplier-buyer relationships, or by common technologies, common buyers or distribution channels, or common labour pools' (Enright 1996: 191). Porter states that 'competitors in many internationally successful industries, and often entire clusters of industries, are often located in a single town or region within a nation (Porter 1990: 154).' Porter gives numerous examples, such as the pharmaceutical industry in Basel (Switzerland) or the cutlery industry in Solingen (Germany).

Following Enright (1996: 191), one may define 'regional clusters' as those 'industrial clusters' whose member firms are in close geographic proximity to each other. It is exactly this subset of industrial clusters which is of particular interest to this volume. Thus, if the authors of this book use the term 'industrial cluster', this should be read as 'regional industrial clusters'. The cluster concept thus characterizes a regional agglomeration of productive and service activities which have a common focus in the sense of a bundle of similar, related activities. A cluster therefore is more than just a sector, insofar as it encompasses the production-oriented services and the infrastructural preconditions. It has to be added at this point that, in the literature, a cluster is generally considered as the dominant core of one region. In the case of multimedia, even in advanced regions, multimedia is only one small cluster among many. To this extent, our use of the cluster concept is a very specific one.

The structure of the book

The inter-regional comparison presented in this book demonstrates that only a few regions host multimedia industries which may be classified as 'pioneers' or 'leading manufacturers'. Most of the regional production complexes can be called either 'routine producers' or 'catching-up regions'. One of the aims of this volume is to verify and deepen this finding by taking a closer look at the factors affecting the development of multimedia as an industry in various regions.

The first part analyses regions which can be called leading manufacturers or pioneers in the multimedia domain. San Francisco (Chapter Two) and the Los Angeles area (Chapter Three) in California must be mentioned here, as well as New York (Chapters Four and Five). As well as analysing the case of San Francisco, Egan and Saxenian in Chapter Two engage in a theoretical discussion of the dynamics of localization and globalization in multimedia, arguing that multimedia is simultaneously an expansion of information technology and a form of cultural expression.

Based upon a broader analysis of the US software industry, it is argued that multimedia is in fact a global production system and will become increasingly global over time. This does not mean that agglomerations will disappear, but the authors suggest that agglomerations with particular types of organizational arrangements will be more likely to persist than others. California's success in high technology domains has been at the centre of a growing body of important research. California is still regarded by many as a 'model region' for the study of future trends in technological and social development. Since a wide range of scholarship on the situation in Southern California already exists, the article on Los Angeles deals with a very specific question, the form and logic of an emerging local labour market for the multimedia and digital visual affects industry. This complements other studies already published by the author Allen J. Scott (see Scott 1996, 1998).

Chapters Four and Five deal with the situation in New York, especially the so-called Silicon Alley. Silicon Alley is not as deeply rooted as the California cluster in the region's economic history, but it nevertheless stands apart from most of the other multimedia locations in the world. Important preconditions for the development include the position of New York as a central location for the media and service industries.

In the second part emerging multimedia clusters are studied. In the regions under discussion, elements of cluster formation can be detected and multimedia-related activities are well established. They do not, however, command the pioneer status of the American regions mentioned above. Chapters Six to Eleven focus on emerging multimedia clusters in Toronto

(Chapter Six), specific parts of North Rhine-Westphalia (notably Cologne) (Chapter Seven), Munich (Chapter Eight), Amsterdam (Chapter Nine), the South East of England (London, Sussex) (Chapter Ten), and Stockholm (Chapter Eleven). Of course this should not be read as an exhaustive list of multimedia clusters, but it is no accident that emerging multimedia clusters can be found primarily in metropolitan areas. The authors furthermore clearly demonstrate that, in spite of the fact that there seems to be a common sectoral governance structure for multimedia, the regional clusters in themselves show markedly different characteristics.

The third part analyses regions which try to establish a multimedia cluster, most often with the help of intensive support from public agencies. Examples of catching-up regions are Cardiff/Wales (Chapter Twelve), Scotland (Chapter Thirteen), Stuttgart (Chapter Fourteen), and Tampere in Finland (Chapter Sixteen). It seems to be a common characteristic of most of these catch-up regions that they attempt to develop a new specialization in multimedia, based on traditional strengths in manufacturing sectors, notably electronics and electrical engineering. The third part ends with a discussion of mainly political efforts in Japan (Chapter Sixteen) and Singapore (Chapter Seventeen).

References

Cairncross, F. (1997) *The Death of Distance. How the Communications Revolution will Change our Lives,* Boston: Harvard Business School Press.
Castells, M. (1996) *The Information Age: Economy, Society and Culture, Volume I, The Rise of the Network Society,* Malden, Mass.: Blackwell.
Enright, M. J. (1996) 'Regional clusters and economic development: a research agenda', in U. H. Staber, N. V. Schaefer and B. Sharma (eds) *Business Networks. Prospects for Regional Development,* Berlin and New York: de Gruyter.
Giddens, A. (1990) *The Consequences of Modernity,* Stanford: Stanford University Press.
Porter, M. E. (1990) *The Competitive Advantage of Nations,* New York: The Free Press
Scott, A. J. (1996) 'The craft, fashion, and cultural-products industries of Los Angeles: competitive dynamics and policy dilemmas in a multisectoral image-producing complex', *Annals of the Association of American Geographers,* 86: 306–23
Scott, A. J. (1998) 'From Silicon Valley to Hollywood: the multimedia industry in California,' in H.-J. Braczyk, P. Cooke and M. Heidenreich (eds) *Regional Innovation Systems,* London: UCL Press.

2

BECOMING DIGITAL

Sources of localization in the
Bay Area multimedia cluster

Edmund A. Egan and
AnnaLee Saxenian

Multimedia: the promise

The past thirty years have been challenging ones for traditional practices of economic development. After decades of uninterrupted economic growth coupled with generally rising living standards, economic expectations about work and wages are changing in the largest economies. Many Western European countries struggle with high unemployment rates. Japan is facing a crisis in core domestic industries and a weakening in lifetime employment policies. The US and Canada, with more flexible labour markets, are experiencing declining wages for most of their populations. The balance between growth on the one hand and rising living standards and economic stability on the other, central to the social contracts of these societies, has been disrupted by a series of changes within these economies since the 1960s. These changes can be analysed along several key dimensions:

The first of these dimensions is technological. The developed economies appeared, by the mid-1990s, to be entering a major period of economic growth associated with the maturing of information technology. The information technology paradigm has now dramatically expanded within the economy, improving the productivity of a far wider range of activities. In terms of regional economic development, this level of technological change offers new opportunities for diversification, but also challenges regions to adopt the latest technology or risk losing competitiveness.

The second dimension is spatial. Improvements in information processing, transportation, and communications technology have created integrated world markets for both consumer and industrial goods and services. The increasing integration of production at the global scale can place tremendous pressures on patterns of local linkages, as imports increase from regions which offer products and services of higher quality or at lower cost. For the advanced regions in particular, continual product innovation has become a necessity because of the inherent cost advantages of industrializing, low-wage nations.

A critical aspect of the globalization of production is the emergence of an international market for informational and cultural services. Since the 1980s, international trade in services – mainly informational and business services – has increased much faster than merchandise trade. As a result, the same kinds of opportunities and challenges that have faced manufacturers since the 1970s – the threat of low-wage competition and the consequent need for continual innovation – are beginning to make themselves felt in the service industries as well.

A third aspect is organization. Many researchers have identified the new networked character of production which is emerging around the world. Industries once dominated by large vertically-integrated corporations are now adopting new, more loosely integrated structures. Large firms and economies of scale still play an important role in many industries, but the overall turbulence of the new technological and market environments have caused both outright vertical disintegration (Scott 1988a, 1988b), and the creation of networks led by large firms (Sabel 1989).

Production networks – ongoing inter-firm ties which involve interdependence, as opposed to anonymous, spot-market transactions – can be either local or global. Most literature has focused on local networks, but organizational forms ranging from transnational corporations to ethnic networks, as well as technological developments such as the Internet, can serve as the basis for global networking. Part of the challenge of assessing the developmental opportunities associated with new technologies such as multimedia involves understanding the trade-offs between local and global networking in a world where everything is networked.

Clearly, these three trends are interlinked. New information and communication technology (fibre optic communications, e-mail, Intranet/Internet hardware and software, etc.) help make both a networked organization and a global production system possible. The globalization of manufacturing and services would be much slower without a movement of large corporations to adopt the networked structure at a global scale (Harrison 1994). And the gains from globalization – both in terms of new markets and sourcing opportunities – drive both key technology industries and increased global alliances and networks.

In this context, interactive multimedia technology has come to be seen as the latest identifiable wave of innovation and potential growth evolving from the information technology revolution. The Internet, an obscure collection of university networks in the 1980s, has become in the 1990s a world-wide interactive communications medium. In the past ten years, a host of hardware and software innovations have increased the capacity of inexpensive desktop computers to produce higher-quality sound, graphics, video, and communications.

The promise of technological visions as virtual reality, Internet-based commerce and a ubiquitous digital communications network raises staggering economic and social possibilities. This is the promise of multimedia.

But what is multimedia at present? What are the advantages that a specialization in multimedia brings to a region? What are the structural and institutional conditions that foster multimedia clusters if, in fact, the industry does tend to cluster geographically? And what can public and private policymakers do to maximize the advantages of a local multimedia industry?

This chapter brings a perspective to these questions from the San Francisco Bay Area, home to Silicon Valley as well as the city of San Francisco. Existing research suggests that it possesses one of the leading multimedia industries in the nation (Scott 1995; Collaborative Economics 1994). Many companies which have been instrumental in developing and commercializing interactive multimedia technology are located in the region. They include Apple, Adobe, Hewlett Packard, Netscape, Sun Microsystems, Electronic Arts, Pixar and cinematic special effects studio Industrial Light and Magic.

The Bay Area's multimedia cluster is not limited to the enabling technology: despite the region's lack of specialization in traditional media industries, it has developed several content clusters which distribute finished multimedia products directly to the consumer. Institutional and informal relationships between different communities in the region have enabled it to develop a very broad cluster. As such it can serve as an ideal model for testing hypotheses regarding the role of both structural and institutional/cultural factors in the growth of multimedia clusters in other regions.

This chapter first develops a definition of multimedia and discusses some key technological trends that have led to its convergence in the 1990s. It includes a broad definition of the multimedia value chain, which will be used to benchmark the Bay Area cluster against other multimedia regions in the US.

The chapter then engages in a theoretical discussion of the dynamics of localization and globalization in multimedia, based on the argument that multimedia is simultaneously an expansion of information technology, and a form of cultural expression. Using a broader analysis of the US software industry, we argue that multimedia is in fact a global production system, and will become increasingly global over time. This does not appear to mean that agglomerations will disappear, but *it does suggest that agglomeration with some types of organizational arrangements will be more likely to persist than others.* After a discussion of the breadth of specialization in the Bay Area cluster, we discuss in detail the relationships between four institutions in the 'Multimedia Gulch' area of San Francisco: multimedia title companies, multimedia authoring software companies, the freelance artistic community, and the non-profit and for-profit art and multimedia schools in the neighborhood. The observable relationships between these groups, we argue, are emblematic of those necessary for the continuing development and breadth in the Bay Area multimedia cluster.

Multimedia as an extension of information technology

Beginning in the mid-1980s, a new type of computer technology entered the lexicon of the industry and exploded onto the mass market in the early 1990s. Known as multimedia, it is generally defined as computing technology capable of simultaneously processing and delivering the range of previous media (text, graphics, sound and video) as a single experience.

Both demand and supply factors played a part in the way that multimedia was anticipated and partially realized. On the demand side, the entertainment and cultural industries in the developed countries have been among the most rapidly growing sectors for at least the last twenty years. On the supply side, very rapid technological development occurred in a number of elements of computer and broader media systems, including among the most significant:

- Operating systems software (32-bit operating systems in PCs, with 64-bit and greater in more expensive workstations).
- Dedicated video and audio processing power (video, game, sound card and RAM).
- Storage (CD-ROMs, leading to digital video disks (DVDs)).
- Display (high-resolution colour monitors, leading to flat-panel display).
- Printing (laser printing, followed by colour laser printing).
- Application software (desktop publishing, image processing, digital audio and video editing).
- Input and output devices (touch screens, graphic scanners, digital cameras, multimedia projectors).
- Networking (from local area networks to Internet/Intranet applications to incipient platforms and applications for televisions and other consumer electronics).

Personal computers – which were really only a decade old in the early 1990s – quickly developed a dramatically enhanced ability to interact with users in more realistic and sensorially compelling ways. The advances are all the more remarkable given that computer graphics was traditionally a marginal field within computer science (Morrison 1995). Some of the most basic routines in today's graphical software, like the algorithms to draw overlapping windows on a monitor, were only invented in the 1970s.

The impact of the new technology was felt, directly or indirectly, in four main ways. First, the multimedia platform of the Internet, the World Wide Web, sent the Net into an exponential growth phase that has produced over 18 million hosts or individual sources of information; this number is expected to rise to more than 100 million world-wide by the year 2001. Although the Internet was growing through primarily academic use during the 1980s, it was innovation in computer languages (Hypertext Markup

Language – HTML – developed at CERN, the European Laboratory for Particle Physics) and computer graphics (the World Wide Web browser, developed at the University of Illinois) that led to its mass-market adoption.

Second, very large corporations in the electronics, cable television, print media, and entertainment industries: Sony, Disney, TCI, Time-Warner, News Corp., Microsoft etc. began experimenting with synergistic joint ventures, partnerships, and acquisitions in preparation for the digital convergence of entertainment and electronics. In this spirit technological ventures such as interactive TV, video-on-demand, and high-bandwidth, set-top modems for television were experimented with, so far with limited results.

Third, the motion picture industry accelerated its reliance upon digital special effects and advanced graphics, video and film processing, and applied the technology in new ways. Finally, the video game industry, which was moribund as recently as the mid-1980s, also became a field of application for the new technology, especially graphics and video. Facing yet another bout of falling margins in the early 1990s, PC vendors looked to differentiate themselves with multimedia enhancements like CD-ROM drives and video and sound cards. Video game makers started developing for that platform in earnest and were joined in the market by a myriad of different educational, entertainment and informational CD-ROMs that melded graphics, video, and sound in new ways. Information technology had begun to establish itself in the lucrative entertainment market, and the multimedia industry was born; combined sales of hardware and software in the US alone were predicted to reach $22 billion by the year 2000 (Frost and Sullivan 1994).

But is multimedia really an industry? It has no single unifying technology and no single market. It is neither exclusively a service nor a product and, if it moves to a network distribution model, it could very well be neither. What prior studies of multimedia have focused on is the composition of *regional multimedia clusters* (Scott 1995, Coopers and Lybrand 1996, Cardoso 1996, Collaborative Economics 1994, IC2 Institute 1996) and here there does appear to be some consensus on the following three core elements of the multimedia production system:

Enabling hardware and software technology As described above, these include specialized hardware and software to enable the development of multimedia content, both for end-users, such as 32-bit operating system or a CD-ROM drive, and for the developers themselves, such as authoring or image processing software.

Multimedia products Typically at present these are packaged CD-ROM products that are distributed through retailers or direct marketing, although for some products, especially lower-end ones, an Internet-based distribution model is emerging.

Multimedia services As is the case with the software industry as a whole, customized services are a considerable share of the total multimedia content business. Such projects may reach outside of the cluster to clients in advertising or other industries or may perform specialized roles within the development of packaged products, such as producing live talent segments for film special effects or video games.

In addition, different researchers consider the following elements to be part of the multimedia production system: traditional media industries, as well as support industries such as venture capital or specialized professional services, trade publications, trade associations and educational institutions. Given the importance of retail distribution, large multimedia publishers that have access to mass-market channels can also play a critical role.

For regional development, the important questions concern: which pieces of the production system take root in which regions? To what extent do agglomeration factors tend to draw different elements together? And what are the dynamics of these processes over time?

For the first question, most empirical analyses agree that multimedia clusters benefit from a combination of creative talent and technology, though the degree to which either is a necessity is a matter for debate. Scott (1995) has shown very clearly that California's success in multimedia is directly related to its specializations in such related industries as film, hardware and software, indicating that prior economic development is an important factor.

With regard to the second question, multimedia appears to share many structural characteristics with industries that have formed flexible production complexes. Innovation is extremely rapid and the limits to communication historically associated with spatial distance may inhibit technological diffusion. Specialization of both final producers and suppliers is a major asset because of the niche character of the markets but these external economies may not occur in many regions. The complexity and lack of standardization in technology and markets favours close user-producer interaction. Inter-disciplinary communication may be enhanced by a shared regional culture and anecdotal evidence suggests that relatively immobile institutions, such as leading-edge educational facilities, may play a critical role in fostering these clusters. All of these factors suggest that we should expect a relatively agglomerated spatial structure of the multimedia production system.

On the other hand, we could cite many examples of a multimedia production system which is spatially dispersed. A typical commodity chain might consist of hardware developed in Silicon Valley and software developed in Seattle and Boston, used by a multimedia developer in London who combines Brazilian music with live action from a Hollywood actor. Moreover, the fact that very different labour inputs are involved at each stage suggests that, if issues of integration are resolved, a spatial division of labour should form in which regions specialize in different elements of a global multimedia production system.

Egan (1997) has argued that an unusual structural characteristic of software – that the same code can be simultaneously produced as a service with high transportation and transaction costs and low economies of scale, or as a package with extremely low transportation costs and extremely high economies of scale – has critical implications for its spatial dynamics. As a service, software obviously tends to agglomerate near customers and forms part of a local cluster. As a package, on the other hand, its market is geographically unlimited; it becomes essentially dissociated from the cluster of which it formed a part as it is sold to many similar clusters.

Software services offer customers a relatively ideal solution at a relatively high development cost. Packaged software companies, on the other hand, offer a standardized solution at a relatively low cost. How low? It depends upon the size of the market because the number of customers determines what the company has to charge to recoup development costs and make a profit. If the market is very small, then a packaged company may not be able to make up in low costs what it gives up in quality. But if the company is, for example, Microsoft and the market is personal computer operating systems, then it can take full advantage of the economies of scale inherent in packaged software. It can undercut competition while earning high margins and obtain a sizable monopolistic advantage as well. As different software market segments grow – multimedia tools are clear examples of this – there is a tendency for packaged software to substitute for services on a product-by-product basis and, consequently, a tendency for local product linkages to be replaced by non-local ones and for global standards to be set.

However, this growth dynamic of packaged software has not meant the end of either software services or the agglomerative character of the industry. An increasingly common software strategy has been to adopt an open-systems approach to software design (Senn 1995). Here packages automate certain elements of the information processing task at hand, while permitting a variety of downstream agents – a software services firm, an end-user or another software product development – to add further functionality to the system in a variety of more specific application domains. For example, a database management system runs on a variety of upstream operating-system platforms and yet also serves as a more specific platform in itself for particular types of database applications.

Open systems permit both the cost-savings associated with packaged software and the potential for greater specification associated with services. The effect on the industry as a whole is to shift its pattern of labour demand and consequently, given the relatively immobile character of labour pools, its spatial pattern. Egan (1997) demonstrated that the US software industry has tended to drift, in relative terms, away from hardware-oriented regions

17

towards the sources of more domain-specific knowledge and towards major downstream users of software. New agglomerations form, and some old ones adjust, on the basis of innovative extensions of existing standardized products, fundamentally stemming from feedback and participation among agglomerations of users, service firms, and packaged software developers. In the context of a growing market, regional concentrations of software do not disappear but are forced to constantly adjust and reinvent themselves, usually by adopting new technologies that were developed elsewhere.

Multimedia tools are examples of such domain-specific software. In response to the new graphics, sound and video technology, and the evident demand for entertainment and cultural products, low-cost, mass-produced elements of open multimedia systems have been developed. These are usually subsets of larger information technology systems. For example, authoring and image processing software by companies such as Macromedia (in San Francisco), or Avid (in Boston), have helped create the multimedia title (CD-ROM) and the multimedia service industries in San Francisco and Los Angeles respectively. Widely-adopted Internet browsers by companies such as Netscape and Microsoft have helped to establish multimedia segments such as video-streaming plug-ins and distributed Internet applications.

Standard upstream software serves to create a large market for compatible downstream specification and, on the supply side, its low cost facilitates its use by compatible downstream developers of these specifications. The effect of these developments is to change the aggregate pattern of labour demand, since low-cost tools substitute for some labour skills. In particular they stimulate the demand for labour at the end of the value chain, where the product is raw information and not software. In multimedia, the value chain ends with content.

Multimedia as an expression of content

In a production system increasingly composed of standard hardware and software elements, the distinguishing characteristic of multimedia products becomes their *content*: the degree to which they harness the power of interactive multimedia in creative and appealing ways. 'Content is King' has become the catch-phrase that many industry experts, including Bill Gates, have adopted as characteristic of the dynamics of the multimedia value chain (Siboni and Kirk 1995). It means that upstream suppliers and downstream distributors are unable to fully extract the value associated with the addition of creative content to the more technically-oriented hardware and software tools which enable but do not define multimedia experiences.

The developing multimedia system offers a technical substitute for some skills (especially programming skills, *on a unit basis*) through the growth dynamic of packaging.[1] At the same time, it raises demand for others, namely the skills of building further extensions to the multimedia system in domains such as entertainment, education and advertising where the technology can be useful. Information technology does not expand into a vacuum but facilitates the expression of existing knowledge/content into a digital medium, as well as fundamentally changing the rules of the game for new creative expression. Hence pre-digital content and content-producing practices are instrumental parts of the evolving system, even as they are transformed. The work of multimedia is the work of becoming digital, of appropriating, creating and re-creating cultural expression within an environment in which it can be endlessly manipulated, customized and processed (Negroponte 1995).

For this basic reason, content regions have a built-in advantage as multimedia centres, especially in an open-market, open-systems context. Since packaged software and hardware are so cheap to reproduce and transport, and since their producers seek to maximize their sales, the natural advantage of nearby users is diminished. Hence the production system *as a whole* tends to be dispersed. The content regions (essentially, those with an existing media industry) have a prior familiarity with the markets in question and have already attracted talented and creative workers and the necessary supporting services and institutions. With cases like the multimedia cluster in Manhattan, we are already witnessing the development of a spatial division of labour in which content regions 'customize', by adding content to, existing multimedia tools.

The addition of content to the information technology system involves other issues, however, because multimedia is more than the extension of information technology: it is also a specific medium, in competition with older media, whose structural characteristics have implications for the organization of the industry. The expanding adoption of the multimedia system for the production and delivery of content is fundamentally driven by the technological changes discussed in the previous section. However, earlier forms of industrial organization, associated with the consolidation of earlier media systems, create institutional pressures within content regions. The resolution of these pressures becomes a *fundamental part* of multimedia's changing geography and technological evolution.

Investment in multimedia technology by established media companies means they are helping to build a system by which their existing market advantages may be weakened. For example, television broadcasting is a natural monopoly (or oligopoly), ultimately, because of the limited number of broadcast channels a television is able to receive. If, on the other hand, telecommunication trends continue to the point that television-quality video can be distributed over the Internet on a one-to-many basis, this will reduce barriers to entry and invite competition in distribution. If the technological trends in multimedia hardware and software continue, then we should expect the production of video and/or multimedia content to decline in price as well.

Nor is television the only such case. Most large media firms – in motion pictures, cable television, music publishing and book publishing – have attained that position on the basis of economies of scale in a distribution system that risks being undermined by the Internet. In such a situation, current media leaders – both firms and regional clusters – may be at risk as many entertainment industries fragment into an array of niches that are largely free from control by either the distribution or production pieces of the value chain. In such a case, the ability of regions rapidly to develop content that appeals to these niches will determine their success in multimedia.

In addition, the creative aspect of multimedia is probably the most spatially concentrated element of any in the value chain. Certainly in the Bay Area the content producers are most heavily concentrated in Multimedia Gulch in San Francisco, in contrast to hardware development which takes place forty miles to the south in Silicon Valley. Part of the success of the region's multimedia cluster, as we will show in the next section, stems from its ability to rapidly create local competencies that fill in the value chain (by providing a locally required labour skill) and can also integrate innovations occurring in vastly different fields (Storper and Walker 1989), in this case, culture and technology.

The Bay Area multimedia cluster in the broader US context

Among the large metropolitan regions vying to be the multimedia capital of the United States, the San Francisco Bay Area is unusually strong in technology and unusually weak in traditional media. Given our earlier discussion, we might expect it to specialize more in the technical aspects of the multimedia production system. In order to investigate this question further, we analysed the spatial pattern of multimedia industries in the Corporate Technology Information Services (CorpTech) directory, which provides very rich industry detail for US technology firms (summarized in Table 2.1).

We classified sixty-seven different technology industries into six stages of the multimedia production system: digital input hardware, specialized multimedia hardware, multimedia development software, multimedia products and services (e.g. finished titles for the consumer and business markets), telecommunications equipment and software, and digital output devices. The categories were chosen both to represent relatively discrete stages in the multimedia development process and also to correspond to different structural requirements (e.g. technology versus telecommunications versus content).

Establishments in each of the six stages were counted in five large US metropolitan areas to benchmark different regions along different parts of the value chain. Telephone area codes were used to define regions.

The results are fairly revealing. Not surprisingly, the Bay Area scores quite highly in the more technical stages of multimedia hardware and software, followed (again not surprisingly) by Los Angeles in the first case and Boston

Table 2.1 Percentage of US multimedia firms in five metropolitan regions, by stage in the value chain, 1997

	San Francisco region	*Los Angeles region*	*New York region*	*Boston region*	*Seattle region*	*Other US regions*	*Total*
Digital input devices	11.4%	11.0%	9.9%	8.8%	2.1%	56.8%	100%
Multimedia hardware	20.4%	10.5%	7.7%	8.1%	1.5%	51.8%	100%
Development software	13.1%	6.4%	7.4%	10.9%	3.0%	59.2%	100%
Multimedia products (CD ROMs)	13.0%	6.1%	7.9%	9.0%	3.7%	60.3%	100%
Telecomms hardware and software	15.6%	7.4%	10.4%	10.0%	1.6%	55.0%	100%
Digital output devices	9.2%	12.1%	12.1%	10.5%	2.5%	53.6%	100%

Source: Corporate Technology Information Services

in the second. Seattle, Microsoft notwithstanding, has not developed a multimedia industry on par with the others, while Greater New York has its greatest specialization in telecommunications and the less specialized manufacturing of input and output devices. Perhaps the biggest surprise is the Bay Area's breadth of leadership in multimedia products which one would expect would have the greatest dependence on an existing media industry.

These results, while not definitive by any means, suggest either that the potential spatial division of labour in multimedia is limited, which tends to run counter to what we already know about New York for example, or that the Bay Area has managed to develop relative strengths in content development without a very large critical mass of traditional media or creative talent. In the next section, the organization of the major content producing area in the Bay Area is discussed to assess that question.

The structure of the multimedia cluster in the city of San Francisco

The Bay Area multimedia cluster is actually a number of highly concentrated clusters linked together in a large metropolitan region. Silicon Valley, in the south of the region near San José, is the home of many fundamental innovations in the history of multimedia and of many leading-edge contemporary companies. At the famed Xerox PARC research facility, graphics and networking innovations that led to the commercial success of companies such as Apple and Sun were developed. Adobe Systems developed the post-script language which facilitated graphics printing, and Hewlett-Packard was an early innovator in laser printing (Cringely 1992). Today, Silicon Valley is home to interactive telecommunications companies such as WebTV (recently purchased by Microsoft), @Home, and C-cube, to video game platform companies like Sega and 3DO, advanced graphic workstation maker Silicon Graphics and Internet equipment makers such as Cisco Systems and Bay Networks. Multimedia and Internet-related businesses have spearheaded another wave of rapid start-ups and employment growth in the valley since the end of the recession of the early 1990s. Within the regional cluster, Silicon Valley tends to specialize, though not exclusively, in the hardware and advanced software segments of the cluster.

San Francisco, roughly forty miles north of the valley, has developed its own vibrant segment of the region's multimedia cluster. Known as Multimedia Gulch, this neighbourhood was historically a light manufacturing and single-room-occupancy hotel area until the early 1980s, when its vacancy rates and warehouse space began attracting artists who needed space to live and work in. Macromedia, now a leading producer of multimedia authoring software, located in the neighbourhood in 1983 and began to develop links to the freelance artist community. This developed into a larger cluster in the early 1990s when the multimedia market expanded. Additional technical and creative talent was added to the external labour market in San Francisco by periodic downsizing at Apple Computer, beginning in the mid-1980s. The long-standing participation of Bay Area resident and Hollywood producer George Lucas, the producer of the *Star Wars* series, was also significant. He recognized early the commercial value of big-budget film productions and now runs Industrial Light and Magic twenty miles north of San Francisco in Marin county.

A recent study by the consulting firm Coopers and Lybrand has provided valuable quantitative information on the structure and growth of the San Francisco multimedia cluster. The study identified 379 companies in the city which were principally involved in multimedia development tools, content design and development (e.g.finished CD-ROMs), content publishing and multimedia services (which may include consultancy as well as customized work). Using a highly suspect methodology, the consultants claimed that 35,000 people in the city work in this industry; the real number is probably in the 12,000 – 15,000 range.[2] Table 2.2 summarizes the results from Coopers and Lybrand's survey of the 379 firms.

These findings are fairly clear evidence that the multimedia area in San Francisco forms a classic cluster or industrial district. It consists primarily of small start-up firms, vertically – and horizontally – disintegrated from existing

Table 2.2 Structure of the multimedia cluster in San Francisco, 1997

Firm size:	
Percentage of companies with 100 employees or more	6%
Percentage of companies with 50–99 employees	11%
Percentage of companies with 26–49 employees	11%
Percentage of companies with 11–25 employees	28%
Percentage of companies with 10 employees or fewer	44%
Total	100%
Year of founding:	
Percentage of companies founded before 1990	10%
Percentage of companies founded 1990–1993	26%
Percentage of companies founded 1994–1997	64%
Total	100%
Location of founding:	
Founded in San Francisco	74%
Founded in San Francisco but plans to leave	1%
Founded elsewhere, moved entirely to San Francisco	14%
Founded elsewhere, established presence in San Francisco	11%
Total	100%
Source of start-up capital:	
Percentage of companies relying on owner capital	75%
Percentage of companies relying on other private equity investment (e.g.venture capital)	11%
Percentage of companies relying on corporate investment	5%
Percentage of publicly-traded companies	4%
Unknown	5%
Total	100%
Revenues:	
Percentage of companies with < $300K annual revenue	34%
Percentage of companies with $300K-$600K annual revenue	14%
Percentage of firms with $600K-$1.8 M annual revenue	20%
Percentage of firms with >$1.8 M annual revenue	32%
Total	100%

Source: Coopers & Lybrand (1998)

companies and industries in the region, with limited access to formal or even venture capital channels. 75 per cent of the companies were started with the private capital of the owners, suggesting that capital barriers to entry are extremely low.

In terms of sectoral composition and growth rates, the Coopers and Lybrand study indicates that the cluster was undergoing a truly remarkable growth period in the mid-1990s, as the data in Table 2.3 report. Overall, revenues grew from $900 million to $2.2 billion in only two years, from 1995 to 1997. Multimedia development tools, which were the largest segment in 1995, were overtaken by content publishing in 1997, with significant increases also found in multimedia services and content design and development.

These trends are important to the arguments we have developed in earlier sections. We would expect San Francisco to specialize in multimedia development tools, given the importance of related hardware and computer graphics innovations to these products. This is, however, the slowest growing segment in the city (although 30 per cent annual growth is not especially slow!). As our comparative analysis in the last section showed, the Bay Area has developed a multimedia content specialization despite its lack of a traditional media industry, and content revenue is increasing more rapidly than revenue from tools. The question remains how this happened.

In 1995 a series of interviews were conducted with multimedia executives and trade associations in San Francisco, aimed at uncovering their companies' reasons for starting up and remaining in the city, as well as providing general insights into industry dynamics. The interviewees suggested that the cluster as a whole consisted not only of tool, content and service companies but also of freelance artists and musicians and large for-profit educational institutions. The workforce is a roughly equal mix of creative and technical workers (see Scott 1995) who, according to our interviews, often experience communication problems.

The area as a whole had many of the organizational characteristics that Saxenian (1994) found to be instrumental in the renewed success of Silicon Valley. The production structure was extremely decentralized, especially for title development companies. In many cases, we were told, firms were formed simply as teams to complete single projects (whether it be a service contract or a CD), and personal networks were instrumental in getting work in this almost entirely external labour market. A recent study of the labour market for the interactive media industry in the Bay Area suggests that content firms

Table 2.3 Growth trends in revenue by segment in San Francisco, 1995 and 1997 ($ million)

	1995	1997	Average annual growth rate 1995–97
Multimedia development tools	416	708	30%
Content design and development	162	454	67%
Content publishing	285	745	61%
Multimedia services	72	293	101%

Source: Coopers and Lybrand (1998)

24

use the film-studio model of organization, in which a firm consists only of a core of experienced managers who, on a project-by-project basis, contract for specialized skills and additional part-time labour (Bay Area Multimedia Partnership – BAMP – 1997). The team disbands after each product. The popularity of the studio model may explain the extremely small size of most multimedia companies and their relative newness, as the Coopers and Lybrand data indicated.

The CD-ROM business in particular is extremely unpredictable and, while a few products make a very large profit, most lose money. Hence few title companies were more than a few months old. The title developers had few local customers; they either sold to a national publisher or did contract work for companies in other industries outside of the region. However, the growth of local publishers since 1995 suggests that this may be changing.

Multimedia appears to be unusual among information technology industries for its propensity to locate in central cities as opposed to suburbs. During the interviews in the neighbourhood we asked about this and were frequently told that most of the technical workers, in particular, preferred a suburban location. The creative and managerial workforce, however, (who mainly lived in the city, if not the neighborhood itself) preferred the urban character of the neighborhood and believed that its stimulation actually resulted in a better product. In fact, the relationships between four major groups appeared to explain both the agglomeration in the urban neighbourhood and the competitive advantage that it facilitated.

First, authoring software companies such as Macromedia were increasingly dependent upon feedback from lead users to help guide the features that would be incorporated in new products. Thus these firms had a policy of sharing early release ideas with local title-developers who were also the main users of the product. From this interaction the authoring companies gained valuable feedback while members of the title developer networks were able to save on learning time by knowing about new features in advance. Almost all of this interaction was handled informally among people in different companies who knew one another. Thus agglomeration gave local companies the advantage of responsive feedback on design features.

Further down the value chain, the relationship between the title developers and the labour pool, especially the freelance artists, was more straightforward: the companies needed creative people on short notice and the artists needed flexible, relatively high-paying work. The highly flexible employment relationship was primarily a function of the sporadic timing of demand for artists, who in turn gained experience by working for several clients.

In a sense, the core of the area is the skills of the labour force, and here the relationships to educational institutions appear to be critical. Firms do not provide these skills: they are too small and their time constraints are too great. As the BAMP labour market survey reported:

EDMUND A. EGAN AND ANNALEE SAXENIAN

The vast majority of people initially employed in this industry taught themselves how to use interactive digital media tools as required for projects. However, as this industry has matured and the job market has become more competitive, workers are expected to possess the skills needed to join the team immediately. In some cases, companies are willing to train exceptionally talented artists who are lacking the latest computer skills.

(BAMP 1997: 2)

The most important specific skills, aside from a temperament conducive to working in an uncertain, pressure-filled and team-based environment, are familiarity with the software used to create content. Since these are constantly changing, continuing formal and informal education is indispensable. Both the entrepreneurship associated with for-profit institutions like the San Francisco Academy of Art and the responsiveness of public institutions like San Francisco State University have been important elements in creating a continuing multimedia education capacity. Moreover, the culture of content development, with its unusual mix of technology and art, and technologists and artists, appears to favour unusually strong communication skills which are often acquired in these unique educational settings. On a more practical level, with almost no formal labour market mechanisms, these schools have become the primary sites for new multimedia workers to begin networking into the industry (BAMP 1997).

Finally, the circuit was completed in the region by the relationship between the authoring companies and the art schools. The new multimedia programs in many cases were supported by the authoring companies (and Silicon Valley hardware developers) who donated supplies and were anxious to have students skilled in their products as they and their employers would be customers once out of school.

The organizational system in place in San Francisco is notable for its overall logic in the absence of any coordinated plan or even any particular long-term formal commitments. It is difficult in fact to imagine what those might be, given the extreme rapidity with which technology changes. Most of the firms are extremely small and, with the possible exception of Macromedia, they do not exert any particular force over other relationships. The various local linkages will persist and deepen in so far as they contribute to the competitiveness of the whole. This responsiveness is associated with private sector initiatives, to be sure, but not exclusively so. According to the BAMP labour market study mentioned above, several of the local state universities have established multimedia curricula in media studies, computer science, and the arts (BAMP 1997).

Policy lessons

In many ways, the Bay Area multimedia cluster is an extension of Silicon Valley but its evolution offers lessons for other regions that do not possess such a level of nearby technical expertise. The Bay Area has been able to diversify its multimedia base: from fundamental innovation in graphics technology to authoring software and to multimedia content without a media industry on the scale of New York or Los Angeles.

In our view there are two basic reasons for this. First, there was no media industry to employ artists, writers, musicians and other creative talent, yet for cultural and historical reasons San Francisco has attracted such people for decades and continues to do so. Thus, the potential labour force for multimedia was not otherwise committed to jobs in established industries, and its labour market was not dominated by companies with potentially ambiguous attitudes towards the technology. Second, a complex educational infrastructure arose very rapidly, through both public and private initiatives, to link these people in concrete ways to the labour demands of a new industry. This infrastructure was itself strongly supported by local technology firms which recognized the advantages of a local testbed of users and also wanted to support the growth of their markets by seeding the schools with their products. Without this supply of computer-friendly artists, and without the set of mediating relationships outlined in the previous section, Silicon Valley alone could not have produced a digital content design industry.

The lesson of San Francisco, then, lies in its ability to link the enabling technology to other knowledge- or content-oriented activities in different industries. Proximity to leading technology companies was certainly crucial in this case but it is not at all clear that it is a necessity for other regions. Multimedia content today has not begun to take full advantage of the opportunities afforded by the technolog, and, therefore, exploring linkages between multimedia and untried industries may be worth pursuing. It is worth pointing out that much of the basic graphics innovation that has driven multimedia entertainment has also been used in fields such as computer-aided design and manufacture, and that industrial design is becoming a major multimedia market. Since the enabling technology is widely traded globally, regions can tailor multimedia development policies to leverage their existing specializations in knowledge, content or media activities.

Such policies do not need to be aimed at developing an export-oriented multimedia cluster like the one in Silicon Valley. It is unlikely that many regions will do so but it is highly likely that most advanced companies will be significant users of interactive communications and, perhaps, multimedia technology. A local multimedia cluster can be viewed as a local competency to enhance the competitiveness of existing industry rather than as a replacement. To this end, companies can and should be encouraged to explore how they can incorporate multimedia into their production and distribution strategies, and governments can help reduce the risk involved with experimentation.

At present, the heavy reliance of multimedia on traditional retail distribution channels gives untapped industries and regions a chance to develop strategies to develop a local multimedia capacity. When and if the World Wide Web becomes a viable distribution channel, however, its global scope could seriously undermine attempts to develop local collaboration between multimedia and other industries: other industries may have significant first-mover advantages. Focusing on new application areas can minimize that risk. On the other hand, media and cultural industries more broadly are highly concentrated in large regions around the world today, where the giants of the old media system are located. Not only do distributional innovations like the World Wide Web potentially erode these older advantages over time but they may lower the threshold on the costs of media/content production, making a broader variety of niche products, and more regions, more viable.

Conclusion

Given the newness of multimedia and the paucity of solid comparative data about its true size, growth and locational patterns, the analysis of particular regional successes in multimedia must be viewed as provisional. San Francisco's very broad multimedia cluster could well thin out as standardiza-tion occurs in key hardware and software tool markets, even if the standard-setters are located in the Bay Area, because they will seek a world-wide market of content developers to sell to. On the other hand, it seems more likely that the organizational arrangements that prevail in Multimedia Gulch and in smaller districts such as Berkeley and Marin County will enable the region to continue to exploit its proximity to more fundamental innova-tions and perhaps even broaden the range of market-standard packaged prod-ucts which have brought so much wealth into the Bay Area. This chapter has aimed to draw some preliminary conclusions and to ask some basic questions about the dynamics of agglomeration and dispersal in multimedia so that the experience of the Bay Area cluster can be used as a basis for policy recom-mendations.

Notes

1 In information technology it is particularly dangerous to assume that tech-nology innovation reduces *overall* employment for skilled workers; certainly nothing of the kind has happened in the software industry, despite (or perhaps because) of the development of automation (i.e. packaged software).
2 Given the distribution of firm sizes reported by Coopers and Lybrand (shown in Table 2.2), it is practically impossible for 379 firms to account for 35,000 employees, which would place the average firm size near 100. Our figure of 12,000 was derived from the firm-size distribution Coopers and Lybrand reported, using the midpoint of each category (and 200 for the > 100 category).

References

Bay Area Multimedia Partnership (1997) *A Labour Market Analysis of the Interactive Digital Media Industry: Opportunities in Multimedia,* prepared for the North Valley Private Industry Council, Sunnyvale, California.

Cardoso, J. A. (1996) 'The multimedia content industry: strategies and competencies', *International Journal of Technology Management* 12, 3: 253-70.

Collaborative Economics Inc. (1994) *The Multimedia Cluster in the Bay Area,* San Francisco.

Coopers and Lybrand (1996) *New York New Media Survey: Opportunities and Challenges of New York's Emerging Cyber-Industry,* New York.

—— (1998) *A Survey of the Interactive Media Industry in San Francisco,* San Francisco.

Cringely, R. X. (1992) *Accidental Empires,* Reading, MA: Addison-Wesley.

Egan, E. (1997) 'The spatial dynamics of the US computer software industry', unpublished Ph.D. dissertation, Department of City and Regional Planning, University of California at Berkeley.

Frost and Sullivan (1994) *World Multimedia Hardware and Software Markets,* Mountain View, CA.

Harrison, B. (1994) *Lean and Mean,* New York: Basic Books.

IC2 Institute (1996) *Austin's Multimedia Industry,* Austin, TX: the IC2 Institute.

Morrison, M. (1995) *Becoming a Computer Animator,* Indianapolis: Sams Publishers.

Negroponte, N. (1995) *Being Digital,* New York: Knopf.

Sabel, C. (1989) 'Flexible production and the re-emergence of regional economies', in P. Hirst and J. Zeitlin (eds) *Reversing Industrial Decline,* Oxford: Berg.

Saxenian, A. (1994) *Regional Advantage,* Cambridge: Harvard University Press.

Scott, A. J. (1988a) *Metropolis,* Berkeley and Los Angeles: University of California Press.

—— (1988b) *New Industrial Spaces,* London: Pion.

—— (1995) 'From Silicon Valley to Hollywood: Growth and Development of the Multimedia Industry in California', UCLA: Lewis Centre for Regional Policy Studies, Working Paper 13.

Senn, A. (1995) *Open Systems for Better Business: Something Ventured, Something Gained,* New York: Van Nostrand Reinhold.

Siboni, R. and Kirk, B. (1995) 'Multimedia juggling act', *Upside* 7, 9: 38-45.

Storper, M. and Walker, R. (1989) *The Capitalist Imperative,* New York: Basil Blackwell.

3

PATTERNS OF EMPLOYMENT IN SOUTHERN CALIFORNIA'S MULTIMEDIA AND DIGITAL VISUAL-EFFECTS INDUSTRY

The form and logic of an
emerging local labour market

Allen J. Scott

Introduction

Since the 1980s, the multimedia and digital visual-effects industry has grown at an extremely rapid pace in California. It is found in two main geographic concentrations in the state, namely, the Bay Area and Southern California (principally in Los Angeles County), with the latter region now moving rapidly into a position of dominance, not only in California but probably in the world at large (Scott 1998).

In its narrowest sense, the multimedia industry can be said to consist of firms that produce two characteristic outputs, namely, compact disks and materials for diffusion over the World Wide Web. These outputs can then be further categorized depending on their substantive content: games, interactive stories, educational and self-help materials, business aids, advertising,and so on. In this sense, the multimedia industry is currently materializing at a point of convergence of all media (visual, textual, and audio) around interactive, digital methods of presentation. The industry can also be defined in a somewhat wider sense that includes not only these activities but all forms of digital enhancement of conventional media and, in particular, a wide range of computerized approaches to graphic design.

It is this larger conception of the industry – the multimedia and digital visual-effects industry – that will predominate in the present study, and all the more so because in the context of Southern California the multimedia industry has developed in close association with the motion picture industry. In particular, computer graphics technologies are rapidly unifying the fields of multimedia, animation and special effects in Southern California; Hollywood feature films and television programmes now routinely depend on ancillary high-technology image-processing operations for their commercial success (PMR 1997).

The remarkable dynamism of Southern California's multimedia and digital visual-effects industry is, of course, closely related to the region's overwhelming and long-standing importance as a centre of the entertainment industry. As such, Southern California represents the country's most densely-developed concentration of specialized workers in such domains as story-writing, visual dramatization and scenario production. It is a place, too, where multimedia content providers can always find a ready supply of subcontract services in film and video production, photography, graphic art, script-writing, musical composition, acting and voice-over, and so on. Even so, with the recent mushrooming of the multimedia industry in the region, many firms are currently reporting an acute shortage of workers with computer graphics skills and other forms of multimedia expertise.

The precise size of the multimedia and digital visual-effects industry in Southern California is extraordinarily difficult to calculate in view of the fact that there is no generally agreed definition of the industry or of how it might be distinguished from functionally adjacent sectors such as motion picture production, publishing, software services and so on.[1] In an earlier study (Scott 1998), I suggested on the basis of the narrow definition of the industry alluded to at the beginning of the second paragraph of this chapter that there was something in the order of 188 multimedia establishments in the entire area of Southern California south of and including Santa Barbara in 1995. However, according to the broader definition of the industry (including all forms of digital visual-effects), the number of establishments in the region can be provisionally estimated at 382. The median size of these establishments is roughly ten employees. The total number of employees in the industry is quite unknown and would be extremely difficult to assess without more complete information on the frequency distribution of employment by establishment. For comparative purposes, it may be useful to note that total employment in Los Angeles County in Standard Industrial Classification (SIC) 781 (motion picture production and services) was 129,863 in 4,416 establishments according to the 1994 edition of *County Business Patterns*.

My specific objective in the present chapter is to describe the shape, form and emergence of the local labour market for multimedia and digital visual-effects workers in Southern California. I shall, in the first instance, attempt to systematize and comment on a large body of survey data about this new and important sector of employment whose lineaments have hitherto remained largely unexplored. In so doing, I shall at the same time be pushing forward on a more general line of research concerned with patterns of space-time filtering of workers through urban production systems and associated questions of the social structure of local labour markets in metropolitan environments (Scott 1984, 1992a, 1992b). More generally, the present investigation seeks to complement the existing literature on regional development processes by offering a number of additional empirical insights into the operation of local labour markets as complex subsystems within dense spatial agglomerations of economic activity (see Scott 1993, 1997).

An empirical framework of investigation

The study of local labour markets is almost always greatly hampered by a dearth of pertinent statistics. It is usually quite difficult to find information about the personal and occupational characteristics of workers on an individual basis, especially where there is a requirement that the data be coded, in addition, by location and sector of employment. Obviously, the best way to obtain micro-data of this sort is by direct questionnaire methods but, even under the best of circumstances, these are expensive and time-consuming. A particular problem in the present context is actually identifying a target population of individuals to be surveyed, especially because there is no official designation of the multimedia and digital visual-effects industry as such. Even when the definitional problem is resolved, the major obstacle of actually delivering questionnaire forms to workers remains.

One possible line of attack is to distribute questionnaires to workers at their place of employment, but this approach runs up against the difficulty of securing cooperation from the firms concerned. It is, in any case, subject to peculiar biases because this method typically results in returns being clumped by firm, a problem that is exacerbated when only a few firms can be induced to participate in the survey, above all when some of them are unusually large in size (Scott 1992b). The alternative method of surveying workers at their place of residence faces the even more daunting problem of constructing at the outset an unbiased list of home addresses. A third approach, which I have used with some success in the past (Scott 1984, 1992a), is to gain access to potential respondents through employee organizations such as unions or guilds, though again strong biases may be expected to enter into any resulting survey when these organizations account for only a fraction of all employees in the selected industry.

Unfortunately, there is no organization in Southern California that claims or even seeks to represent all multimedia and digital visual-effects workers in the region; and there is none that comes close to embracing a majority of these workers. That said, there are various interest groups in the region whose members are either employed in the industry or are actively seeking jobs in it. Two of these interest groups are of particular significance here because they are fairly large in size and because, taken together, their membership appears to provide a fairly good representation of employment structures in the industry. Each of these groups is a local chapter of a wider international society. They are:

32

- IICS (International Interactive Communications Society). The objectives of IICS are to provide information, professional support and skills development for individuals across the spectrum of the interactive arts and technologies business. Its membership is recruited broadly from professionals in multimedia, computing, telecommunications, education, online services, media, publishing and entertainment. In total, the IICS has thirty-four individual chapters throughout the world. When this study was initiated in the summer of 1996, the Los Angeles chapter had a membership of 612.
- SIGGRAPH (Association of Computing Machinery's Special Interest Group on Computer Graphics). Like IICS, SIGGRAPH is dedicated to providing information, professional assistance and training, but to a rather more narrowly defined membership. This is focused primarily, but not exclusively, on computer graphics specialists. There are twenty-six chapters of SIGGRAPH world-wide. The Los Angeles chapter had 820 members when this project started.

Despite the fact that IICS members are drawn from the entire spectrum of occupations in the industry (including business and financial operations, production management, writing and so on), while SIGGRAPH tends to be rather more technically-oriented, there is some overlap of membership between the two. Neither of the two organizations provides an exhaustive or unbiased window onto local labour markets in the multimedia and digital visual-effects industry but together they probably yield as comprehensive a picture as it is possible to obtain at the present time with limited resources. The advantage of basing the study on two different but complementary organizations is that the information they offer provides a degree of focus that would otherwise assuredly be lacking if we looked only at one of them in isolation.

With the full cooperation of the officers of the local chapters of IICS and SIGGRAPH, a standard questionnaire was mailed to all members over the second half of 1996. The total number of responses received back from IICS was 171 (a response rate of 27.9 per cent) and from SIGGRAPH 159 (a response rate of 19.4 per cent). These response rates are fairly representative for this kind of survey, though the sharp and statistically significant difference between the two rates obtained here remains inexplicable.

In the absence of any definitive information on the social characteristics of the underlying population of workers, we have no way of assessing what specific biases may exist in the questionnaire returns, though it is probably safe to assume that bias of some sort is present. Accordingly, the results reported below need to be treated with due caution. In view of this warning, I shall refrain in this study from premature generalization of the survey results. Even so, the main findings, taken simply on their own terms, tell us much about at least significant fractions of the labour force in this burgeoning industry and its associated employment structures in Southern California. They are generally consistent with information gathered in a parallel series of some twenty-five face-to-face interviews with representatives of multimedia and digital visual-effects firms in the region.

A concise geographic and demographic profile of questionnaire respondents

In Map 3.1, I have mapped out the residential locations of all questionnaire respondents together with a set of isolines indicating the generalized spatial pattern of the digital visual-effects industry in Southern California. The residences of questionnaire respondents are depicted individually in Map 3.1. Any given isoline in this figure represents a locus of points with identical levels of accessibility to establishments in the multimedia and digital visual-effects industry. Accessibility is defined here as $\sum d_j^{-1}$, where d_j is the distance from any arbitrarily given point to the jth establishment in the industry. The analysis was restricted to just Los Angeles and Orange counties (which between them account for a total of 311 establishments), with address data for individual establishments taken from a wide variety of directories and business guides.

Map 3.1 clearly highlights the locational build up of the multimedia industry in and around Santa Monica and the western part of the City of Los Angeles together with an axis that extends eastward and northward through Hollywood and Burbank and then turns back toward the west through the San Fernando Valley. A very minor outlier of the industry can be observed in Orange County to the south. The figure reveals the existence of a remarkable spatial correspondence between the distribution of respondents' residences and the general locational structure of work-places. This same observation is corroborated by questionnaire data which indicate that the median commuting time for IICS respondents is fifteen minutes and for SIGGRAPH respondents twenty minutes.

This kind of tight spatial relationship between employment places and the residential locations of workers is, in general, a persistent feature of local labour markets in the large metropolis, even in Los Angeles which is often (mistakenly) seen as being a more or less fluid commuting shed across its entire extent. The correspondence is magnified in the present instance by the fact that the demographic features of questionnaire respondents match closely the generalized social profile of the residential neighbourhoods of the western reaches of the Los Angeles metropolitan area.

Questionnaire respondents can be represented for the most part as a rising cohort of successful professionals in which women play a noticeable and presumably increasing role. A total of 39.9 per cent of IICS respondents and 29.1 per cent of SIGGRAPH respondents are female. As shown by Table 3.1, most of the individuals who returned a questionnaire are in their thirties, the median age being thirty-nine for IICS and thirty-seven for SIGGRAPH

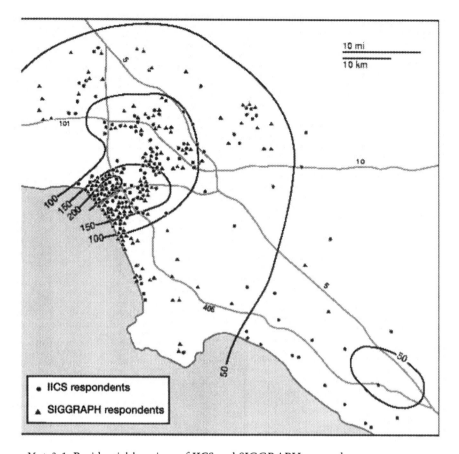

Map 3.1 Residential locations of IICS and SIGGRAPH respondents
Source: Author's survey
Notes: Isolines indicate overall accessibility to multimedia establishments in Southern
California.
Major freeways are shown.

respondents. (It may well be that workers in the multimedia and digital
visual-effects industry as a whole are actually somewhat younger than these
figures would suggest, and we should be alert to some possible bias in the
sample here).

Both groups of respondents are overwhelmingly dominated by whites,
with Asians, Hispanics and African-Americans representing disproportionately small percentages of all respondents (Table 3.2). Annual salaries are
high: the median salary for IICS respondents is $55,000, and for the more
technically-oriented SIGGRAPH respondents, $70,000 (Table 3.3).

Only about a quarter of all respondents were actually born in Southern
California. The remaining three quarters were for the most part born not

Table 3.1 Age of questionnaire respondents

Age	IICS (%)	SIGGRAPH (%)
20–24	0.6	2.6
25–29	8.5	14.1
30–34	20.1	28.2
35–39	22.6	18.6
40–44	19.5	13.5
45–49	16.5	9.6
50–54	4.3	7.1
55–59	4.9	2.6
60–64	2.4	1.9
65+	0.6	1.9
Number of usable responses	164	156

Source: Author's survey

Table 3.2 Racial and ethnic characteristics of questionnaire respondents

Racial/ethnic category	IICS (%)	SIGGRAPH (%)
White	92.4	88.0
Asian	1.3	7.7
Hispanic	4.4	1.4
African-American	1.9	2.8
Number of usable responses	158	142

Source: Author's survey

only outside the region but also outside the state. Of IICS respondents, 6.1 per cent were born in a foreign country, with the corresponding figure for SIGGRAPH being 21.2 per cent. Most of these foreign-born respondents came from Asia, Canada, and Europe. The relatively high proportion of foreign-born personnel in the work-force is no doubt in part a reflection of the reported shortage of computer graphics skills in both California and in the country at large (see also the section below on spatial mobility).

Employment and recruitment patterns

The sectoral distribution of employment

A classification of individual sectors in which questionnaire respondents are employed is laid out in Table 3.4. This classification is quite consistent with

Table 3.3 Income distribution of questionnaire respondents

Income bracket ($000)	IICS (%)	SIGGRAPH (%)
<20	7.7	10.7
20–30	5.1	6.7
30–40	11.5	9.4
40–50	17.9	9.4
50–60	16.7	9.4
60–70	9.0	6.7
70–80	5.1	11.4
80–90	5.1	8.7
90–100	3.8	6.7
100–110	5.1	7.4
110–120	1.3	3.4
120–130	2.6	2.7
>130	9.0	7.4
Number of usable responses	156	149

Source: Author's survey

the broader definition of the multimedia and digital visual-effects industry offered in the introduction to this chapter. A clear majority (79.0 per cent) of all questionnaire respondents are employed in a core group of sectors, with the balance being employed in sectors that are at best only marginally connected to the multimedia and digital visual-effects industry (see Table 3.4).

Core sectors are multimedia (in the narrow sense), motion pictures /TV/video, special effects, animation and so on. Note that the IICS respondents are heavily concentrated in the multimedia sector as such, whereas SIGGRAPH respondents tend to gravitate more to a nexus of sectors involving motion pictures, special effects and animation, where their high levels of computer graphics skills are in particularly high demand at the present time. Non-core sectors of employment reported by respondents are education, the defence industry, legal services, health services and miscellaneous industries. Even in these non-core sectors, however, respondents tend to occupy jobs that in one way or another involve multimedia skills and techniques.

There is, in addition, some filtering of individuals from non-core to core sectors, with education and the defence industry being the most common points of origin. Thus, (combining data for both IICS and SIGGRAPH), 30.8 per cent of the twenty-six respondents who reported that their previous job was in education shifted into core multimedia and digital visual-effects sectors, as defined. The corresponding figure for the twelve respondents whose previous job was in the defence industry is 25.0 per cent. While these figures are small, they nevertheless suggest that the Los Angeles area as a

Table 3.4 Sectors of employment of questionnaire respondents

Sector	IICS %	SIGGRAPH %	Combined %
Core sectors:			
Multimedia	42.4	12.6	27.6
Motion pictures/TV/video	11.1	14.0	12.5
Special effects	0.0	20.3	10.1
Animation	0.7	17.5	9.1
Software design	5.6	5.5	5.6
Multimedia consulting and training	6.9	1.4	4.2
Advertising	5.6	2.1	3.9
Telecommunications	2.8	2.1	2.5
Graphic design	2.1	2.1	2.1
Printing and publishing	2.8	0.0	1.4
	80.0	77.6	79.0
Other sectors:			
Education	8.3	4.9	6.6
Defence industry	2.1	9.1	5.6
Legal services	2.8	0.7	1.8
Health services	0.7	2.8	1.7
Miscellaneous	6.3	4.9	5.6
	20.2	22.4	21.3
Number of usable responses	144	143	287

Source: Author's survey

whole probably has important reservoirs of experienced potential job-seekers ready to move into the multimedia and digital visual-effects industry. The questionnaire data indicate that, once individuals are employed in core sectors, any subsequent job shifts tend to be virtually entirely within the core itself.

Employment, occupations, and computer skills

Almost all questionnaire respondents are currently employed in full-time jobs (see Table 3.5). A very significant number (20.3 per cent) of IICS respondents are engaged in freelance activities, whereas only 7.3 per cent of SIGGRAPH respondents are so employed.

The much higher percentage of SIGGRAPH respondents occupied in regular salaried employment can no doubt be explained in terms of the demand for firm-specific human capital in the motion picture, special effects and animation industries (in which SIGGRAPH respondents are mostly employed). Firms

Table 3.5 Some general employment characteristics of questionnaire respondents

Variable	IICS		SIGGRAPH	
	value of variable	*number of usable responses*	*value of variable*	*number of usable responses*
Per cent employed	94.7	168	98.0	158
Per cent employed full-time	85.8	163	96.6	146
Per cent working freelance	20.3	157	7.3	155
Median length of time with current employer (years)	2.0	148	2.0	140
Median length of time engaged in multimedia work (years)	3.0	161	4.4	148

Source: Author's survey

such as Disney Interactive, Dreamworks, Sony Pictures and Warner Digital insist upon high levels of intrafirm teamwork and product designs that are safeguarded by copyright and trade-mark provisions. Such firms are thus likely to prize a captive labour force that can be socialized and supervised more easily than freelance workers.

For both respondent groups, the median length of current job tenure is two years. IICS respondents claim to have been employed in the industry as a whole for 3.0 years, with SIGGRAPH respondents claiming 4.4 years. In addition, over their entire employment experience in the multimedia and digital visual-effects industry, IICS respondents have worked for an average of 2.82 firms, and SIGGRAPH respondents for an average of 3.4 firms. These figures suggest that there is some modest but not excessive employment instability in the industry.

The occupational characteristics of questionnaire respondents are laid out in Table 3.6. Detailed descriptions of typical occupations in the multimedia and digital visual-effects industry can be found in Regan and Associates (1997) and Vivid Studios (1995). The only occupation noted in Table 3.6 that requires further commentary here is the production/direction category, which refers to occupations (at various levels of seniority) where the main responsibility for design, organization and execution of multimedia and digital visual-effects work (including website construction) resides. Specialized programming and animation/graphic design occupations are broken out as distinctive categories in their own right in Table 3.6. In practice, there are rarely sharp divisions of occupational function in the multimedia and digital visual-effects industry, and the information laid out in the table needs to be interpreted with a high degree of flexibility.

For the most part, the data arrayed in Table 3.6 are unsurprising. Most workers in the industry are engaged in central production, direction,

Table 3.6 Occupations of questionnaire respondents

Occupation	IICS (%)	SIGGRAPH (%)
Owner/senior management	24.8	7.3
Business/financial/sales	18.5	4.7
Production/direction	26.1	20.7
Programming/technical support	12.1	25.3
Animator/graphic designer	7.0	38.0
Writer	5.1	0.7
Other	6.4	3.3
Number of usable responses	157	150

Source: Author's survey

programming, animation and graphics occupations. A distinction between
IICS and SIGGRAPH respondents becomes increasingly evident as the
present discussion moves forward. The former group is patently more entrepreneurial and business-oriented, in the sense that it is marked by a relatively
high proportion of owners, managers and individuals in
business/financial/sales occupations. The latter group is much more focused
on technical occupations such as programming, animation and graphics.

This distinction between the two groups of respondents may be further
elaborated in terms of their differential command of computer skills. Almost
two-thirds of all respondents indicated that they had some computer programming proficiency, with the two most commonly known languages for
IICS respondents being Hyptertext Markup Language (HTML) (39.2 per
cent) and Lingo (22.8 per cent), and for SIGGRAPH respondents, C/C++
(40.1 per cent) and HTML (37.0 per cent). HTML is an easily learned and
widely used language for building web pages; Lingo is a medium-level programming language with applications in the areas of both graphics and business; and C/C++ is a fundamental programming language requiring
significant technical expertise on the part of the user. Once again, then, the
two groups emerge with significant overlap, but with IICS veering to the less
technical and SIGGRAPH to the more technical side of the industry.

Spatial mobility and job recruitment

As I have already intimated, most of the questionnaire respondents were born
outside Southern California. Even more significantly, roughly half of all respondents received their highest level of education outside the region and, for the
most part, outside the state. Furthermore, 3.8 per cent of IICS and 6.1 per cent
of SIGGRAPH members were educated in a country other than the United
States. These data signify, once again, that the multimedia and digital visual-

effects industry in Southern California is highly dependent on human capital imported from outside the region. Nevertheless, once they enter the Southern Californian labour market, workers in the industry tend to become quite rooted in the region. Thus, of all respondents (i.e. the majority) who stated that their current job is not the first job they have ever held, as many as 83.0 per cent indicated that their previous place of employment was in Southern California.

Job recruitment patterns in the multimedia and digital visual-effects industry are displayed in Table 3.7, and they are much alike for both groups of respondents. Observe that the data in the main body of the table are defined as percentages of employed workers only (i.e. excluding founders of firms and the self-employed). By far the greater proportion of all workers in the industry are recruited either on the basis of information provided by friends or organizational contacts or by means of direct communication between the employer and the prospective employee. This observation is consistent with other studies of recruitment patterns, where it has been found that most information about job openings travels in one way or another by word of mouth (Granovetter 1974, Scott 1992a). Advertising also accounts for a modest share of actual recruitment in the industry, with a perhaps anomalously high frequency among IICS respondents.

Education, training, and professional organizations
Education and training

Table 3.8 reveals that the majority of questionnaire respondents have high levels of educational qualification. Most respondents have at least a four-year

Table 3.7 Method of recruitment of questionnaire respondents to their current jobs

Recruitment method	IICS (%)	SIGGRAPH (%)
Friends or organizational contacts	37.2	43.3
Contact initiated by employer	22.7	23.9
Contact initiated by employee	12.7	14.2
Advertisement	17.3	9.0
Job fair	1.8	5.2
Employment agency	8.2	2.2
School placement	0.0	2.2
Number of cases for above variables	110	134
Number of founders of firms or self-employed	28	11
Number of usable responses	138	145

Source: Author's survey

Table 3.8 Highest level of education attained by questionnaire respondents

Level of education	IICS (%)	SIGGRAPH (%)
High school	0.6	3.2
Two-year college	7.2	12.3
Four-year college	38.6	49.0
Master's degree	45.2	27.7
Doctoral degree	8.4	7.7
Number of usable responses	166	155

Source: Author's survey

college degree and significant numbers have acquired Master's degrees. About half of all respondents graduated with their highest degree in 1985 or later.

The educational majors completed by questionnaire respondents are laid out in Table 3.9. If we gloss over the by now familiar differences between IICS and SIGGRAPH respondents, the data presented in this table indicate that most of them have received educations that are highly appropriate for careers in the multimedia and digital visual-effects industry. Well over fifty per cent of them majored in such fields as film, graphics, business and computer science, while significant numbers of the rest majored in engineering, fine arts, social science and liberal arts. Educational pathways

Table 3.9 Educational majors completed by questionnaire respondents

Major	IICS %	SIGGRAPH %	Combined %
Film, theatre, TV, broadcasting	27.5	13.4	20.7
Graphics, computer graphics, animation	3.8	25.5	14.2
Business	20.6	6.7	13.9
Engineering, mathematics, science	6.3	19.5	12.6
Computer science	5.0	14.1	9.4
Fine arts, architecture	6.3	12.1	9.1
Social sciences	10.0	4.0	7.1
Liberal arts, languages	9.4	3.4	6.5
Education	5.0	0.7	2.9
Law	4.4	0.0	2.3
Medicine, health care	1.9	0.7	1.3
Number of usable responses	160	149	309

Source: Author's survey

into the industry are thus multiple, but nevertheless rather clearly focused on the artistic, business or technical skills most in demand by employers.

There is also a remarkable wealth of relevant educational and training establishments in the region. Of those respondents who took their highest degree in Southern California, as many as 34.0 per cent graduated from the University of California at Los Angeles, followed by the University of Southern California (13.9 per cent), California State University at Northridge (9.0 per cent), Art Centre Pasadena (5.0 per cent), and California State University at Fullerton (3.5 per cent), (see Table 3.10). The remainder graduated from some twenty-three different colleges and universities scattered throughout the region.

Additionally, 70.2 per cent of IICS respondents and 55.3 per cent of SIG-GRAPH respondents indicate that they have taken at least one part-time course in multimedia or computer techniques since graduation. The lower figure for SIGGRAPH respondents is no doubt a function of their already relatively high level of technical expertise upon graduation. The institutions providing the part-time courses taken by respondents are exhibited in Table 3.11. Respondents were asked to name these institutions in an open-ended fashion and the answers are arrayed in Table 3.11 simply by number of mentions, without any attempt to correct for multiple mentions by any one respondent.

Some of the institutions noted in the table are conventional colleges and universities, some are private establishments providing in-house programmes or vendors offering special training, and others are professional associations of different kinds (including unions and guilds). The miscellaneous categories shown in the table represent bundles of institutions that received only one mention each. The information in Table 3.11 informs us that there is a rather surprising number and diversity of possibilities for part-time training in the multimedia and digital visual-effects industry in Southern California, with the University of California at Los Angeles again leading the way.

Table 3.10 Educational institutions from which questionnaire respondents obtained their highest degree (Southern Californian institutions only)

Educational institution	IICS %	SIGGRAPH %	Combined %
University of California, Los Angeles	34.6	33.3	34.0
University of Southern California	15.4	12.1	13.9
California State University, Northridge	7.7	10.6	9.0
Art Center Pasadena	0.0	12.1	5.6
California State University, Fullerton	1.3	6.1	3.5
Others	41.0	25.8	34.0
Number of usable responses	78	66	144

Source: Author's survey

Table 3.11 Institutions (in Southern California only) from which questionnaire respondents have taken part-time courses in multimedia techniques, arranged by number of mentions

Institution	IICS	SIGGRAPH	Combined
Colleges, universities and professional schools:			
University of California, Los Angeles, Extension	36	57	93
Learning Tree University	3	4	7
Art Center Pasadena	4	1	5
University of California, Irvine	3	2	5
New Horizons	2	2	4
California State University, Long Beach, Extension	0	4	4
Santa Monica College	0	4	4
Orange Coast College	0	2	2
The Learning Annex	0	2	2
Mount Sierra College	0	2	2
California State University, Northridge	2	0	2
University of Southern California	0	2	2
West Coast University	2	0	2
Miscellaneous colleges, universities, etc.	21	18	39
In-house training or product vendor programmes:			
Silicon Studio	14	4	18
Alias	5	0	5
AVID	0	2	2
Microsoft	0	2	2
Miscellaneous in-house training or product vendor programmes	15	13	28
Professional associations (including user groups):			
American Film Institute	12	23	35
SIGGRAPH	9	0	9
IICS	2	5	7
Los Angeles MacIntosh Users' Group	2	3	5
Society of Motion Picture and Television Engineers	0	2	2
Women in Film	0	2	2
Directors' Guild of America	0	2	2
Miscellaneous professional associations	3	9	12

Source: Author's survey

The abundance of educational and training opportunities offered in the region for those seeking careers in the multimedia and digital visual-effects industry suggests that there is a significant degree of institutional responsiveness to the current high demand for relevant skills and aptitudes in Southern California. If there is a labour shortage in the industry at the present time, this is perhaps less a function of the absence of basic instructional infrastructures than a consequence of the sudden recent surge in the demand for appropriately-trained labour. The danger in responding to this shortage by increasing the number of educational and training programmes in the region is that it may result in a long-term over-supply of labour. The main objectives of policy in this regard should not be so much to expand the number of programmes as to improve the quality of those that exist, while ensuring that minority groups are able to gain better access to them.

Professional organizations

Questionnaire respondents were asked to list in open-ended format all the professional associations, unions and guilds to which they belong. The answers to this query are tabulated in Table 3.12 which is arranged simply in terms of the number of times each organization was mentioned.

Table 3.12 suggests that multimedia and digital visual-effects workers are

Table 3.12 Affiliations of questionnaire respondents with professional associations, guilds and unions, arranged by total number of mentions

Association, guild, union	IICS	SIGGRAPH	Combined
SIGGRAPH	18	—	18
IICS	—	8	8
Society of Motion Picture and Television Engineers	10	9	19
International Alliance of Theatrical and Stage Employees (various locals)	0	14	14
Bar associations	10	0	10
Women in Film	7	0	7
Women in New Technologies	7	0	7
International Television Association	7	2	9
Institute of Electrical and Electronics Engineers	5	14	19
International Animated Film Society	2	6	8
Los Angeles MacIntosh Users' Group	2	3	5
Writers' Guild of America	5	0	5
Directors' Guild of America	3	0	3
Miscellaneous	130	155	285

Source: Author's survey

notably gregarious on the professional front. Respondents are joined together in webs of intersecting affiliations in a wide variety of formal organizations (including IICS and SIGGRAPH) as well as in many different informal support groups. Note that eighteen IICS respondents claimed to be members of SIGGRAPH while eight SIGGRAPH respondents claimed to be members of IICS, a finding which suggests that while there is some redundancy in the survey data reported here, it is fairly limited.

In general, the organizations noted in Table 3.12 play an important role in the local labour market. They provide corporate representation of their members' interests, they offer training programmes of various types, and they ensure that critical information about new technologies, skills, job opportunities and so on circulates rapidly through the local labour market. Recall from the earlier discussion that a significant proportion of questionnaire respondents obtained their current jobs through organizational contacts.

The local labour market and regional economic development

The labour market for workers in the multimedia and digital visual-effects industry in Southern California is highly distinctive in its overall structure, and it has emerged in its present form via complex processes of space-time filtering of individuals through a series of geographic and institutional staging points. It is made up for the most part of rising professionals of both sexes, but with a very low representation of minority ethnic and racial groups. Workers in the industry are well educated and trained, and they earn notably high incomes on average. While it is always possible that the survey method used here to gain information about the local labour market may have yielded a very one-sided view of its general make-up, more casual data collected in firm interviews corroborate the broad conclusions offered here. It is conceivable that some bias may have entered into the two sample groups in the matter of age but, even here, the degree of bias is probably not unduly great.

The local labour market that has grown up around the multimedia and digital visual-effects industry in Southern California is endowed with rich institutional infrastructures. Workers themselves appear to be extremely involved in job-enhancing extra-work activities, including the pursuit of part-time training. Above all, they are joined together in many different criss-crossing networks of association through which they are able to collectivize their individual experiences, knowledge, information, contacts and so on. They thus generate organizational frameworks that supplement general processes of worker socialization and job mobility. Such networks have been found to be an important basis of worker expertise and innovative activity in other industries and other regions, whether it be in the case of semiconductor engineers in Silicon Valley (Saxenian 1994) or international finance workers in the City of London (Thrift 1994) or even visual artists in New York (Montgomery and Robinson 1993).

In fact, local labour markets typically function not only as simple adjuncts to specialized regional economies but also as critical sources of the agglomeration economies that keep them functioning as dynamic and tightly-organized spatial units. When they work well, they ensure that trained and acculturated workers with frequently up-dated agglomeration-specific know-how are constantly supplied to employment places.

In the present study, I have not examined in any detail those aspects of this question that have to do with the attitudes, habits and practices of workers in the multimedia and digital visual-effects industry or, more generally, with the culture-generating capacity of cities and its expression in the character of local labour markets and local economic development at large. As a simple matter of observation, this capacity and its recent flowering in the cultural economies of major metropolitan areas is now becoming a significant element of contemporary world capitalism (see Molotch 1996, Scott 1997).

The multimedia and digital visual-effects industry will almost certainly become one of the driving forces behind the continued growth of urban cultural economies in future years and Los Angeles – with its highly developed entertainment complex – is already a major centre of the industry. In the light of this remark, further research on the elusive issue of place-specific forms of worker socialization is urgently needed, and nowhere more so than in the burgeoning cultural-products industries where subtle processes of habituation of the labour force are critical to overall economic success.

Notes

This research was supported by a grant from the Office of the Vice-Chancellor for Research, University of California, Los Angeles. I am grateful to Jeffrey Boggs, Howard Harrington and Zack Lynch for their able research assistance on this project. I also wish to thank the Los Angeles chapters of IICS and SIGGRAPH for their cooperation in making this research possible.

1   The industry is not currently recognized in the US Standard Industrial Classification.

References

County Business Patterns (1994) Washington D.C.: US Department of Commerce, Bureau of the Census.

Granovetter, M. S. (1974) *Getting a Job: A Study of Contacts and Careers,* Cambridge, MA.: Harvard University Press.

Molotch, H. (1996) 'LA as product: how design works in a regional economy', in A.

J. Scott and E. Soja (eds) *The City: Los Angeles and Urban Theory at the End of the Twentieth Century*, Berkeley and Los Angeles: University of California Press.

Montgomery, S. S. and Robinson, M. D. (1993) 'Visual artists in New York: what's special about person and place?' *Journal of Cultural Economics* 17: 17–39.

PMR (1997) *Making Digits Dance: Visual Effects and Animation Careers in the Entertainment Industry*, Los Angeles: The PMR Group, Inc.

Regan and Associates (1997) *A Labour Market Analysis of the Interactive Digital Media Industry: Opportunities in Multimedia*, San Francisco.

Saxenian, A. (1994) *Regional Advantage: Culture and Competition in Silicon Valley and Route 128*, Cambridge, MA.: Harvard University Press.

Scott, A. J. (1984) 'Territorial reproduction and transformation in a local labour market: the animated film workers of Los Angeles', *Environment and Planning D: Society and Space* 2: 277–307.

—— (1992a) 'The spatial organization of a local labor market: employment and residential patterns in a cohort of engineering and scientific workers', *Growth and Change* 23: 94–115.

—— (1992b) 'Low-wage workers in a high-technology manufacturing complex: the Southern California electronics assembly industry', *Urban Studies* 29: 1231–46.

—— (1993) *Technopolis: High-Technology Industry and Regional Development in Southern California*, Berkeley and Los Angeles: California University Press.

—— (1997) 'The cultural economy of cities', *International Journal of Urban and Regional Research* 21: 323–9.

—— (1998) 'From Silicon Valley to Hollywood: the multimedia industry in California', in H. Braczyk, P. Cooke, and M. Heidenreich (eds) *Regional Innovation Systems*, London: UCL Press.

Thrift, N. J. (1994) 'On the social and cultural determinants of international financial centres', in S. Corbridge, N. J. Thrift, and R. L. Martin (eds) *Money, Power, and Space*, Oxford: Blackwell.

Vivid Studios (1995) *Careers in Multimedia*, Emeryville, CA.: Ziff-Davis Press.

4

MULTIMEDIA NETWORKS, GLOBALIZATION AND STRATEGIES OF INNOVATION

The case of Silicon Alley

Wolf Heydebrand

Introduction

This chapter offers a sociological portrait of 'Silicon Alley', a highly dynamic metropolitan multimedia industry cluster of over one thousand firms that has emerged in lower Manhattan since the early 1990s. About half (48 per cent) of the nearly five thousand multimedia firms in the entire New York area are relatively recently established corporations whose main business is either to create new media products and services or to use them in a novel manner.

By definition, the concepts of new media or multimedia refer to products and services combining the video, audio and print/graphic dimensions of computer technology, telecommunications and content that can be used interactively by consumers and business users. The products and services of multimedia firms include content design and development; consulting in such areas as marketing, design, and technology; content packaging and marketing, including CD-ROM publishing and online/Internet services; content distribution, such as online/ Internet; electronic commerce such as financial services; software development and 'generic' applications, including information retrieval and management; and content creating tools such as audio recording, design and illustration.

The organizational dynamics of this new segment of advanced producer and business services are unusual, to say the least. About two-thirds of the firms have been in business for three years or less, and about 30 per cent have been newly established over a period of eighteen months from March 1996 to September 1997. During this last period, about one-sixth (17 per cent) of the firms have dropped out as independent entities either by merger, relocation or bankruptcy.

Besides providing a description of the structure and dynamics of this new segment of the post-industrial services sector, my purpose is to concentrate on the special affinity between innovative corporate strategies and certain structural characteristics of the new inter-firm networks that are central to this dynamic process. I focus on the expansion of the new media industry in Manhattan since 1992, its economic effects on the tri-state region (New York, New Jersey and Connecticut), its internal structure, the typical organizational profile of its new innovative firms, and the emerging competitive effects of the new media on the old media.

The growth of 'Silicon Alley' before and after 1992

From the perspective of urban sociology in general, and the theory of regional economic development and innovation in particular, the case of New York City is rather atypical, if not unique. New York has been an economically thriving metropolis for a long time (the fiscal crises of 1975, 1987 and the early 1990s notwithstanding). It is a central site for a region already leading in the development of post-industrial and especially business services as well as communications and entertainment. It has a highly concentrated clustering of multimedia firms whose development, while contributing to the regional economy, can be said to feed mainly on their own success, thus creating a highly dynamic and self-sustaining, almost autonomous, development.

The New York City multimedia industry participates actively in the process of globalization. It continues to attract investment from domestic and transnational financial centres, is an exporter of multimedia services, and thus benefits from a highly competitive-cooperative-integrative environment without as yet showing signs of being overly fragmented, over-integrated, or destroyed by these processes. During the 1990s, it has been a case of growth feeding on growth. The central causal assumptions of the theory of industrial districts, that production and service networks will generate innovative regional economic growth (Becattini 1990, Bergman et al. 1991, Camagni 1991, Amin and Thrift 1992), are therefore supported from the start. In the case of New York, indeed, they are somewhat tautological since the process already occurs at a high level of 'institutional thickness' and sustained development rather than starting out from ground zero.

In this Chapter, I will briefly highlight the importance of pre-1992 economic developments in New York as a 'global city', describe the explosive growth of multimedia services and their effects on the region since 1992, analyse the special features of multimedia firms and networks, and discuss some of the likely consequences of new media growth for the older media.

New York's pre-1992 economic development in the context of a 'global city'

Like most major world cities, New York has experienced a disproportionate growth of the service sector (relative to manufacturing) since the early 1970s (Sassen 1991: 166; Castells 1996: 201-33). Within that sector, business, commercial or producer services have been the fastest growing and transnationally most relevant component (Noyelle and Dutka 1988). The leading producer services are the FIRE services, i.e. financial (banking), insurance and real estate, as well as accounting and consulting, advertising and legal services. To these must be added communications and a host of other business services such as administration and management, research and development, personnel and security, not to mention maintenance, cleaning, and related 'personal' services.

Nationally, total employment in the United States grew from 77 million in 1970 to 117 million in 1991 (52 per cent), whereas producer services jumped from almost 6.3 million in 1970 to 16.35 million in 1991 (160 per cent) (calculated from data provided by Manuel Castells, as reported by Sassen 1994: 56-9; see also Castells 1996: 282, Table 4.1). Within the category of producer services, the two fastest growing items during this twenty-year period were legal services (211 per cent) and miscellaneous business services (314 per cent). A persuasive case can be made that a significant part of this dramatic expansion of producer services is due to the concentration of transnational corporate headquarters in global cities like New York (Sassen 1994: 68–74).

As mentioned, the growth of the post-industrial urban service economy has not been one of unbroken monotonic increases. In the mid-1970s, the New York City government experienced an unprecedented fiscal crisis which was 'solved' only by subordinating the 'sovereignty' of financial decisions on credits and expenditures to the Municipal Assistance Corporation. This was a financial control board constituted and heavily influenced by banks, investment houses and other financial institutions. From 1977 to 1987, New York City's share in the national employment level in producer services declined slightly from 8.3 per cent to 7.6 per cent, due in part to the municipal fiscal crisis and in part to an increasing dispersion of such services regionally and nationwide. The ten-year decline varied slightly among services, from insurance (6.5 to 4.8 per cent), real estate (10.1 to 7.5 per cent) and business services (8.4 to 6.2 per cent) to legal services (9.4 to 8.2 per cent). Only banking and finance remained stable at 11.7 per cent during this period (Sassen 1991: 148-50, Table 6.15). It should be noted that, in all of these figures, Manhattan always shows a higher concentration of services than New York City as a whole.

After the October 1987 stock market crisis, there was a sharp decline in employment as well as considerable restructuring in the securities and banking industry, including mergers among large domestic banks. Employment in banking fell from 169,000 in 1989 to 157,000 in 1991, a drop of 7.6 per cent. Nevertheless, the growth of foreign investment and banking continued to ensure New York's role as a leading world financial centre. The city retained six of the world's top ten securities firms as of 1990 (Sassen 1994: 75), not to mention the continued importance of Wall Street, the New York and American Stock Exchanges, the Dow Jones Company (ranking as the world's fortieth largest media corporation which includes the *Wall Street Journal*) and numerous other business and financial service enterprises.

New York City was and is, of course, also the media capital of the United States, where some of the nation's largest publishing firms, television networks and advertising agencies are located (see also Castells 1989). 'These corporations', as Moss and Ludwig (1991: 245) put it, 'produce the information and images that are communicated across the country and the world, in the form of newspapers, magazines, books, and radio and television programmes. The presence of information-intensive firms in New York City contributes to the economic well-being of the city' and serves 'the larger metropolitan region surrounding the city itself'.

As of 1988, the four major daily newspapers (*Daily News, New York Newsday, New York Post*, and *New York Times*) had a total circulation of about 4.6 million (Moss and Ludwig 1991: 246). City residents can receive at least fifteen television stations without subscribing to cable TV and there are fifteen AM and twenty-three FM radio stations. Moss and Ludwig (1991: 250) identified eighty foreign language newspapers serving the city's vast and growing immigrant population. Cable television has grown from two cable TV franchises for Manhattan in 1971 to four franchises serving all the boroughs since 1986.

Yet Moss and Ludwig (1991: 264–5) point out that the riches of media coverage in the city are double-edged: 'a small number of firms control the major television channels, radio syndicates, and major daily newspapers. On the other hand, a multiplicity of grassroots media outlets . . . have emerged to counter the inadequate coverage and appeal of the mainstream, and often national, media'. There is a growing disparity between the traditional television and print media that serve the area and the highly diverse ethnic and minority groups that make up the majority of the city's population. 'Moreover, there is growing bifurcation of the media, with the city-wide print and television increasingly serving the affluent middle class within the city and surrounding region, while radio and community newspapers serve specific ethnic and minority groups' (ibid: 265). It stands to reason that this social division will continue to be reflected in the bifurcation of old and new media consumers since educational differences, as well as the costs of equipment and access, are likely to restrict the new media market to those with adequate economic resources and cultural capital. Unfortunately, continued global economic expansion is likely to exacerbate the existing socio-economic inequality within cities as well as among them. There are also growing disparities in the stratification among sub-national, national, and transnational regions.

52

The growth of Silicon Alley since 1992

The traditional media have always been concentrated in urban areas and have played an important role in the economic and cultural life of cities like New York for many decades. The last few years, however, have witnessed the explosive growth of a qualitatively different symbiosis of information technologies, structural innovations and cultural creativity which has come to be known as the 'new media', multimedia, or cyber-industry. To be sure, personal interaction and participation remain distant ideals in these new media, but they provide a new technical infrastructure in which interactive and response capacity is a central, built-in feature. One could view the electronic bulletin board and interpersonal e-mail as transitions to these new computer-integrated forms. Local area networks and, finally, 'The Internet' and its subsets, such as the World Wide Web with its websites, home pages and voice-audio-video-graph-print combinations have become emblematic of a new interactive virtual reality and the notion of 'virtual communities' (Poster 1997, Roesler 1997). Multimedia products and services represent a new symbolic environment, a 'culture of real virtuality' (Castells 1996: 364-75). While there is plenty of myth-making that surrounds the secrets of the Internet and the new media, there is a tangible and highly profitable infrastructure of producers and providers that constitute the core of this cyber-industry (Sassen 1997).

Multimedia firms, as described in the following account, include companies specializing in entertainment software, those providing online/Internet services, CD-ROM title developers, website designers and an assortment of related production and service networks connecting suppliers, producers, distributors and consumers. Advertising, marketing, entertainment, education, publishing and video-film production are the new media providers with core businesses outside the new media. It is useful to distinguish at least three layers of the New York cyber-industry: the corporate giants, the new media industry as a whole, and its most creative and volatile subset, Silicon Alley. In reality, these layers are, of course, interrelated.

The corporate giants

New York is home to seven of the world's largest multimedia firms including Time Warner (ranked number 1), Viacom (4), Advance Publications (15), National Broadcasting Co. (NBC) (19), the Columbia Broadcasting System (CBS) (24), The Hearst Corporation (37), and Dow Jones and Co. (40) (see Hachmeister and Rager 1997). Each of these giant corporations consists of several subsidiaries: they are the result of multiple mergers and acquisitions and are continuously involved in processes of reorganization and restructuring. The world's largest media firm Time Warner, for example, includes Turner Broadcasting (and the popular CNN) since 1995 and holds the Manhattan Cable TV franchise. Time Warner had a total of 72,500 employees in 1995. In the same year it had a total media transaction volume of $25.37 billion but, significantly, due to a large volume of corporate debt, in fact made a net loss of $124 million.

Viacom Inc., the fourth largest media corporation with a $17 billion transaction volume and 81,700 employees, had a net profit of $163 million for 1995. It controls a variety of subsidiaries, including Paramount Pictures, the Blockbuster Video chain (film and video game rentals, acquired in 1994) and a host of cable-TV networks (MTV, Showtime, Nickelodeon, Nick at Nite and ten other channels, some of them joint ventures), film, multimedia, publishers and entertainment park groups. In 1996 Viacom entered into a joint venture with the Kirch-Group in Germany. Should the Internet ever become accessible via home television, a corporation like Viacom would be well situated to reap enormous profits from its wide-ranging corporate network.

Still another well-known example is Dow Jones and Co., the fortieth largest media firm world-wide. It includes *The Wall Street Journal* (WSJ), Business Information Services, the WSJ Television Group, the Dow Jones Investor Network and the business journals *Barron's* and *Smart Money*. In 1995, it had 11,200 employees in over 100 countries and a transaction volume of $2.284 billion, with a net profit of $190 million.

It goes without saying that each of these corporate giants constitutes the core of a series of partly hierarchical, partly lateral inter-firm production, service and supplier networks (Bagdikian 1987; see also Harrison 1994: 171, who speaks of 'production networks as an expression of concentration without centralization'). The New York Times, for example, is represented among Silicon Alley firms by its subsidiary The New York Times Electronic Media Company which is headed by a content development specialist and has sixty employees (*Silicon Alley Reporter* 1998: 42; henceforth cited as *SA Reporter*). Sony, the sixth largest media concern world-wide, has had an 'entertainment' subsidiary Sony Online Ventures Inc. since 1995 (ibid.).

Finally, Microsoft maintains three subsidiaries in Silicon Alley with an undisclosed number of employees (Microsoft Multimedia Productions, Microsoft Sidewalk.com and Microsoft Developer Relations Group).

It is likely that the new media industry will increasingly be dominated by an ever-smaller number of large, transnational enterprises. Despite a large number of new entries into the industry, many of the small multimedia firms to be described below will ultimately become integrated into the larger firms by joint ventures and strategic partnerships or will develop into sizeable corporations themselves through mergers and acquisitions (see Barnouw *et al.* 1997; Hazen and Winokur 1997).

The New York area new media industry

The new media industry as a whole provided 105,771 full-time equivalent jobs in 1997, including 55,973 (53 per cent) in New York City proper

(Coopers and Lybrand 1997: 47–8). The eighteen-month increase from the end of 1995 to mid-1997 alone amounted to 48 per cent for the whole area and 105 per cent for the city proper.

The breakdown for the type of employment in 1997 was as follows: of the total of 105,771 employees, 56 per cent were full-time, 21 per cent part-time and 23 per cent freelancers. While the category of freelancers has remained stable, the proportion of part-time employees jumped from 12 to 21 per cent in eighteen months, whereas the proportion of full-time employees shrank from 64 per cent to 56 per cent (Coopers and Lybrand 1997: 5).

In April 1996, the big accounting and consultancy firm Coopers and Lybrand had estimated that new media area employment as a whole would increase by at least 100 per cent by the end of 1998. So far, the increase has been 50 per cent for about half of that three-year period and about 200 per cent since 1992. Thus, despite criticisms of the firm's methods and projections as inflated and advocacy oriented (it was criticised as an 'industry booster'), it is worth noting that most of the figures reported for 1997 have been remarkably close to the earlier projections and that the firm cannot be faulted for lack of accuracy.

The economic picture points to a success story as well. A total of 4,259 area firms generated $3.8 billion in gross revenues in 1995 (these totals for the new media industry include related firms in New Jersey and Connecticut). The corresponding figure for 1997 is 4,881 firms generating $5.7 billion, a 50 per cent increase. Manhattan alone, with 2,128 or 44 per cent of all the new media enterprises, generates $2.8 billion or almost half of the area's gross revenues derived from new media products and services. This represents a 56 per cent increase in revenues over 1995 for the Manhattan enterprises, which tend to be larger than those located outside Manhattan and New York City.

However, there has been a significant structural change in the New York area industry in the eighteen months from April 1996 to October 1997 that signals a rapid increase in economic concentration. Significantly, '1996 was the year of the shakeout in Silicon Alley'; '1997 was . . . the year of continued consolidation' (SA Reporter 1997: 3). For example, in 1995–96, the ratio of large multimedia firms with annual revenues of over $5 million to those under $5 million was .235 or 235 per thousand. By 1997, in contrast, this ratio had shrunk to .0526 or 53 per thousand. This amounts to a four-and-a-half-fold increase in corporate concentration in a year and a half.

This means that while the 250 largest multimedia firms or business units make up only about 5 per cent of all New York area firms, they account for 72 per cent of the total revenues. Moreover, since the percentage of revenues spent outside the local economy increases with firm size, a growing portion of the $4.1 billion generated by the 250 largest multimedia corporations in 1997 was spent outside the New York economy (all figures calculated from data provided in Coopers and Lybrand 1996: 31, 1997: 9, 31–2). To be sure, the total number of firms increased during the period in question, but the size distribution has become more skewed.

Another type of concentration, this one related to the Internet itself, can be ascribed to the 'normally' high corporate density of metropolitan areas. Not surprisingly, Manhattan is also 'the hub for the Internet with almost 150,000 Internet hosts in New York County' (Moss 1996: 11). More importantly, in 1997 New York City had the largest Internet presence with 17,579 registered domains or 4.2 per cent of the national total (Moss and Townsend 1997: 3). A domain represents a single organizational entity or naming authority such as 'nyu.edu' which is used by thousands of computer work stations and e-mail addresses at New York University alone (ibid.). According to Moss and Townsend (1997: 5), 85 per cent of the domain registrations are commercial domains that use the abbreviation '.com'. The remaining 15 per cent are domains like '.org', '.gov', and '.edu'.

Manhattan alone had 15,139 or 86 per cent of the area's registered domains. With a population of over one and a half million, Manhattan had a 'domain density' of 9.9 (ibid.). Only San Francisco had a higher domain density (10.2), although it has only half of the actual number of registered domains (7,518 to Manhattan's 15,139). Thus, the five American cities with the largest number of domains and the highest domain density are Manhattan, San Francisco, Seattle (4,080), Dallas (3,988) and Boston (3,981).

Silicon Alley

The district that is most interesting and relevant for purposes of this chapter is 'Silicon Alley', which comprises the southern third of Manhattan. It represents the area south of 41st Street which is constituted by the 30s and 20s, the Flatiron District, Chelsea, Greenwich Village and the East Village, the Lower East Side, Soho and Downtown. The latter includes Wall Street, the New York and American Stock Exchanges, the World Trade Centre, and the famous 55 Broad Street building with its broad bandwidth, high-speed wiring which is home to many firms.

The 'institutional thickness' of this geographical area is proverbial and illustrates the embeddedness of Silicon Alley firms in a rich economic, social and cultural environment. For example, many of Silicon Alley's multimedia service and training networks involve institutions of higher education such as New York University and its Tisch School of the Arts Centre for Digital Multimedia, now the Centre for Advanced Technology with its famous Interactive Telecommunications Program (ITP). Directed by Professor Red Burns of NYU, the ITP has produced a number of top executives in Silicon Alley, including Jaime Levy (Electronic Hollywood), Howard Greenstein (now director of the Microsoft Developer Relations Group), Rebecca Odes and Esther Drill of gURL, and Stacey Horn of Echo, a virtual community firm. Burns began her career in 1971 when she founded the Alternate Media Centre at the Tisch School which is also nationally known for its outstanding film and video training programmes.

Other examples of New York's rich array of training networks are the NYU Taub Urban Research Centre, the NYU Stern School of Business and the Courant Institute of Mathematics with its computer facilities. In addition, there are various research institutes, colleges, business and law schools (some of them part of the City University system) as well as smaller educational establishments such as the Parsons School of Design (New School of Social Research), the Fashion Institute of Technology and Pace University, to name just a few. Some of these institutions are themselves connected by network ties among teaching and research faculty, the supply of new student cohorts and the placement of graduates.

As mentioned before, publishing houses, advertising agencies, and a host of older media conglomerates complement this densely structured service environment. Many of these institutions pre-date the multimedia revolution, but there is no doubt that the new media industry and the highly saturated educational environment benefit from each other.

Silicon Alley comprises 1,106 new media establishments, which represent 52 per cent of all new media businesses in Manhattan and generate $2.8 billion in gross revenues (Coopers and Lybrand 1997). An increasing number of these firms provide specialized products and services. Thus, the average number of products and services provided in 1995–96 was 3.6, but dropped to 2.4 in 1997. 84 per cent of the firms provide content design and development as a core product/service (Coopers and Lybrand 1997: 36). The other top six products and services provided by firms in descending order are consultancy (37 per cent), content packaging and marketing (34 per cent), content distribution and transport (22 per cent), software development (20 per cent), content creation tools (17 per cent), and electronic commerce (16 per cent).

In terms of their service relationship to various market segments, the firms in this area are most closely associated with advertising and marketing (59 per cent), entertainment (37 per cent), information/reference (43 per cent), education (31 per cent) and financial services (28 per cent) (Coopers and Lybrand 1997: 36). The largest business customer segments besides publishing, advertising, new media and information technology are entertainment, financial services, telecommunications, education, broadcasting, retailing and other business and commercial services.

Publishing, new media, information technology, financial services and telecommunications saw the largest amounts of growth, between 14 per cent and 48 per cent, after 1995-96. The increase in the share of financial services (48 per cent), new media (39 per cent) and information technology (33 per cent) illustrates the tendency for Silicon Alley growth to feed on itself. Smaller customer industry segments such as health care, culture and government also experienced disproportionately large increases; government, for example, almost doubled its share from 8 to 15 per cent.

A close-up view of Silicon Alley firms

Besides the many network ties, alliances, partnerships and joint ventures that are characteristic of firms in the multimedia industry, there are also larger associational entities that reflect the phenomenal growth of the Silicon Alley cluster. For example, the Flatiron Partners venture capital group has more than 120 'associates'; there are over two thousand members of the New York New Media Association (NYNMA) located at 55 Broad Street. The scale of growth is also reflected in the number of subscribers to the *Silicon Alley Reporter* itself, an industry journal that was established in late 1996 and published its tenth issue in the winter of 1997-98. In the following account, I draw on a number of these indigenous sources of information, given the absence of a comprehensive empirical study of Silicon Alley to date.

The latest membership directory of the NYNMA provides perhaps the best illustration of the great diversity of firms located in Silicon Alley. Of the 2,058 members listed for Fall 1997, 1,878 designate their primary business within one of sixty-five product and service categories. If this total of 1,878 corporate members is taken as a base (clearly non-random, but probably fairly representative), one arrives at the following distribution in declining order of frequency.

1   The largest category is constituted by a total of 573 digital media firms which represents 30.5 per cent of the 1,878 firms. Of these 573, almost one-third (10 per cent of the total) are in web services and design. Another third (9.2 per cent) are in online news and information, almost 5 per cent in CD-ROM development, and almost 4 per cent in advertising design.

2   Financial services constitute the second largest group with 202 (10.8 per cent) of the 1,878 firms. Banking, venture capital and investment make up the lion's share of this category with 142 firms (70 per cent). Accounting, financial management and consultancy come in second with fifty-eight firms (29 per cent).

3   A third major category is represented by a variety of professional services. By far the largest group here is legal services (132 firms, or 7 per cent of the total 1,878). This is followed by management consulting (84 firms or 4.5 per cent), and marketing and promotion (83 or 4.4 per cent). 'Recruitment' accounts for 76 firms (4 per cent); this probably includes the important networking activity of talent and head hunting. Finally, there is advertising and sales (66 firms or 3.5 per cent). All other professional service firms account for 3.9 per cent of the total.

4   The print media (newspaper, magazines, and book publishing) are repre-

sented by an astonishing 113 firms (6 per cent). This suggests that old media corporations are likely to have new media subsidiaries and that there is a considerable degree of interpenetration of old and new media rather than outright competition. The additional 64 broadcast media firms, especially radio and network and cable TV, could be seen as similarly bridging the old and new media sectors. The same is true of professional services like graphic design, photography and writing.

5   Finally, there are 103 software development firms (5.5 per cent of the total), a category that includes publication and distribution, interactive software and contract consulting.

These groupings reflect the organizational and corporate diversity of Silicon Alley, not necessarily the shares in profits or total value added. The diversity of products and services is obvious and is reflected in the sixty-five separate categories in terms of which the 1,878 firms are listed.

Some industry clusters outside New York have a fairly high degree of area specialization. This is reported, for example, by Allen Scott (1995: 6, Table 2) in his work on the San Francisco Bay Area in Northern California (business applications and information repositories) and the Los Angeles/Hollywood centred area in Southern California ('self-enhancement' products). Silicon Alley markets seem to combine and integrate both of these specialty areas and appear generally to be more highly diversified than either of the two California area clusters. Unfortunately, the product market categories represented by Scott's 431 California firms are not commensurable with the categories used by the Coopers and Lybrand study or the NYNMA directory. Hence, there is no easy way to compare the findings of Scott's meticulous study short of a systematic comparison and replication.

Another way of looking at the 'typical' Silicon Alley firm is provided by a listing of 100 top multimedia executives and their firms published in the tenth issue of the *SA Reporter* (1997). This is by no means a random sample but it does represent the range of both successful and struggling multimedia firms and provides a behind-the-scenes look at the dynamics of this unusual industry cluster. I have selected forty firms from the 100 entries published and believe they can serve as a basis for constructing a kind of 'ideal type'.

Half of these 'typical' Silicon Alley firms are in the business of producing 'content' and thus represent the more creative aspect of multimedia service production. The other half are in design, advertising and marketing, public relations and accounting, software, virtual communities and chat groups. Among these forty firms, the average number of employees is twenty-two, with a range from two to fifty-five. The average age of the Chief Executive Officer is thirty-two years, with a range from twenty-three to forty-six. Finally, the average length of time the firms have been in business is twenty months with one firm being barely six months old.

Four companies out of the 100 listed and not included in the above ideal-type profile are significantly larger: the average number of employees is 168. They are in accounting and financial services (Coopers and Lybrand New Media Group), Internet advertising (*DoubleClick*), commerce, content and software (*N2K*), and 'online community' content (*iVillage*). They have been in business for an average of two and a half years, with the average age of the executive being forty-eight years.

By contrast, the typical Silicon Alley firm is small and entrepreneurial, relatively young, and headed by a relatively young executive/owner. Most of these Silicon Alley firms, however, share the feature of extensive 'networking', be it in the form of mutual client and supplier relationships, subcontracting, joint ventures, partnerships or strategic alliances. Informal cooperation is also of course a common pattern.

It is worth noting that Coopers and Lybrand's demographic profile for 1997, based on all 4,881 multimedia firms in the New York area, is only marginally different from the above ideal type. Their 1997 report shows that 60 per cent of all firms have their primary business in content design and development. These firms generate about 50 per cent of the industry revenues. The average age of the new media top executive is forty years. In addition, the report emphasizes the network structure of the industry, in that new media firms show a 'high degree of reliance on suppliers and subcontractors' (Coopers and Lybrand 1997: 30). New media firms are also shown to have a relatively young workforce; 36 per cent of the employees are under thirty years old and another 35 per cent are between thirty and forty. Only 38 per cent of the employees, however, are female (ibid.: 41).

Finally, in the absence of an in-depth empirical study of Silicon Alley, one may draw upon a gradual accumulation of a fund of knowledge and 'wisdom' by knowledgeable participants and observers. One of these is Thomas Hirschfeld (1997: 66–8), a journalist who provides an informative description of some of these firms. For example, *AdOne Classified Network* collects classified ads from hundreds of newspapers across the US and publishes them on a single website. Users can search *AdOne* not only by category and region but much more narrowly by type of house, car, job or other commodity. *Atnet* (Apparel and Textile Network) provides business-to-business communications. Through 'virtual showrooms' and company directories that can be searched by product and price, businesses in the fashion industry can locate suppliers and customers. *Data Downlink* is a service for business users. It aggregates quantitative information such as economic figures, industry statistics, company financial data and market facts, and makes it available to subscribers who can download the data directly from the web. *Index Stock Photography* functions as an electronic photo-research centre for advertising agencies, publishers, and others. The 'Riddler' website of *Interactive Imaginations* entertains visitors with trivia contests, crossword puzzles and other games. Playing is free and real prizes are offered, but the games take players on tours of other websites whose owners pay *Interactive Imaginations* for the traffic.

According to Hirschfeld, the service is very popular and serves as a marketing tool for consumer-focused businesses.

iVillage was originally founded by a partnership of executives from the magazine industry, cable home shopping and other services. It publishes 'magazines' on the Internet for sharply defined consumer groups one of which (*Parent Soup*), for example, gives parents medical advice, guidance from child-rearing experts, news and other information. It organizes online 'chat groups' where parents can discuss particular issues with one another while being offered child-related merchandise for online sale. Founded in January 1996 with $14 million in venture capital, *iVillage* got into rough water within a few months and had another capital infusion of $21.5 million in June 1996. In November 1996, all of *iVillage's* sites were integrated at a separate site called *Life Soup* devoted to parenting, health and work from a women's perspective. 'A convergence of message boards, chat areas, and "advertorials", the sites are integrated with commerce zones and sold to advertisers on claims of 51 million page views per month' (*SA Reporter* 1997, 10: 14).

Juno provides almost a million consumers with free electronic mail services in return for showing them advertisements while they are writing or reading messages. *Medscape*, supported by advertising from pharmaceutical manufacturers and others, is an Internet site for doctors. It has some 200,000 members. For a fee, users can get important information, including journal articles and research abstracts.

N2K (*Need to Know*), founded in 1995 and one of the large Silicon Alley firms mentioned above, operates some of the major music-related websites where browsers can hear excerpts from new releases, learn what their favourite artists listen to, and buy from a vast assortment of CDs. Such new media services are highly competitive vis-à-vis the old media firms, as Hirschfeld points out; for example, traditional stores have begun to offer some of these services but cannot match *N2K's* selection and convenience as well as the scale and scope of the Internet. Like *iVillage* and other firms, *N2K* encountered some rough going in the beginning, but seems to have recovered after 1996. It established sales alliances with America Online, Netscape, MTV, @Home, PointCast, AT&T, and WebTV and added a software component with *e-mod (encoded music online delivery),* a technology that plays CD-quality music over the Net (*SA Reporter* 1997, 10: 20).

The nature and importance of multimedia networks (MMNWs)

In discussing the network structure of clusters like Silicon Alley, it is useful to distinguish analytically between the technical information infrastructure or technical networks, on the one hand, and social networks on the other. *Technical networks* such as computer or telecommunications networks (e.g. local area nets and the Internet as a whole, as the net of nets) are 'technical' in the sense of requiring computers (hardware), the necessary programs (software), protocols (traffic rules) and electronic or optical telecommunications connections for purposes of access and use. One of the quantum differences of these networks from the one-to-one connection between users of a conventional telephone system lies in their one-to-infinitely-many simultaneous, multimedia, interactive capability. For the remainder of my discussion, I will treat these technical networks as given (for a useful overview, see Latzer 1997).

Social networks are the specific weblike patterns of informal social relationships among different nodes, as constituted by persons, firms, organizations, and other collective actors (agents, agencies) (Keupp and Röhrle 1987: 7, Knoke and Kuklinski 1982, Schenk 1984: 37, Wellman and Berkowitz 1988, Scott 1991). Among social networks, I want to further distinguish between *emergent* ('natural', expressive) and instrumental or *strategic networks* (formed for explicit purposes such as exchanging information, obtaining resources or solving problems) and concentrate mainly on the latter (see also Sydow 1993).

Inter-firm production and service networks (such as intercorporate and interorganizational networks among multimedia firms, their suppliers, distributors and corporate customers) are prime examples of consciously enacted strategic alliances and economic networks (Harrison 1994). While such networks could conceivably develop and function without the technical infrastructure discussed here, the scale and scope of their operations are vastly enhanced by the availability of the Internet.

There are, of course, other important types of strategic networks, such as quasi-governmental and policy networks (Grimm 1994, Heritier 1993, Knoke 1990, Lauman and Knoke 1987, Marin and Mayntz 1991, Pappi, 1993), and the clandestine networks of organizational, governmental and élite corruption as well as organized crime (Shapiro 1984, Gambetta 1990, Simon and Eitzen 1990, Yeager 1991, Benz and Seibel 1992, Erman and Lundman 1992, Tonry and Reiss 1993). In all of these cases, there is likely to be an underlying 'milieu effect' which results from the embeddedness of actors in a common social environment or subculture ranging from simple and homogeneous to highly diverse and multiplex settings (Amin and Thrift 1992, Braczyk and Schienstock 1996, Castells and Hall 1994, Granovetter 1985, Grabher 1993, Harrison *et al.* 1996, Maillat 1991, Saxenian 1994, Schamp 1995).

A third, intermediate category of networks are either strategically produced by, or emerge more or less randomly from, technical networks. As such, they can be said to be the social by-products, as it were, of techno-social linkages. I call such technically based or net-induced social structures *socio-technical networks*. They are characterized by a great variety of purposes, contents, themes or orientations. Socio-technical networks are 'virtual communities' in the dual sense of representing a community of interacting 'netizens' whose connection to each other is nevertheless based on mere cybernetic links (see also Iglhaut *et al.* 1996, Mitchell 1995). Thus, in talking about socio-technical networks, it seems important to analyse the origins and nature of the technical infrastructure of networks separately from their generative, productive and innovative effects on organizational and social network formation. One should distinguish the technical aspect from effects such as the creation of specialized electronic markets, target groups, interest associations and value-adding partnerships (Johnston and Lawrence 1988). Similarly, since the development of markets, hierarchies, groups and associations from any kind of prior social network involves a process of formalization and institutionalization, it too requires a separate logic of analysis (also see Powell 1990: 322, Benz 1993, Zintl 1993).

While technical, social (especially organizational and interorganizational) and socio-technical networks can be analytically distinguished, this is not quite so easy in actual practice. As Hoogvelt and Yuasa (1994) point out in a comparison of Japanese and Western conceptions of information technology, technical information networks cannot be easily separated from production and organizational technology. They argue that 'in the West, the absence of a psycho-cultural infrastructure comparable to that which enables Japanese network capitalism to operate, has resulted in the conviction that information technology is not primarily part of production technology, but mainly organizational technology. As organizational technology, it is designed to overcome the "precarious" dependency which the new systems of production entail and which, in the Japanese context, as we have shown, are relatively unproblematic. The function of electronic data processing (EDP) and electronic data interchange (EDI) in particular is organizational: providing procedures, communication and memory patterns and ways of linking, controlling and coordinating personnel and companies with one another and with machines. Emerging patterns of hierarchization of EDI flows are important determinants of future constructs of power and regulation' (Hoogvelt and Yuasa 1994: 299, also see Deutschmann 1996).

In sum, there are many types of techno-social linkages in the sense that the nature and capacities of computer networks have consequences (or create opportunities) for the formation, structure and operation of social networks. (On a 'sociology of the Internet', see Gräf and Krajewski 1997, especially the papers by Gräf 1997 and Schack 1997, also Jones 1995.) It is in this latter capacity that the Internet and its constituent sub-nets can be seen as factors in the acceleration of competition and innovation. Self-reinforcing processes are set in motion in which competition leads to cooperation and further integrative social network formation. This, in turn, may stimulate innovation and competition at a higher level. Something like this has undoubtedly animated the phenomenal growth of the new media industry in Silicon Alley in the last half decade.

The negotiated work agreements of multimedia networks

In the strategic social and socio-technical networks among the multimedia firms of Silicon Alley, we find all the well-known types of relationships characteristic of production and service networks. They range from relatively open and informal cooperative arrangements among producers, service providers or suppliers (see e.g. Richardson 1972, Mariti and Smiley 1983) to strategic alliances and joint ventures. They also include the more formal and long-term aspects of relational contracting (Macneil 1978, 1985) and the bi-lateral agreements of quasi-firms (Eccles 1981). The mixed and often contradictory nature of some of these relationships in terms of formal–informal, contractual–noncontractual, managerial—competitive or cooperative–competitive elements is indicated in such terms as managed competition, managed trade and negotiated market relations, mutual advantage and profit sharing, mutual transparency and joint target costing (Weber 1995, Schmidt 1996).

Relational business practices, however, have a tendency to marginalize or bypass formal contractual ties, seeking to get a maximum of cooperation, effort and response out of interactive episodes or partnerships with a minimum of formal commitments, institutional obligations or legal consequences (Macauley 1963, Kaufman Winn 1994). Yet interactive and relational practices in service settings in general, and in knowledge-intensive services in particular, have a much broader significance for social network formation involving co-producers, service providers, clients, consultants and related expert services. Insofar as the participants and members of such interactive network-based practices develop and share a common definition of the situation (the terms and conditions, expectations and rules, definitions and standards, rights and obligations which make these practices possible), they can be said to have a *negotiated work agreement* that tacitly governs their interactions and relations. (See Steinert's (1984, 1994) 'Arbeitsbündnis' or 'Interaktionsbündnis'; see also the notions of the 'definition of the situation' and 'negotiated order' from symbolic interactionist theory and 'making sense together' from ethnomethodology).

It is these more or less implicit work agreements that are the core of multimedia networks. In contrast to the analytical separation between process and product in manufacturing, the product of human services inheres in the process of providing the service itself. The quality of the customized performance is constituted in part by the nature and quality of a human relationship. This process typically involves a kind of co-production based on intensive symbolic interaction and negotiation between two or more people, for example between the service provider and the client.

Human professional services, from medicine and law to teaching and consulting have always been based on this model of more or less cooperative interpersonal negotiation in a somewhat ambiguous, indeterminate, non-routine situation. In such settings, it is understood that experts, due to their technical know-how (or one might say, 'professionals, due to their technical autonomy and their monopoly over skill and knowledge'), exercise a certain degree of influence over clients which hovers between persuasion, charisma and the substantive rationality of professional authority.

As the vast literature on the professions and professional practice shows, however, social expectations, negotiated agreements and implicit contracts can also be disrupted or negated by asymmetrical power relationships or, more precisely, by the conversion of knowledge into power. Misunderstandings and distortions based on unequal power relationships may already be present at the time so-called 'agreements' and 'contracts' are negotiated. They may develop later during the course of the 'consummation' of the negotiated relationship. It goes without saying that asymmetry and inequality of resources and power underlie most problems in the 'fulfilment' of contracts. This is an endemic modern condition that tends to surface also in other fairly institutionalized relationships such as employment and marriage contracts. Formal legal definitions and contractual arrangements were historically designed to stabilize such problems.

In the knowledge-intensive settings of contemporary high-tech production and service systems, the work of 'symbolic analysts' (Reich 1991) is frequently evaluated in terms of the specific interpersonal skills and performance they exhibit in the process of providing a service (see Seron 1996 on the social dimensions of solo and small-firm legal services). As Powell (1990: 300) puts it with respect to network forms of work, 'certain forms of exchange are more social – that is, more dependent on relationship, mutual interest and reputation – as well as less guided by a formal structure of authority'.

While trust plays an important part in such settings, the partly cooperative, partly competitive situation is often sufficiently ambiguous to warrant a more or less rational recourse to the terms and conditions of the work agreement. In other words, strategic social networks do not, and probably cannot, operate merely on 'blind trust' but are contingent and conditional on some reflexive evaluation of the 'performance' in and of the service relationship. (See also Bradach and Eccles 1989, and Gambetta 1990 whose performance-based concept of trust has a similar kind of rational twist). This is likely to be even more true of socio-technical networks and virtual communities, in which the anonymous and liberating nature of the virtual reality produced may also generate a degree of social distance, if not estrangement. Let me illustrate these considerations with some examples of typical service network structures that one is likely to encounter both within and among firms in the multimedia industry.

Project networks in advertising and consulting

In a typical advertising or consulting agency, a given project is organized around both business and management functions. These are centred in a client consultant and his or her account as well as an associated technical and creative organizational unit consisting of a technical or art director, a copy writer and a creative director. Contact with the client is maintained by the consultant who brings the client's viewpoints and wishes into the agency and provides the project team with the appropriate conceptual and technical specifications.

Since teams are sometimes working on different projects and accounts at the same time, there is a good deal of ongoing restructuring and rotation in the division of labour. The agency may resemble a loosely-coupled network of activities or 'adhocracy' rather than a professional bureaucracy with its hierarchy of specialists. Occasionally, in-house teams are asked to compete against each other, especially when customized campaigns are developed to attract a new client.

An ad agency may either provide (make) or outsource (buy) needed support services such as print, film and video, interactive online computer screen design, EDP and direct dialogue marketing. There may be independent management consultants and trend researchers who specialize in certain markets or 'future trends' and who mediate between client firms and ad agencies. Short-term technical services may be provided by freelancers who often develop personal relationships with creative personnel in a multitude of different agencies and who constitute a crucial resource in local multimedia markets.

In many of these cases, the project teams must contact and activate these external service providers and develop social networking skills to use them effectively. Thus, the external relationship between agency and market is constantly pulled into the agency itself; economic principles of competition and the control of transaction costs may assume the function of internal organizational direction and control, especially when agencies are dependent on powerful clients.

The network form of organization also governs the constitution of more external 'core teams' or 'integrated communication networks' among firms. A powerful client, in consultation with an ad agency, may initiate and finance the development of an *ad hoc* project network pulling together various firms for the production of advertising campaigns involving music, film or other performance media, promotion, and public relations. Different networks may be put together for different purposes. Clearly, it is in the agency's interest to be able to have a number of such multimedia service suppliers available at short notice and to develop long-term relationships with them. However, shifts in market trends, clients, and the constant need to weigh make-or-buy decisions also generate a degree of rotation, turbulence and change. Project networks and core teams, therefore, do not necessarily exist for long periods of time or have a determinate structure and stability. Indeed, the term 'core team' has sometimes been viewed as too static and may give way to terms like 'integrated communication agencies' or 'integrated communication networks'.

In advertising, project networks within and between agencies and clients are usually connected by local area computer networks which parallel or supersede the traditional connections by telephone. An agency may have 'internal' computer networks ('Intranets') both for in-house staff located in its various branches and for its clients, although cross-access may be limited. Usually, of course, both staff and client networks are also connected to the Internet.

Other knowledge-intensive service networks

It should be clear that the kinds of service and project networks described above are not simply an added element of traditional organizational forms in knowledge-intensive and multimedia services. Service and project networks constitute the core structure of a new type of organization of work in which cooperation across institutional boundaries becomes a new force of production, creativity, and innovation. This understanding informs research on a variety of advanced producer and business services and their inter-firm networks. It is relevant to fields such as management consultancy, corporate auditing, and tax, legal, and marketing consultancy; computer and EDP services, software development, communication, and marketing services, as well as advertising in a number of different countries (see van Dinteren *et al.* 1994, especially Howells 1990, Gentle and Howells 1994, Monnoyer-Longe and Mayere 1994, Powell, Koput and Smith-Doerr 1996, Strambach 1993, 1994, 1997, Starbuck 1992: 730–3).

The work organization of services in these areas is characterized, according to Strambach (1993: 36), by an intensive process of cooperative interaction and exchange of information between service provider and client which derives from the client's need for explanation, clarification, interpretation and detailed instructions. Clients in this service sector demand a highly particularized and individualized 'product'. Their specification results, in part, from the cognitive nature of the tasks to be processed and the non-routine problems to be 'solved'. It also, in part, comes from the very availability and increased use of new information and communication technologies themselves. Such highly specialized products-as-processes can, in turn, often be provided only by a cooperative arrangement between service provider and one or several suppliers. The service process has to be adapted to the specific needs and circumstances of the corporate client. 'Only then can a qualitatively optimal problem solution be achieved from the perspective of the client. From the perspective of the service provider, on the other hand, a high degree of adaptation and flexibility is required' (Strambach 1993: 36, see also Davidow and Malone 1993, Fagerberg 1995).

Strambach (1993: 46–9) concludes that knowledge-intensive firms use network structures in order to respond effectively to complex and dynamic work situations and to adapt to rapidly changing external environments. By using combined network strategies (e.g. cooperation and externalization) flexibly, they establish a competitive advantage over those firms that do not use network structures.

These conclusions agree broadly (provided production and service networks are analytically distinguished from marketing networks) with those of other students of interorganizational networks such as Berkowitz (1988), Faulkner and Anderson (1987) and Perrow (1992; for useful reviews, see Mizruchi and Galaskiewicz 1994 and van Dinteren 1994). A particularly interesting formulation of a typology of *social networks in marketing* comes up with the concept of 'stakeholders' (other than consumers') networks not under the control of the firm' (Arabie and Wind 1994: 258). The authors state that 'companies are adopting the concept of the hollow corporation (citing Wilson and Dobrzynski 1986) which suggests that, through strategic alliances and outsourcing, the firm can obtain many of the functions it requires without having to perform all of them internally, and there is increased interest in . . . the management of a network of organizations' (ibid.). Obviously, there are analytical parallels between the notions of the 'hollow corporation', the highly networked Type 1 service network (Strambach 1993), the 'borderless enterprise' (Picot *et al.* 1996), the 'virtual enterprise' (Davidow and Malone 1993) and the 'lean supplier system' (Weber 1995), even though one could quibble over the analytical differences between 'system' and 'network'.

Thus, the process of learning, adaptation and managerial transformation with respect to networking appears to complement the population-ecological process of selection of those organizational forms that opt for network-based innovations (see also Picot *et al.* 1989, 1996, and Meckl and Rosenberg 1995). Moreover, in addition to their technical or socio-technical aspects, such networks have a social character that appears to have a particularly innovative potential which renders multimedia networks phenomena of more than technical interest (Ortmann 1990, Feldhoff *et al.* 1994, Weltz and Ortmann 1992). One aspect of this development is the strategic significance that Peter Drucker and others (e.g. Hamel and Prahalad 1994, Reich 1991) have ascribed to knowledge-intensive human capital, a type of capital vastly enhanced in the context of social and socio-technical networks.

Another aspect is the blurring of boundaries among firms and between them and their environments, a theme developed by neo-institutionalist organization theory (Powell and DiMaggio 1991) but not yet fully articulated with the theory of social networks except for Powell's (1990, 1994, 1996) seminal contributions. Finally, there is the question of the spatial/global and longitudinal/historical dimensions of interorganizational network formation and development, especially when viewed in terms of the transitions from inter-firm competition to possible later stages of cooperative, exchange and oligopolistic or neo-corporatist networks and, ultimately, hierarchical or transnational integration (Galbraith 1971,

Friedmann 1988, Harrison 1994). Much of this work – in tandem with the object it describes – finds itself *in statu nascendi* insofar as the intimate connection between economic globalization and the emergence of strategic alliances and networks is only now evolving. It is as yet barely studied or understood (but see Petrella 1996 and Harrison 1994 for analyses of global network relations).

The competition between old and new media firms in Silicon Alley

The putative competitive advantage of multimedia firms in Silicon Alley is a particularly fascinating issue when it is viewed through the Schumpeterian lens of 'creative destruction' (Garud and Lant 1996). There seems to be little doubt among the 'new media partisans . . . not just the militantly non-conformist employees of the start-up companies themselves but their whole support network of venture capitalists, lawyers, landlords, consultants, accountants . . . that new media are destined to triumph over old media' (Hirschfeld 1997: 68). Hirschfeld adduces five basic reasons for this scenario.

1   Since Internet users spend forty to forty-five hours per month online (Coopers and Lybrand 1996), they tend to cut back on the most time-consuming old media activity: television viewing.
2   Television and other ad-supported old media will lose advertising dollars as their mass audiences are reduced by the new media's ability to offer advertisers 'narrowcasting', the capacity to reach carefully targeted audiences through socio-technical networks. Through a kind of 'informating' process, that is, the possibility of collecting background information on Internet users through user-search practices (e.g., while clicking on an advertisement on the web), firms can build up invaluable data sets on specific target groups.
3   New capabilities such as 3-D simulations or cheap, high-quality video-conferencing (already used for pornographic purposes) promise to be expanded for business- and family-oriented mass market applications.
4   Although the old media conglomerates own large sets of valuable content (e.g. the Hollywood film files originally brought to Time Warner Inc. by Warner Bros. and Ted Turner), these assets are not easily turned into a competitive advantage since re-tailoring or translation of old content for new media use appears to be dragging. Hirschfeld (1997) observes that 'video games based on movies usually fail, and websites created by old magazines [cannot compete against new] start-ups'
        New media, in turn, can create 'brave new worlds of content' and can 'customize content for individual users in a way that no old-media company can'. Hirschfeld continues:

Above all, the new media allow subscribers to create their own content, to build the sense of 'electronic community' that many customers want. In thousands of so-called 'chat rooms', the content consists of never-ending conversations . . . about everything from car repair to knitting to politics, offering far more variety and personal contact than a conglomerate's polished product. These 'rooms' make money by charging chatters per minute or by displaying print ads. The king of such communal, subscriber-created content is America Online (AOL) which . . . is like a digital bartender, bringing like-minded people together and collecting more money the longer they schmooze.

(Hirschfeld 1997: 69)

It is estimated that by the end of 1997, AOL had more subscribers in Manhattan than Manhattan Cable and more New York subscribers than the *New York Times*. Clearly, newspapers and other local media are beginning to see the writing on the wall.

5   The old media conglomerates, finally, may find it difficult to change their corporate cultures and transform their corporate structures. They have large operating units and multi-level hierarchies that obstruct the flow of information, resist the processes of constant reorganization and restructuring so typical of the new networked corporate entities, and are ill-adapted to start new programmes and projects on short notice.

Hirschfeld (1997: 69) points out, however, that the sheer money and power invested in the old media conglomerates may prove to be a formidable source of resistance for some time to come. Old-media revenues have still been growing even as some giants like Time Warner, which is participating simultaneously in both old and new media markets, operate in the red (due largely to a huge debt service). The traditional entertainment industry is 'an export powerhouse, second only to aerospace' (ibid.). Advertising itself is a potent factor in the relatively low cost of using television and radio as compared to start-up costs of the (ever-changing) computers and the new media subscription fees, and established big media firms may still have the advantage of name recognition, large mass audiences and huge advertising budgets.

Some difficulties may also face the new media in terms of the undue cost and amount of time spent individually on the Internet as well as some degree of cultural resistance to becoming a 'netizen' in a virtual community, factors that appear to be even stronger in Europe than America. Old media corporations may, however, seek to conquer the new rivals by integration, as has already been suggested by the extent to which large corporations like the *New York Times*, Sony, Time Warner and the big national TV networks have managed to put their foot in the door and begun to operate simultaneously in old and new media markets.

Nevertheless, the 'war between old media and new will be fought in every segment of the industry', according to Hirschfeld (1997: 70), and estimates as to the likely outcome require a differentiated analysis. All print media are most vulnerable to competition from the new media because computerized texts offer new possibilities as compared to paper. Searchability by subject, author, date or specific publication, and capabilities like alphabetization, archiving, filtering and electronic cutting and pasting are powerful alternatives to traditional modes of using print media. Newspaper advertising and, hence, newspaper circulation stand to lose the most in comparison to the ad-listings-cum-pictures and other information offered by the World Wide Web.

Magazines, however, may be better prepared for the threat from the interactive periodicals called 'zines' because they have their own websites and can meet the competition on its own turf, for the time being. For example, Time Warner's Pathfinder 'allows visitors to chat on topics related to Time Inc.'s various magazines, to communicate directly with reporters and photographers on key stories, and even to play games related to the subject matter' (Hirschfeld 1997: 71). Here the new versus old media competition takes place within the belly of the beast itself.

In the case of the book market, the verdict is mixed. The book industry, currently growing at 5 per cent annually, also partakes of both old and new media advantages. Books are still easier to read the old-fashioned way as compared to consuming them on the computer, but they can be marketed and bought more easily via the new media, for example through the one million title 'virtual inventory' of Amazon.com in Seattle. As a result, large publishers and distributors profit more from the Internet than do ordinary bookstores.

In contrast to newspapers, magazines and books, business information services are among the most profitable segments of the new media industry and generate $31 billion in annual revenues for companies in the New York metropolitan area (Hirschfeld 1997: 72). 'Business information naturally lends itself to on-line delivery' (ibid.) which, due to lower costs, benefits the owners of content such as McGraw Hill, Dun and Bradstreet, Dow Jones and Thompson Business Services.

As to the film, music, TV and radio industries, Hirschfeld believes that they 'will feel the new media's effects later than the print industries, but they will feel them even more profoundly, for reasons that Thomas Edison would find very familiar' (ibid.). Clearly, the new technologies need a while to be perfected and to catch on but, once they do, technological 'breakthroughs such as high-speed connections over cable TV lines, TV sets with built-in web software, and "hybrid" CD-ROM's that combine copious data with online updates' (ibid.) will sweep the field, mainly because of lower costs. This is particularly significant in the area of film, where 'Hollywood studios (most owned by New York-based conglomerates) now routinely use supercomputers to generate special effects' (ibid.), making previous techniques and practices of the film industry obsolete. In the recorded-music industry (as in the book industry), the new media effects derive from distribution and marketing, not production. Since 'music is already in digital form thanks to compact disk technology, customers will soon be able to download entire albums directly onto their hard drives over the Internet (something they will eventually be able to do with movies too)' (ibid. 72–3).

Broadcast television and cable TV will be affected by the new media, but in opposite ways. Hirschfeld (1997: 73) reports that 'in 1995, Americans spent slightly more buying PCs than TVs, and TV usage fell 40 per cent on average after the purchase of a household's first PC', a fact likely to hit the country's four major New York-based TV networks. Cable TV networks, on the other hand, will benefit from the broadband data lines into homes, ultimately capable of delivering data a thousand times faster than a fast telephone modem. 'Speed matters', argues Hirschfeld (ibid.), 'not only because consumers get responses more quickly but also because multimedia content containing too much information to download effectively over phone lines will soon be available'.

Radio is the only old medium likely to continue to serve the same audiences that have always been listening: the millions who drive to work and those in low-income and minority groups who, as Moss and Ludwig (1991) point out, have little or no access to other media, especially in expensive new forms.

In sum, the competition between old and new media may enhance rather than destroy the field, partly because it may occur more and more within rather than between media conglomerates such as Time Warner Inc. As Hirschfeld's informative analysis suggests, the Internet provides for cheaper and more effective marketing and distribution at the expense of newspapers and broadcast television. At the same time, however, the Internet will increase the value of ideas and thus enhance the cultural significance and economic scope of the multimedia industry as a whole.

Interim conclusion on multimedia networks

The multimedia networks of Silicon Alley are, to some extent, spin-offs from the producer-services sector and the information technologies that have developed since the 1970s and contributed to spectacular global expansion since 1992. Multimedia networks are, of course, not the only factor in the process of economic and financial globalization, but they are a significant and indicative part of it and have grown at the same dramatic pace in the last few years. Yet this is not all. Multimedia networks in global nodes such as New York City are themselves centres of self-activity, organizational learning and high-density interaction with other units. It would, therefore, be too simple to describe them as merely a link in a one-dimensional, mono-causal, or unidirectional chain of 'value creation' (Fuchs and Wolf 1997: 32) in which they are seen to influence the creation, diffusion and adoption of technical and social innovations, or to determine regional economic development.

Multimedia networks are, rather, part of a process of mutual causation. In other words, they are self-organizing core structures in a series of relationships of partly competitive, partly cooperative interactivity with other production and service networks. As members of networks in a transitional phase between competition and integration, actors in multimedia networks may indeed perceive greater benefit from temporary cooperation rather than single-minded competition and conflict. This is reflected in slogans like 'everybody benefits', 'rising water lifts all boats', 'increasing the size of the pie as a collective strategy is more important than competition for the pieces'. In a period of global block formation, such arguments are particularly persuasive. Given the central location of Silicon Alley in one of the world's major cities, the various multiplier effects and synergies of such a combination of cultural and economic density tend to translate into the kind of positive feedback loop I mentioned before.

The multimedia industry, by its very nature, tends to contribute to a new culture industry which is in the business of providing new images, interpretations and meanings of what is happening globally at the same time that it offers redefinitions of changing cultural traditions and practices at the national, regional and local level. Thus, the new multimedia-based culture industry benefits from the very social and economic reality it helps to describe and define in the virtual reality of cyberspace.

Discussion and conclusion

The short historical trajectory of New York's Silicon Alley shows the tremendous potential for sustained economic development of production and service networks in general, and of multimedia networks in particular. The new production and service networks, whether in Europe, Japan or the United States, exemplify the dual role of being part of economic globalization and at the same time constituting the backbone of reactive regional development strategies in the face of global competition. In this dual role, they are supported and their effects augmented by the new media industry.

The special nature of interactive virtual communication makes multimedia networks into something more than a sub-category of service networks. Because of their technical capabilities and socio-technical convertibility as well as their strategic significance in the new culture industry, multimedia networks provide an additional level of communicative capacity and cultural sophistication. They are networks of networks. As such, their effect seems to reach beyond the conventional advantages of agglomeration because they are in the business of self-enhancement and creative self-representation.

Moreover, they may harbour the key not only to self-transformation, but to local/institutional and regional/socio-economic transformation. Network formation normally benefits from cultural homogeneity and other categorical similarities among actors as well as homophily in their choices.

Multimedia networks, however, appear to thrive on diversity and difference, thus encouraging collective learning and experimentation as well as creativity and innovation under conditions of freedom of speech and self-expression. If their accessibility were not so frequently limited by virtue of unequal resources, education and other restrictions of cultural capital, they could become the medium of a liberal-democratic culture *par excellence*.

The case of Silicon Alley, however, is difficult to separate from other aspects of the unique context in which it is embedded. New York's conditions of organizational density are hard to duplicate in regional clusters that find themselves in the incipient stages of economic development. The experience of Silicon Alley points to the kinds of potential synergies that emanate from a diversified economic and cultural context. Even a limited constellation, such as a mid-sized urban environment with two or three institutions of higher education, research and development, and creative-technical training (art, computers, design, film, music), one or two major employers sponsoring a series of production, supplier, and service networks, and a few networks of multimedia firms self-sufficient enough to constitute a relatively autonomous, but attractive basis for further development, would be a viable baseline for any regional cluster. Examples from the American heartland are the 'Research Triangle' of North Carolina or the urban-regional high-tech clusters around Ann Arbor, Atlanta, Austin, Baltimore, Bloomington, Boston, Houston, Ithaca, Madison, New Haven, Princeton, San Francisco, Seattle and Washington. None of these cities are particularly large or even comparable to New York, but they all have either a major research university, or a state government or major employer large enough to anchor some other knowledge-intensive service network or multimedia venture. The crucial factor seems to be the avoidance of a highly specialized or homogeneous, single-industry base which might be internally networked, but not sufficiently diversified.

All of these cases also benefit from the active participation and encouragement of local, state, and sometimes interstate or regional economic development agencies and policies. For the State of New York, these roles are performed by the Office of Economic Development in the State Office of Management and Budget, Albany, N.Y.; the New York City Mayor's Office of Economic Development which is highly pro-active in attracting out-of-state and foreign venture capital and arranging for tax credits and tax abatements; and the Port Authority traditionally active in planning tri-state infrastructure and advanced economic development.

In addition, a multicultural and multi-ethnic urban environment always seems to have an edge over culturally and ethnically homogeneous settings if only because the latter tend to be boring, offer a limited quality of life in terms of choices of entertainment and life-styles, and are often artistically, culturally and intellectually impoverished. Multicultural university towns, by contrast, have often proved sufficiently attractive for young urban professionals to provide the right kind of dynamic, liberal, youthful, future-oriented milieu.

If this sounds like an advertisement from a local chamber of commerce or from a regional economic development corporation, it is perhaps not so far from the mark because these characteristics also figure in the 'quality-of-life' ratings of cities, their demographic composition and their economic growth rate. All told, the new multi-layered types of social and socio-technical networks discussed here seem to fit well with this larger socio-cultural diversity. Multimedia networks tend to spring up and develop in a relation of mutual causation and transformation with the rich, image-laden and meaning-producing texture of cities, and thus also help to create and reflect the current dynamics of global change.

Note

For helpful comments on an earlier version of this chapter, I want to thank the participants of the International Workshop on Regional Economic Restructuring and Multimedia, especially Phil Cooke, Gerhard Fuchs, Meric Gertler, John Pavlik, Åke Sandberg, Allen Scott, and Hans-Georg Wolf; my colleague Doug Guthrie; and four anonymous reviewers.

References

Amin, A. and Thrift, N. (1992) 'Neo-Marshallian Nodes in Global Networks', *International Journal of Urban and Regional Research* 16: 571–87.

Arabie, P. and Wind, Y. (1994) 'Marketing and Social Networks' in: S. Wasserman and J. Galaskiewicz (eds) *Advances in Social Network Analysis,* Thousand Oaks: Sage.

Bagdikian, B. (1987) *Media Monopoly,* Boston: Beacon.

Barnouw, E. *et al.* (1997) *Conglomerates and the Media,* New York: The New Press.

Becattini, G. (1990) 'The Marshallian industrial district as a socioeconomic notion', in F. Pyke, G. Becattini and W. Sengenberger (eds) *Industrial Districts and Interfirm Cooperation in Italy,* Geneva: International Labour Office.

Benz, A. (1993) 'Commentary on O'Toole and Scharpf: The Network Concept as a Theoretical Approach', in F. W. Scharpf (ed.) *Games in Hierarchies and Networks,* Frankfurt: Campus.

Benz, A. and Seibel, W. (eds) (1992) *Zwischen Kooperation und Korruption: Abweichendes Verhalten in der Verwaltung,* Baden Baden: Nomos.

Bergman, E. M., Maier, G., and Tödtling, F. (eds) (1991) *Regions Reconsidered: Economic Networks, Innovation, and Local Development in Industrialized Countries,* London: Mansell.

Berkowitz, S. D. (1988) 'Markets and market-areas', in B.Wellman and S. D. Berkowitz (eds) *Social Structures: A Network Approach,* New York: Cambridge University Press.

Braczyk, H. J. and Schienstock, G. (eds) (1996) *Kurswechsel in der Industrie: Lean Production in Baden-Württemberg,* Stuttgart: Kohlhammer.

Bradach, J. L. and Eccles, R. G. (1989) 'Price, authority and trust: from ideal types to plural forms', *Annual Review of Sociology* 15: 97–118.

Camagni, R. (1991) *Innovation Networks: Spatial Perspectives,* London: Belhaven Press.

Castells, M. (1989) *The Informational City,* Oxford: Blackwell.

—— (1996) *The Rise of the Network Society,* Oxford: Blackwell.

Castells, M. and Hall, P. (1994) *Technopoles of the World: The Making of the 21st Century Industrial Complexes,* London: Routledge.

Coopers and Lybrand Consulting (1996) *New York New Media Industry Survey: Opportunities and Challenges of New York's Emerging Cyber-Industry,* New York: New York New Media Association.

Coopers and Lybrand Consulting (1997) *New York New Media Industry Survey: Opportunities and Challenges of New York's Emerging Cyber-Industry,* New York: New York New Media Association.

Davidow, W. H. and Malone, M. S. (1993) *Das Virtuelle Unternehmen: Der Kunde als Co-Produzent,* Frankfurt and New York: Campus.

Deutschmann, C. (1996) 'Lean production: der kulturelle Kontext', in H. J. Braczyk and G. Schienstock (eds) *Kurswechsel in der Industrie: Lean Production in Baden-Württemberg,* Stuttgart: Kohlhammer.

Eccles, R. (1981) 'The quasifirm in the construction industry', *Journal of the Economic Behaviour of Organizations* 2: 335–57.

Erman, M. D. and Lundman, R. J. (eds) (1992) *Corporate and Governmental Deviance. Problems of Organizational Behaviour in Contemporary Society,* 4th ed., New York: Oxford.

Fagerberg, J. (1995) 'User-producer interaction, learning, and comparative advantage', *Cambridge Journal of Economics* 19: 243–56.

Faulkner, R.R. and Anderson, A.B. (1987) 'Short-term projects and emergent careers: evidence from Hollywood', *American Journal of Sociology* 92: 879–91.

Feldhoff, J., Hessinger, P. and Schlinkert, P. (1994) *Wandel des Betriebs durch Informationstechnologie,* Frankfurt: Campus.

Friedmann, H. (1988) 'Form and substance in the analysis of the world economy', in B. Wellman and S. Berkowitz (eds) *Social Structures: A Network Approach,* New York: Cambridge University Press.

Fuchs, G. and Wolf, H.-G. (1997) *Regionale Erneuerung durch Multimedia? Arbeitsbericht* 74, Stuttgart: Akademie für Technikfolgenabschätzung in Baden-Württemberg.

Galbraith, J. K. (1971) *The New Industrial State,* 2nd ed., Boston: Houghton Mifflin.

Gambetta, D. (ed.) (1990) *Trust: Making and Breaking Cooperative Relations,* Oxford: Blackwell.

Garud, R. and Lant, T. (1996) 'Dynamics of innovation in Silicon Alley: public and business policy associated with the emergence of multimedia technology in Silicon Alley.' First draft of proposal, New York: Stern School of Business, New York University.

Gentle, C. and Howells, J. (1994) 'The computer services industry: restructuring for a single market', *Journal of Economic and Social Geography* 85: 311–24.

Grabher, G. (ed.) (1993) *The Embedded Firm: On the Socioeconomics of Industrial Networks.* London and New York: Routledge.

Gräf, L. (1997) 'Locker verknüpft im Cyberspace – Einige Thesen zur Änderung

76

sozialer Netzwerke durch die Nutzung des Internet', in L. Gräf and M. Krajewski (eds) *Soziologie des Internet,* Frankfurt and New York: Campus.

Gräf, L. and Krajewski, M. (eds) (1997) *Soziologie des Internet. Handeln im Elektronischen Web-Werk.* Frankfurt and New York: Campus.

Granovetter, M. (1985) 'Economic action and social structure: the problem of embeddedness', *American Journal of Sociology* 91: 481–510.

Grimm, D. (ed.) (1994) *Staatsaufgaben,* Baden-Baden: Nomos.

Hachmeister, L. and Rager, G. (eds) (1997) *Wer beherrscht die Medien? Die 50 größten Medienkonzerne der Welt,* München: C. H. Beck.

Hamel, G. and Prahalad, C. K. (1994) *Competing for the Future,* Boston: Harvard Business School Press.

Harrison, B. (1994) *Lean and Mean: The Changing Landscape of Corporate Power in the Age of Flexibility,* New York: Basic Books.

Harrison, B., Kelley, M., and Grant, J. (1996) 'Innovative firm behaviour and local milieu: exploring the intersection of agglomeration, firm effects, and technological change', *Economic Geography* 72: 233–52.

Hazen, D. and Winokur, J. (1997) *WE the Media: A Citizen's Guide to Fighting for Media Democracy,* New York: The New Press.

Heritier, A. (ed.) (1993) *Policy-Analyse: Kritik und Neuorientierung.* Politische Vierteljahresschrift 24, Sonderband.

Hirschfeld, T. P. (1997) 'The Coming Showdown in Media City' *City Journal* 7 (Winter): 66–8.

Hoogvelt, A. and Yuasa, M. (1994) 'Going lean or going native? The social regulation of 'lean' production systems', *Review of International Political Economy* 1, 2: 281–303.

Howells, J. (1990) 'The internationalization of R & D and the development of global research networks', *Regional Studies* 24: 495–518.

Iglhaut, S., Medosh, A. and Rötzer, F. (eds) (1996) *Stadt am Netz: Ansichten von Telepolis,* Mannheim: Bollmann.

Johnston, R. and Lawrence, P. R. (1988) 'Beyond vertical integration – the rise of the value-adding partnership', *Harvard Business Review* 1988 (July-August): 94–101.

Jones, S. (1995) *CyberSociety: Computer-mediated Communication and Community,* Thousand Oaks, Cal.: Sage.

Kaufman Winn, J. (1994) 'Relational practices and the marginalization of law: informal financial practices of small businesses in Taiwan', *Law and Society Review* 28: 193–232.

Keupp, H. and Röhrle, B. (eds) (1987) *Soziale Netzwerke,* Frankfurt: Campus.

Knoke, D. (1990) *Political Networks: The Structural Perspective,* Cambridge University Press.

Knoke, D. and Kuklinski, J. H. (1982) *Network Analysis,* Beverly Hills: Sage.

Latzer, M. (1997) *Mediamatik - die Konvergenz von Telekommunikation, Computer und Rundfunk,* Opladen: Westdeutscher Verlag.

Laumann, E. O. and Knoke, D. (1987) *The Organizational State: Social Choice in National Policy Domains*, Madison: University of Wisconsin Press.

Macaulay, S. (1963) 'Non-Contractual relations in Business', *American Journal of Sociology* 28: 54–71.

Macneil, I. R. (1978) *Contracts: Adjustment of Long-term Economic Relations Under Classical, Neoclassical, and Relational Contract Law*, Northwestern University L.R., 854–905.

—— (1985) 'Relational contract: what we do and do not know', *Wisconsin Law Review* 3: 483-526.

Maillat, D. (1991) 'The innovation process and the role of the milieu', in E. M. Bergman, G. Maier and F. Tödtling, (eds) (1991) *Regions Reconsidered: Economic Networks, Innovation, and Local Development in Industrialized Countries*, London: Mansell.

Marin, B. and Mayntz, R. (eds) (1991) *Policy Networks*, Frankfurt: Campus.

Mariti, P. and Smiley, R. (1983) 'Cooperative agreements and the organization of industry', *Journal of Industrial Economics* 31: 437–51.

Meckl, R. and Rosenberg, C. (1995) 'Neue Ansätze zur Erklärung internationaler Wettbewerbsfähigkeit', *Zeitschrift für Wirtschafts- und Sozialwissenschaften* 155: 211–31.

Mitchell, W. J. (1995) *City of Bits: Space, Place, and the Infobahn,* Cambridge: MIT Press.

Mizruchi, M. S. and Galaskiewicz, J. (1994) 'Networks in interorganizational relations' in S. Wasserman and J. Galaskiewicz (eds) *Advances in Social Network Analysis,* Thousand Oaks, Calif.: Sage.

Monnoyer-Longe, M. C. and Mayere, A. (1994) 'Networks in knowledge-intensive firms', *Journal of Economic and Social Geography* 85: 303–15.

Moss, M. (ed.) 1996. *The Changing Telecommunications Environment and New York City.* New York: Taub Urban Research Centre, New York University and Carnegie Corporation, Program on Science, Technology and Government.

Moss, M. and Ludwig, S. (1991) 'The Structure of the Media', in J. Mollenkopf and M. Castells (eds) *Dual City: Restructuring New York,* New York: Russell Sage.

Moss, M. and Townsend, A. (1997) *Manhattan Leads the 'Net Nation',* New York: NYU Taub Urban Research Centre.

New York New Media Association (1997) *Member Directory.*

Noyelle, T. and Dutka, A. B. (1988) *International Trade in Business Services: Accounting, Advertising, Law, and Management Consulting,* Cambridge, Mass.: Ballinger.

Ortmann, G. (1990) *Computer und Macht in Organisationen: Mikropolitische Analysen,* Opladen: Westdeutscher Verlag.

Pappi, F. U. (1993) 'Policy-Netze', in A. Heritier (ed.) *Policy-Analyse: Kritik und Neuorientierung.* Politische Vierteljahresschrift 24, Sonderband.

Perrow, C. (1992) 'Small network firms', in N. Nohria and R. Eccles (eds) *Networks and Organizations: Structure, Form, and Action,* Boston: Harvard Business School Press.

Petrella, R. (1996) 'Globalization and internationalization: the dynamics of the emerging world order', in R. Boyer and D. Drache (eds) *States Against Markets: The Limits of Globalization,* London and New York: Routledge.

Picot, A., Laub, U. D. and Schneider D. (1989) *Innovative Unternehmensgründungen: eine Ökonomisch-empirische Analyse,* Berlin: Springer.

Picot, A., Reichwald, R. and Wigand, R. (1996) *Die Grenzenlose Unternehmung,* Wiesbaden: Gabler.

Poster, M. (1997) 'Elektronische Identitäten und Demokratie', in S. Münker and A. Roesler (eds) *Mythos Internet,* Frankfurt: Suhrkamp.

Powell, W. (1990) 'Neither market nor hierarchy: network forms of organizations', *Research in Organizational Behaviour* 12: 295–336.

Powell, W. and DiMaggio, P. (eds) (1991) *The New Institutionalism in Organizational Analysis,* Chicago: University of Chicago Press.

Powell, W., Koput, K. and Smith-Doerr, L. (1996) 'Interorganizational collaboration and the locus of innovation: networks of learning in biotechnology', *Administrative Quarterly* 41: 116–45.

Powell, W. and Smith-Doerr, L. (1994) 'Networks and economic life', in N. Smelser and R. Swedberg (eds) *The Handbook of Economic Sociology,* Princeton: Princeton University Press.

Reich, R. (1991) *The Work of Nations: Preparing Ourselves for 21st Century Capitalism,* New York: Knopf.

Richardson, G. (1972) 'The organization of industry', *Economic Journal* 82: 883–96.

Roesler, A. (1997) 'Bequeme Einmischung, Internet und Öffentlichkeit', in S. Münker and A. Roesler (eds) *Mythos Internet,* Frankfurt: Suhrkamp.

Sassen, S. (1991) *The Global City,* New York, London and Tokyo: Princeton University Press.

—— (1994) *Cities in a World Economy.* Thousand Oaks, Calif.: Pine Forge Press.

—— (1997) 'Cyber-Segmentierungen. Elektronischer Raum und Macht', in S. Münker and A. Roesler (eds) *Mythos Internet,* Frankfurt: Suhrkamp.

Saxenian, A. (1994) *Regional Advantage: Culture and Competition in Silicon Valley and Route 128,* Cambridge: Harvard University Press.

Schack, M. (1997) 'Telearbeit und Internet', in L. Gräf and M. Krajewski (eds) *Soziologie des Internet,* Frankfurt and New York: Campus.

Schamp, E. W. (1995) 'Arbeitsteilung, neue Technologien und Regionalentwicklung', in D. Barsch and H. Karrasch (eds) 49. *Deutscher Geographentag,* Stuttgart: F. Steiner.

Schenk, M. (1984) *Soziale Netzwerke und Kommunikation,* Tübingen: Mohr.

Schmidt, G. (1996) 'Lean production – konzeptionelle Überlegungen zu einer Zauberformel', in: H. J. Braczyk and G. Schienstock (eds) *Kurswechsel in der Industrie: Lean Production in Baden-Württemberg,* Stuttgart: Kohlhammer.

Scott, A. J. (1995) 'From Silicon Valley to Hollywood: growth and development of the multimedia industry in California', Los Angeles: UCLA, Lewis Centre for Regional Policy Studies, Working Paper, 13.

Scott, J. (1991) *Social Network Analysis,* Thousand Oaks, Calif.: Sage.

Seron, C. (1996) *The Business of Practicing Law,* Philadelphia: Temple University Press.

Shapiro, S. (1984) *Wayward Capitalists: Target of the Securities and Exchange Commission,* New Haven: Yale University Press.

Silicon Alley Reporter (1998) Issue No. 10 (Winter).

Simon, D. R. and Eitzen, S. (1990) *Elite Deviance,* 3rd edition, Boston: Allyn and Bacon.

Starbuck, W. H. (1992) 'Learning by knowledge-intensive firms', *Journal of Management Studies 29:* 713–40.

Steinert, H. (1984) 'Das Interview als soziale Interaktion', in H. Meulemann (ed.) *Soziale Realität im Interview,* Frankfurt: Campus.

—— (1994). 'Am unerfeulichsten ist der Kunstskandal, der ausbleibt: Anmerkungen zu 'Arbeitsbündnissen' in der Kunst, besonders des 20.Jahrhunderts', Vorwort zu: C. Resch, *Kunst als Skandal: der Steirische Herbst und die Öffentliche Erregung,* Wien: Verlag für Gesellschaftskritik.

Strambach, S. (1993) 'Die Bedeutung von Netzwerkbeziehungen für Wissensintensive Unternehmensorientierte Dienstleistungen', *Geographische Zeitschrift* 81: 35–50.

—— (1994) 'Knowledge-intensive business services in the Rhine-Neckar Area', *Journal of Economic and Social Geography* 85: 354–61.

—— (1997) 'Wissensintensive unternehmensorientierte Dienstleistungen – ihre Bedeutung für die Innovations- und Wettbewerbsfähigkeit Deutschlands', *Vierteljahreshefte zur Wirtschaftsforschung* 66: 230–42.

Sydow, J. (1993) *Strategische Netzwerke: Evolution und Organisation,* Wiesbaden: Gabler.

Tonry, M. and Reiss, A. (eds) (1993) 'Beyond the law: crime in complex organizations', *Crime and Justice Series* 18, Chicago: University of Chicago Press.

van Dinteren, J. (1994) 'Introduction', *Special Issue on Business Services and Networks. Journal of Economic and Social Geography,* 85: 291–95.

van Dinteren, J. *et al.* (eds) (1994) 'Special Issue on Business Services and Networks', *Journal of Economic and Social Geography* 85.

Weber, H. (1995) *Management und Logik des schlanken Zuliefersystems.* Kaiserslautern: Universität Kaiserslautern, FG Soziologie, discussion paper, 501.

Wellman, B. and Berkowitz, S. D. (eds) (1988) *Social Structures: A Network Approach,* New York: Cambridge University Press.

Weltz, F. and Ortmann, R. G. (1992) *Das Softwareprojekt. Projektmanagement in der Praxis,* Frankfurt and New York: Campus.

Wilson, J. W. and Dobrzynski, J. H. (1986) 'And now, the post-industrial corporation', *Business Week,* 3 March 1986.

Yeager, P. (1991) *The Limits of Law: the Public Regulation of Private Pollution,* Cambridge: Cambridge University Press.

Zintl, R. (1993) 'Commentary on O'Toole and Scharpf: networks as a challenge for theory', in F.-W. Scharpf (ed.) *Games in Hierarchies and Networks,* Frankfurt: Campus.

5

CONTENT AND ECONOMICS IN THE MULTIMEDIA INDUSTRY

The case of New York's Silicon Alley

John V. Pavlik

Focus of this study

The focus of this study is on the growing multimedia industry located in a geographic region known as the 'Silicon Alley' of New York. As noted by Fuchs and Wolf (1997), multimedia is usually defined in technical terms. In this sense, it signifies a combination of a variety of media (at least three of the following: text, graphics, moving pictures, audio, etc.) available in a digitized format that can be accessed interactively. We consider multimedia to be a networking technology. Our definition is geared toward the end product of a potential multimedia value chain or value network in which a variety of actors can be present. These actors include, among others, network operators (for online multimedia), hardware producers (servers, computers, etc.), the media industry, service providers, content providers, software producers and the entertainment industry.

In the case of New York's Silicon Alley, an area comprising Manhattan south of 41st Street, the multimedia industry, as defined by Fuchs and Wolf (1997), is generally referred to as 'new media'. Notably, in its October 1997 study, Coopers and Lybrand report that the vast majority (76 per cent) of New York's new media firms are primarily involved in interactive multimedia content and design. The remainder (24 per cent) are involved indirectly in the multimedia industry, in fields such as multimedia marketing (9 per cent), software development (5 per cent) or enabling services, such as design consultancy (11 per cent). As Coopers and Lybrand sum up the situation, 'Businesses primarily involved in content design and development are the predominant players in New York's New Media industry' (Coopers and Lybrand 1997: 7). Therefore, in this chapter, the term 'multimedia' will be used to describe what in New York is generally referred to as 'new media.'

Fuchs and Wolf (1997) also note that corporations that become active in multimedia can be of at least three types:

1   Traditional technology corporations that use multimedia for problem solving.
2   Established corporations that move into new business fields (e.g. traditional content providers in television or publishing).
3   New corporations being established in the multimedia, or new media, field.

Types two and three are the focus of this study, and represent the core of the multimedia industry in New York. Type three is especially important in New York. One study (Coopers and Lybrand 1997) shows that 68 per cent of New York's new media, or multimedia, firms have been in business for three years or less, and 30 per cent have been established only in the past eighteen months.

A global multimedia capital

New York has emerged in the 1990s as a global capital of the multimedia, or new media, industry. The Coopers and Lybrand study (1997) reveals that the New York region is home to 4,881 companies that develop and market multimedia software, online entertainment, World Wide Web sites on the Internet and other digital content and services. Most of these are small entrepreneurial firms but others are off-shoots of large media and technology companies. Together, they employ more workers in New York than the traditional media industries of television, book publishing and newspapers, each of which has been in retrenchment in recent months and years. Multimedia employment, including full-time, part-time and freelance, has more than tripled in five years, from 28,500 in 1992 to 71,500 in 1995 and to 105,771 in 1997. It is expected to top 144,000 by the end of 1998 (Coopers and Lybrand 1997: 47). In comparison, a similar study of the multimedia industry in San Francisco found that some 2,200 new media companies employed more than 62,000 workers in 1995 (Bay Area Multimedia Partnership 1997).

Freelance employment is expected to grow especially rapidly in the New York multimedia market, with Coopers and Lybrand projecting 50 per cent growth in the next three years (1997: 54). Multimedia firms also expect to rely increasingly on remote workers, especially for creative staff; the Coopers and Lybrand study shows this growing from 10 per cent today to 16 per cent in the next three years (1997: 56). Furthermore, in 1997, the multimedia industry based in the tri-state area of New York, New Jersey and Connecticut generated some $5.7 billion in gross revenues. One half of this, or $2.85 billion, was generated in New York City alone, a 50 per cent growth rate since 1995 (Coopers and Lybrand 1997: 5).

A variety of factors have contributed to the rapid ascendancy of the new media, or multimedia, industry in New York, including many of the institutional conditions suggested by Amin and Thrift's (1992) notion of 'institutional thickness'. New York's relatively compact borough of Manhattan provides the geographic proximity conducive to the development of a new industry. For example, as a cultural, media and financial world capital, New York offers the growing multimedia industry a teeming pool of young designers, artists, writers and programmers well positioned to exploit the dynamic diffusion of personal computers and the Internet (Moss 1996). New York's compactness also facilitates the use of support services of regional actors in research, education, economic, promotional and technology transfer. These factors are especially important to the multimedia industry, which is dominated, at least in the early stages, by small and medium-sized companies (Junne 1995, Fuchs and Wolf 1997).

The Coopers and Lybrand study (1997: 10) identifies the three areas where multimedia executives view New York as most competitive: access to editorial/artistic talent; access to customers; and image and credibility. The study also identifies the three most important elements of location attractiveness: availability of technology infrastructure; image and credibility; and overall costs of doing business. In this case, New York scores highly on infrastructure and image, but poorly on the third element, costs. This is where public policy can play an important role.

The number of multimedia businesses by geographic segment also reflects the central importance of Manhattan, and an area within it known as 'Silicon Alley', in the growth of the New York's multimedia industry. Almost half (44 per cent or 2,128) of the multimedia businesses in the New York tri-state area are located in Manhattan, with much smaller portions located in other parts of New York City (10 per cent or 473), New York metro (14 per cent or 696) New Jersey (20 per cent or 974) and Connecticut (12 per cent or 610) (Coopers and Lybrand 1997).

The heart of New York's multimedia industry lies south of 41st Street Manhattan and includes Chelsea, Greenwich Village, Soho and Wall Street. The area was dubbed 'Silicon Alley' by new media pioneer Mark Stahlman. Manhattan's multimedia map is presented in Map 5.1. Of Manhattan's 2,128 multimedia/new media establishments, 1,106 are in Silicon Alley, while just 451 are in Midtown (north of 41st Street and south of 59th, the lower end of Central Park) and 571 are in uptown Manhattan (ibid.: 27). The numbers of New York multimedia/new media jobs are similarly skewed, with 23,390 in Silicon Alley, 13,445 in Midtown and 11,993 Uptown.

The presence of numerous traditional media companies also supports the development of the multimedia industry. Among these are seven of the world's largest media companies, including Time Warner (ranked 1), Viacom (4), Advance Publications (15), National Broadcasting Company (NBC) (19), the Columbia Broadcasting System (CBS) (24), The Hearst Corporation (37) and Dow Jones and Co. (40) (Heydebrand 1998: 13, Hachmeister and Rager

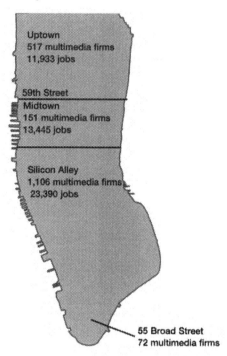

Map 5.1 Manhattan's multimedia industry
Source: Coopers and Lybrand 1997

1997), as well as the *New York Times*. All of these are actively involved in
multimedia enterprises in New York. New York is also the undisputed media
capital of the United States (Heydebrand 1998). Many of the nation's largest
publishing firms, television networks and advertising agencies are headquartered in New York. These companies produce much of the 'multimedia'
content of the traditional and new media.

One significant example of the synergy brought about by the convergence
of traditional publishing companies and the burgeoning multimedia industry in New York is the emergence of Silicon Alley companies specializing in
producing online multimedia content for women. Development of content
for women represents one of the fastest growing sectors of online communications around the world. Jupiter Communications reports in a study
(Wheatley 1997: 1) that women represent 32.5 per cent of users online. It
predicts that 'the women online will steadily increase, reaching nearly 47 per
cent by the year 2000.'

As a result, many multimedia producers have begun focusing much of
their marketing effort toward women. For example, 'By mid-1996 all four of
the major consumer online services – AOL, CompuServe, MSN and

Prodigy – had established special areas for women,' reports Jupiter (ibid.: 103). Further, Jupiter has identified the fourteen leading producers and providers of online multimedia content for women, six of which are located in New York (either in Silicon Alley or in the tri-state metropolitan area), including Prodigy (White Plains, NY), HomeArts (a Hearst company featuring Planet Lunch, a multimedia cafe with recipes, comics, interactive wine navigator and more), Lifetime (a spin-off from Lifetime Entertainment, which creates the Lifetime channel on television), Condenet (Conde Nast Publications), Herspace (Downtown Digital), Cybergrrl Webstation (Cybergrrl Internet Media).

Local and regional government policy has played a limited role in the growth of New York's multimedia industry, yet promises to expand its impact in the near future as city and state agencies consider providing reduced taxes and investment incentives to multimedia companies. They are also encouraging investment in high-speed data lines. One example of the city's public sector interest in this regard is explored later in this paper.

Regional industry clusters

The industry has flourished in New York because of the city's ample pool of young designers, artists, writers and programmers who are fluent in digital technology and thus able to take advantage of the rapid spread of personal computers and the Internet. Porter's (1990) notions of regional factor endowments and regional demand factors are particularly evident in the case of multimedia industry clusters in New York. A variety of resources, including human, intellectual, physical, capital and infrastructure all reflect the regional factor endowments endemic to New York and supportive of a growing multimedia industry. Similarly, regional demand factors for multimedia content are particularly strong in New York. As of 1996, for example, sixty-one Fortune 500 companies have their headquarters in New York State, twenty-three in New Jersey and twenty-two in Connecticut; thus more than 20 per cent of the largest companies in the US are headquartered in the New York region.[1] There are also numerous institutional consumers as well as a large individual consumer base.

Innovation networks

Also spurring the growth of a regional economy based on multimedia are innovation networks in New York. One emerging network that is examined in this paper is based at Columbia University, where a collaborative team of engineers, computer scientists, journalism, business and education scholars are finalists for a multimillion-dollar grant from the National Science Foundation to create an Engineering Research Center (ERC) in multimedia in New York City. The proposed ERC involves not only advanced engineering research in multimedia but must satisfy extensive National Science Foundation (NSF) requirements documenting technology transfer to the New York business, educational and journalism communities.

Columbia University received the very first ERC awarded by the NSF in 1984, establishing the Center for Telecommunications Research (CTR), out of which emerged a number of patented technologies including MPEG-2, the global standard for compressed digital video. Columbia is now in the forefront of the development of future generations of MPEG compression technology, including MPEG-7. The ERC effort has spurred the development of an innovation network incorporating a variety of educational, research, business and governmental actors. Representatives of these various institutional actors met in June, 1997, at the New York Information Technology Center (NYITC) to begin building a cooperative strategic plan to support Columbia's effort to secure the ERC award.

Adding momentum to this effort is Columbia's receipt of a US$2.5 million computer equipment award from the Intel Corporation. Intel has awarded Columbia the grant for use in its multimedia research efforts and will supply the university with hundreds of state-of-the-art Pentium II computers and related peripheral devices over the next three years.

Latency period

Although there has been marked growth in the multimedia industry since 1992, there were signs of retrenchment in late 1996 and early 1997. A number of multimedia start-ups either filed chapter 11 bankruptcy protection or downsized, such as iVillage, which in April 1997 (Chervokas and Watson 1997) laid off almost 20 per cent of its fifty-five employees and began restructuring its electronic commerce operation. Coopers and Lybrand (1997: 6) report that 17 per cent of New York's multimedia firms 'have exited the market during the past eighteen.months'. They further report that businesses generating US $1 million or less in new media/multimedia revenues annually 'have grown significantly as a proportion of the regional total,' from 63 per cent in 1995 to 83 per cent in 1997. Larger companies still represent the bulk of the multimedia business, with those more established US$5 million enterprises accounting for a majority (US$4.1 billion) of the local new media/multimedia industry revenues (ibid.: 32). However, these figures suggest that 'smaller firms have absorbed employees migrating from larger firms that have restructured or eliminated their new media units' (ibid.: 9).

Investors have retreated sharply from the second-tier Internet start-ups such as Voxware. Originally named Advanced Communications Technologies Inc., the company achieved considerable success and attracted much attention in 1995 when it was renamed Voxware Inc.. Reinventing itself as an Internet company, Voxware moved into an office park in Princeton, N.J., where it lured researchers from MIT and Bell Labs. In October 1996, Netscape Communications Corp. and Intel Corp. invested one million dollars in Voxware, and the company had an initial public stock offering (IPO) that raised an additional $20 million (Lohr 1997).

Since the company's early success, however, Voxware has struggled. It lost $6.3 million on revenues of $5.1 million for nine months ending in March 1997. As of 6 June 1997, its stock closed at $4.6875, down 37 per cent from the IPO price of $7.50 a share.

This pattern is not unique to Voxware. Morgan Stanley and Co.'s analysis of fifty-seven Internet company IPOs since the public offering of Netscape shows that the stock-market value of these companies had fallen $1.2 billion. Just thirteen of them were trading above their offering price as of early June 1997.

Does this evidence mean that the multimedia industry is dying? Not at all, at least in New York. Instead, it is likely that there is a period of latency that a new industry such as multimedia must endure, in which a critical mass of what Amin and Thrift (1992) call 'institutional thickness' is established to support the long-term financial viability of the new industry. Evidence suggests that this is happening in New York's multimedia industry.

A variety of institutional factors have been coalescing in New York to the point of critical mass in late 1997. Foremost is the telecommunications infrastructure in the region, which is heavily wired with high-bandwidth fibre-optic cabling and increasingly rich in reliable wireless technology, including digital personal communications services (PCS) and local multipoint distribution (LMDS). The latter is a wireless technology similar to cellular technology which only recently received federal regulatory permission to be deployed in New York City (Landler 1997). Like cellular telephony, it transmits a signal from a central tower to a small antenna. However, LMDS transmissions bounce off buildings, making the technology well suited to the canyons of New York. LMDS also offers a broadband wireless pipe capable of delivering many types of communication services says Shant S. Hovnanian, the 38-year-old founder of Cellularvision, the company that has the LMDS licence to operate in New York. Cellularvision currently uses LMDS technology to transmit television pictures, but soon expects to use the wireless infrastructure to deliver phone conversations and Internet access to small dishes mounted on windowsills throughout New York.

The city is also home to a number of major technology companies that have long been in the forefront of communications and computing. These include AT&T, number seven on the Fortune 500 list of US corporations with $74 billion in revenue in 1996, and the recent spin-off from the former AT&T Bell Labs, Lucent Technologies. The International Business Machines Corporation (IBM) has its headquarters in Armonk, NY, in Westchester County, the county adjacent to and immediately to the north of New York City. With revenues of some $75 billion in 1996, IBM ranks sixth on the Fortune 500 list of US corporations. Also headquartered in the New York metropolitan region is the General Electric Corporation (GE), which owns the NBC television network and has its corporate offices in Fairfield, Connecticut. GE ranks fifth on the Fortune 500 with $79 billion in revenues in 1996. GTE Corporation, forty-first on the Fortune 500 list with $21 billion in revenues in 1996, is headquartered in Stamford, Connecticut. New York's local telephone company, Nynex, ranked ninety-first on the Fortune list with $13 billion in revenue in 1996, is merging with Bell Atlantic, ninety-ninth on the Fortune list with $13 billion in revenue in 1996, making the combined telecommunications behemoth worth some $26 billion in revenues and catapulting it to twenty-seventh on the Fortune 500 list.

Many of these companies have invested heavily in research and are investing in the multimedia industry as well. They have also supported academic research and education in the region. This is reflected in the important multimedia programmes housed at Columbia University (e.g., the Center for New Media in the Graduate School of Journalism, the Columbia Institute for Tele-Information in the Business School), New York University (the Interactive Telecommunications Program) Fordham University (The Donald McGannon Research Center), the New York Law School (with a programme in new media law and regulation) and elsewhere.

In addition to the technological and communications infrastructure, other institutional forces are reaching a critical mass for supporting the multimedia industry. An intriguing illustration comes from the banking and financial services industry, where for many years most efforts to launch online banking drew little consumer interest. Communications analyst John Carey, founder of Greystone Communications, has long observed the development of online banking. He concludes that earlier efforts failed less for technical reasons than for a strategic one (Carey 1996): most early online banking efforts set the price for the service too high and, as a result, few consumers were interested. The efforts of the mid-1990s set the price at the right level: no charge. As a result, a growing number of consumers equipped with a home computer and modem are now using online banking at financial giants such as Citibank (headquartered in New York) to usher in a new era in electronic financial services.

More importantly, this success is creating even greater potential for the multimedia industry, which is banking on the growth of secure online commerce as an economic cornerstone of the fledgling industry. Analysts expect online commerce to grow substantially in the next five years. Forrester Research Inc. of Cambridge, Mass. predicts business-to-business commerce on the Internet will reach $66 billion by the year 2000, up from $600 million in 1996. Consumer-based online commerce has even greater potential. Robert W. Pittman, Chief Executive Officer of America Online Networks, the largest Internet Service Provider with more than eleven million subscribers as of September 1997, estimates his company alone will transact $66 million in electronic commerce in the third quarter of 1997 (Braverman 1997).

New York is the home to a great many other leading financial institutions, ranging from the Chase Manhattan Corporation to the Morgan Stanley Group, as well as the US headquarters of many international financial behemoths such as Credit Suisse First Boston. As such, it has a very strong financial infrastructure to support the multimedia industry. This infrastructure is beginning to provide the necessary investment capital to propel the growth of the industry.

This is illustrated by an event that occurred in August of 1996: Fred Wilson received $50 million from Chase Manhattan Bank and the Softbank Corporation to launch Flatiron Partners, instantly making it one of the largest venture capital firms in New York specializing in investing in Internet companies. (Chen 1997) Since then, Flatiron, Chase and Softbank have made six multimedia investments totalling $22.7 million. Most have been in multimedia start-ups in New York's so-called Silicon Alley.

Other important venture capital operations in New York with a multimedia interest include Venrock Associates, the venture-investment arm of the Rockefeller family; Discovery Fund, the venture-investment operation of the City of New York. Coopers and Lybrand, one of the so-called 'big six' accounting firms headquartered in New York, reports that venture capital investment in New York City software, electronics and multimedia companies jumped more than 100 per cent, from $49.5 million in 1995 to $111.3 million in 1996, further demonstrating the growing critical financial mass of the region's multimedia industry.

In addition, some 400 people attended the second annual two-day New York City Venture Capital Conference on 9 July 1997 'to hear business pitches, discuss trends in venture capital financing and mull the state of New York's new-media industry,' reports one observer (Chen 1997). This reflects nearly a fifty per cent increase in attendees from the 1996 conference which drew 280 delegates. The conference was proposed by the public sector, including New York City Mayor Rudolph Giuliani, noted conference organizer Charles Millard, president of the New York City Economic Development Corporation.

Another important aspect of the critical mass infrastructure in New York necessary to the maturation of the multimedia industry is the knowledge infrastructure of the region. This takes many forms, including higher education, which produces both technical research and necessary training for human resources, conferences, seminars, workshops, conventions and expositions, and research on the emerging multimedia industry itself. Also worth noting are the variety of newsletters and other online reports covering developments in Silicon Alley, including *@NY, AlleyCat News* and the *Silicon Alley Reporter*.

Coopers and Lybrand has conducted a series of pioneering studies assessing the scope and prospects for growth of the booming multimedia industry centred in New York. Paid for by Empire State Development Corporation, a state agency, the Coopers and Lybrand study represents the first detailed accounting of the burgeoning multimedia industry in New York. The study confirms other indicators of the growth of the multimedia industry, such as the rise of the New York New Media Association, a trade group founded in 1994 with some 2,100 members. .

Other research firms headquartered in New York are expanding their research activities on the multimedia industry. Importantly, the studies conducted by these firms provide the kind of knowledge necessary for other businesses to invest in and utilize multimedia companies and resources.

Simmons Marketing Research Bureau (SMRB), for example, is a firm specializing in collecting, analysing and publishing data on media usage patterns as associated with various demographic and consumer purchase profiles. On 11 June 1997, SMRB hosted a breakfast meeting at its New York headquarters in the Ogilvy and Mather building (O and M is one of the world's leading advertising agencies) to brief its corporate clients on a new study planned for later that year: to expand its measurement of multimedia behaviours into its annual research series. The study includes comprehensive measures of online media usage patterns, ranging from the amount of time spent online and the online service used to content-based websites visited, such as the *New York Times* on the Web, Pathfinder and MSNBC. It also provides various demographic and other user data (Incalcatera 1997). These data are useful for companies seeking to utilize multimedia, such as online multimedia publications, to advertise and market their products. This 'knowledge infrastructure' is essential to the economic growth and viability of the multimedia industry.

A.C. Nielsen Co., also headquartered in New York, is expanding its measurement of online multimedia publications as well, providing ratings data useful to marketers attempting to employ multimedia in their overall media strategies.

New York innovation multimedia network

Perhaps the most compelling evidence of the growing critical mass of the multimedia industry comes in the form of the effort led by Columbia University to create a National Science Foundation-funded ERC in multimedia at the University. Key to obtaining the ERC award is Columbia's securing widespread collaborative support for the mission of the ERC throughout the New York region. Essentially, this means building a strong innovation multimedia network throughout the New York metropolitan region. To date, a broad cross-section of institutional players have aligned themselves voluntarily with the effort, seeing the ERC as a potential catalyst to propel New York as a global multimedia capital. Among the institutional players are the public sector, including the city (mayor's office), the state of New York (governor's office) and the United Nations (Department of Public Information, which represents 185 countries). Support also comes from the financial investment and services community, including venture capital and banking; technology companies; major media companies; multimedia start-ups; arts and culture groups and industry associations.

Collaborators in the New York multimedia innovation network met on 13 June 1997 at the New York Information Technology Center in the heart of Silicon Alley. The meeting was hosted by William Rudin, owner and developer, and John Gilbert, Chief Technology Officer, NYITC. Rudin has developed the NYITC as a principle catalyst or incubator for the growth of New York's multimedia industry, especially its so-called Silicon Alley where hundreds of multimedia start-ups are headquartered. NYITC offers turnkey, state-of-the-art voice, video and data transmission capabilities. It is one of the few buildings in the world to offer a combination of satellite accessibility, single- and multi-mode fibre optics to the desktop, high-speed category five copper wire, video conferencing and Internet access from DS-3 to fractional T1 connectivity, from 10 to 100 megabits per second bandwidth.[2] As a result, NYITC has drawn seventy-two multimedia tenants, ranging from behemoths such as IBM to multimedia start-ups such as K2Design, an interactive multimedia design firm, and @NY, a leading online news report covering Silicon Alley. The 55 Broad Street concept is not limited to New York's Silicon Alley, however, nor is it necessarily limited to New York. As Jason Chervokas and Tom Watson observe:

> Bill Rudin backed into the development of The New York Information Technology Center at 55 Broad Street. But having spent $40 million on the superwiring of the building, Rudin saw the light. Today he's an evangelist for wired real estate and he's got the ears of New York's entrenched real estate establishment. The result is not only a new wired building on Wall Street, another in London, and a spate of knock-offs around the city, but also an ambitious plan to build and wire a midtown office space for Reuters that will surely be a milestone building as New York evolves into the information age, the way the Flatiron Building signified something about 19th century New York.
>
> (Chervokas and Watson 1997)

Present at the planning meeting on 13 June were the CEOs of ten Silicon Alley multimedia companies: Netcast, Intercom, Let's Talk Business, LPNY, Infosafe, Second Line Search, Microsoft Multimedia, N2K, Duck Corporation, I/O 360. Joining them were representatives from the public sector, including Charles Millard, President of New York City Economic Development Corporation and David Klasfeld, Chief of Staff of the Office of the Deputy Mayor for Planning and Community Development.[3]

Together, this group outlined a cooperative, voluntary plan to form an active network of business, government and academic partners to facilitate the ERC effort of Columbia University, recognizing that obtaining the ERC funding would not only catalyze the University's multimedia research effort but also help in the transfer of technology and technology application to multimedia business in New York.

Among the policy options the city and state may consider in this context are:

1 Broad-based tax reductions for multimedia companies.
2 Equity investment incentives.
3 Incentives for low cost space.
4 Greater local loop competition.
5 Intellectual property tax clarification.
6 User friendly tax reduction/elimination.
7 Business support programmes, especially in terms of technology and infra-structure support services.
8 Telecommunications tax reduction/elimination.
9 Building rewiring incentives.
10 Incubator facilities.

Beyond this core group the ERC effort has drawn more than eighty other corporate partners both large and small, including AT&T, Bannister Productions Inc., A.H. Brown Enterprises, Cavanaugh Communications Digital Media Interactive, Dynamind, General Instrument, GTE, LG Electronics, Lucent Technologies, Microunity, Net.Content Inc., New York Now, Panasonic, Philips North America, Propp Productions Inc., Sanyo Multimedia USA, Select Media, USAR Systems and Vivo Software.

A number of major media companies based in New York have also taken initial steps to become involved in the ERC effort. Among those are Viacom, which has given the Centre for New Media a $15,000 gift to fund a project using the Omnicamera to generate an original omni-video story for use on the web. The Omnicamera is a new camera invented by Columbia University Computer Science Professor Shree Nayar. It is the first video camera that can shoot an entire 360 degree field of vision in real time, allowing multiple viewers to simultaneously pan, tilt or zoom anywhere in the entire field of view.

NBC Desktop Video has made a tentative commitment to join the Centre in a collaborative project in which an Omnicamera would be placed in one or more stock exchanges around the world as a test of the viability of the camera to deliver on-demand live interactive multimedia content. Sports Illustrated Online, a Time Warner company, has expressed interest in using the Omnicamera on an experimental basis to provide interactive multimedia coverage of various sporting events via the web.

The *New York Times* on the Web is similarly interested in conducting a news project using experimental technology being developed at the multimedia centre at Columbia. Together, these major media companies represent a significant institutional force in the New York multimedia industry. Their commitment to the ERC will provide substantial momentum to the project.

One notable public sector participant in the ERC effort is the United Nations which is headquartered in New York. The UN Department of Public Information is especially interested in two aspects of the ERC effort. First is the potential for technology transfer from the ERC research to a global community. This has the potential for much economic and cultural benefit, especially in developing nations. Second, and a corollary to the first, is the potential impact of the ERC effort in multimedia on developing international partnerships and collaboration. These two dimensions suggest a means by which a regional industry, such as multimedia in New York, can strengthen its position in an increasingly global marketplace by extending an innovation network from a local to an international arena.

Conclusion: three stages of institutional development

The development of the multimedia industry in New York is dependent on a variety of important institutional factors. These include the direct effects of the geographic proximity of a very wide range of organizations. Just as important, however, are the benefits of the formation of innovation networks and the industrial clusters to which they give rise.

In this context, the New York region is evolving through three distinct stages (see Table 5.1). First is the initial formation of the multimedia industry, which can trace its beginnings to a variety of institutional foundations. These include the major media and technology industry which have a long history in the region, the financial institutions of the region and its advanced telecommunications infrastructure. This period captured considerable attention, anticipation and speculation, resulting in considerable investment in a wide variety of multimedia start-ups.

Inevitably, this stage was followed by a slight downturn, or levelling off, where retrenchment, mergers and acquisitions realigned the playing field. This second stage, which has dominated the New York market since the summer of 1996, suggests, at least on the surface, that the multimedia industry might be dying. It appears to signal a loss of potential, reduced growth and ultimate failure of a possibly over-hyped new industry. However, the reality is that this second stage is one in which a critical mass is being generated on a variety of institutional fronts. This stage might better be thought of as a latency period, in which institutional players are forming critical alliances or innovation networks to support the long-term viability of the multimedia industry.

This second stage is now nearing its completion, and the next twelve to eighteen months will see the emergence of a third stage of multimedia industry maturation. The multimedia industry will surge forward with steady, sustainable growth. Hype will be replaced by viable business opportunities.

Table 5.1 Institutional forces shaping multimedia industry growth in New York: principal institutional influences

Stages	Regional factor endowments						
	Financial	Content	Technology companies	Education	Small entre-preneurs	Public	I–networks
1 Early growth	x	x	X	x	XX		
2 Latency, critical mass	X	X	XX	X	X	x	X
3 Stabilization, steady growth	XX	XX	XX	XX	x	X	XX

Source: Author's research

Note: The size and number of 'X's' indicates the relative importance of an institutional factor at each stage of development of the new media industry in New York.

In fact, a recent report released by New York University shows that New York City now has more than 17,000 registered commercial and non-profit domains on the Internet, double the number in its closest rival multimedia capital, San Francisco (Johnson 1997).

New technology and innovation will continue but will be developed through collaborative efforts linking academic researchers, industry partners and public sector players, facilitating both technology transfer and successful implementation of those multimedia technologies.

An example is the development of a new company called Cyclovision, which is headquartered in New York's Silicon Alley but grows out of acade-mic research at Columbia University. Cyclovision is the multimedia start-up company whose mission is to develop, licence and market the Omnicamera. The company was set up in June 1997, manufactured its first Omnicameras in July, and had orders for more than 200 units by August.

Cyclovision represents the beginning of a third stage of development in the regional New York multimedia industry. It illustrates the development of institutional forces that helped define a new industry. These forces have evolved into an innovation network that facilitated a necessary critical mass to support the multimedia industry, and ultimately spawned a business model in multimedia viable for long-term health and stability.

A vital final step in this evolution is the development of broad-based public sector policies that support the multimedia industry in New York. To date, few multimedia companies in New York have applied for or received public sector support. Coopers and Lybrand (1997: 70) report that only 18 per cent of multimedia companies have applied for or received any public support to date, with most of those falling into five categories: financing; technical assistance; business administration support; training/

employment credits; and investment incentives/credits. Among the critical public sector initiatives are: first, entrepreneurial tax relief, including real property tax abatements and commercial rent tax reductions; second, establishment of a public-private equity investment fund for City-based multimedia businesses (Mayor Guiliani has established a multimedia advisory panel to consider placing US$75 million in such a fund); and third, a 'CyberSymposium' which the city and state are planning in cooperation with Columbia's ERC effort. Together, these public policy initiatives will help ensure the viability of sustainable growth in New York's multimedia industry.

Notes

The author acknowledges the research assistance of Jared Goldstein, Masters in Business Administration candidate, Columbia University School of Business.

1 From the Fortune website, www.fortune.com, as of July 22 1997.
2 From the NYITC website at www.nyitc.com.
3 See http://www.ci.nyc.ny.us/nyclink/htm/edc/home.html.

References

Amin, A. and Thrift, N. (1992) 'Neo-Marshallian Nodes' in Global Networks, *International Journal of Urban and Regional Research*, 16, 4: 571–87.
Bay Area Multimedia Partnership (1997) *A Labour Market Analysis of the Interactive Digital Media Industry: Opportunities in Multimedia*, prepared for the North Valley Private Industry Council, Sunnyvale, California.
Braverman, A. W. and America Online, Inc. (1997) *Internet Industry Report,* Credit Suisse First Boston, June 24. New York.
Carey, J. (1996) 'Consumer Adoption of Internet Technologies', Speech at the Centre for New Media, November 11, New York.
Chen, D. W. (1997) 'Venture capital showing faith in Internet's future', *The New York Times,* 10 July.
Chervokas, J. and Watson, T. (1997) @NY newsletter. December 26, 1997; 2 May 1997.
Coopers and Lybrand Consulting (1997) *New York New Media Industry Survey: Opportunities and Challenges of New York's Emerging Cyber-Industry*, New York: New York New Media Association.
Fuchs, G. and Wolf, H.-G. (1997) 'Regional re-juvenation with the help of multimedia?' Stuttgart: the Centre for Technology Assessment in Baden-Württemberg.
Hachmeister, L. and Rager, G. (eds) (1997) *Wer beherrscht die Medien? Die 50 grössten Medienkonzerne der Welt,* München: C.H. Beck.
Heydebrand, W. (1998) 'Multimedia networks and strategies of innovation: The case of New York', Chapter 3 in this volume.

Incalcatera, T. (1997) 'Simmons consumer online usage study', Simmons Marketing Research Bureau, New York.

Johnson, K. (1997) 'Study says New York business embraces the net', *The New York Times,* 30 September.

Junne, G. (1995) 'Global cooperation or rival trade blocs', *Journal of World-Systems Research* 9, Jg 1.

Landler, M. (1997) 'Wireless service may be coming soon to a windowsill near you', *The New York Times*, 7 July.

Lohr, S. (1997) 'Ups and downs of a second-tier Internet start-up', *The New York Times,* 9 June.

Moss, M. (1996) 'The changing telecommunications environment and New York City: a policy report based on a three session colloquium', sponsored by New York University, Program on Science, Technology and Government, funded by the Carnegie Corporation of New York.

Pittman, R. W. (1997) 'Briefing for investors and analysts', Credit Suisse First Boston Seminar, 29 May 1997, New York.

Porter, M. E. (1990) *The Competitive Advantage of Nations,* New York: Free Press.

Wheatley, A. (1997) *Women Online: Developing Content and Advertising for an Emerging Market*, New York: Jupiter Communications.

6

THE DIGITAL REGIONAL ECONOMY

Emergence and evolution of
Toronto's multimedia cluster

Shauna G. Brail and Meric S. Gertler

The establishment of a digital regional economy

As capitalist economies around the world emerge from the current round of fundamental restructuring (Webber and Rigby 1996), new forms of economic activity have arisen to capture the attention of scholars and policy analysts alike. Dominant among these is the group of activities associated with a new techno-economic paradigm based on microelectronics, information and communication technologies (Freeman and Perez 1988, Freeman 1991).

Earlier scholarly research recognized this shift by focusing first on the geography of microelectronics-based industries such as semiconductors, computers, telecommunications equipment and consumer electronics (see, for example, Hall and Markusen 1985, Angel 1994), and subsequently on the geography of computer software production (Cornish 1997). More recently, attention has shifted to other sectors of economic activity downstream from the actual production of hardware and software. As the applications of these new core technologies diffuse and spread throughout the wider economy, the list of sectors affected by this fundamental transformation has grown steadily.

Multimedia production represents one of the more noteworthy examples of this recent development. In the past few years, it has come to be recognized as a fast-growing component of some of North America's largest metropolitan economies, with significant concentrations of activity in San Francisco and Los Angeles (Fortune 1996, Scott 1997), New York (Krantz 1995, Coopers and Lybrand 1996) and elsewhere (see Brail 1998 for a review of recent evidence).

Toronto has emerged as the predominant centre of multimedia in Canada, and a major North American concentration of activity in this industry. In this chapter, we document the emergence, organizational structure and geography of Toronto's multimedia cluster. Our primary objective is to understand the forces and dynamics that have been responsible for driving its evolution. In particular, we are keen to determine if the emergence of this multimedia sector represents a 'clean break' from past economic activity, or if instead it has been produced by a strongly path-dependent, evolutionary process (Nelson 1995), building on the foundation of the region's older industries. If the latter scenario is more likely, then this raises a crucial question about the extent to which public policy intervention can play a role in spurring the development of a multimedia cluster (and what forms that policy might have taken in Toronto's case).

Following on from this last theme, considerable attention has been dedicated recently to the role of institutions and forms of governance in promoting the emergence of innovative economic regions. Storper (1997) builds his analysis of new regional growth phenomena around the concepts of 'convention' and 'untraded interdependencies' to capture the mechanisms which facilitate the cooperation and information-sharing between firms that is deemed necessary to support innovative production. Amin and Thrift (1994) have coined the term 'institutional thickness' to reflect the conditions under which individual firms are most likely to act in a socially coherent and consistent way for mutual benefit.

Morgan (1995) sees such characteristics as distinguishing 'learning regions' from other types. In such regions a set of public and private, formal and informal institutional arrangements combine to encourage inter-firm learning, which Morgan argues is an important regionally-based source of competitive advantage. Finally, Saxenian (1994) argues that distinctive 'regional cultures' have emerged within countries like the United States, and that these cultures play a large part in shaping the growth trajectories of individual regional economies.

In much of this recent literature, there is a strong contention that the forces supporting inter-firm interaction, cooperation and learning will be especially important in those industries which are subject to rapidly changing and variegated demand conditions, and in which production processes can be readily disaggregated along vertical lines. On the basis of the limited evidence available thus far, the multimedia sector appears to share these basic characteristics.

Arguments based on the idea of institutional thickness imply that successful approaches to the promotion of such industries must depend on the direct building up of institutions closely related to the sector's development. These arguments stand in contrast to another approach that emphasizes the influential role of broader, overarching regulatory frameworks. In this alternative view, the wider regulatory environment determined by policy structures at higher spatial scales (especially the national and provincial/state levels) is seen as having the potential to create either conducive or unsupportive conditions within which a particular industry (or set of characteristic industrial practices) might develop (see for example Christopherson 1993, Wever 1995, Gertler 1997, Lane 1997).

In this chapter, we argue that the emergence of Toronto's multimedia cluster exhibits a very strong regional-evolutionary dynamic, since its growth appears to have been squarely dependent on the prior development of a wide range of supporting activities and industries. There is very strong evidence that this new activity has emerged from Toronto's rich mixture of pre-existing, design-intensive and knowledge-based economic activities: graphic and visual arts, publishing, advertising, television, film, video and audio production, animation, computing and software production, and financial services. Furthermore, the industry is strongly tied to local specialized suppliers and labour markets, as well as to the Toronto region's large portfolio of corporate clients in finance, advertising and the media. We argue that, because of its very strong connections to these older sectors of the regional economy, the inherent growth potential of multimedia activity in Toronto is considerable. Nevertheless, it is constrained, at least in the short- to medium-term, by a shortage of more highly skilled and experienced personnel.

We argue further that local associative action has played a significant role in the industry's successful emergence in Toronto. Until now this has taken the largely informal and 'private' form of inter-firm networking within a vertically disintegrated production chain and has been largely unmediated by local industry-specific institutions. Nevertheless, public policy – particularly the broader, macroregulatory environment shaping cultural policy in Ontario and Canada – has played a crucial role in stimulating the development of the wide array of cultural industries on which the multimedia cluster's emergence clearly depends. These industries function as a source both of key inputs and of demand for multimedia products. Furthermore, at the regional level, the key public institutions supporting the industry's development are local colleges and universities producing skilled labour in a wide range of fields, many of which are not directly targeted to multimedia production *per se*. Hence, we conclude that the initiatives of organized producer associations and recent targeted initiatives of local and provincial governments have to this point lagged behind, rather than led, the industry's development.

For the purposes of this chapter, we define multimedia as the merging of traditional audio, visual and print media through digitization in an interactive format. Our study of multimedia firms includes established corporations that have moved into the field of multimedia such as graphic design companies, computer software developers and book publishers. It also comprises newly developed 'multimedia-only' firms, whose core business offering is the development and production of multimedia products based on CD-ROM, Internet/Intranet, kiosks and so on. We do not consider established firms in traditional industries that use multimedia applications and/or technology to enhance their operations as 'multimedia firms.'

Size, situation and structure of Toronto's multimedia industry

Studies of the Canadian multimedia industry have documented the fact that the Toronto area has the largest number of multimedia firms in Canada, followed by Quebec (centred in Montreal) and British Columbia (centred in Vancouver)

(IMAT 1995, Centre for Image and Sound Research 1995). At the national level, our estimates indicate that the Toronto area alone contains between two and three times more multimedia firms than either Quebec or British Columbia.[1]

Toronto's pre-eminence in the hierarchy of Canada's centres of multimedia activity stems in part from its position as Canada's largest metropolitan area, with a 1994 population of 4.5 million (Greater Toronto Area Task Force, 1996). It is also the location of choice for many national and international corporations, financial institutions and other business services. Table 6.1 shows that 38 per cent of the Toronto Census Metropolitan Area labour force works in managerial, professional and technical positions, and an equal percentage of the labour force is employed in business/personal services. As we shall argue below, Toronto's economic focus on management and business services helps to set the framework for the growth, development and focus of the region's multimedia industry, since activities such as advertising, banking, other financial services and corporate management constitute a key market for multimedia products.

However, these aggregate figures fail to convey a key aspect of the Toronto economy that is absolutely fundamental to the emergence and strength of multimedia production in the region: namely, its status as Canada's major centre for cultural industries and related activities. The Toronto region

Table 6.1 Toronto Census Metropolitan Area employment

Toronto CMA employment by occupation (1993)	Number	Per cent
Managerial	676,600	38
Clerical	320,500	18
Sales	183,100	10
Service	210,400	12
Manufacturing	270,700	15
Other	105,100	6
Total	1,766,400	99*
Toronto CMA employment by industry (1993)		
Manufacturing	303,100	17
Construction	89,100	5
Communications/utilities	123,300	7
Trade	286,600	16
Financial, insurance, real estate	189,600	11
Business/personal	671,300	38
Public administration	93,600	5
Other	9,800	1
Total	1,766,400	100

Source: Statistics Canada
Note: * does not equal 100 due to rounding.

possesses by far the largest concentration of activity in film, television, video and audio production, music recording, book and magazine publishing, and live theatre in the country. In fact, the region is now the third largest centre for film and television production in North America, after Los Angeles and New York (Ministry of Culture, Tourism and Recreation 1994). Moreover, as Figure 6.1 shows, these activities are supported by the presence of other key sectors which, taken as a whole, can be viewed as forming a richly developed entertainment, media and publishing cluster.

Many of this cluster's individual elements provide important product and service inputs for multimedia production. For example, Toronto is a major

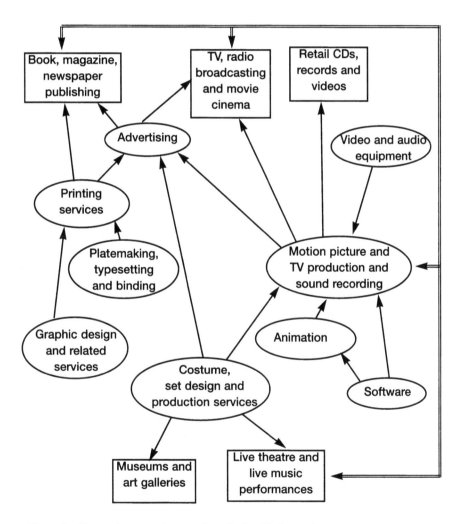

Figure 6.1 Toronto's entertainment / media / publishing cluster

North American centre for software production, home to companies such as Alias/Wavefront (recently acquired by Silicon Graphics in California) which specialize in producing software for film and video animation. Other local firms such as Nelvana are major international players in the production of animated features, and their continued success has been supported by the presence in the region of world-renowned educational programmes in animation offered by institutions such as Sheridan College. As our analysis in later sections of this chapter will show, the film production, sound recording and live music/theatre industries represent important local suppliers to the multimedia sector. Other elements of this local cluster constitute both content providers and customers for the multimedia industry. Prime examples include museums, art galleries, and book and magazine publishers.

It is within the context of this rich and deep collection of cultural industries that the Toronto multimedia industry's development must be understood. Moreover, as we shall argue in the penultimate section of this chapter, the most important public policies supporting multimedia activity were not designed or implemented with the needs of this sector in mind. Rather, they have provided general stimulus to the development of 'background' cultural industries through a series of national and provincial policies designed to nurture the development of home-grown film, television, music and publishing industries while also protecting Canadian cultural activities from the deluge of American products.

A database of multimedia firms in the Province of Ontario was developed in an effort to determine the size and geographical distribution of the multimedia industry in the province.[2] A total of 421 multimedia firms were confirmed to be in operation in the province in February 1997. Table 6.2 displays the intraprovincial location of multimedia firms in the database. In total, 319 or 76 per cent of all firms were located in the Greater Toronto Area (GTA). 62 per cent of all firms located in the province were situated in the central municipality of Toronto.[3]

Maps 6.1 and 6.2 show the geographic location and metropolitan

Table 6.2 Multimedia firms in the province of Ontario

Location	Number of firms	% of province
Metropolitan Toronto	259	62
Rest of GTA	60	14
Rest of southern Ontario	47	11
Ottawa region	42	10
Other	13	3
Province total	421	100

Source: Brail 1998

clustering of multimedia firms in the Toronto area. Map 6.1 depicts the spatial distribution of multimedia firms within metropolitan Toronto. As Map 6.2 shows, the largest numbers of firms are located in older industrial areas generally, the area south of Queen Street surrounding the urban core. Table 6.3 provides a breakdown of the number of multimedia firms in the Greater Toronto area. It highlights the clustering of 81 per cent of the area's multimedia firms in metropolitan Toronto, with 61 per cent located in the central part of the city. These maps and tables show the strongly urban nature of the multimedia industry as well as the marked intra-urban clustering of multimedia firms in older industrial areas of the urban core. Site visits to many of these locations confirm that these firms do in fact favour old industrial and warehouse buildings that had been vacated by businesses leaving the central area for more suburban sites.

Characteristics of Toronto area multimedia firms

In order to learn more about the activities, organization and location patterns of multimedia firms, a survey was distributed to all firms in the database located in the Greater Toronto Area during February and March 1997. The survey was distributed by e-mail to 286 firms and sent by regular mail to twenty-five firms with no e-mail addresses.[4] The survey was also posted on a Canadian website that is widely used for accessing information on multimedia, and this enabled firms to access the survey on the Internet, regardless of whether they were on the research database or not.[5]

This approach was used in an attempt to ensure all 'eligible' firms had access to the survey despite the lack of an inclusive, recognized listing of multimedia firms. It also served as a way of adding new firms to the research database. Due to typically low barriers to entry and exit within the industry, the population of multimedia firms is prone to rapid change, and several responding firms indicated that they had been in business for less than one year. We are confident that the survey results reflect the industry as a whole, in the light of our industry knowledge and continuous work and discussion with representatives and experts from more than seventy multimedia and related firms dating back to February 1996.

Table 6.3 Multimedia firms in the Greater Toronto Area

Region	Number of firms	% of GTA
Greater Toronto Area	319	100
Metropolitan Toronto	259	81
Outer zone	64	20
Central zone	195	61

Source: own calculations

Map 6.1 Multimedia firms in Metropolitan Toronto
Source: Map: GCM Services Inc., Data: Brail (1998)

Queen
Street

Map 6.2 Multimedia firms in downtown Toronto
Source: Map: GCM Services Inc., Data: Brail (1998)

Toronto's multimedia industry has emerged relatively recently. Survey results indicate that the median age of all firms currently involved in multimedia is five years. However, the average firm in the Toronto area began to work in multimedia only in 1993. To further emphasize the youth of the industry, consider that fully 40 per cent of firms were established in 1994 or later.

Previous studies of multimedia have identified a strong relationship between multimedia, computing and cultural industries (IMAT 1995, Scott 1997) and the results presented here appear to support such claims. Furthermore, the results highlight the fact that multimedia and related industries are not mutually exclusive and that both types of activities can be successfully carried out within the same firm. The majority of firms (64 per cent) reported that they combine multimedia work with other types of work. The most common types of work combined with multimedia include related industries such as software development, graphic design, printing and publishing, broadcasting and video, music, advertising and marketing, and computer based training.

Table 6.4 indicates that the overwhelming majority of firms do not target all of their products towards one market sector. The sector which commands by far the most attention is the corporate market, with 60 per cent of firms gearing more than half of their work towards corporate products. This is not surprising, considering that the Toronto area is the single largest centre for headquarters of both national and international corporations in Canada, as well as the focal point of the national financial services industry and many other producer and business services. Firms targeting the entertainment, edutainment and education categories tend to focus on products geared towards several markets and clients. The health sector is the one sector in which most firms do not participate. It is also, however, one of the newest sectors among

Table 6.4 Product focus (%)

Product focus:	Corporate	Entertainment	Edutainment*	Education	Information	Health
All	8	2	2	11	5	0
Most	52	16	12	18	24	4
Some	24	33	32	27	35	31
None	9	18	27	24	15	35
No Answer**	7	31	27	20	21	30

Source: Brail 1998
Notes: N = 85

    Bold = largest per cent in category.

    * Edutainment products represent a combination of both education and entertainment-based content.

    ** The figures presented under the heading of 'No Answer' in this table and in subsequent tables most likely correspond to an answer of 0 per cent. However, they are reported separately in order to present the results as unambiguously as possible. See endnote 6 for discussion on interpreting Tables 6.4–6.6.

those listed for which multimedia products are being developed.

Table 6.5 clearly shows that Toronto's multimedia firms are strongly focused on custom products.[7] Three-quarters of all firms indicate that half their work or more is developed exclusively for custom clients, representing the 'business service' focus of the region's multimedia industry. Conversely, these figures show that most firms produce few or no mass market products. In other words, the bulk of multimedia work carried out by Toronto area firms involves the development of custom products.

Table 6.6 reveals the platform focus in the area, that is the medium through which the multimedia product is distributed. The table indicates that very few firms focus solely on one platform type. Most respondents indicated that their work is divided between at least two platforms. Games consoles were by far the least common. This is in many ways an expected result as games development is a very expensive mass market undertaking that requires access to finance, markets, distribution channels and, increasingly, the support of large corporations. With respect to the other five platform foci the most common appears to be Internet/Intranet, followed by CD-ROM, hard disk and floppy disk and then kiosks.

Table 6.5 Client focus (%)

Client focus	Custom	Mass market
All	43	6
Most	32	14
Some	14	**26**
None	7	25
No Answer	4	29

Source: Brail 1998
Notes: N = 85
   Bold = highest per cent in category.

Table 6.6 Platform focus (%)

Platform focus	CD-ROM	Internet /Intranet	Kiosks	Hard disk	Floppy disk	Game console
All	7	7	0	0	2	0
Most	21	29	5	7	4	0
Some	**46**	**44**	32	**38**	36	7
None	19	15	**40**	35	**38**	**62**
No answer	7	5	23	20	20	31

Source: Brail 1998
Notes: N = 85.
   Bold = highest per cent in category.

SHAUNA G. BRAIL AND MERIC S. GERTLER

In aggregate, these results clearly show that Toronto's multimedia industry is strongly focused on the development of customized, interactive
multimedia products using a combination of platforms. Although it caters to
several different markets, the corporate market emerges as the most important of these. The depth and diversity of the type of work being carried out
by the local industry is considerable. This may be a reflection of the industry's flexibility and adaptability towards new product development based on
similar technology, and its capacity to tailor products towards a multiplicity
of end users with different interests and needs.

Features and practices of employment in multimedia

The data in Table 6.7 show the breakdown of workers by employment status.
While the majority of employment in multimedia is full-time, more than
one-quarter of all employees (excluding those in the largest firm) are contract
employees, with short-term contracts (essentially freelancers) comprising the
bulk of contract activity. There has been a slight increase in the proportion of
full-time employment over the past year, with small subsequent declines in
part-time and short-term-contract employment shares. Full-time employment in firms has increased by 20 per cent between 1996 and 1997, while

Table 6.7 Employment in multimedia

| | Total employment | | Excluding largest firm | |
	1997	1996	1997	1996
Full-time (FT)	1,028	816	658	516
	(72)	(70)	(63)	(61)
Part-time	143	123	123	98
	(10)	(10)	(12)	(12)
Long-term contract	77	67	77	67
	(5)	(6)	(7)	(8)
Short-term contract	184	167	182	167
	(13)	(14)	(18)	(20)
Total	1,432	1,173	1,040	848
Average total employment	18	16	13	12
Average FT employment	13	11	8	7
Median total employment	6	4	6	4
Median FT employment	3	2	3	2
	n = 81	n = 73	n = 80	n = 72

Source: Brail 1998
Note: Figures in brackets represent percentage share of employment in each column.

108

median full-time employment in firms has increased by one person during the same time.

From Table 6.8, it is again clear that small establishments are numerically prominent in this industry. The data also show that the size distribution of full-time employment has remained relatively stable between 1996 and 1997, though there is some growth in the employment share exhibited by the largest firms.

According to Table 6.9, creative workers are the most common full-time employees (38 per cent), followed by management/sales employees. Technical positions comprise about one quarter of total full-time employment. Similar proportions are evident for part-time employment, as far as creative and technical posts are concerned, though fewer part-time employees work in management and sales, while more are classified as 'other'. 'Other' employees generally include clerical and office support staff. Again, employees working on the creative aspects of multimedia projects comprise the majority of both long- and short-term contract workers in the industry, followed by technical and then management/sales employees. Overall, creative employees form the core of multimedia employment with 42 per cent of all jobs falling into this category. This is followed by the

Table 6.8 Employment by size of firm

	Number of firms			
	Full-time employment		Total employment	
Employment size category	1997	1996	1997	1996
1 person	23 (29)	21 (29)	8 (10)	10 (14)
2–5 persons	28 (35)	26 (36)	27 (33)	28 (38)
6–10 persons	13 (16)	12 (17)	17 (21)	10 (14)
11–20 persons	6 (8)	7 (10)	13 (16)	12 (16)
21–49 persons	6 (8)	4 (6)	13 (16)	11 (15)
50 +	3 (4)	2 (3)	3 (4)	2 (3)
	n = 79	n = 72	n = 81	n = 73

Source: Brail 1998
Note: Figures in brackets represent percentage share of employment per column.

Table 6.9 Employment by job type and skill category (excluding largest firm)

	Creative (%)	Technical (%)	Management /sales (%)	Other (%)
Full-time	38	24	31	7
Part-time	35	25	18	22
Long-term contract	50	33	17	0
Short-term contract	64	30	4	2
All employees	42	25	25	8

Source: Brail 1998

technical and management/sales categories, each contributing 25 per cent of total employment.

The geography of suppliers and markets

Firms participating in the survey indicated that on average more than three-quarters of their suppliers, by dollar volume of sales, are located in the Toronto area, with almost one-fifth of supply purchases taking place within the same neighbourhood as responding firms (see table 6.10). Outside the Toronto region, Ontario and the rest of Canada account for an average of some 13 per cent of supply purchases, followed by the United States. Customers are slightly less concentrated in the Toronto area than suppliers, but nevertheless, firms surveyed indicated that an average of 62 per cent of their customers by sales volume are located in the Toronto area. The international focus of the multimedia industry is reflected more strongly in the customer base than in the supplier base, with respondents indicating that an average of 18 per cent of sales are to clients located outside Canada.

The overwhelming majority (92 per cent) of the firms reported that they were initially established in the Toronto area. However, 23 per cent of firms indicated that they also have offices outside the area.

More than half (52 per cent) of the survey respondents indicated that they had had at least one previous location in the Toronto area. The vast majority (68 per cent) of these firms indicated that their reason for moving was that their prior premises were too small (see Table 6.11). Another important trend (consistent with our earlier findings concerning size and age) is indicated in the finding that 29 per cent of the respondents had moved away from home offices. Finally, 22 per cent of the firms indicated that they had moved to be in a more central location. This response confirms again that intra-urban factors do play a role in the industry's location patterns, further emphasizing that central locations are an enduring feature of the industry, rather than acting solely as an incubator for firms first starting out. Other reasons that

Table 6.10 Location of suppliers and customers by sales volume

Location	% of suppliers	% of customers
Same neighborhood	19	10
Toronto area including neighbourhood	**78**	**62**
Rest of Ontario	7	11
Rest of Canada	6	9
United States	8	13
Outside North America	1	5

Source: Brail 1998
Note: Bold = highest per cent in category.

respondents cited for moving included the opportunity to purchase space, the merging of firms and non-renewal of leases, and the desire to be closer to suppliers and clients.

Emergence and evolution of Toronto's multimedia cluster

Face-to-face interviews with principals and senior staff at selected multimedia firms in the Toronto region were conducted to add greater depth to the survey results and to explore other issues not well suited to a questionnaire format. The sample was selected to capture the full diversity of sizes, locational choices and type of work.[8] Interviews were also conducted with civil servants and politicians at the municipal, provincial and federal levels of government, as well as with a series of association leaders. These interviews have furthered our understanding of how and why Toronto's multimedia industry has emerged and developed its present shape and structure.

Table 6.11 Reasons for firm moves

Reasons for firm moves	%
Space too small	68
Moved from home office	29
More central location	22
Lower rent	17
Less central location	2
Other	24

Source: Brail 1998
Note: Some respondents indicated more than one reason.

Multimedia's origins

As indicated earlier, multimedia represents the convergence of several industries, most notably those related to the information and communication technology and creative sectors. The background education and work experiences of multimedia firm principals provide a telling display of the range of linkages between multimedia and related industries.

Table 6.12 hints at the significance of multimedia's strong association with 'older' sectors such as publishing, advertising, film/television/radio, financial services and graphic design, in addition to linkages with 'newer' sectors of the regional economy including software development, computer hardware, robotics and other information technology intensive industries.

Demand conditions: from regional to export markets

Not only have large multimedia clusters developed as a result of strong historical linkages to related industries, but the early emergence of multimedia clusters has also been shaped by local demand conditions. Highlighting the

Table 6.12 Range of firm founders' backgrounds prior to entering multimedia

Media and communications	*Computing and technology*
Advertising	Computer sciences
Audio visual	Computing
Broadcast television	Engineer
Digital video	Manage technology-related companies
Film and broadcast	Physics
Pre-press	Robotics, automation
Publishing	Scientist
Sound recording	Software development
Television, film and radio	
Art and design	*Finance, insurance and management*
Art as a hobby	Banking (training)
Art college	Finance and insurance
Fine arts teacher	MBA
Interior design	Marketing and sales
Graphic design	
Music	
Painter/artist	
Other	
Sociology professor	

Source: Brail 1998
Note: N = 29.

motors of their respective regional economies, Scott (1997) identifies the specialization of San Francisco area firms in the development of corporate-based multimedia products, while noting that Los Angeles-based firms are more specialized in producing for the entertainment sector. Similarly, the New York industry is supported through its connections to the advertising, publishing and entertainment industries (Coopers & Lybrand 1996). The Toronto cluster is no exception to this pattern of industry specialization being defined by the structure of the local economy.

On the demand side, the growth of Toronto's multimedia industry, especially in its early stages of development, has been largely a function of demand for new media products from locally headquartered national and international corporations. Survey results reviewed earlier indicated that clients remain highly localized, with 62 per cent of respondents' customers by sales volume being located in the Toronto area and a further 11 per cent located elsewhere in the province. 18 per cent of sales are exported to clients outside Canada, with the majority going to the United States, followed by Europe and Asia.

Conditions associated with local demand have led to the start-up of several multimedia firms and also to the redevelopment of firms previously working in other related fields. Gord Gower, President of Mackerel Interactive, a thirty-person multimedia firm, described the demand conditions which initiated their multimedia work as follows:

> About six months after we started the business [a design firm], we did an interactive piece using Hypercard to promote the design business, and more people wanted us to do interactive programs for them than do straight paper based designs. That caused a change in the business. Really, by about 1992-93 we weren't doing any traditional design anymore, we were doing all interface design.[9]
>
> (Interview)

Another Toronto multimedia firm, Integrated Communications and Entertainment Inc. (ICE), was formed as a communication services firm specializing in graphic design and the production of live events. Peter Nikitopoulos, Marketing Director of the 108-person firm, says that ICE was launched into new media as the result of a client's request:

> In 1986 when Apple Canada came on board as a client, we were producing slide shows for corporate clients. At the time they said 'We don't want you guys to use these slides any more, they're archaic. We want you to use this new thing called multimedia.' And they introduced our designers to an electronic presentation format. They trained our people on it and we created what we believe was one of

the first multimedia presentations for Apple. Apple was one of our big clients back then. They really sort of launched us way ahead of our time into multimedia and multimedia presentations.

(Interview)

Local demand has not acted to support all firms in the industry. Several interviewees commented that much of the local corporate sector is often very slow to adopt new technologies and/or take risks associated with marketing and financing interactive projects. This was true of both customers and financiers. Other interviewees identified the problem of technology adoption as a challenge to the industry, noting that the ability to convince potential clients that they should use multimedia as a business tool is a skill that takes time to develop.

Another factor supporting the development of the local industry is the proximity of multimedia firms to potential clients. As firms must in many cases seek out and sell themselves to potential clients, this proximity improves their chances for meeting people and helps them to maintain networks in which they learn about work opportunities. There is also the perception that it may in fact be easier to work with locally-based firms. Harold Feist, President of 2D Art Systems, describes looking for a distributor to market a children's CD-ROM series that he produced. Though he was negotiating with both a local and an international company, he chose to go with the local company, and thus far in his business all his clients have been located in the GTA. Feist says, 'So far, physical geography has been the main thing. Proximity. Despite how easy it would be, theoretically, to collaborate long distance, I find there's a need to meet face-to-face throughout the process' (interview).

Clients may also prefer to work with locally based firms, underlining the importance of meeting face-to-face with suppliers, despite the fact that proximity to the client or supplier is often not necessary during production. According to Bill Sweetman, a multimedia consultant and 'idea guy' at the one-person firm, Electric Eye Multimedia:

It has been my observation that clients, and my clients, tend to pick locally. I've seen that when I've been hired by companies to recommend suppliers, I'll ask them: 'Does it matter where they are?' and they'll say, 'Well, we'd rather have a firm in our town.' I think it's perceived as expensive to have the supplier out of town and I think they feel if they're out of town they can't keep an eye on them. I'm not saying that's true but I think that's the perception.

(Interview)

114

The same feature that has helped to support the growth of a local industry has also helped several Toronto area firms to branch out geographically into other markets. Several of the larger Toronto firms have opened offices elsewhere in response to client location. For example, Digital Renaissance opened an office in New Brunswick in order to better serve their largest client, New Brunswick Telephone. ICE opened an office in New York's 'Silicon Alley' to show their commitment to one of their largest clients, IBM.[10] In explaining ICE's New York office, Peter Nikitopoulos says:

> Although you can do everything over the Internet, they [clients] actually want to know there's an office down the street. Some of them will not give you the business unless they know you have a presence, some sort of physical presence in the neighborhood.
>
> (Interview)

Other Toronto firms have also opened offices in places such as Ottawa, Vancouver, San Francisco and Boston. This is not to say, however, that only firms with international offices will be able to branch out into extra-regional markets. As with other business service industries, however, firms that want to maintain long-term relationships with valuable clients are finding that physical proximity to the client is important. This seems to matter, especially to large clients, although, on the other hand, several firms cite examples of clients they have worked for both locally and internationally where they met face-to-face only once, or never, and conducted all their work over the telephone, Internet etc.

Most Toronto area multimedia firms producing mass-marketed, consumer-based products have actively exported their products soon after their establishment, as the Canadian market is generally not considered large enough to make the expensive development process profitable. A number of different experiences have led to the pursuit of export markets.

Perception of a crowded local market

> Exporting has grown quite a bit over the last three years. It's very important. There just isn't really the work in Canada to support the business, because of the size and because of the business realities that we're working in now as a larger, small company. [Export strategies have] grown out of the Toronto marketplace only because there's a lot of really small firms and it's just easier for them to pick up the jobs in Toronto; in a lot of ways it's hard for us to compete with them because they compete on a price basis.
>
> (Interview with Gord Gower, Mackerel Interactive,
> 55 per cent of clients located in US)

Active pursuit of export markets

> The retail market for children's CD-ROM based products is extraordinarily difficult, although we've been quite successful in what we've done. Our work is, I think, now in twelve or thirteen languages. We've had very much an international focus on what we do, but the North American market is extremely difficult. We find partners with whom we work in various countries
>
> (Interview with Karen Anderson, President of Interlynx Multimedia, 90 per cent of whose clients for children's products are international)

Passively developed export opportunities through local subsidiaries

> We've generally won that [European export] business . . . through the Canadian subsidiary of a company . . . and won business from the parent firm based on work that we've done for the subsidiaries. That's actually a growing part of the business, which is kind of interesting because we never see these people.
>
> (Interview with Aurel Langlois, ElectraMedia, 20 per cent of whose clients are in Europe and Asia)

Other firms are actively pursuing exports but find that there are some barriers which tend to slow the process down. For instance, James Rossiter, Executive Director of Knowledge Connection Corporation, a non-profit organization geared towards developing and disseminating information on interactive distance-based learning, notes that:

> It does take quite a long time, in my experience, to develop international projects. Partly it's a trust factor. I don't mean that quite as boldly as it sounds. I think it just takes time for people who are working at a long distance and over cultural divides to feel comfortable working with another organization.
>
> (Interview)

Supply conditions: sources, skill, and regional strengths

Our earlier review of survey results showed that suppliers to Toronto's multimedia industry are highly concentrated in the region (78 per cent of suppliers by sales volume are located within the Toronto area, and 19 per cent are located in the same neighbourhood as multimedia firms). Recalling further that the median full-time staff of multimedia firms is three persons, linkages to supplier industries are obviously critically important. The survey also revealed that, on average, 24 per cent of all work is contracted out. Figure 6.2 shows that more than two-thirds of firms (69 per cent) subcontract out all musical composition; 59 per cent of the firms subcontract out all voice-over work; and 48 per cent of the firms subcontract out all cinematography. Conversely, 90 per cent of the firms indicate that customer service is conducted in-house; 64 per cent of the firms do all their content research in-house; and just under half of the firms indicate that all programming, artwork and illustration, writing and editing is done in-house.

The creation and development of multimedia products requires highly trained talent and multiple skills, which generally means that there are several people and/or firms working on the creation of each product. The most commonly cited type of supplier is a freelancer: someone with specialized talent who is hired on a contract basis, as needed, per project. Many survey respondents indicated that the most critical types of supplier to their firms are freelancers or firms with particular artistic or technical expertise. Freelancers also work with one another on projects. Brett Maraldo, Principal of Plexus Interactive, a one-person multimedia firm/freelancer, comments on the way in which he works with other multimedia freelancers:

> I have colleagues that I've met through clients and work. They've become friends to some degree, you know, work-related type friends. So we go out for a beer every once in a while, just check up on what

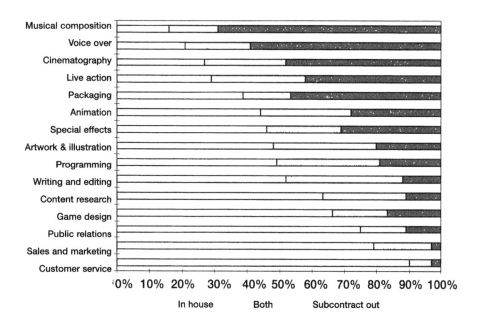

Figure 6.2 Make or buy?

117

each other's doing, and then if a contract comes along we'll use each other as resources to get the work done. . . . None of us say no to a contract, so if there's something I can't do I know that there's people that can do it. So I'll say 'yes' and then just subcontract out to my colleagues. And they do the same.

(Interview)

According to Stuart Ross, President of Bindernagel-Ross New Media, a mid-sized multimedia firm catering to Fortune 500 companies,

Multimedia is not an individual skill, it's a group skill. To really produce, to live up to the potential that multimedia or interactive multimedia offers, you have to approach it from a multidisciplinary approach. Which means you do not have a single individual that is capable of sitting behind a computer in the basement with Macromedia Director and becoming the writer *and* the author *and* the programmer, and the animator and the graphic designer. It's almost a metaphor for the business itself that it requires a group of people to come together and combine all these different skills that we use to create products. We try not to be experts in everything. If there's audio work to be done we will go out to an audio post-production studio, certainly video we handle the same way. All of those are sub-trades that have their own craftspeople that we work with. So some of the major media categories like audio and video, we subcontract out to.

(Interview)

Aurel Langlois, Director of Electramedia, a mid-sized firm that has produced both corporate products and a successful interactive game, classifies the firm's alliances with other sectors as follows: the most important inputs by dollar figure are from outside consultants such as designers, programmers, camera people and sound composers. The second most important suppliers are outside video and post-production services. Finally, suppliers of raw materials and consumables such as computer hardware, software and blank CD-ROMs round off the linkages that support the firm's activities.

Another form of 'multimedia firm' is one that develops multimedia products to enhance its core business. For example, Irwin Publishing is an educational publishing firm that produces CD-ROMs which are supplementary to the core of their business, educational textbooks. Rather than set up an in-house multimedia department, Irwin Publishing hires or subcontracts locally based multimedia firms to do all of the technical delivery and programming required. Brian O'Donnell, President, notes that some of their suppliers, who include replicators, graphic designers, artists, illustrators and freelance editors, are 'not necessarily associated with the multimedia industry. They work for all media

118

industries. So I mean they might be hired by the multimedia industry one day and a cereal manufacturer or an ad agency the next.' This statement underscores a key point: that the skills required for the development of multimedia products include both industry- and non-industry-specific talent.

Not surprisingly, large multimedia firms contract out proportionately less work to freelancers and specialist experts than small and mid-sized firms as they have larger numbers of in-house staff to draw upon for expertise and skill. Marketing directors for two multimedia firms each with over 100 employees confirmed this view, indicating that their main outside suppliers are in computer software and hardware as well as production and post-production companies.

Finally, most firms indicate that they also hire suppliers such as lawyers, accountants and couriers to provide general business services. These services tend to take up proportionately less time and money than specialist expertise and computing needs, however.

Though the costs of start-up in multimedia are typically low, which reduces barriers to entry into the industry, access to financing for further development and growth poses difficulties for many firms. Financing for multimedia firms is difficult to secure for two main reasons. First, multimedia is a knowledge-based industry making it difficult to measure the value of a firm's assets by traditional accounting methods. Second, as a relatively new industry with no long-term history or track record, it is seen by many major financial institutions as too risky an investment. This situation is beginning to change slowly, as venture capitalists and some banks are learning more about the opportunities presented by multimedia and are beginning to invest in the industry.

The regional labour market

In terms of the presence of skilled labour to feed into and support the local multimedia industry, interview respondents generally indicate that there is an excellent labour supply for multimedia and supporting industries in the Greater Toronto Area, with two main exceptions: senior multimedia personnel and highly skilled programmers. The availability of well-trained creative and technical people is greatly facilitated by the presence of numerous educational and training institutions in the region. Some of these offer multimedia specializations; others are less specialized but still provide much-needed talent for the multimedia sector. According to Michael Shostak, Vice President of Marketing at Digital Renaissance:

> It's [the GTA] kind of unique probably in North America because we have a very good influx of creative people and places like Sheridan College are putting out really good quality candidates, and you have a good influx of technical people, and you have the University of Toronto

and Waterloo and some pretty internationally well-known schools that produce engineers and programmers and the two kind of meet in the centre. So it's great for both those areas. . . .There's a lot of candidates at a junior level. It's tough to find senior people, people with experience in this industry, because it is such a new industry. So there's a lot of bright, Waterloo engineering students but there's not a lot of engineering people out there with a couple years experience in our industry, working in multimedia. Same thing with graphic design. . . . Especially someone in the sales, marketing, business management areas as well. There's very few people who have combined knowledge of this industry and a business background. Really, it's part of the failure of a lot of companies in this industry, because they have a lack of people with business savvy that understand this industry.

(Interview)

In many respects the lack of senior level multimedia personnel is a catch-22, as the industry has not been around long enough to produce a significant number of senior personnel. Interviewees also expressed the criticism that, despite the number of educational and training institutions offering multimedia programmes directly or indirectly relevant to multimedia in the region, most programmes are oriented towards beginners rather than towards the development of intermediate or advanced skills.

John King, Director of the Bell Centre for Creative Communications (BCCC), a local college with multimedia training programmes, acknowledges this problem but notes that it is partly a function of the industry itself.[11] According to King, the people capable of teaching advanced courses are too busy working on multimedia projects of their own. King adds that there is no significant demand for the advanced courses that are currently offered at BCCC as some of the large US industry players such as Industrial Light and Magic prefer to hire skilled, entry-level practitioners whom they can then train on their own proprietary systems.

The Toronto area is acknowledged by virtually all survey and interview respondents as an important source of expertise and suppliers to the multimedia industry. In part this reflects Toronto's cosmopolitan status as a hub for culture, education, business, infrastructure and other amenities. Aurel Langlois, Director at Electramedia, says of Toronto: 'This is the hot spot for multimedia in the country. There's a lot of talent available here, either specific to new media or to the ancillary or the other media that constitute multimedia.' Frank Abrams, President of Flying Disc Entertainment, concurs:

We're not really taking widgets and turning them into product, we're taking people's talents, artistic talents, programming talents and using that. Specifically with artists they tend to congregate in larger cities, they tend to not have cars, they tend to be poor, sort of the starving artist thing is very much a reality and they tend to sort of struggle in that respect. If you are located conveniently and it's a really great place to work and a great place to live, then you're likely to attract better talent to work for you.

(Interview)

Nurturing multimedia's growth: public policy and associative action

We have argued in the preceding sections of this chapter that the development and current health of Toronto's multimedia sector must be seen as depending heavily on the region's collection of pre-established activities in the arts, media, entertainment and business services. It should therefore come as no surprise that the most significant public policy initiatives in support of the multimedia industry are those that have nurtured the development of Toronto's (and Canada's) cultural industries in general.

Given Canada's proximity to the United States and its openness to American cultural influences in many forms, the central thrust of federal and provincial public policy since the 1960s has been to shelter home-grown Canadian culture from the English-language 'onslaught' from south of the border. This has been achieved through a number of programmes and policies designed to encourage the production of Canadian cultural products. Most prominent among these is the policy enacted through the federal government's chief regulatory body, the Canadian Radio-Television and Telecommunications Commission (or CRTC). This agency significantly expanded the domestic market for Canadian cultural products through its 'Canadian content' regulations, which require television and radio stations to include a certain minimum amount of Canadian-produced programming in their regular schedules. This policy is widely acknowledged as having stimulated the development and efflorescence of domestic industries in television production, music recording and composing (Ministry of Culture, Tourism and Recreation 1994), with much of this activity developing in Toronto (as well as Montreal and Vancouver).

In a similar vein, both the federal and Ontario governments have established agencies to promote the domestic production and foreign distribution of Canadian films. Telefilm Canada, the National Film Board, the Ontario Film Development Corporation and Ontario's Film Investment Program have been recognized for their catalytic role in nurturing this industry and, indirectly, the specialized supplier activities that constitute the rest of Toronto's film, television and sound recording cluster (Ministry of Culture, Tourism and Recreation 1994). These agencies, in association with aggressive marketing efforts from the City of Toronto's own Film and Television Office, have also been responsible for luring a very substantial amount of film and television production to the Toronto region from the United States.

Book and magazine publishing has also benefited directly from federal and provincial government support, through preferential taxation, postage/distribution and advertising regulations, as well as direct operating subsidies. Foreign investment in publishing has been more tightly regulated (and limited) than in virtually any other sector of the Canadian economy (Ministry of Culture, Tourism and Recreation 1994). Once again the Toronto region, as the nation's pre-eminent geographical concentration of book and periodical publishing firms, has enjoyed the positive effects flowing from this aspect of cultural policy.

We would contend that this unusually comprehensive policy framework, enacted by senior levels of government in Canada out of a long-standing concern to promote home-grown culture, has almost single-handedly nurtured the development of Toronto's entertainment, media and publishing cluster. It has created the enabling conditions for the emergence of multimedia production in Toronto, a development assisted by government support for the rich regional endowment of educational institutions in visual arts, computer science and related fields noted earlier. Against this backdrop of crucial – though indirect or largely unintended – public support for the sectors on which multimedia 'feeds', other public sector measures explicitly designed to nurture this sector's development pale in comparison.

The emergence of the multimedia industry has not gone unnoticed by governments and policymakers at the federal, provincial and local levels. While some efforts have been devoted to institution-building and the encouragement of associative action, most public policy approaches have thus far been largely focused on information gathering and consultation processes, with some support also going towards export market development.

In addition to conducting periodic surveys of the multimedia industry, Industry Canada (the federal government's industry ministry) has supported the development of a promotional CD-ROM listing Canadian multimedia firms which was distributed at MILIA '97, an annual multimedia conference held in Cannes, France. To support the development of Canadian multimedia exports, the Department of Foreign Affairs and International Trade also posts information officers with multimedia industry expertise in American centres of multimedia activity, including New York, Chicago, Boston, Los Angeles and San Francisco.

More explicit attempts by public agencies to build 'institutional thickness' have, thus far, yielded little in the way of concrete results. The NDP government (ruling Ontario from 1990 to 1995), as part of its Industrial Policy Framework, stimulated the development of a series of 'sectoral strategies' along broadly corporatist lines. These involved participation of firms, organized labour and other major industrial stakeholders (Wolfe and Gertler 1998). Among the various strategies to support individual industrial sectors, three (in computing, culture and telecommunications) addressed issues related to the support of a multimedia industry. The cultural industries strategy had the expressed goal 'to develop an industry-government frame-work that will enable Ontario's cultural industries to take a lead role in developing new multimedia products and in using new systems to distribute traditional cultural products' (Ministry of Culture, Tourism and Recreation 1994: 46). The cultural industries strategy recommended the creation of a centre to promote strategic alliances and other collaborative initiatives between local industry players and to develop Ontario's reputation as a leader in the development of world-class multimedia content. However, the new (Conservative) government was elected shortly after the development of the sectoral strategy plans, and very few of the recommendations were ever fully implemented.

Currently, at the provincial level, the Ministry of Economic Development, Trade and Tourism is working in conjunction with the Ministry of Citizenship, Culture and Recreation to develop recommendations for public policy initiatives in support of the multimedia industry. The current government's approach to economic development is to eliminate barriers to businesses' growth, rather than to support business development financially. The two Ministries are working with a group of multimedia industry leaders, termed the 'Digital Media Champions Group', to create a framework for future policy directions for the industry, though the group's recommendations will not be binding upon the government.

While government financial support for the industry is limited, a provincial tax credit was recently introduced for firms working in the field of animation. Other ways through which the government supports the industry's growth and export efforts are through the development of promotional materials touting the industry's regional strengths, and by sponsoring booths in international trade fairs, reducing participation costs and increasing international networking opportunities for participating firms.

At the local level, efforts by governments within the GTA to stimulate the development of a multimedia sector 'from scratch' indicate just how difficult a task this is. They also indicate how distance-sensitive are many of the activities performed in the production of multimedia products. As Maps 6.1 and 6.2 indicated, Toronto's multimedia industry is strongly focused on the districts immediately adjacent to the most central areas of the region. Such areas offer an attractive array of physical and locational assets: an abundance of vacant, relatively cheap and funky 'loft-style' space in old industrial buildings; close proximity to major customers in the downtown corporate and financial core; easy access to key suppliers and potential collaborator firms in the visual arts, graphic design, software, video and audio production sectors.

Against this overall pattern, consider the case of East York, a borough of the (former) Municipality of Metropolitan Toronto whose principal industrial zone is located a mere ten kilometres from the downtown core of Toronto.[12] This municipality is currently pursuing an economic development plan aimed at revitalizing its industrial areas in response to the loss of traditional industry. One of the largest firms to leave in recent times is Alcatel, a company whose wire and cable plant employed over 400 people and occupied over one million square feet of space (Prue 1996). East York has devised an economic development plan aiming to create a 'New Media Village' by promoting the existence of fibre-optic cable in the area and waiving development charges for businesses (Godfrey 1996: 2). Thus far, however, these attempts to trigger the relocation and indigenous development of multimedia firms in the area have failed to produce the desired result.

In addition to the policy efforts being undertaken by governments, a series of private and public-private institutions have also developed in an effort to harness the growth potential of multimedia and help support the industry's growth.

The Interactive Multimedia Arts and Technologies Association (IMAT) is a national organization headquartered in Toronto that represents the multimedia industry in Canada. Despite its national focus, however, the industry's members are highly centralized in Toronto, Montreal and Vancouver. IMAT was established in January 1995, as a result of the merger between the Canadian Computer Graphic Artists Association and the International Multimedia Development Association. Its mandate is: 'to generate jobs for the multimedia and cultural sectors; to create an environment for economic development; to bridge the gap between information technology (IT) and culture; to foster Canadian content; and to represent emerging technologies' (IMAT 1996: 6).

To this end, IMAT holds monthly meetings in Toronto, publishes a quarterly newsletter and advertises jobs in the industry. It currently has over 600 members; 85 per cent are located in the Toronto area, and a further 10 per cent in other parts of Southern Ontario. Several interview respondents praised IMAT for catering to new entrants to the industry by providing a forum for learning about working in multimedia, but criticized it for failing to support established firms or to provide a strong voice for the industry in public policy matters. IMAT is hoping to address this problem, with the election of a new board and president. The hope is that it will continue to serve the needs of its individual members by organizing and coordinating meetings and networking opportunities, while at the same time broadening its role in matters that affect the industry as a whole such as public policy initiatives.

Two other organizations that support the multimedia industry as part of their larger mandates are the Information Technology Research Center (ITRC) and Smart Toronto. ITRC is a provincially funded Centre of Excellence, which brings university researchers together with private companies to share information and collaborate on research. It sponsors monthly 'Web breakfasts' where speakers discuss current research and state-of-the-art technology related to the development of the web, and includes multimedia content in their programme offerings of annual meetings, training seminars and special events.

Smart Toronto is a public–private organization, initiated to promote the

GTA's development in information-technology industries. Smart Toronto is bringing together industry players to work on improvements to the technological infrastructure in the region. These include increasing the availability of high-bandwidth services, working on programmes to link investors with new media firms, and promoting the strength of the GTA's information technology industries world-wide at conferences and conventions such as MILIA.

Despite the work of both Smart Toronto and ITRC, many of the multimedia employees and principals interviewed were unaware of the existence of these organizations or of their efforts to support the regional multimedia industry. This suggests that the more formalized and public forms of associative action have, to this point, tended to lag behind, rather than lead, the multimedia industry's development.

Findings and implications for policy and theory

The survey and interview results presented here comprise the first in-depth study of the Toronto area multimedia industry. They provide useful information for other centres of multimedia activity on the background history of the industry's emergence, the significance of backward and forward linkages with local area firms, and insights into the locational clustering of firms in older, traditional industrial areas. Both the survey and interview results emphasize the fact that the multimedia industry remains strongly linked to local suppliers and clients in the urban core. Intra-urban location appears to be a critical variable for firm development due to the importance ascribed to ease of access to related and supplier industries, freelancers, potential employees, amenities and educational and training facilities, because it facilitates interaction and networking with clients. This helps to explain the clustering of multimedia firms in older industrial areas of the urban core as evidenced in Maps 6.1 and 6.2. Firms which do not seem to place as much significance on location were those with stronger linkages to export than to local markets, firms producing mass marketed goods, and firms with networks of suppliers that are not centred on Toronto. These were the minority in the Toronto case study.

The evidence presented here suggests that the broader, macroregulatory framework of Canadian (and Ontario) cultural policies has provided the most important public sector stimulus to the development of Toronto's multimedia sector. Furthermore, this case study suggests that the simple targeting of multimedia firms alone for assistance is not enough to support the development of a multimedia industry. The development of the industry has been shown to be strongly path-dependent. It relies on talent from diverse backgrounds, and the industry continues to depend on the services of specialized expertise in traditional media, programming, arts and related fields. The presence of multiple and diverse education and training institutions, and access to cultural amenities and services, has also helped the industry to

SHAUNA G. BRAIL AND MERIC S. GERTLER

develop in Toronto, a characteristic this region seems to share with New York City, San Francisco, Los Angeles and other major North American centres of multimedia production.

It is difficult to imagine a competitively structured multimedia industry that is not supported by these features. The structures required to support the industry run far deeper than the availability of technology and related infrastructure. Therefore, public policy initiatives need to address a wide range of multimedia and related support linkages in an effort to encourage the industry's existence. In light of these issues, it seems fair to say that multimedia alone cannot be a panacea for economic development. The richly developed supplier and client networks on which the industry's emergence and continuity rely are an integral part of any regional multimedia cluster.

The implications of this research for the literature on the geography of economic activity are twofold. First, this research supports and reinforces the conclusions of earlier research (Kutay 1989, Capello and Gillespie 1993, Coffey 1996, Graham and Marvin 1996, Graham 1997): industries based on information and communications technology still rely heavily on interpersonal networks and strong backward linkages leading to agglomeration in urban centres. In this sense, we concur with Kutay (1989: 376), who concluded some time ago that 'high tech economic development is not a solution to the decline of mature industrial regions . . . policy would be more realistic if economic development strategies are built upon the stronger components of the existing regional economy'. The convergence of technology and creative sectors, and the history of large city-regions as centres of culture (Scott 1998) further reinforce the importance of urban locations for multimedia activity. The networks that the managers of multimedia firms describe as being critical to their development and survival are not so much networks of multimedia firms but rather of related firms and institutions.

A second and related point concerns the issue of institutional thickness. It is clear that, to this point, the industry in Toronto has developed despite lacking local depth or thickness in the institutions that might engender inter-firm cooperation. It appears that the industry's growth, to this point, has been largely a function of favourable policies supporting cultural industries nationally and provincially rather than strong institutional structures (apart from education and training centres). The associative behaviour that does exist is primarily of an informal nature, in the form of loose associations between cooperating firms. Whether or not the industry can maintain its competitive advantage without further strengthening its associative institutional structures, is uncertain. Indeed, in the face of current and future threats to the integrity of Canada's cultural policies, arising from increasingly common challenges from the United States, Europe and the World Trade Organization (Scoffield 1998), the industry may soon be forced to pursue more associative strategies with greater vigour.

Notes

The authors wish to thank the Social Sciences and Humanities Research Council of Canada for its support of this research through a Doctoral Fellowship and a strategic grant. We would also like to thank Prof. Philip Coppack, Ryerson Polytechnic University, for his assistance in geocoding Maps 6.1 and 6.2. We would also like to acknowledge the time taken by survey respondents and interviewees for completing the survey and participating in interviews. Finally, thanks are due to Gerhard Fuchs, David Wolfe and the referees for valuable comments on an earlier draft of this chapter.

1 These estimates are based on our analysis of two national databases: the Industry Canada Strategis (http://www.ic.gc.ca) database and the Multimediator Canadian Developer's Directory (http://www.multimediator.com).

2 The database, survey and interviews being described in this paper derive from Shauna Brail's (1998) Ph.D. research on the emergence of the Toronto multimedia industry.

   The database was developed by combining lists of Ontario multimedia firms from six sources:

   1 The Interactive Multimedia Arts and Technologies Association Members' Directory (1996).
   2 Firms who classified themselves within the multimedia industry in the Industry Canada Strategis website as of January 1997 (http://strategis.ic.gc.ca).
   3 Firms listed in the Canadian Developers Directory on the multimediator website as of January 1997 (http://www.multimediator.com).
   4 Firms with listings in the 1996 'Guide to Multimedia Services' advertising section in *Marketing Magazine*.
   5 Firms with listings in the same publication, 1997.
   6 Firms listed as new media producers and creators in the 1995 *Canadian Directory of New Media in the Cultural Sector*.

3 During the course of this research, the provincial government introduced a bill to amalgamate what was previously a regional government 'Metropolitan Toronto' comprised of six local municipalities (including the central 'City of Toronto') into one municipality, to be called 'Toronto'. For the purposes of this research, the pre-amalgamation municipal boundaries are used. The GTA is used here as the most extensive definition of the Toronto region, being comprised of Metropolitan Toronto and the four adjacent regional municipalities. The GTA's total population is 4.5 million.

4 The field of 319 multimedia firms in the GTA was reduced to 311 firms at this point in the research process as we were unable to locate three firms, one mailed survey was returned by the post office, and four firms indicated they were not working in multimedia.

5 A total of eighty-five usable responses were received. Of those, eighty-one were respondents from the electronically distributed survey and four were respondents to the mailed version. Seventeen surveys were received from firms that were not on the initial database. This represents a response rate of 22 per cent for the electronically distributed surveys (not including the responses from the seventeen

non-database firms), and an overall response rate of 21.5 per cent (mailed and electronically-distributed surveys).

6 Survey respondents were asked to rank activities in one of the following four percentile groups per category (listed horizontally): All = 100 per cent of their work falls under this category; Most = between 51 and 99 per cent of their work falls under this category; Some = between 1 and 49 per cent of their work falls under this category; None = 0 per cent of their work falls under this category. The numbers presented in all columns to the right of the left hand column represent the proportion of firms whose work falls within each percentile group, per category. Hence (as an example), 18 per cent of respondents indicated that Education products comprised more than half (but less than 100 per cent) of their sales.

7 Custom products are those that have been commissioned by a specific client and tailored for their particular needs. Mass market products are those that are developed by a multimedia firm with the intention of selling these products in standard form to a large number of consumers.

8 The sample of interviewed firms was chosen according to: size (1, 2–20, 20+ employees); intra-urban location (downtown, midtown, fringe); and multimedia composition of their work (multimedia only or multimedia component). In total, 44 interviews were conducted with representatives of multimedia firms, government and related associations.

9 Mackerel Interactive Media declared bankruptcy shortly after this interview, following a merger and the subsequent demise of both the parent and sister companies which left Mackerel without sufficient cash flow to continue operating.

10 Silicon Alley is the term coined to describe an area in Manhattan dominated by new media firms and activity. See the chapters in this volume by Heydebrand and Pavlik.

11 BCCC is the result of a partnership between Centennial College (a local college) and a group of companies involved in digital communications, including Bell Canada, Silicon Graphics Canada Inc., Alias Wavefront and Sony of Canada.

12 The Borough of East York is the smallest municipality in the GTA, and adjacent to the City of Toronto. It has experienced job losses due to the relocation of several large companies to newer industrial spaces.

References

Amin, A. and Thrift, N. (1994) 'Living in the global', in A. Amin and N. Thrift (eds) *Globalization, Institutions and Regional Development in Europe,* London: Oxford University Press.

Angel, D. (1994) *Restructuring for Innovation: The Remaking of the US Semiconductor,* New York: Guilford Press.

Brail, S. (1998) '"New" media in '"old"' urban areas: the emergence and evolution of Toronto's multimedia cluster', Ph.D. thesis, Department of Geography, University of Toronto.

Canadian Heritage (1995) 'Canadian directory of new media in the cultural sector', Canada: Minister of Supply and Services.

Capello, R. and Gillespie, A. (1993) 'Transport, communications and spatial organisation: future trends and conceptual frameworks', in G. Giannopoulos and A.

Gillespie (eds) *Transport and Communications Innovation in Europe,* London and New York: Belhaven Press.

Centre for Image and Sound Research (1995) *Study of the New Media Industry in British Columbia,* Vancouver: Price Waterhouse.

Christopherson, S. (1993) 'Market rules and territorial outcomes: the case of the United States', *International Journal of Urban and Regional Research* 17: 274–88.

Coffey, W. J. (1996) 'Employment growth and change in the Canadian urban system, 1971-94', Working Paper No. W(02), Ottawa: Canadian Policy Research Networks.

Coopers and Lybrand Consulting (1996) *New York New Media Industry Survey.* New York: New York Media Association.

Cornish, S. (1997) 'Product innovation and the spatial dynamics of market intelligence: does proximity to markets matter?', *Economic Geography* 73: 143–65.

Freeman, C. (1991) 'Networks of innovators: a synthesis of research issues', *Research Policy* 20: 499–514.

Freeman, C. and Perez, C. (1988) 'Structural crises of adjustment: business cycles and investment behaviour', in G. Dosi *et al.* (eds) *Technical Change and Economic Theory,* London: Pinter.

Fortune (1996) 'It's glitz, not guns, behind California's comeback', *Fortune,* 5 February: 53–4.

Gertler, M. S. (1997) 'The invention of regional culture', in R. Lee and J. Wills (eds) *Geographies of Economies,* London: Edward Arnold.

Godfrey, J. (1996) 'Your voice in Ottawa', *Constituency Newsletter,* September.

Graham, S. (1997) 'Cities in the real-time age: the paradigm challenge of tele-communications to the conception and planning of urban space', *Environment and Planning* A 29: 105–27.

Graham, S. and Marvin, S. (1996) *Telecommunications and the City,* London and New York: Routledge.

Greater Toronto Area Task Force (1996) *Greater Toronto: Report of the GTA Task Force,* Ontario: Queen's Printer for Ontario.

Hall, P. and Markusen, A. R. (1985) *Silicon Landscapes*, London: Allen and Unwin.

IMAT (1995) (Interactive Multimedia Arts and Technologies Association) 'Survey of the multimedia industry in Canada', Ottawa: Industry Canada and IMAT.

—— (1996) '1996 directory of members and services', Ottawa: Interactive Multimedia Arts and Technologies Association.

Krantz, M. (1995) 'The great Manhattan geek rush of 1995', *New York* 28, November 15: 34–42.

Kutay, A. (1989) 'Prospects for high technology based economic development in mature industrial regions: Pittsburgh as a case study', *Journal of Urban Affairs* 11, 4: 361–77.

Lane, C. (1997) 'The social regulation of inter-firm relations in Britain and Germany: market rules, legal norms and technical standards', *Cambridge Journal of Economics* 21: 197–215.

Marketing Magazine (1995) 'Guide to multimedia services 1995', *Marketing Magazine,* 18 December: 16–21.

Marketing Magazine (1996) 'Guide to multimedia services 1996', *Marketing Magazine,* 16 December: 11–17.

Ministry of Culture, Tourism and Recreation (1994) *The Business of Culture: A Strategy for Ontario's Cultural Industries,* Toronto: Queen's Printer for Ontario.

Morgan, K. (1995) 'The learning region: institutions, innovation, and regional renewal', Papers in Planning Research 157, Cardiff: Department of City and Regional Planning, University of Wales.

Nelson, R. R. (1995) 'Recent evolutionary theorizing about economic change', *Journal of Economic Literature* 33: 48–90.

Prue, M. (1996) 'Why Alcatel killed Leaside plant', *Town Crier,* February.

Saxenian, A. (1994) *Regional Advantage: Culture and Competition in Silicon Valley and Route 128,* Cambridge, Mass.: Harvard University Press.

Scoffield, H. (1998) 'EU taking Canada to WTO in film dispute' *Globe and Mail,* 21 January, B4.

Scott, A. J. (1997) 'The cultural economy of cities', *International Journal of Urban and Regional Research* 21, 2: 323-39.

—— (1998) 'From Silicon Valley to Hollywood: the multimedia industry in California', in H.-J. Braczyk, P. Cooke and M. Heidenreich (eds) *Regional Innovation Systems,* London: UCL Press.

Storper, M. (1997) *The Regional World,* New York: Guilford Press .

Webber, M. J. and Rigby, D. L. (1996) *The Golden Age Illusion: Rethinking Postwar Capitalism,* New York: Guilford Press.

Wever, K. S. (1995) *Negotiating Competitiveness: Employment Relations and Organizational Innovation in Germany and the United States,* Cambridge, Mass.: Harvard Business School Press.

Wolfe, D. A. and Gertler, M. S. (1998) 'The regional innovation system in Ontario', in H.-J. Braczyk, P. Cooke and M. Heidenreich (eds) *Regional Innovation Systems,* London: UCL Press.

7

BETWEEN REGIONAL NETWORKING AND LONESOME RIDING

Different patterns of regional
embeddedness of new media sectors in
North Rhine-Westphalia

Josef Hilbert, Jürgen Nordhause-Janz and Dieter Rehfeld

Introduction

The new media have come under the scrutiny of business firms and politicians alike. Politicians hope that the new multimedia industries will create high-paying jobs, business people see the new media as a means to enhance the competitiveness of their firms in conventional markets, or as a tool for the development and design of new products or services. Despite such hopes and wishes, the future prospects of this industrial sector remain uncertain. Up to now, neither the technology, the articulated preferences of corporate customers and private consumers, nor the regulatory frameworks suggests a definite path of development (see Riehm and Wingert 1995, DIW/Prognos 1995).

With these uncertainties in mind, it is likely that regional patterns of new media industrial development will vary widely. This does not mean, however, that an unlimited range of development paths is feasible. On the contrary, innovation theory and regional development research suggest that sustainable innovation is most likely to succeed where it is regionally embedded with both conventional, well-established industries and firms interlinked with the multimedia sector. Accordingly, regions that profit from new multimedia developments have shown a proven ability to address the needs of at least two groups. The first comprises industries, firms, customers or consumers who are willing to make use of new technological opportunities. The second includes those new media firms which are willing to address and collaborate with firms from traditional industries, with the aim of tentatively identifying and developing potential products and services (see Braczyk *et al.* 1998, Fritsch and Ewers 1985, Gregory and Urry 1985, Henke*l et al.* 1984).

This chapter investigates the validity of 'regional embeddedness' as a necessary condition for new media business development, using the case study of North Rhine-Westphalia (NRW) and some of its sub-regions. In terms of population size and economic relevance, NRW is the most important state in Germany. As far as new media businesses and the theoretical hypothesis outlined above are concerned, it is interesting to study NRW for at least two reasons. First, in contrast to many other states and regions that aim to develop new media industries, NRW has both a large and flourishing new media industry and a great deal of experience in new media-related industrial policies. Second, methodologically, a case study analysis of NRW presents a useful platform from which to launch sub-regional comparisons among sub-regions with diverse economic traditions and profiles which share a common media policy, regulatory framework and cultural background. Compared to international comparative studies, an intra-state comparative analysis of regional patterns of embeddedness suffers less distortion from intervening political, regulative or cultural variables.

The first part of this chapter (an economic profile) presents general background information about NRW to demonstrate the utility of the case. The next part (multimedia in NRW) outlines a definition of multimedia and specifies the databases used. The third part (a bird's-eye view) gives an overall profile of the new media industry and its development in NRW. This is the background for a detailed look at very specific cases in three different NRW sub-regions in the fourth part (regional profiles). The concluding section (multimedia in the Ruhr area) tries to draw conclusions from the NRW case study for assessing industrial policy as well as multimedia business development prospects.

North Rhine-Westphalia: an economic snapshot profile

NRW, one of Germany's sixteen federal states (Länder), is situated in the heart of Europe, bordering Belgium and the Netherlands. With a population of 17.8 million (1994), NRW is the most populous state in Germany and its most significant industrial region. Approximately 25 per cent of (West) German GNP, 27 per cent of its industrial output and 28 per cent of exports originate in NRW. The leading industrial sectors are chemicals, mechanical engineering, electronics and electronic engineering, the automotive industry and the food industry. A third of Germany's top 500 international companies have their headquarters there. There are also more than 500,000 small and medium-sized enterprises.

By and large, the economic profile of NRW and its different sub-regions is characterized by diversity and change. Business activities cover almost all existing sectors and branches, ranging from coal-mining and energy (in the Ruhr area) to traditional industries such as furniture (in the Lower Rhine area as well as in eastern Westphalia) to food processing (in the Münsterland) and to modern service industries. In such a broad and differentiated economy, it is difficult to identify any prime factor driving the dynamics of change. Nevertheless, two important trends have emerged.

First, as in almost all advanced industrial countries and regions, there is a noticeable economic shift from manufacturing to services (see Table 7.1). In this context, production-oriented services and social services account for most of the new jobs.

Second, the above-average decline in such traditional sectors as mining, steel and parts of the investment goods sector is the main reason for the changes that can be seen in the regional economy. The decline of these traditional industries in NWR is particularly marked in the Ruhr area, the industrial heart of both NRW and Germany. This area has a third of NRW's population and industrial output and is still dominated by its traditional sectors: coal-mining and steel. Although these sectors employ fewer than 200,000 people, the production networks, concepts and regimes in this area are still characterized by traditional patterns (see Table 7.2).

One prominent example is the case of mechanical engineering. More than 30 per cent of this sector in the Ruhr area is directly linked to the coal-mining industry, especially Ruhrkohle AG, the dominant coal-mining company. Most of these companies are small and medium-sized firms which depend to a high degree (50 to 90 per cent of turnover) on business with Ruhrkohle AG and are thus affected by its investment decisions. It is estimated that one job

Table 7.1 Sectoral employment in North Rhine-Westphalia and West Germany: percentage changes 1980 to 1996

	W. Germany*	NRW
Agriculture	-14.0	12.3
Energy, mining	-5.9	-34.3
Industry	-13.9	-19.7
Construction	-9.8	-14.3
Wholesale and retail	10.4	8.0
Transport and communication	10.2	15.4
Financial institutions and insurance	27.4	15.9
Other services	47.5	45.8
Total	8.3	2.5

Source: Bundesanstalt für Arbeit; own calculations.
Note: * excluding North Rhine-Westphalia.

Table 7.2 Developments in North Rhine-Westphalian and (West) German industries 1993 (1980 = 100)

	Companies		Employment		Turnover	
	NRW	W. Germany*	NRW	W. Germany*	NRW	W. Germany*
Mining	65.4	75.0	61.0	68.2	100.8	83.8
Basic goods	97.3	80.0	71.5	88.1	103.7	134.7
Investment goods	110.3	109.9	92.2	96.3	166.6	181.2
Consumer goods	87.7	80.1	85.0	79.6	159.5	149.9
Food and beverage	103.5	90.4	105.1	98.3	163.3	156.7
Total	100.3	91.9	83.2	91.1	136.0	159.2

Source: LDS; Bundesanstalt für Arbeit; own calculations
Notes: * Excluding North Rhine-Westphalia.

in the coal-mining industry supports 1.3 additional ones in related economic sectors (Lehner *et al.* 1988).

The problems of structural change and renewal in the Ruhr area have caused problems for the economic performance of NRW in general. As Table 7.3 indicates, total employment in NRW grew less than the West German average. To a large extent this weaker performance can be attributed to labour market developments in the Ruhr area. Unemployment in NRW (12 per cent) is above the (West) German average (10.6 per cent) with a peak of 14.9 per cent in the Ruhr area.[1]

Although these regional and sectoral peculiarities show some important trends of structural change in NRW, there are also remarkable developments which indicate a shift from the traditionally-structured regional economy to a new economy which is based on future-oriented markets. One prominent example is the environmental protection industry which accounted for about 100,000 jobs (Nordhause-Janz and Rehfeld 1995) in 1993. Another example that is described in more detail in this chapter is the multimedia sector.

Multimedia in North Rhine-Westphalia: definitions and data bases

While the term 'multimedia' is certainly one of the most cited and 'hyped' words dominating debates about the future of advanced industrial societies, its overuse has obscured its specific economic and developmental definition. At first it was hardly more than a technical concept, but took on a wider meaning as the discussion on multimedia increasingly centred around the emergence of a new economic sector and new business clusters. Although many different prognoses on market volumes and jobs exist, there is no official definition of what multimedia means in a sectoral sense. In a technical sense multimedia applications are characterized by three important features:

Table 7.3 Employment in North Rhine-Westphalia, Ruhr area and West Germany (1983 = 100)

	NRW	*Ruhr area*	*W. Germany**
1983	100.0	100.0	100.0
1984	99.7	98.6	100.1
1985	100.4	98.7	101.5
1986	101.8	99.3	103.3
1987	102.9	99.3	104.9
1988	103.9	99.1	106.1
1989	105.7	100.1	108.0
1990	109.3	102.4	111.9
1991	112.5	104.4	116.0
1992	113.6	104.8	117.8
1993	111.5	102.2	116.1
1994	109.5	99.2	114.5
1995	108.7	97.5	113.0
1996	107.1	95.7	112.2

Source: Bundesanstalt für Arbeit; own calculations
Note: * excluding North Rhine-Westphalia.

- Interactive usage.
- Integration of different media types.
- Treatment and storage on the basis of digital technologies.

This summary of basic features illustrates that the multimedia has a typical cross-sectional character not only in a technological but in a sectoral sense. The production of multimedia applications requires the combination of goods, services and competencies of different actors and sectors. In particular, this demand for combination and cooperation can be regarded as the main reason why some analysts speak of a *production chain multimedia*, combining the audio visual and print media sector, advertising companies, hardware and software producers and telecommunication providers (Booz *et al.* 1995; DIW/PROGNOS 1995).

Following this broad understanding of multimedia, our analysis in most parts is based on a definition of a sectoral view as shown in Figure 7.1. To compare the NRW multimedia sector to other German federal states we will use a tighter definition which covers only companies engaged in the core fields of multimedia, such as CD-ROM producers, online-publishing, Internet and telecommunication services.

To define a multimedia sector is one thing, but to assemble and analyse relevant quantitative data is much more difficult. As Figure 7.1 demonstrates, multimedia covers not only companies in the industrial sector but also a range of companies in the service sector. Unfortunately, official

135

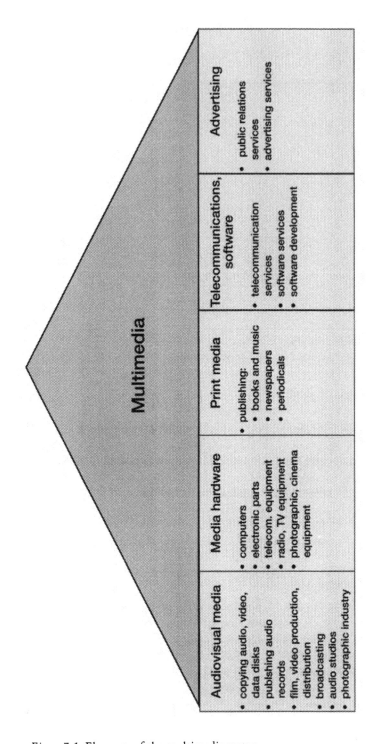

Figure 7.1 Elements of the multimedia sector

statistical data in most cases are not published in an adequate sectoral depth. Only the German turnover tax statistics, which are published every two years, contain significant sectorally disaggregated data. In this context two other difficulties regarding the contents of these data must be mentioned. First, information gathered from the turnover tax statistics is limited to the number of enterprises and the turnover achieved. Second, regionally disaggregated data may conflict with data protection regulations. Accordingly, statistical offices are often restricted in their abilities to offer data in the desired disaggregated form.

Due to these limitations we use several databases referring to the company level as a second source. These databases were collected by the Institut für Arbeit und Technik (IAT) and cover information on more than 5,000 individual companies of the multimedia sector in NRW.[2]

Multimedia in North Rhine-Westphalia: results from a bird's eye view

Although estimates of multimedia market volumes and developments differ according to the definitions they are based on, some common trends over recent years can be detected. Compared with the total economy, the market for multimedia products and services has shown above average growth and many experts are convinced that this increase will continue in the future, even if the expected growth rates appear rather moderate (Booz *et al.* 1995, DIW/PROGNOS 1995).

A first look at the situation in NRW indicates that the multimedia sector has reached a significant economic scale and is challenging the importance of the most relevant industrial sectors (see Table 7.4). According to the turnover tax statistics, which include companies and freelances with a taxable turnover of more than 32,500 DM per year, about 34,000 multimedia companies or freelances are located in NRW with an overall turnover of more than 130 billion DM. The turnover per enterprise shows that the multimedia sector consists predominantly of small and medium-sized enterprises. More than 36 per cent are engaged in the telecommunications, telematics sector and in various fields of audio visual media. All in all, the NRW multimedia sector at present accounts for more than 210,000 jobs.

A closer analysis, based on the core parts of the multimedia sector, shows that about 24 per cent of the German multimedia companies are located in NRW (Table 7.5). Together with Bavaria, where more than 20 per cent of the German multimedia sector is located, NRW can be regarded as one of the German multimedia centres.

NRW companies offer a broad range of different multimedia services in a sector where full service and a wide supply range seems to be typical. This is all the more surprising as most of the companies are relatively young. 60 per cent of the enterprises of the core multimedia fields have been engaged on the multimedia market for five years or less.

Table 7.4 Number of enterprises, turnover and employed persons in the North Rhine-Westphalian multimedia sector 1996

WZ description	Multimedia sector	Number of enterprises	Turnover in 1,000 DM	Employed persons
	Audio visual media	3,555	6,786,212	19,000
Publishing: audio-records		45	59,332	
Copying: audio disks and tapes		171	1,299,743	
Copying: audio/data disks and tapes		46	30,877	
Photographic industry		1,733	704,672	
Film and video production		782	1,026,421	
Film and video distribution		540	440,981	
Broadcasting		123	3,162,802	
Audio studios		60	16,694	
Technical services for entertainment		55	44,690	
	media hardware	1,465	9,186,499	79,000
Computers		480	1,551,343	
Electronic parts		325	3,868,020	
Telecomunication equipment		488	3,037,601	
Radio, TV, video receiving equipment		122	557,185	
Photographic, cinema, projection equipment		50	172,350	
	print media	1,958	18,137,694	30,000
Publishing: books and music		676	8,650,557	
Publishing: newspapers		107	4,196,198	
Publishing: periodicals		461	3,842,636	
Publishing: others		714	1,448,303	
	advertising	18,032	21,388,490	26,000*
Market- and opinion research		663	2,378,698	
Public relations		7,968	6,111,847	
Advertising services		9,401	12,897,945	
	telecommuni-cations, software	9,198	75,239,128	58,000
Telecommunication services		174	62,746,452	
Hardware consultance		506	245,031	
Software consultance and development		1,280	1,991,888	
Other computer services		6,391	9,314,381	
Online databases, maintenance/ repair of computers and office machinery		131	91,385	
Other hardware and software services		716	849,991	
Multimedia total		34,208	130,738,023	212,000
NRW economy (excl. multimedia)		554,099	1,886,504,587	6,985,30
Multimedia as % of total economy		6.17	6.48	2.86

* only advertising services.
Sources: LDS, Statistisches Bundesamt Mikrozensus 1996, IAT database telecommunication providers; own calculations, including freelancers.

Table 7.5 Regional distribution of German multimedia companies 1997: regional share of multimedia segments in % multimedia segment

	CBT	CD Rom titles	Electronic commerce	Electronic catalogues	Intranet applic.	POI, POS terminals	Online marketing	Online publishing	Games	Telecom. services	Multimedia total
Baden-Württemberg	12.9	12.5	15.7	14.9	14.2	14.2	14.0	13.6	13.6	11.9	12.6
Bavaria	27.3	25.2	21.6	23.0	25.2	22.8	22.9	25.6	21.2	16.1	20.6
Berlin	6.7	6.3	5.4	6.1	5.5	7.3	6.8	8.4	7.0	3.7	6.3
Hamburg	4.6	8.8	10.3	6.9	9.3	7.8	9.7	8.7	12.2	4.7	7.0
Hesse	12.7	10.6	10.5	9.8	10.2	10.8	10.8	9.1	13.0	13.6	11.7
North Rhine–Westphalia	21.9	22.0	22.2	24.2	22.8	24.3	23.3	20.8	22.6	25.2	23.9
Other former German federal states	9.0	9.6	11.4	10.1	8.9	8.6	9.3	9.8	7.8	14.8	11.5
New German federal states	5.0	5.0	3.0	5.0	3.9	4.2	3.2	3.8	2.6	9.9	6.4
Germany	100	100	100	100	100	100	100	100	100	100	100
Germany absolute numbers	480	819	370	753	508	548	472	711	345	975	2574

Sources: IAT database multimedia NRW, IAT database telecommunication providers.

Because of the overall importance of multimedia, many hopes for the creation of new jobs are connected with this sector. This is particularly true of those regions of NRW, such as the Ruhr, which are confronted with economic problems.

A more detailed look at the sub-regions, however, clearly demonstrates that these expectations are not justified in all cases. On the contrary, as Table 7.6 shows, multimedia only plays an important role in some of the regions. One is the Rhine area, particularly Cologne and Düsseldorf which represent the two centres of the NRW multimedia sector. These two regions account for more than 39 per cent of multimedia companies.

Düsseldorf and Cologne show interesting differences in company structures. Whereas Cologne's profile is characterized by a greater number of enterprises which are engaged in the field of audio visual media, Düsseldorf's sectoral structure is more diversified. It has a stronger position in media hardware, which to a great extent derives from its importance as a headquarters location of multinational companies from Japan. Most of the new competitors of the German Telekom are located in Düsseldorf; this is one reason for its relatively strong position in the telecommunication sector. Finally, Düsseldorf is one of Germany's most assertive advertising centres (Belzer and Michel 1998).

A rather special feature can be observed in the region of Ostwestfalen-Lippe where, among other enterprises, two global actors, Siemens-Nixdorf and the Bertelsmann AG, are located.

While the overall quantitative data seem to support the existence of a multimedia sector, such quantitative data do not by themselves demonstrate the viability of sustainable multimedia industrial clusters. A more detailed analysis of three different NRW sub-regions will provide a basis for evaluating the 'take-off' point for multimedia cluster development.

Multimedia in North Rhine-Westphalia: a detailed look at regional profiles

Multimedia in Cologne: clustering in progress

Without any doubt, the most promising and expanding media cluster in NRW is located in Cologne. The roots of this cluster originate from a specific set of conditions. First of all, Cologne is the location of the Westdeutscher Rundfunk (WDR), the second-largest broadcasting company in Europe. In addition, Cologne is well known for its very broad and attractive cultural milieu, the development of which was closely linked to the expansion of the WDR. In the 1960s, the electronic recording studios of the WDR attracted artists like John Cage, Nam June Paik and Karlheinz Stockhausen, followed by ambitious gallery managers who organized the first world-wide art fair in Cologne. As a result of this engagement, Cologne grew up to be one of the

Table 7.6 Regional distribution of North Rhine-Westphalian multimedia firms 1996 (in per cent of each multimedia subsector)

	Audio visual media	Hard-ware	Print media	Adverti-sing	Telecomms, software	Total
Hochsauerlandkreis, Kreis Soest	1.7	2.5	2.0	1.7	1.4	1.7
Central Ruhr Valley/Bochum*	3.7	4.0	4.0	3.8	4.7	4.1
Dortmund/Unna District/ Hamm*	5.0	6.1	4.1	4.5	5.0	4.7
Märkische region	2.2	4.8	2.1	2.7	2.8	2.7
Siegen	0.8	3.2	1.3	1.5	1.8	1.6
Ostwestfalen-Lippe	6.9	8.5	7.7	8.2	8.3	8.1
Towns of the Bergisches Land	3.7	6.8	3.2	4.1	3.3	3.9
Düsseldorf/Central Lower Rhine	20.8	17.5	18.6	22.4	17.9	20.6
Mühlheim/Essen/Oberhausen*	5.7	5.0	6.9	6.1	5.2	5.8
Lower Rhine	5.2	6.9	5.2	5.6	5.9	5.7
Aachen	5.0	8.9	4.9	5.4	8.6	6.3
Bonn	5.9	4.2	10.9	5.7	8.1	6.9
Cologne	25.5	12.8	19.7	18.0	17.6	18.5
Emscher-Lippe*	3.4	3.3	2.6	3.4	3.4	3.3
Münsterland	4.4	5.7	6.7	6.2	6.0	6.0
* Ruhr area	20.1	23.1	19.7	20.5	21.1	20.7
North Rhine-Westphalia weighted average	4.7	5.8	5.0	5.0	5.3	5.2

Sources: LDS; IAT database telecommunication providers; own calculations.

most dynamic art locations in the world (Krings 1988). Finally, its proximity to Bonn, the former German capital, and Brussels, the location of the EU-Commission, made Cologne attractive as a base for the headquarters of a broad range of media associations.

Figure 7.2 illustrates the development of the media cluster in Cologne. After a rather slow but continuous rise in the 1950s, the sector started to boom in the 1970s and 1980s. Film production and service companies and – especially in the 1990s – companies engaged in multimedia-oriented productions (see Media-Guide 1997) predominated. Above all, this dynamic development was the result of deregulation measures opening up the TV and radio market for private companies. The state government of NRW announced that it would open the new frequencies for TV first of all to those companies that are located in NRW.

The establishment of the German RTL headquarter in Cologne functioned as a catalyst for the Cologne cultural and media seedbed. More and more

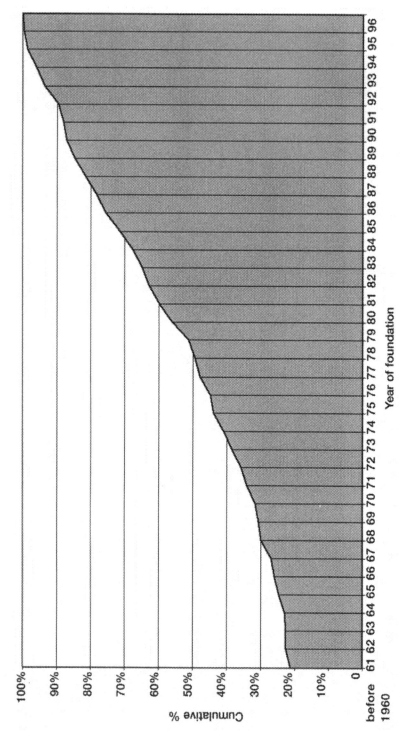

Figure 7.2 Year of foundation of companies active in multimedia in Cologne *Source:* IAT Database Multimedia NRW

broadcasters followed RTL; some relocated their headquarters from Munich or Berlin to Cologne. Regional suppliers specialized on media-related services and today the most prominent world-wide media companies, Sony, Warner Brothers, EMI, Pioneer, Bertelsmann and so on, are highly visible in Cologne (see Rehfeld and Wompel 1997).

Of course, the expansion of the media cluster in Cologne also followed from political decisions. Media deregulation kick-started a boom among private broadcasting companies in Germany with the NRW state government offering enticing incentives for companies such as RTL to establish facilities in Cologne. However, it must be noted that other state governments in Germany, Lower Saxony for example, tried to do the same and failed. NRW was in an optimal position because a third of (West-) German TV-viewers live there. And, as shown above, Cologne was ready for the boom.

When the boom in Cologne started, the work of the local political managers was simple but effective: the media park, a facility for the new media companies, became well known as the first ambitious public-private-partnership project in Germany (see Mayer 1994). The newly-founded Media University turned out to be a source of many creative artists. The local savings-bank (Stadtsparkasse) supported the foundation and location of new media companies. The local agencies for economic development provided information and discussions. Their input in turn stimulated other actors.

Two aspects of these political activities have to be considered. First, the cluster-related activities started only when the rise of the media cluster could no longer be ignored by local authorities, who were rather doubtful about its potential until the mid-1980s (Stadt Köln 1985). Second, since political initiatives only began at a late stage, we have to point out that regional and local politics did not initiate this cluster, though they made an important contribution towards accelerating its development.

In the light of the success of this media cluster, the local authorities in Cologne started looking out for further clusters. Today, the City of Cologne presents itself as Communication City (Stadt Köln 1995) and aims to initiate a new media boom. The extent to which Cologne meets preconditions for this are encouraging. As shown above, it has a dominant position in NRW in nearly all new media sectors. Nevertheless, the realization of these potentials does not only depend on regional economic potential.

The chances for, and the structure of, a cluster are closely linked to company strategies. In this respect, our research shows a trend among Cologne companies to combine network management, software development, organizational advertisement and other production-related services to a potential cluster that we call organizational management. Companies from very different sectors, such as insurance, facility management, electricity, network providing, advertising or hard- and software companies, have the same focus: how to use new media in organizing integrated networks, providing system management, giving advice in related organizational questions and developing value-added services (Mehrwertdienste) for their new customers. Some of them concentrate upon billing, others upon infrastructural services and most of them are in search of integrated strategies.

The market is not yet fully developed and most companies use their contacts with Cologne companies in order to open up lead markets. The Cologne IBM subsidiary, for instance, has a strong focus on integrated hardware, software and organizational system management especially for established Cologne sectors such as insurance, media or the chemical industry (see Rehfeld and Wompel 1997).

The situation is more competitive than cooperative. Nevertheless, there are synergies. New companies order headhunters to recruit qualified managers. In some cases like software and multimedia, informal circles are established. Everybody is interested in everybody else's strategies. It is not certain, however, whether or not a new production cluster will arise or not. Most of the activities are organized in the context of the individual firms. A political initiative might help to start a regional discussion to promote the development of a new media cluster, but the politicians are hesitating again. The local authorities concerned with industrial development focus on multimedia in general rather than on production clusters, and talk more about technology and infrastructure than about markets.

Interestingly, there are very few linkages between the established media cluster in Cologne and new activities in organization management. The highly integrated media cluster is regarded primarily as a customer, not as a partner. Some publicly-funded institutions provide qualified personnel and research for both clusters; perhaps multimedia will grow at the borderline of the two.

Neither regional anchorage nor regional modernization impact: the lonesome riding of Bertelsmann in the multimedia business

A somewhat different picture can be drawn if we take a more detailed look at Ostwestfalen-Lippe, another NRW sub-region, and its most prominent economic actor, the Bertelsmann Corporation. Without any doubt, this corporation is among the biggest and most powerful media enterprises in the world. It employs about 58,000 people and operates world-wide. Its strongest pillars are the European and US–American markets, although sales in Latin America as well as in Asia are increasing. The 1995–96 business report outlines five branches: books (publishing houses and book clubs), entertainment (audio and video), newspapers and magazines, printing and media-related services and – last but not least – new media.

Most of the competitors of Bertelsmann have their headquarters in world-famous and hyper-busy megacities such as New York, Los Angeles, Tokyo or Paris. In contrast, the headquarters of the Bertelsmann-holding are based in Gütersloh, a small and rather undistinguished town of around 100,000 inhabitants in Ostwestfalen, the rural eastern part of NRW. In other words, Bertelsmann is a high-stake global player with a provincial base.

At present, new media is only a new and small area of activity for Bertelsmann. The whole corporation employs only about 2,500 to 3,000 people in this field (of these, around 900 work for Bertelsmann/AOL: 300 in Germany and 600 in France and the UK). However, Bertelsmann considers interactive, multimedia online services to be a key to future growth in media businesses. Within a couple of years, multimedia-based products will account for 30 to 50 per cent of the corporation's turnover growth according to estimates in the 1995–96 business report. Therefore, Bertelsmann has done a great deal to develop competencies, capacities and power in this area. The aim is to become a leading high-potential global actor in all parts of the multimedia production chain, including network development and provision, via online services, of content and Internet services.

Probably the best known activity is the Bertelsmann/AOL joint venture. With about 350,000 subscribers in Germany and 1,000,000 in Europe (spring 1998), AOL Bertelsmann Online has become one of the top European online services and Internet providers. Bertelsmann AOL Germany is located in Hamburg, with a support and call centre located in Eiweiler (close to Saarbrücken). The UK and French services are based in London and Paris; both have a joint service centre in Dublin, Ireland.

In the summer of 1997, Bertelsmann/AOL took over the European private customer relation services of CompuServe with 850,000 subscribers. The two firms – Bertelsmann/AOL and CompuServe (Europe) – will not be integrated; they plan to develop different profiles. Bertelsmann/AOL will focus on entertainment and family-related services, CompuServe on academic and professional users.

At least four Bertelsmann firms are important in terms of new media infrastructure and technology. Media Ways – a fully-owned subsidiary of Bertelsmann – was founded to push network development and network technology. Innovative Internet solutions are the main business of Telemedia, a Gütersloh-based service provider which has some strategic alliances with leading technology providers such as IBM, Sun and Oracle. With respect to the (technical) design of products, Bertelsmann has a Hamburg-based subsidiary called New Media and holds 75 per cent of the shares of Pixelpark, a leading production firm for multimedia products located in Berlin.

Another interesting business in new media is the development and service of multimedia solutions for process or product improvement. EPS (Bertelsmann electronic printing service) is noteworthy in this field. The firm is located in Gütersloh and specializes in multimedia-based document management for printing industries. It has been developed in response to a demand that grew out of the printing firms and publishing houses within the Bertelsmann holding.

For information or content provision, Bertelsmann is collaborating with a wide variety of customers. If there are market opportunities for innovative services but no competent provider, Bertelsmann sometimes tries to develop new products by collaboration. An example for this is BSG (Bertelsmann Springer Gesundheit), a joint venture of Bertelsmann and Springer, a publishing house with much relevant experience in health and medical literature. BSG provides private and professional customers with online information services in health and medicine.

As mentioned above, the Bertelsmann headquarters and some of the Bertelsmann firms are located in and around Gütersloh, in Ostwestfalen (i.e. in the eastern part of NRW), and Bertelsmann is the biggest employer in the region. Approximately 8,500 (out of 58,000) Bertelsmann employees work there. Besides strategic and administrative activities, the majority of the Gütersloh-based workforce is active in traditional media businesses such as book clubs, printing (of books, magazines, CDs, and CD-ROMs), marketing and distribution.

The importance of Bertelsmann to Ostwestfalen does not mean that this region is dominated by media enterprises. Ostwestfalen is the location of several other enterprises, some of which have been very successful in recent years in both national and international markets. These enterprises are active in a number of different sectors and branches, with particular strength in food processing, furniture industry and mechanical engineering. Specific customer-supplier or other collaborative relations or arrangements among the leading firms of these sectors are not known. Overall, the economic performance of the region and its leading firms has been above average during the last two decades. Perhaps it makes sense to say that Ostwestfalen is characterized by some very successful but lonesome-riding hidden champions, and that this region itself is a hidden champion among German and European regions.

This picture holds true with respect to the media business. Besides Bertelsmann there are several other enterprises in this industry (e.g. publishing houses specializing in calendars, time schedules and diaries), but there are neither systematic nor accidental linkages among these firms. There is one very significant exception: the customer-supplier-relations between the different Bertelsmann firms. Although Bertelsmann subsidiaries are not obliged to cooperate with each other, they normally do. As insiders report, cooperation within the family is made easier by a strongly defined corporate identity, joint management training and the development of exchange programmes.

The Bertelsmann new media activities are geographically dispersed. Basic technologies and services are developed and delivered by Gütersloh-based firms. Online services, content development and providing are carried out by firms located in big cities and well-known media regions like Hamburg, Paris or London. Labour intensive services (call centres) are situated in cheap labour regions (Saarland or Ireland).

Although the new media activities of Bertelsmann in Ostwestfalen are significant, their regional impact seems to be rather marginal. As quantitative data and qualitative interviews show, the performance of this region in the new media business is average or even better, both in the development of multimedia and in the exploitation of new media for rationalization and improvement of traditional business. This is not due to Bertelsmann and its Gütersloh-based new media subsidiaries. These firms are not engaged in joint ventures with other firms in the region; customer–supplier relations within the region hardly exist. Knowledge transfer from Bertelsmann to other firms in the region by people moving from Bertelsmann to other employers are rare because, in terms of wages, working conditions and corporate identity, Bertelsmann is one of the most attractive German companies. As a Bertelsmann official put it when asked to outline the linkages to the Gütersloh region in the new media business: 'The only foot we have in Ostwestfalen is our employees'.

Multimedia in the Ruhr area: heterogeneity in search of synergy

It may seem surprising that an old industrial region like the Ruhr area, well known for a long-standing crisis in its industrial core sectors (see Rehfeld 1993, 1995), is engaging in multimedia. Unemployment rates in this region are still significantly above the German average and unemployment rates in the steel and coal sector will continue to rise in coming years. The need for new industrial activities and for the creation of new jobs is evident.

In former regional development concepts some years ago, only a few isolated remarks concerning multimedia could be found. Considering the regional distribution of multimedia companies in NRW, one could assume that this lack of emphasis is unrealistic.

Because of many positive and enthusiastic job prognoses and dynamic developments in other NRW regions like Cologne, many political and regional actors regard the multimedia sector as a promising field for new jobs and regional restructuring. In this context the NRW state government and the local actors in the Ruhr area started to consider the potential of new media as an important contribution to the restructuring of the Ruhr area. In the late 1980s the government started the 'Teletech NRW' programme and accelerated its activities to promote new media in NRW in 1995. The aims of these programmes are:

- Establishment of media firms in the regions of NRW.
- Sponsorship for the film and television industry.
- Opening up of the multimedia market as a part of a state initiative for media in NRW.
- Sponsorship for media projects in urban development (e.g. the media centre in the Düsseldorf Harbour, and the Cologne Media Park).

- Sponsorship for training in media skills for the employees of the media industry and the users of media in application fields or private households (e.g. the building of the European Centre for Media Competence).
- Sponsorship for the organization of media events (e.g. the Media Forum NRW).
- Sponsorship for the external promotion of the industry (e.g. participation in film festivals and the television fair in Cannes) (*Media Guide* 1997: 1).

Compared with other industrial policy programmes, the focus on projects opening up the market for new media makes a particular difference. The installation of an ambitious infrastructure combined with the promotion of lead-user concepts has been successful in NRW in promoting new sectors like the environmental industry (see Nordhause-Janz and Rehfeld 1995). It has involved a large number of established and newly-founded new media companies. Some of the core projects include the Ruhr area. One of these projects is located in Gelsenkirchen and, under the leadership of o.tel.o, aims at the installation and exploitation of all new media services such as online, teleco-operation, teleconferences, interactive TV and so on. More than a third of the other projects are located in the Ruhr area, especially in Dortmund and Duisburg, and involve large companies as well as local suppliers. The Ruhr area projects include a research institute for telecommunication in Dortmund, an electronic fair system in Essen, the wireless local loop in Duisburg and a multimedia project in Gelsenkirchen (see MWMTV 1997).

Another project was not part of the media promotion programme of the NRW state government but attracted great public interest. This was the opening of the film and leisure park 'Movie World' in Bottrop (region of Emscher Lippe) in 1996. This park is a joint venture of Warner Brothers and the Siemens-Nixdorf Company and was supported by the NRW government. Yet, it will be very hard for Bottrop to compete with the established studios and multimedia facilities in Cologne.

Besides these political activities, another factor that affects the prospects for multimedia in the Ruhr area must be taken into account: the economic activities of major companies, some of whom have started to engage extensively in the multimedia sector. Four of the five biggest newcomers in the field of telecommunication are located in NRW, and two of them have their company's headquarters in the Ruhr Area. The strength of these companies, especially those involved in energy supply, is in their data networks. For internal use they were allowed to build up their own data networks and are well-placed to meet the deregulation of the telecommunications sector. Apart from the former monopolist Deutsche Telekom AG they are the only providers of a wide-ranging telecommunication infrastructure in Germany.

But infrastructure is only the starting point for further ambitions. The structure of the consortia and their strategic alliances has been changed many times during the last few years in the hope of finding the right way to become a global actor. In 1996, at least one provider seemed to have found a final organization: The Düsseldorf-based VEBA and the Ruhr-area-based RWE established the joint venture o.tel.o in order to shape the new market. The business fields of this new company cover the full range of telecommunication and related services.

In some ways, the strategy of the new telecommunication companies presents a paradigm for a regionally based diversification strategy (see Rehfeld 1993). Enterprises use their traditional competence in network organization and management to invest in this new market. However, in other terms, this strategy also represents the traditional spatial division of labour in the Ruhr area. The headquarters of the new companies are located in Düsseldorf, the capital of NRW and the traditional location for most headquarter-related functions concerned with the Ruhr area. Related functions such as products, services and innovative telecommunication solutions are located in Essen, Bochum and Dortmund. But o.tel.o possesses further sites and agencies all over Germany; in Cologne in particular the development and operation of the telecommunication network accounts for about 600 employees.

All in all, looking at the overall picture of multimedia in the Ruhr area, one is reminded much more of scattered islands of various sizes than of the rise of a new production cluster. Centres of activity are largely confined to Cologne, Düsseldorf and their neighbourhoods and the most innovative companies are located there. Moreover, there are general limits in the cluster-building potentials of new media. First of all, new media is associated with infrastructure. Providers and service activities have to be organized in a strong spatial relation and cannot be exported like traditional products. Therefore, we can expect a broad spatial dispersion of multimedia-related activities and only a few functions will generate clusters that can be observed, for example in Cologne.

Multimedia activities, however, are important to support the structural change in the Ruhr area. New companies have a base to join the market, the infrastructure is excellent and, last but not least, new media will soon be available for companies in other industrial sectors. From this point of view the regional prospects for multimedia must be evaluated in terms of new infrastructure and innovative applications but not in terms of industrial clusters.

Industrial policies for innovation and the development of multimedia enterprises: experience from North Rhine-Westphalia

Although multimedia has been on the agenda of business people and industrial policymakers for several years, it is still considered to be a promising growth area. In the context of this debate, some fundamental questions concerning the development, governance and self-governance of complex innovation processes have been posed. The main focus of this debate can be summarized in terms of the need for, and difficulty of, collaboration and the different strategies relevant to different regions:.

The need for collaboration   Many ambitious, far-reaching and promising innovation projects can hardly be realized by a single firm. Instead, a complex and flexible collaborative arrangement of actors from different firms, branches and sectors is needed. The drive for cooperation has many different reasons, one of them being that advanced technical solutions can only be realized by technology fusions (Kodama 1991). Another pressure for collaboration seems to result from increased competition and time pressure. A step-by-step development of products and components in one firm may risk being overtaken by simultaneous inter-firm engineering arrangements.

The difficulty of collaboration   Cooperation across firm and sector borders seems very difficult to achieve. Lonesome riding traditions, different professional backgrounds, significant concertation (transaction) costs and, last but not least, a lack of trust, i.e. the fear of being exploited by an unfair partner, prevent many firms from collaborating. If industrial policy wants to promote collaboration in order to develop employment and welfare, it has to produce policies to initiate, facilitate and support it. As yet it is rather unclear what a promising strategy looks like although there seems to be some evidence that regions can play a crucial role. It is assumed that the density of regional interaction routines provides a fertile ground for both the development of inter-firm and inter-sectoral synergies (be it by accident or by strategy) and the emergence of trust.

Types of region   In order to understand inter-regional differences in innovation and the development of new business clusters, two types of region can be distinguished. In the first, there are sectors that have essential capacities to contribute significantly to new business activities. The second type of region tries to develop new areas of business by attracting firms from abroad and by encouraging new business start-ups. It seems evident that the first strategy is more promising than the second.

Some regions aim to attract investment by outlining the demand, needs and purchasing potentials of their population. This concept could be an alternative, but is in any case a good starting point for innovative activities, and seems to be particularly relevant for a new industry like multimedia that is still looking for new applications and mass markets. If a region is willing to realize advanced pilot projects, this could mean the mobilizing of many new customers and might attract research and development investment from large multinational firms (Meyer-Krahmer and Reger 1997).

Thus different types of region may be characterized by different types of industrial policy: one approach is to let new media emerge from related

150

business activities; another is to attract new media business by promising lead-use mass demand for new applications.

Conclusions

Evaluating both the development of new media enterprises in NRW (and its sub-regions) as well as new media-related industrial policies, given hypotheses and reflections can be specified and further developed.

First, it is not possible to develop a new media business cluster out of nothing. Up to now, only some regions have been significantly successful in contributing to leading edge technology and application development as well as in generating an above-average impact on the regional labour market. Such regions are deeply rooted in multimedia-related sectors such as traditional media, computers, network development and provision, and have strong user branches such as financial services and retail trade. The alternative strategy, to attract new media business investment by promising lead-use mass demand (as discussed earlier above), is practiced in the Ruhr area. This seems helpful with respect to keeping an old industrial area up to date with advanced technologies. However, it is wishful thinking to suppose that the new media will become a new regional specialization (with more than regional relevance) and create a new growth and job machine (as it was the case with pollution control industries).

Second, although the lead-use approach will not be able to develop new media clusters in regions without strong roots in new-media-related sectors, its relevance should not underestimated. If a region has sufficient potential in related sectors and multimedia technology, it could be worthwhile to activate them by fostering lead-use strategies. The relevance of such lead-use strategies will increase. Until now, the main focus of multimedia enterprises has been on technology and infrastructure: nowadays the need to develop mass markets by attractive applications is becoming more and more relevant. Unless such mass markets develop, it seems impossible to realize a sufficient return from past investment or to raise further investments.

A third factor that should be considered is collaboration. In order to promote competitiveness, as the Bertelsmann activities in new media show, there is a functional equivalent to regional clusters and inter-firm collaboration: namely, cooperation within a multinational corporation. Bertelsmann succeeded in becoming an internationally relevant new media provider by developing traditional firm activities as well as by acquisitions and joint ventures. With respect to both technical issues and basic services (call centres), Bertelsmann can exist and prosper without intensively collaborating with other firms in the regional neighbourhood.

The situation with respect to application development and content providing is quite different. In this case, synergies resulting from close and sometimes even informal collaboration with neighbouring firms are essential. Therefore Bertelsmann subsidiaries in these businesses are located in traditional media capitals like London, Paris, Berlin and Hamburg.[3] Overall, the Bertelsmann strategy seems to be adequate to guarantee the success and growth of the corporation itself. The modernization impact on the economy at its headquarters, however, is rather marginal.

Finally, the most relevant push for multimedia in NRW was obviously caused by the liberalization of broadcasting and telecommunication markets in Germany and Europe. This allowed potential actors to engage and to invest in the region, resulting in a wide variety of new media firms, initiatives and projects in NRW. This was possible because the NRW economy, particularly the Cologne region, had many strong roots in all sectors that are relevant for new media.

In contrast to the basic decisions for liberalization, regional policies are of minor importance. Nevertheless, regional policy programmes and initiatives can significantly contribute to facilitating and speeding up the development. This can be shown in particular by evaluating the Cologne case. Although considerable sums of public money went into projects and initiatives to develop the new media business in this region, the most positive support probably came from two rather informal factors. First was the traditional and symbolic openness of Cologne, seen in the posture of business people and politicians towards innovation in media. Second, there were a variety of political initiatives to bundle different but complimentary actors and resources to support joint innovative activities. With respect to the design and implementation of such joint innovation projects, it was not so much the 'round table' of all related and affected interests that brought about progress. Instead, multilateral commitments, innovative alliances of selected innovation promoters (business people, researchers, politicians and civil servants) were essential. To develop their own careers such people need success, and this interest causes them to go for risky joint projects. Such projects are essential for regional progress. At the regional level such 'benevolent conspiracies' seem to be more promising than 'round tables'.

Notes

1 All data June 1997 according to Landesarbeitsamt North Rhine-Westphalia and Bundesanstalt für Arbeit.
2 At the moment these databases contain information about firm locations, production and serve programmes, year of firm foundation, sectoral information and, in some cases, information on firm size and turnover.
3 The location of AOL Bertelsmann Online in Hamburg was probably not a decision against Cologne, the NRW media capital. One of the main intentions was to place the new online service next door to Gruner and Jahr, the Bertelsmann publishing house for newspapers and magazines.

References

Belzer, V. and Michel, L. P. (1998) 'Der Multimedia Standort Düsseldorf', Arbeitsbericht Nr. 98, Stuttgart: Akademie für Technikfolgenabschätzung in Baden-Württemberg.

Booz, Allen and Hamilton (1995) 'Zukunft Multimedia. Grundlagen, Märkte und Perspektiven in Deutschland', Frankfurt a.M.: Institut für Medienentwicklung und Kommunikation.

Braczyk, H.-J., Cooke, P. and Heidenreich, M. (eds) (1998) *Regional Innovation Systems*, London: Routledge.

DIW/PROGNOS (eds) (1995) *Künftige Entwicklung des Mediensektors*, Basel and Berlin: Duncker and Humblot.

Fritsch, M. and Ewers, J. (1985) 'Telematik und Raumentwicklung. Mögliche Auswirkungen der neuen Kommunikationstechnologien auf die Raumstruktur und Schlußfolgerungen für die raumbezogene Politik', Schriften der Gesellschaft für regionale Strukturentwicklung, Bonn: Gesellschaft für regionale Strukturentwicklung.

Gregory, D. and Urry, J. (eds) (1985) *Social Relations and Spatial Structures*, Basingstoke: MacMillan.

Henkel, D., Nopper, E and Rauch, N. (1984) *Informationstechnologie und Stadtentwicklung*, Stuttgart u.a.: Kohlhammer

Kodoma, F. (1991) *Analysing Japanese High Technologies: The Techno-Paradigm Shift*, London and New York: Pinter.

Krings, E. (1988) 'Die Metropole – Der Horizont', in Agentur für Recherche und Text (ed.) *Kultur Macht Politik. Wie mit Kultur Stadt/Staat zu Machen ist*, Köln: Kölner Volksblatt Verlag.

Lehner, F., Nordhause-Janz, J. and Schubert, K. (1988) 'Probleme und Perspektiven des Strukturwandels der Bergbau-Zulieferindustrie', Working Paper, Arbeitsgemeinschaft für angewandte Sozialforschung und Praxisberatung (ASP), Bochum.

Mayer, M. (1994) 'Public-Private-Partnership – eine neue Option und Chance für die kommunale Wirtschaftspolitik?' in R. Roth and H. Wollmann (eds) *Kommunalpolitik. Politisches Handeln in den Gemeinden*, Opladen: Leske and Budrich.

Media-Guide (1997) 'Film, Funk, Fernsehen, Telekommunikation, elektronische Medien in Nordrhein- Westfalen', Köln: Messe-Treff-Verlag GmbH.

Meyer-Krahmer, F. and Reger, G. (1997) 'Konsequenzen veränderter F&E-Strategien für die nationale Forschungs- und Technologiepolitik', in A. Gerybadze, F. Meyer-Krahmer and G. Reger (eds) *Globales Management von Forschung und Innovation*, Stuttgart: Schäffer-Poeschel.

Ministerium für Wirtschaft, Mittelstand, Technologie und Verkehr des Landes Nordrhein-Westfalen (ed.) (1995) 'Kultur- und Medienwirtschaft in den Regionen Nordrhein-Westfalens', 2. Kulturwirtschaftsbericht NRW, Düsseldorf: MWMTV Nordrhein-Westfalen.

Ministerium für Wirtschaft, Mittelstand, Technologie und Verkehr des Landes Nordrhein-Westfalen (ed.) (1997) 'Media NRW: Projekte', Düsseldorf: MWMTV Nordrhein-Westfalen.

Nordhause-Janz, J. and Rehfeld, D. (1995) *Umweltschutz 'Made in NRW'*, München: Rainer Hampp Verlag.

Rehfeld, D. (1993) 'The "Ruhrgebiet": Patterns of economic restructuring in an area of industrial decline', Future of Industry Paper Series, FOP 373, Brüssel.

—— (1995) 'Disintegration and reintegration of production clusters in the Ruhr area', in P. Cooke (ed.) *The Rise of the Rustbelt,* London: UCL Press.

Rehfeld, D. and Wompel, M. (1997) 'Künftige Produktionscluster im Raum Köln. Gutachten im Auftrag der Stadtsparkasse Köln', Graue Reihe des IAT, Gelsenkirchen: Institut für Arbeit und Technik.

Riehm, U. and Wingert, B. (1995) 'Multimedia. Mythen, Chancen und Herausforderungen', Abschlußbericht zur Vorstudie, Karlsruhe: Büro für Technikfolgen Abschätzung beim Deutschen Bundestag (TAB).

Stadt Köln (ed.) (1985) 'Wirtschaftsentwicklung und Arbeitsmarkt in Köln. Analyse, Perpektive', Programm, Köln: Stadt Köln.

—— (1995) 'Kommunikationsstadt Köln', Köln: Stadt Köln.

8

MULTIMEDIA

Profiling and regional restructuring of Munich as an industrial location

Detlev Sträter

Industrial development in the Munich area

The Munich area has always been regarded as one of the most vital economic regions in the Federal Republic of Germany.[1] Compared to other German conurbations, Munich has even managed to cope relatively well with the crisis since the early 1990s. It was already an important industrial location prior to the Second World War, with a brewery industry that was export-oriented even at that time, as well as a quite considerable machine building industry. However, Munich's actual economic boom did not come about until the early 1960s. More or less free from so-called obsolete industries, Munich and its environs have experienced a huge industrial and social structural upheaval within the past twenty-five to thirty years.

Since the achievement of full employment in the early 1960s, the number of employees in the city and environs of Munich (see map 8.1) has continuously risen to approximately 1.3 million.[2] The increase has primarily been in the Munich periphery during the past twenty years, although more than two-thirds of the jobs, approximately 850,000, are still situated in the core of the city itself.

The sectoral structure has changed with this general growth in employment. The manufacturing and service sectors once employed almost equal numbers, but the proportion of persons employed in the manufacturing sector has decreased to a quarter while the service sector now accounts for three out of four employees. This remarkable increase is Munich-specific to the extent that it is not only production-oriented but primarily technology-oriented. It has resulted in a remarkable rise in the level of qualified labour in the region ('academization'). There has also been a considerable externalization of technical activities: an indication of flexibilization strategies and a corresponding cooperation intensity (Biehler *et al.* 1994: 14).

This structural change towards 'post-fordistic' industrial structures has

Map 8.1 The Munich region

Source: Bayerisches Staatsministerium des Inneren and Bayerisches Staatsministerium für Landesentwicklung und Umweltfragen

been supported by numerous public and private training and research institutions, by the communication and transport infrastructure, and by highly developed 'soft location factors'. In comparison to other agglomeration areas in Germany, the Munich location has the additional advantage of offering an attractive leisure-time and recreational area in its immediate and outer environs, as well as in the proximity of the Alps.

The Munich area in comparison to other locations of the media and communication industry

Apart from these production/service complexes, an important media industry has developed in Munich. Alongside Cologne, Hamburg, Düsseldorf and Berlin, the Munich area is considered one of the most important media centres in Germany. Each of these four conurbations has a stronger special-ization than Munich in specific sectors of the media industry (e.g. the news-paper sector in Berlin, the magazine sector in Hamburg, the radio and TV sector in Cologne, and the advertising sector in Düsseldorf). The Munich area, in contrast, has achieved prominence across a wide range of media and communication sectors. Among the four agglomerations, Munich boasts the broadest media range and the greatest functional diversity.

In comparison to Berlin, Hamburg and Cologne, Munich has an extremely strong competitive position as a telecommunication and media location. The location advantages of the Munich area (Referat für Arbeit und Wirtschaft 1997: 31) are especially evident in the telecommunication and information technologies, software production, electronic media hard-ware and television. 'Munich is represented in the various sub-sectors of the telematics and media sectors in a balanced manner, which in a great num-ber of sub-segments has resulted in a leading role and in an adequate presence in virtually all of them' (ibid.).

The media industry in the Munich area and the trend towards 'multimedia'

Among the important media locations in the Federal Republic, Munich is certainly the 'Number one' (MedienStadt München 1996: 4). This was already ascertained in the first study 'Media City Munich' dated 1983 and confirmed in the two subsequent studies conducted in 1988 and 1995. Approximately every tenth employee in the Munich area is currently employed in the media sector. The study entitled 'MedienStadt München III' (Media City Munich III) was jointly commissioned by the City of Munich and the Chamber of Industry and Commerce (IHK) for Munich and Upper Bavaria and published in 1996. It shows that in the City of Munich and its environs there were 101,000 persons in full and freelance employment in 6,700 enterprises in the printing, film/radio/TV and advertising sectors. Their turnover amounts to 25.1 billion DM. Since the first study in 1983 the figures have doubled, not only as regards employment but also as regards the number of enterprises and turnover.

Between 1988 and 1995, a total of 28,440 new jobs were created in the media industry ('Medienstadt München' 1996: 7). In 1995, 72,060 persons were employed in this sector as full-time staff and 28,700 as freelances. Compared to 1988 and 1983, the share of freelances among all employees has continually grown to approximately 30 per cent at present.

Since 1988 the number of enterprises has increased by 60 per cent; between 1993 and 1995 1,200 new media enterprises were established. Since 1988 the turnover of the industry has risen to 25.1 billion DM, an increase of 8 billion or a 47 per cent increase. This does not take into account the turnover generated by non-Bavarian and foreign subsidiaries.

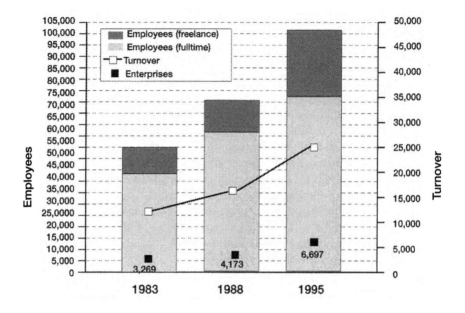

Figure 8.1 Enterprises, employees and turnover of the media industry, Munich 1995
Sources: 'Medienstadt München I' (1985) and 'MedienStadt München III' (1996)

In the same period, capital expenditure has risen from 893 million to 4.2 billion DM (projected for 1994), representing an almost five-fold increase (see fig. 8.1).

About half of the approximately 6,700 media enterprises in the Munich area (1995) are active in the advertising industry (3,078), a further 2,074 are associated in some way or other with the printing media. Approximately 1,500 (every fourth enterprise) are associated with film/TV/radio etc. The printing sector is the largest industry in the media sector, not only in terms of the number of employees (38,000 or 53 per cent) but also as regards turnover (11.3 billion DM or 45 per cent). It is primarily the publishing sector that contributes to growth (more than 8,000 employees), while the printing sector itself, above all the pre-print stage, is declining. Approximately one-fifth of employees (13,800) work in the advertising sector and the industry's turnover is in proportion to this (4.9 billion). In contrast to the previous years analysed, printing and the film/radio/TV sectors managed to increase their percentage for 1995 while the advertising industry had to face a loss of approximately 5 per cent.

The media industry is characterized by small and medium-sized companies interspersed with some large-scale enterprises. Only about thirty enterprises can be referred to as large media-industry enterprises although even these, in comparison to other industrial enterprises, are of a rather modest size. About 90 per cent of the Munich-based media enterprises generate a turnover of under 10 million DM, half have a turnover of under 1 million DM, and a third produce an annual turnover of 250,000 DM or less.

More than half of the media enterprises consist of independent contractors and are therefore not listed in the commercial register. These include two-thirds of all enterprises in the advertising industry, but only a third of those in the printing sector. Approximately half of the radio/film/TV/video sector is made up of small enterprises (MedienStadt München 1996: 7).

Due to the digitization of the information, communication and transmission technologies, the various media sectors have started a process of integration and mergers. Innovative multimedia products and services are emerging at the interface between the traditional media sectors of audio media (sound), visual media (picture, movies) and printing media (text). The producers needed only a few years to create a multimedia industry (in the narrow sense). Although there is neither a generally valid classification and distinction of the economic multimedia segment nor a clear definition of its contents, it is largely agreed that the terms integration, interaction and networking may be used to describe three multimedia directions or qualities (see Chapter One).

Integration is promoted by digitization from a technological point of view and by the liberalization of the media and telecommunication markets from the point of view of economic policy. It is an ongoing process which involves an increasing number of sectors of the economy. The media industry is currently merging with the information and telecommunication industries, which has led to the coinage of the term 'TIME industry' (telecommunication, information technologies, media industry and entertainment). In view of this tendency the approximately 14,000 employees in the enterprises and companies of the computer and telecommunication technologies must be included, so that in 1995 approximately 115,000 persons were employed in the TIME sector. The total number of employees in the city and environs of Munich is 940,000.

Figures based on the number of employees paying social insurance (taking into consideration the statistical error margin) show a steady development, with a slight regression in some manufacturing technologies but an overall increase (see Figure 8.2).[3]

Historical preconditions

The media and communication industry in Munich has various technological, economic and political origins. These include the precision mechanical/optical and the printing industries. Inventions and developments made in Munich in the late eighteenth and early nineteenth centuries promoted the establishment of enterprises concerned with the manufacturing of cameras, lenses and photographic material (Rodenstock, Perutz, Linhof and Agfa as well as Arnold and Richter-ARRI).[4] Munich's political role as state

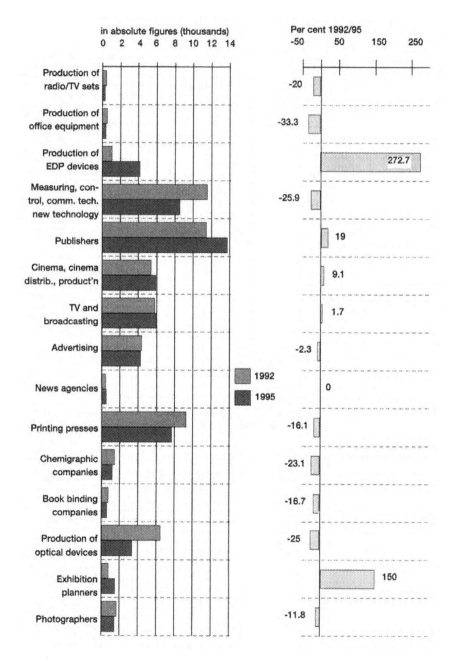

Figure 8.2 Employees in the telematics and media industries (city of Munich and environs) in 1992 and 1995

Source: Referat für Arbeit und Wirtschaft 1997: 19

Note: Subject to payment of social insurance contributions

capital and the central function of the city for its environs and indeed all of Bavaria have always enhanced the theatre and other cultural institutions such as museums as well as a broad range of training facilities.

Before the Second World War, the electrical engineering industry was already represented by numerous enterprises in Munich. It received a decisive impetus immediately after the end of the war with the move of the head-quarters of Siemens AG from Berlin to Munich and the resulting expansion of the Munich plant. The enterprise currently employs approximately 35,000 people in the Munich area.

The growth of the defence industry in the Munich area in the 1960s and 1970s also attracted a large number of foreign companies, in particular American electronics enterprises (Texas Instruments, Digital Equipment, Motorola and others), who have established subsidiaries (responsible for mar-keting, customer service and training) and some production facilities in the Munich area. A broad range of software companies has settled and developed around them (including Microsoft Deutschland in Unterschleißheim and CompuServe in Unterhaching, an Internet provider that has recently been taken over by AOL).

The fact that Munich is one of the most important training and research locations in Germany is a decisive condition of development and an impor-tant location factor. More than 100,000 students are enrolled at ten universi-ties and colleges. Particularly close links have been established between Technische Universität München and industrial enterprises.

Munich also holds a predominant position as regards extra-university research.[5] Those groups whose headquarters are situated in Munich have concentrated their research and development facilities there.[6]

This concentrated research and development competence provides an employment and labour market climate for high-tech development in Munich which thus directly or indirectly benefits from the communication and media sectors. This enhances flexibility, especially among more highly-qualified personnel and increases their opportunities for transferring to other enterprises. This, in turn, contributes to the diffusion of knowledge and experience.

Location requirements and location factors of the communication industry

The attractiveness of Munich for the media and communication industries is based on a number of special, primarily 'soft' location factors, which are either general 'location advantages' or the concentrated presence of elements which are important to the industry. These include:

- Proximity to a great variety of media providers and users.

- A comprehensive range of qualified staff and a creative labour pool ('good people').
- A broad range of training facilities and sites for media and communication professions.
- A well-established media and communication infrastructure.
- An urban ambience (regarded as a fertile ground for creativity and diversity).
- The image as an area boasting concentrated media and communication competence, thus attracting other professionals.
- Support by state and local governments for the media and communication industry.
- An attractive residential and leisure environment; the Munich conurbation is the 'sunbelt' of the Federal Republic.

A survey showed that 85 to 90 per cent of the media enterprises were satisfied or extremely satisfied with the location (MedienStadt München 1996: 17). The agglomeration Munich *per se* with its (media) diversity is emphasized as being the most important location factor. 'The prime aspect is Urbanity – with a capital U' (MedienStadt München 1996: 4). The fact that other media producers and providers are also located *in situ* is regarded by enterprises as the main asset. It enhances close customer relations and offers numerous opportunities for contact with customers and sub-contractors. The pool of qualified labour, an efficient transportation network, the size of the local community and the unbureaucratic attitude of the local authorities are also of great importance to them. Location disadvantages are also mentioned (expensive location, high rents - both for residential and business premises - considerable competition, high taxes) but none of these aspects outweighs the advantages of the location.

In a current study by the IMU Institute and the Catholic University of Eichstätt, experts constantly refer to the positive aspect of agglomeration size, geographic proximity, media diversity and urban environment. These factors all contribute to a creative environment for which the sectoral media diversity in the Munich location prepares the ground.[7] A thriving urban culture is the expression, prerequisite for and result of this creative process. Proximity offers interaction advantages, facilitates many immediate face-to-face contacts and thus enhances and secures the availability of information.

Media producers require an urban environment which enables their largely freelance employees freely to organize the working-time during which the task at hand is to be fulfilled. Many of them are not unwilling to work at night in order to be able to spend their days elsewhere. The separation of day and night work becomes blurred, and the same applies to the separation between work and non-work. This mode of working and living is possible in a city region offering creativity and stimulating diversity but not in residential and commercial deserts situated on the fringe of the agglomeration.

Core areas of the media industry and multimedia activities

As already mentioned, the media and communication sector in the Munich area consists primarily of small and medium-sized companies. It is grouped around a very few production service cores that represent a considerable percentage of the media employees and is, moreover, important for the orientation of the media and communication policies in Munich. It will be useful to detail the most important protagonists of the communication and media industry.

Newspaper publishers

Five daily newspapers with a total circulation of 1.2 million copies are published in Munich. The national *Süddeutsche Zeitung* is published by Süddeutscher Verlag, owned by five publisher families. One of them, the Friedmann family, also publishes the tabloid *Abendzeitung*. Münchner Pressehaus is the second largest newspaper publisher. It publishes the *Münchner Merkur*, which is primarily distributed in southern Bavaria, and the tabloid *tz*. The south German editorial office of *BILD-Zeitung* is also situated in Munich.

There are various interrelations between the publishing companies, particularly in the form of printing cooperation but also through interlocking capital arrangements. For the print publishing companies, expansion towards the new media is an attempt to open up further exploitation channels in addition to the traditional media such as newspapers, magazines or books. As is the case with other newspapers and magazines, the articles of the *Süddeutsche Zeitung* are also available online. The Süddeutsche Verlag issues a TV magazine *SZett* (which is fed into the programme of the privately-owned TV broadcasting company VOX situated in Cologne). It also holds a share (26.4 per cent) in the Munich radio station Radio Gong 2000 and in the regional programme slots of RTL and SAT.1 (Süddeutscher Verlag 1996). Münchner Pressehaus (*Münchner Merkur, tz*) has acquired the local radio station Charivari and the local TV station M1.

Magazine publishers

Judged by the number of editorial offices, titles and publishing companies, Munich ranks second after Hamburg in the magazine publishing sector. In 1983 the Burda Verlag moved the editorial head office of the *Bunte* magazine from Offenburg in Baden-Württemberg to Munich. The editorial offices of other magazines already located in Munich but spread throughout the city area were merged with the Bunte editorial office at the same time. Other editorial offices were moved from Stuttgart to Munich. The news magazine

Focus, published by Burda Verlag, has been the most successful new venture in the German weekly magazine market in the last few years.

According to media analysis '96, the Burda group ranks third among the ten major German publishing ventures. Approximately 800 out of a total of 5,000 full-time employees are on the Burda payroll in Munich compared to a mere 380 employees in 1983. The Burda group has concentrated a substantial share of its radio, TV and multimedia activities in its subsidiaries Burda New Media and Burda Broadcast Media, both housed in Munich. The Burda Verlag for example also produces the TV magazine *Focus TV* (in the 'virtual' studio of Bavaria Film GmbH in Geiselgasteig) which is broadcast by the privately-owned TV station Pro Sieben.

Important magazines are produced in the Munich location for the Hamburg publishing companies Grunerand Jahr, a Bertelsmann subsidiary, as well as for the Heinrich-Bauer-Verlag. Some of these magazines have also acquired offshoots in the electronic media sector. Besides general public magazines, numerous specialized publishing companies are located in the Munich area.[8] Their publications focus on telecommunication issues and high-tech products. Most of the computer and PC magazines available in Germany are produced and published in Munich.

Book publishers

Munich is second only to New York in global book publishing. 12,000 new titles are issued annually by 319 book publishers. A quarter of all the books produced in Germany are published in Munich. Although not all of the books published in Munich are also printed there, its position is strengthened by the printing industry located in Munich. The same applies to the wide range of agencies and other service providers in sectors ranging from photography and graphic arts to distribution. Publishers view 'new media' or 'multimedia' as an opportunity for opening up additional channels of exploiting traditional contents by means of technologically novel information media. The question for publishing companies is to what extent they themselves can make use of and control the new technologies and the associated new distribution channels, or whether these have to be opened up by third parties.

With its book and music production, the Bertelsmann group, situated in Gütersloh, constitutes an essential node in the media industry complex of the Munich area. Bertelsmann is one of the biggest media groups in the world with a turnover totalling more than 22 billion DM in the business year of 1995–96. In Munich, Bertelsmann Buch AG, together with its publishing subsidiaries, has approximately 1,500 employees. Bertelsmann AG achieves the bulk of its turnover with music, entertainment and multimedia. Its product line is integrated in the BMG Entertainment AG, which also has its headquarters in Munich.

BMG Entertainment International holds a 14 per cent share in the global music market and continuously expands into non-music oriented entertainment sectors, such as video and interactive entertainment. The subsidiaries of BMG Entertainment in the Munich area include BMG Ariola Media, Ufa Musikverlage, Ufa Video and BMG Entertainment TV. It has interests in the radio firms RTL2 (8.5 per cent) and Antenne Bayern (16 per cent) and in the Arbor TV film production in Tutzing (74 per cent).

Further important publishing companies in the Munich area include R. Oldenbourg Verlag (with publishing company, graphic industries and data systems divisions) with approximately 1,700 employees; Bruckmann Verlag, with F. Bruckmann Medien GmbH as a media subsidiary; Langenscheidt-Verlag, which currently also distributes a major part of its language tuition programmes on CD-ROM; and publishing companies like Markt und Technik, Magna Media and Franzis', who have focused on electronics, computers and PCs.

Film/radio/television

Munich is the leading centre for film and TV production in Germany. 34 per cent of this industry's turnover in Germany is generated in Bavaria, primarily in the Munich area. Two-thirds of all feature film producers in Germany are located there. The film/radio/TV sector boasts the highest growth rates in personnel among all sub-sectors of the media and communication industry. The granting of licences to privately-owned radio and TV programmes by the authorities has opened up a new sphere for capital investment. This comes primarily from the printing and publishing sectors as well as the licensing of media products and recently also from the trading sector. In addition to the established public stations Bayerischer Rundfunk and Landesstudio Bayern of ZDF and the privately-owned Bavaria Film GmbH, an important electronic media constellation developed in Munich during the 1980s when the Radio and TV sector was liberalized. The availability of a large number of radio and TV channels has opened up new, additional presentation and advertising opportunities. Yet there is also a need for additional programmes and adequately qualified staff.

The activities of the Kirch group (film licence trading, film production, film dubbing) have given rise to the TV station Pro Sieben with its subsidiary Kabel 1 and the sales station H.O.T., a joint venture with Quelle Versand. DF-1, the first German TV channel based on digital transmission technology, and Deutsches Sportfernsehen (DSF) are located in the immediate vicinity of the studios of Bayerischer Rundfunk and ZDF in the northern outskirts of Munich. The two TV stations RTL2 and tm3, the latter generally regarded as catering primarily for women, have also started operation. The local TV station tv-münchen, originating from TV weiß-blau, has opened up a transmission centre east of Munich.

165

Bayerischer Rundfunk (BR), a public radio and TV station, is integrated into ARD (Arbeitsgemeinschaft der Rundfunkanstalten Deutschlands). In addition to its share in the Erstes Deutsches Fernsehen programme and the 'Third Programme' (Bayerisches Fernsehen), it broadcasts five radio programmes. With regard to a regional multimedia cluster, one has to mention the cooperation with *Süddeutsche Zeitung* as regards text archives, the merging of the BR studio capacities with the ZDF subsidiary FSM (Fernsehstudio München) and Bavaria Film (see below) and a corporate participation in Bavaria Film decided on in summer 1997 (Will 1996: 28).

With the acquisition of the transmission rights for films like *La Strada* and *Casablanca* in the 1950s, Leo Kirch laid the foundation for one of the largest film and media licensing enterprises in the world. In the 1970s and 1980s Kirch founded numerous subsidiaries and acquired majority shares in film and TV productions as well as dubbing enterprises, film distribution companies, cinemas, licensing agencies and other enterprises. The Kirch group employs 1,400 people, of whom approximately 800 work in the Munich area (Kirch Gruppe 1996).

In the late 1980s and early 1990s the Kirch group also expanded into the TV business. Kirch currently holds 43 per cent of the privately owned TV station SAT.1, 66.5 per cent of Deutsches Sportfernsehen (DSF), 25 per cent of Hamburg pay-TV station Premiere and 100 per cent of the digital TV station DF-1.[9] His son, Thomas Kirch, increased his share in Pro Sieben Media AG to 60 per cent when it went public in July 1997 (Röper 1997). Moreover, he owns 40 per cent of the local TV station tv-münchen and one-third of the teleshopping station H.O.T. (Home Order Television).

Kirch's television flagship is the TV station Pro Sieben, located in Unterföhring. It was founded in 1988 after the purchase of the Munich news station Eureka TV and started transmission in early 1989. In 1992 Pro Sieben acquired the station Kabel 1 as a subsidiary. Pro Sieben is the only TV provider of the Kirch group that operates in the black; with a turnover of 1.67 billion DM in 1996 the station earned a profit of approximately 170 million DM. In July 1997 the station went public as Pro Sieben Media AG. Thomas Kirch acquired further shares so that the direct Kirch stake in the station now amounts to 60 per cent. The new name is indicative of an entrepreneurial development that commenced in 1993 and expanded the activities and business segments of the station to include almost the entire multimedia sector.

In the radio sector a comparable supplier expansion has taken place in the last ten to twelve years. Parallel to the expansion of the public Bayerische Rundfunk from three to five programme segments, a privately-owned broadcasting network has been established with Antenne Bayern as a second regional broadcasting station located in Unterföhring, as well as a number of local broadcasting stations including Radio Gong 2000, Radio Arabella, Radio Energy, Radio Charivari, Radio Two Day and scene radio stations like Radio Feierwerk and Radio LoRa among others.

166

The Bavaria Film premises have existed since 1919 in Geiselgasteig, the Grünwald suburb on the southern outskirts of Munich. These premises are among the largest film production sites in Europe. Refounded in 1959 as Bavaria Atelier Gesellschaft, the Bavaria Film area serves as a production and service institution for German and foreign film and TV productions. Bavaria Film GmbH boasts the whole range of state-of-the-art film and video recording facilities, as well as film laboratories, dubbing studios, distribution departments, and other facilities. The Bavaria studio has approximately 2,000 employees and in 1996 achieved an annual turnover of 277 million DM.

Westdeutscher Rundfunk (with Westdeutsches Werbefernsehen) and Südwestdeutscher Rundfunk Stuttgart are the majority shareholders of Bavaria Film GmbH. The remaining shareholders include banks and insurance companies. This association of Bayerischer Rundfunk and Bavaria Film is supposed to give a boost to the media location Bavaria. In spring 1997, Bavaria and ZDF combined their studio capacities to form the Bavaria-Film und Fernsehstudio GmbH, the largest studio association in Germany. As well as ZDF and Bavaria, the Bayerische Landesanstalt für Aufbaufinanzierung also has a share in this. Hitherto the ZDF studios had been subsidiaries of the FSM Fernsehstudios in Unterföhring. The new company has 14 studios and 200 employees. Its services are expected initially to generate a turnover of 30 million DM.

The advertising industry

The advertising industry is represented to a lesser extent in the Munich area than in other locations. Among the fifty advertising agencies with the largest turnover in Germany in 1996, fifteen were located in Frankfurt, eleven in Hamburg, ten in Düsseldorf and only six in Munich. The biggest Munich advertising agency, Heye and Partner GWA, with a turnover of approximately 48 million DM, ranks 16th, up three ranks compared to the previous year. It has approximately 200 employees. The business segments of the advertising industry are changing with the new media and communication technologies. The trend points towards marketing consultation and access to the electronic advertising market. Here a segment is developing in which advertising agencies will increasingly compete against multimedia producers and suppliers in the foreseeable future.

Multimedia

The multimedia sector in its narrow sense can be defined as including production companies and service providers for offline and online applications (such as CD-ROM games, computer-based training (CBT), archiving systems, Internet and Intranet, etc.). It is currently made up of at least 150

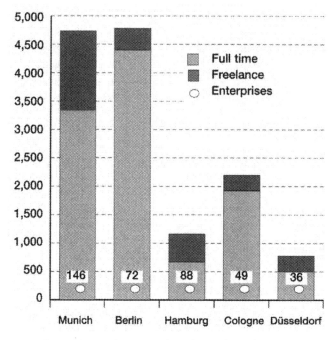

Figure 8.3 Enterprises and personnel in the multimedia sector in Munich, in comparison to Berlin, Hamburg, Cologne and Düsseldorf 1995

Source : Multimedia-Jahrbuch (1996); *Referat für Arbeit und Wirtschaft* (1997): 31.

enterprises with about 5,000 employees (full-time and freelance staff) in the Munich area.

The Munich area has become the leading centre for multimedia taking the number of multimedia development and production companies and their staff as indicators (see Figure 8.3). The wave of newly-established companies in this sector peaked between 1992 and 1996. About ninety of today's multimedia enterprises were founded during this period. Most of them were originally established as multimedia agencies; others came into existence as a result of the re-orientation of existing producers and service providers or of expansion strategies aimed at including multimedia applications. The third part of the multimedia sector foundation was laid by spin-offs of subsidiaries or hiving-off parts of large media and telecommunication groups, such as Siemens and Burda publishers.

Siemens-Nixdorf Informationssysteme AG (SNI) is a fully owned subsidiary of Siemens AG located in Munich. It was established by Nixdorf AG in Paderborn (subsequently taken over by Siemens) and the information and communication sectors of Siemens AG. Approximately 7,400 people work at the SNI headquarters in Munich. In autumn 1996, SNI opened the new business area of 'Advanced Services & Media' (ASM), in which the enterprise interest in the multimedia market segment was combined with the areas of computer-based training, Internet and Intranet, teleworking and telecooperation. It includes consultancy, design and operation of the corresponding multimedia services and is targeted mainly at multimedia concerns of medium-sized and large-scale industries (Siemens-Nixdorf 1996). In 1996, SNI founded the Computertraining und Services GmbH Munich as well as the Waste and Recycling Information Services GmbH (WARIS) in Grasbrunn near Munich. This is the first global waste and recycling exchange that - by using the Worldwide Waste Management Information System (WWI) in the Internet - offers both information and a business platform for an optimization and recycling of resources to suppliers, inquirers and service providers of the waste disposal industry as well as the authorities concerned.

Many multimedia companies see themselves as advertising agencies using specific media technology platforms (CD-ROM, Internet, Intranet). Another part of the enterprises is - just like book publishers - concerned with the production and distribution of information (modern history, edutainment, language courses, games); a further aspect is drawing up concepts for the communication between enterprises ('business to business').

The majority of the enterprises active in the multimedia sector are small and very small enterprises. Two-thirds of all enterprises (128 entries in *Multimedia-Jahrbuch* 1998) employ up to twenty persons (full-time employees and freelances). One-quarter of all enterprises have twenty to fifty employees. This means that over 90 per cent of all multimedia enterprises employ fewer than fifty people. Only 3 per cent (four entries) have between fifty and 100 employees, while only 5 per cent (six entries) have between 100 and 300 employees. The German branch office of the Internet and software company Oracle in Munich distorts this picture: they have approximately 1,300 employees, more than a quarter of all those employed in the multimedia sector in the Munich area. The other large-scale enterprises also include companies with a range of interests in addition to multimedia. They are included among the multimedia sector only because they provide services for the multimedia sector by offering facilities for training or further education.

Although the market currently continues to expand, especially where online multimedia applications are concerned, the multimedia sector as a whole seems to have entered a phase of consolidation, particularly among major enterprises. The number of new business starts has decreased. The same decline is seen in the growth of employment and turnover, which in some cases has been enormous in the last few years. Enterprise structures have sometimes not been able to catch up with the fast-moving development of the industry and need to be adapted. Some multimedia agencies are trying to promote growth and the use of their existing resources by restructuring their enterprises, part of which developed in a rather unsystematic manner during the boom in the early years. They are also trying to stabilize their customer relations. However, even these in-house consolidation efforts are not sufficient for some of the major multimedia agencies. Enterprises try to meet increased financing requirements (a rising share of fixed costs) by gaining support from well-funded external shareholders, by company take-over bids or by going public. At the same time, agreements on the medium and long-term management of key accounts make the enterprises more aware of the need for security.

The initial upswing and the specific profile of the multimedia sector is closely related to the existing manufacturing and service structures prevailing in the high-tech Munich location. During their start-up phase, almost all multimedia agencies worked for one or several large Munich enterprises, drawing up offline or online company and product presentations or training projects for them. Working for enterprises in the automotive and electrical engineering industries, publishing houses and banks, and for the television and film industry in the Munich area has led to an orientation towards specific technologies and programming in the multimedia industry. Coping with these tasks often provided the multimedia agencies with so much thrust that they have been able to go beyond southern Bavaria and do business on a national or even international scale. Nevertheless, most Munich-based multimedia agencies continue to focus on the south of Bavaria.

Although multimedia enterprises in general have to regard most of the other multimedia agencies as competitors, these enterprises maintain an open relationship which is due, among other things, to the continuing expansion of the multimedia market. In principle, every enterprise is able to cooperate with any other enterprise and in fact will do so if a project requires a competent partner for tackling specific tasks. Competence is the decisive factor in cooperation even if the search for potential partners is often limited to a circle of enterprises whom the company already has found to be completely satisfactory. A large number of the multimedia agencies try to specialize in specific areas of know-how, thus identifying a niche for themselves where, although the competitive pressure is remarkable, they enjoy some degree of shelter from it.

Multimedia is a fast-moving industry. The requirements to be met by the enterprises are changing fast. The life-span of multimedia know-how is extremely short, and those responsible for professional training often cannot update courses as quickly as the industry requires. The qualifications required to work in an enterprise are therefore imparted to a large extent by the enterprises themselves. Formal professional education is not an absolute requirement for new employees. Prerequisites include skill, talent, the ability to work in a team and the readiness to meet new challenges. The output-oriented approach pursued by multimedia agencies requires creative, flexible, ambitious, adaptable and - in general - young employees who will take on the tasks involved in a project as their own and be ready to commit themselves beyond traditional working (time) rules. Some of the employees work as freelances or regular freelances, and some routinely work at home and are connected online to the enterprise.

Until now, enterprises have been able to meet their demand for new creative thinkers when they need to expand their skeleton staff by tapping a broad-based and diversified regional labour market. They are only faced with bottlenecks when recruiting qualified programmers. Staff seldom move from one enterprise to another on account of a generally very positive working atmosphere, though such movement might be desirable to ensure a continuous restoration of the creative potential. Independent freelances are often highly qualified in a specific segment (for example 3D applications) and work for several companies at the same time.

Most multimedia agencies regard all forms of Internet or Intranet presentations as their particular strategic spheres of multimedia activities in the future. They focus on the business-to-business sector, that is the design and handling of commercial relations between the protagonists in the enterprises. A broad range of activities will open up in this area within the next few months and years, while the private household demand for online services will only increase significantly after a sustained improvement in convenient online features. This will incur communication costs.

Although multimedia enterprises must (still) be considered as belonging to a small segment of the labour market and the industry, their innovative potential is expected to promote the restructuring of the location and to provide further positive employment impulses to the Munich labour market.

Telecommunication

As the telecommunication sector was liberalized, this market was subject to substantial changes. New business start-ups, alliances and cooperation between enterprises characterize the sector. The information and communication sector in Europe is expected to overtake the automobile industry by the year 2000.

When the Bavarian utility group Bayernwerk AG was privatized in 1994, the utility company VIAG AG took over the majority share from the Free State of Bavaria in 1994. At the request of the Bavarian Government, it subsequently relocated its headquarters from Düsseldorf to Munich. It founded the VIAG Interkom GmbH, as a joint venture together with British Telecom in May 1995. In June 1997, VIAG Interkom already had 700 employees and is expected to expand its workforce to approximately 9,000 by 2006.

As a telecommunication provider, VIAG Interkom offers the international language and data services 'Concert' in Germany, a joint venture between British Telecom and the US MCI Communications Inc., which is aimed at providing with global communication services to international enterprises. Technical services through the link-up of fixed networks and mobile phones are also expected to be offered to private clients. In February 1997 the enterprise was granted the fourth German mobile phone licence E2.

Public authorities also wish to participate in the expected telecommunication boom. The restructuring of the postal and telecommunications services in mid-1996 broke the monopoly on the transmission channels in the telecommunication network. It is now possible for owners of efficient data transfer networks other than Telekom – above all public and private utility companies – to make their networks available. In July 1996 representatives of the City of Munich, Bayernwerk Netkom GmbH, Bayerische Landesbank and Stadtsparkasse München signed a partnership agreement to found a joint city network telecommunication company M'net.[10] Currently based on 50 km. of fibre optic cables and 1,800 km. of copper cable, M'net has developed its own telecommunication service. Apart from basic services such as the link-up of computer centres and local mainframe networks, M'net is also involved in the implementation of value-added services and video conferences. The Bavarian Ministry of Industry and Technology has earmarked 3.3 million DM for the sponsoring of its trial runs (Bayerische Staatsregierung 1997: 17).

An indication of the importance of the Munich data processing and telecommunication enterprises is also given by their presence at important computer fairs. At the CeBit 1995 in Hanover, 498 enterprises from the Munich area were represented, making up 12.2 per cent of all German exhibitors (Referat für Arbeit und Wirtschaft 1996: 23).[11] The annual 'Systems' trade fair takes place in Munich and is one of the leading information and communication trade fairs in Europe that links technology and contents. It provides an international forum for producers and suppliers of hard- and software in the EDP and communication sectors.

Production and working conditions

Unlike other industrial production, the product of the media industry or of multimedia constitutes the unique output of a creative, innovative formation process. Let us distinguish the (multi-) media product from its carrier medium - newspaper, magazine, book, film, radio broadcast, CD-ROM, Internet presentation, etc. - and focus on the content that is to be conveyed by means of the medium. The content is essentially the individualized output of a constantly new and diversified creative process although the related manufacturing technology reaches an ever increasing - in some cases even high - level of standardization. Right up to the point where it is reproduced, the media product is the result of a craftsman-like manual design process.

The media formation and production process primarily consists of projects which produce 'interaction goods'. It is frequently achieved not by an individual (as in the case of a novel) but by cooperation and joint action, partly by formally independent creators, in an organized cooperation process such as a film or video production, a music production or a CD-ROM production.

Cooperation is a primary principle in the creation of media products; without it very few would come into existence. The more the media production process resembles an industrial production process (as in the production of a daily newspaper) the more cooperation is required within an enterprise. The more it represents a unique event (as in the production of a feature film) the more likely it will be a cooperative process between numerous different partners led by one management. This cooperation is flexible and temporary; the personnel involved in production differ according to the form and purpose of the product. The team is disbanded after the termination of the project to re-form for a different project in a different constellation. Qualification and flexibility of those involved is an essential factor. Urbanity and a creative environment are the most important conditions for the creation and formation process of an 'interaction product'.

The media sector has always evinced a high proportion of so-called self-employment activities in comparison to other industries (consider the actors, journalists, graphic artists, photographers and other persons employed in the film, radio, publishing and theatre sectors). This is due to the fact that the media product is a cooperative project. Behind the forms of free cooperation, a broad range of diverse employment opportunities is evident. In some cases it is a matter of so-called 'make-do' independence: an employment relationship where in fact there is a high dependency on the individual employer and little or no creative liberty is granted to independent work.

In almost all new working places created in the media industry, vacancies are currently apparent, just as recently vacated posts in which hitherto full-time employees were active are metamorphosing into working places for freelance employees. At the same time the tendency towards multiple employment increases; hence the employment in different, parallel spheres of activity.[12]

Changing qualification and training requirements

There has been a change in qualification requirements with regard to employment in the traditional and 'new' media sectors. While traditional commercial professional knowledge and professional experience decline in importance, the requirement for skills and qualification in EDP-supported working places increase. This is the case not only in the hitherto traditional printing sector but also in the various categories of the new media.

Apart from the expansion of existing professional profiles to include EDP know-how in training and further education, new professional profiles arise by way of the integration of hitherto subdivided activities. Thus it will not be possible in future to carry out activities without formal training ('learning by doing'), as in the initial phase of the 'new' media industry. Here, too, the requirement for specifically designed training courses in the new multimedia sectors in training centres especially established for this purpose will increase.

The diversity of qualification in the Munich area is supported, safeguarded and funded by a broad range of training and further education facilities for media professions. In its scope and diversity this is the equal of any in other media locations in Germany. Apart from the established training facilities, some of which have existed for decades, a number of new training and further education facilities have been created in the last few years to cater to the changing media landscape. No fewer than thirty different (high) school and further education facilities can be listed, not counting the numerous private actors' studios in Munich (see Table 8.1). These initial professional training facilities include those listed in Table 8.1.

The expansion in the telecommunication sector in the last few years and the boom that will undoubtedly result from the loss of Deutsche Telekom AG's telecommunication monopoly in 1998 threaten to lead to a shortage of specialized labour in the Munich area as far as the telecommunication suppliers are concerned. Siemens AG is a case in point. In July 1997 Siemens had 200 vacancies in the telecommunication sector. By the year 2000 the company will employ an additional 3,000 telecommunication specialists. Multimedia enterprises are complaining about a noticeable lack of qualified programmers. Meanwhile, the number of students in such subjects as information technology, electrical engineering and communication engineering has continuously declined both at the Ludwig Maximilians and the Technische University of Munich as well as at senior technical colleges. The current number of enrolled students is 3,800, which is an indication of a considerable shortfall of newcomers. Hence enterprises like Siemens have increasingly started to boost their recruitment programmes in the form of mobile information fairs at the Technical University and the Fachhochschule München.

Multimedia infrastructure

Apart from the entrepreneurial protagonists immediately involved in the media and communication industry, a network of supplementary facilities, associations, regular events and other infrastructural conditions has developed for their support. Its density and diversity is a further indication of the importance of the media and telecommunication cluster in the Munich area. This multimedia infrastructure includes interest groups and other associations, including public or semi-public institutions, to support and monitor prize awards and other events.

Associations

In the Munich multimedia cluster, numerous associations come together to represent and try to implement the interests of their respective customers (in

Table 8.1 Professional training facilities

Institution	Supporting organization
Institut für Kommunikations-wissenschaft (previously: Zeitungswissenschaft)	Munich University (State of Bavaria)
Institut für Theaterwissenschaft	Munich University (State of Bavaria)
Hochschule für Musik	State of Bavaria
Deutsche Journalistenschule	Public and private TV and radio stations, newspaper and magazine publishers, Deutscher Journalisten-Verband (Association of German Journalists), Industriegewerkschaft Medien (media trade union), Evangelische Medienakademie (Protestant media academy)
Hochschule für Fernsehen und Film (HFF)	State of Bavaria
Akademie der Bayerischen Presse	Bayer. Journalistenverband (Association of Bavarian Journalists), Verband Bayer., Zeitungsverleger (Association of Bavarian Newspaper Publishers), Verband der Zeitschriftenverlage in Bayern (Association of Magazine Publishers in Bavaria)
Bayerische Akademie der Werbung	Non-profit institution sponsored by thirty enterprises, associations, chambers, Bayerische Landeszentrale für neue Medien (BLM)
Bayerische Akademie für Fernsehen	Bayer., Staatsministerium für Unterricht, Kultur, Wissenschaft und Kunst (Bavarian State Ministry for Education, Culture, Science and Art), privately owned broadcasters, BLM, numerous enterprises
Bayerische Theaterakademie im Prinzregententheater	State of Bavaria
Fachakademie für Fotodesign	State of Bavaria
Otto-Falckenberg-Schule (Fachakademie für Darstellende Kunst)	City of Munich
Mediadesign Akademie	Privately-owned training institution (mediadesign CAD Trainingscentre München GmbH)
Burda Journalistenschule	Privately-owned magazine group (Burda)
BLR Dienstleistungsgesellschaft für Bayerische Lokal-Radio-programme mbH & CoKG	Privately-owned radio broadcasters

Table 8.2 Associations

Sector	Association
Printing and publishing sector	Verband Bayerischer Verlage und Buchhandlungen e.V. Verband Bayerischer Zeitungsverleger e.V. Verband der Zeitschriftenverlage in Bayern e.V. Landesverband Bayern der Industriegewerkschaft Medien Presse Club München e.V. Club Wirtschaftspresse e.V. München
Advertising sector	Konferenz der Akademien für Kommunikation, Marketing, Medien Arbeitsgemeinschaft der ARD-Werbegesellschaften
Film industry	Wirtschaftsverband der Filmtheater e.V. Bayern Verband der Szenenbildner, Filmarchitekten und Kostümbildner in Europa e.V. Grünwald Verband Deutscher Schauspieler-Agenturen Interessenverband deutscher Schauspieler e.V. Verband Deutscher Filmexporteure e.V. Export-Union des Deutschen Films e.V. (EXU) Verband Neuer Deutscher Spielfilmproduzenten e.V. (55 producers/production firms out of 115 members are based in Munich)
TV and radio broadcasting sector	Verband Privater Bayerischer Fernsehanbieter (VPGBF), Freising Verband Bayerischer Lokalrundfunk Vereinigung Bayerischer Rundfunkanbieter Arbeitsgemeinschaft Privater Rundfunk (APR) Lokal-Fernsehen München e.V., Unterföhring Kommunikationsverband Bayern e.V. Bundesverband Deutscher Fernsehproduzenten e.V. (52 out of 134 German members are based in the Munich area)
Theatre and music business	Verband Deutscher Schauspieler-Agenturen Landesverband Bayerischer Tonkünstler e. V. Interessenverband deutscher Schauspieler e.V.
Performing rights organizations (ensure adherence to copyright regulations)	Gesellschaft für Musikalische Aufführungs- und mechanische Vervielfältigungsrechte (GEMA) Gesellschaft zur Wahrnehmung von Film und Fernsehrechten mbH (GWFF) Verwertungsgesellschaft (VG) Wort Clearingstelle Multimedia Verwertungsgesellschaft mbH (CMMV) Verwertungsgesellschaft der Film und Fernsehproduzenten mbH (VFF) Verwertungsgesellschaft Bildkunst
Labour unions	Industriegewerkschaft Medien – Landesbezirk Bayern

general, professional groups or groups of companies) with regard to other social groups, the state and administration or the public. (See Table 8.2.)

In August 1995, the Deutscher Multimedia Verband e.V. (dmmv) with headquarters in Munich was established by several multimedia entrepreneurs, including some based in Munich.[13] They realized that there was a need for joint action in the multimedia sector, above all as regards quality control, legal and training issues, quotation and calculation issues. The association has also been designed to maintain contact between industry, politics, the authorities and the press. By early 1997 the dmmv had already expanded to an interest group representing more than 220 members of the German online and offline multimedia industry. A survey dating from October 1996 shows that thirty-one of the 118 associated multimedia enterprises come from the Munich area.

Supervisory and coordination institutions

The Bayerische Landesanstalt für neue Medien (BLM), as the second public corporation in the radio and TV sector in Bavaria licences and supervises private radio and TV providers (BLM 1995). The Münchner Gesellschaft für Kabelkommunikation (MGK), Unterföhring, is responsible for the technical assignment of broadcasting frequencies to the private radio and TV stations in Munich and Bavaria.

The 'Münchner Kreis' (Munich circle), founded a decade ago, is an association for communication research. It is one of the most important institutions of this kind in Germany, organizes specialized conferences and conventions, and focuses and represents the interests of the telecommunication sector.

Events

A great number of events are held in the Munich area every year. These provide information on new developments in sub-sectors and offer an opportunity for meeting important protagonists of the media and telecommunication sector. These events include:

*   'Medientage München', one of the most important media-political conferences in Germany.
*   'Internationale Frühjahrsbuchwoche'.
*   The associated event 'Werbegipfel München'.
*   'BLM Rundfunkkongress'.
*   The 'Systems' trade fair.
*   CINEC, previously known as ShowBIZ Europe, an international trade fair for film technology.
*   'Münchner Filmfest' held in summer every year. It is one of the leading

festivals of Europe's film industry alongside Cannes and the biennial film festivals in Berlin and Venice.

Political frame conditions that help promote the media, multimedia and TIME industries

Prize awards demonstrate the attention and esteem bestowed on an actor, a product or a sphere of activity. In Munich, for example, the 'Bayerischer Filmpreis', the 'Bayerischer Fernsehpreis' and the 'Deutscher Videopreis' awards are granted by or with the support of the State of Bavaria. The City of Munich regularly awards various literature prizes.

Munich was slow to realize the importance of the media and telecommunication industry for the future economic development of the area and for years treated all innovative private media in a somewhat reserved manner. Recently, however, it has made great efforts to support and encourage activities in this sphere. The city of Munich for instance holds a 40 per cent share in the 'Internationale Münchner Filmwochen GmbH', which organizes the Munich film festival. The Bavarian State Government also sponsors the film industry. In 1980 it inaugurated a Bavarian film-sponsorship programme and established the 'FilmFernsehFonds Bayern' (film/TV fund Bavaria), without which hardly any film project could be implemented in Munich.

'Bayern Online' is an initiative of the Bavarian State Government, which has 100 million DM to support telecommunication. The aim is to stimulate the use of modern telecommunication technologies and telematic services in Bavaria and to create or promote the use of the corresponding network structures and network capacities. Sixteen pilot projects have been designed to provide impulses for a speedy implementation and to intensify the use of telecommunication technologies and services.

The Bavarian State Government uses the 'Bayern Online' project to exert influence on industrial policy so as to speed up the introduction and dissemination of information and communication technological networks, services and applications in Bavaria. 'Bayern Online' presents itself as a programme opening the multimedia market, the targets of which are negotiated and stipulated between the representatives of industry, science, politics and administration largely without the participation of the public.

Conclusions

It can be stated that a comprehensive, broad media and telecommunication cluster which includes both the software and hardware sectors has crystallized in the Munich region. Technological, economic and political conditions have had a positive effect on the formation of this cluster. It is apparent that - due to the entrepreneurial and infrastructural conditions prevailing in the

Munich area - the multimedia sector (in its narrow sense) is going to expand and will gain even greater importance.

Recent technological developments (the expansion of digital information, communication and production technologies) and political decisions (liberalization/privatization of the media and telecommunication provider markets) support the integration of the media industry and the information and telecommunications industries into what is generally referred to as the TIME industry. Even if this is only discernible in outline, conditions are favourable for developing network-like interrelations between the protagonists and sub-segments of the 'multimedia sector' (in its broader sense).

The traditional borders between individual industries are blurring as new and pre-existing firms merge. The multimedia sector integrates traditional media industries (e.g. printing and publishing), the film industry, radio and TV with the electronics and telecommunication sector of the metal and electronics industries, the distribution sector for media technology and media products, and cultural production.

The stabilizing multimedia complex is becoming more and more attractive to external protagonists. To an extent hardly matched by any other agglomeration in Germany, the Munich area offers a range of advantages for the media and telecommunication protagonists. These include a flourishing urban environment and a creative working atmosphere, a subtly differentiated, broad range of qualifications, short distances for face-to-face contacts, and other favourable conditions. Many protagonists who have relocated their enterprise headquarters in the Munich area have at the same time enhanced the reputations of their enterprises. Sometimes this enhancement of reputation is the main reason for a move to the Munich area.

The multimedia cluster offers not only ephemeral but above all immediate material advantages, for example as regards the application of digital production and transmission technology against the background of a broad range of knowledge and experience in the micro-electronics and computer technology sectors at the location.

The media enterprises located in Munich are paying close attention to political initiatives in, for example, North Rhine-Westphalia or the new Länder which aim to improve the innovation and location conditions for their (multi-)media industries. In so doing, they also point out that the past development of the media and telecommunication industries in Munich has for the most part been self-generated by the market without any support from economic policies.

The economic success of the media and telecommunication location in the Munich area has hitherto received political support mainly by means of establishing and safeguarding favourable infrastructural and 'climatic' conditions. State programmes have only recently been initiated by industrial and structural policies and used in a target-oriented manner to promote key projects of the media and telecommunication industries and speed up their implementation and distribution. These programmes include the FilmFörderungsFonds Bayern and 'Bayern Online'. It is not only the subsidizing of the media and telecommunication technologies that plays a role in this respect but also the efforts to enhance the position of Munich and Bavaria as compared to other national and international media centres.

Multimedia enterprises are somewhat sceptical about the 'Bayern Online' programme in particular. They do not have great expectations of the support of the multimedia sector by political measures. Small enterprises often gain no benefit from state-subsidized programmes. The market requirements facing the multimedia sector as regards speed and flexibility hardly correspond to the traditional political support instruments and procedures, which are felt to be rigid and slow. According to multimedia agencies, it would be useful if politics and administration were more flexible in adapting their own procedures to the ways of working prevailing in the multimedia sector and in the TIME industry.

Notes

1 The Munich region includes the city of Munich and the districts of Munich, Dachau, Ebersberg, Erding, Freising, Fürstenfeldbruck, Landsberg and Starnberg.
2 Employees subject to payment of social insurance contributions.
3 The official employment statistic is only of limited use for an analysis of media and telematics employment. Communication technology is only classified in conjunction with measurement and control technologies; telecommunication services are not listed separately. Deutsche Telekom AG continues to be listed together with the postal and bank service of Deutsche Post AG yet, on the other hand, the civil servants are not included in Telekom' s employment rate. Furthermore, neither self-employed staff nor freelances are listed, nor are the proprietors of small enterprises although their number is relevant. Trade with media and telematics goods and services is also not listed; see Standortbewertung (1997: 20).
4 'Arriflex', which is manufactured in Munich, is one of the best and most sought-after professional film cameras.
5 The two important para-state research societies are located in Munich: Max-Planck-Gesellschaft (key sector: basic research) has its head office and five of its scientific institutes there, and the Fraunhofer-Gesellschaft (key sector: applied research) has its head office and two scientific institutes. Furthermore, Fraunhofer-Management-Gesellschaft, GSF Forschungszentrum Umwelt und Gesundheit GmbH (GSF Research Centre Environment and Health GmbH) as well as DLR-Deutsche Forschungsanstalt für Luft- und Raumfahrt e.V. have their headquarters in Munich or are at least represented with research institutes.
6 Approximately 15,000 out of the 35,000 Siemens employees in the Munich area and approximately 6,000 out of 23,000 BMW employees are involved in research and development. In addition to its headquarters, Daimler Benz Aerospace (DASA) has established its research and development centre in

Ottobrunn near Munich. Enterprises such as Krauss-Maffei, MAN Technologie, MTU, Rohde and Schwarz and other enterprises of the electrical engineering, communication and transmission technology industries have also established their central research and development institutes in Munich.

7   'Regional Networks and Regional Labour Market: Cumulative Processes of Circular Causes?', a joint project of the IMU Institute, Munich, and the Catholic University Eichstätt on behalf of Deutsche Forschungsgemeinschaft (DFG) 1996-99.

8   These include the publishing company IDG, Magna Media, Vogel Verlag, Ziff, Weka, Franzis', Markt und Technik.

9   Kirch holds a further 20 per cent of SAT.1 through his participation in the Axel Springer Verlag. Indirectly he owns a further 7 per cent so that he holds a share of more than 50 per cent in SAT.1.

10 Stadtwerke München holds a 45 per cent share, Bayernwerk Netkom and Bayerische Landesbank a 25 per cent share each and Stadtsparkasse München a 5 per cent share of M'net. The City of Munich and the Free State of Bavaria, the owner of Bayernwerk AG until its sale to VIAG, each hold half of the M'net shares.

11 For comparison, those from Hamburg made up 5.2 per cent, Berlin 4.5 per cent and from Cologne only 3.5 per cent.

12 There are multimedia enterprises in the Munich area where the proprietor is the sole employee. All other employees are in fact directly associated with the enterprise but enjoy freelance status.

13 The dmmv moved to Düsseldorf in July 1997.

References

Bayerische Landeszentrale für Neue Medien (BLM) (1995) 'Entwicklung, Förderung und Veranstaltung von privaten Rundfunkangeboten in Bayern', München: Bayerische Landeszentrale für Neue Medien.

Bayerische Staatsregierung (1997) Bulletin 1997, *Bulletin der Bayerischen Staatsregierung* 8, 18 April 1997.

Biehler, H., Brake, K. and Ramschütz, E. (1994) 'Standort München. Sozioökonomische und räumliche Strukturen der Neo-Industrialisierung', IMU-Studien Bd. 20, Munich: IMU-Institut.

BLM (1995) *Entwicklung, Förderung und Veranstaltung von privaten Rundfunk-angeboten in Bayern,* ed. Bayerische Landeszentrale für Neue Medien, Munich.

Graf, J. (ed.) (1996) *Multimedia Jahrbuch 1996 mit CD-ROM. Das Jahrbuch der inter-aktiven Medien. Produzenten und Dienstleister in Deutschland, Österreich und der Schweiz,* Munich: Hightext Verlag.

Graf, J. (ed.) (1998) *Multimedia Jahrbuch 1998 mit CD-ROM. Das Jahrbuch der inter-aktiven Medien. Produzenten und Dienstleister in Deutschland, Österreich und der Schweiz,* Munich: Hightext Verlag.

Kirch Gruppe (1996) 'Facts & Figures – 40 Jahre Kompetenz und Kreativität', Munich: Kirch Gruppe.

MedienStadt München (1985) Industrie-und Handelskammer für München und

Oberbayern (IHK) 'MedienStadt München I', IHK-Schriftenreihe 1, Munich: IHK.

—— (1990) Industrie-und Handelskammer für München und Oberbayern (IHK) 'MedienStadt München II'. IHK-Schriftenreihe 1. Munich: IHK.

—— (1996) Industrie- und Handelskammer für München und Oberbayern (IHK) 'MedienStadt München III', IHK Schriftenreihe 1. Munich: IHK.

Referat für Arbeit und Wirtschaft (1997) 'Standortbewertung für die Stadt München im Bereich Telematik und Medien', Untersuchung der Prognos Consult GmbH, Veröffentlichungen Referat für Arbeit und Wirtschaft 59, Munich: Referat für Arbeit und Wirtschaft.

Röper, H. (1997) 'Formationen deutscher Medienmultis 1996', *Media-Perspektiven* 5: 226–55.

Siemens-Nixdorf (1996) 'Daten und Fakten 1995/96', München: Siemens-Nixdorf.

Süddeutscher Verlag (1995) 'Geschäftsbericht', Munich: Süddeutscher Verlag.

Will, H. (1996) Absage an Privatisierung – BR beteiligt sich nicht an geplanter Studio GmbH von ZDF und Bavaria, *M 11*, 28.

9

MULTIMEDIA AND UNEVEN URBAN AND REGIONAL DEVELOPMENT

The Internet industry in the Netherlands

Richard Naylor

The rise and rise of the Internet

If asked the question, 'What do you understand by the term 'multimedia'?' nine out of ten respondents, I contend, would answer: 'the Internet'.[1] More seriously, while it is clear that the Internet is just one element within the multimedia sector, the ready conflation of the two terms would be understandable. After a number of distinctly underwhelming predecessors and contemporaries (laser disc, CDi and to some extent, CD-ROM) the Internet, put simply, appears to be 'the real McCoy': the technology that will finally begin to realize the potential of digitally mixed media on a grand scale, and provide substance to claims regarding the increasing 'convergence' between the telecommunications, computing and media industries.

The Internet is both a new medium for the development of interactive, narrow- and broadcast content and a 'meta-carrier' for existing products and services such as software, voice telephony, video and audio material. Many of the Internet's possibilities were unthinkable or impractical even three years ago but its products and services have proliferated at a remarkable speed. Successive technological solutions allied with dramatic increases in infrastructure investment have fuelled and sustained the enormous growth of the network itself, a network that has been 'doubling in size with each successive year since 1988 . . . a far greater growth rate than any communications medium or consumer electronic product at any time in history' (*Screen Digest* 1995: 82).[2] The Internet, then, necessarily looms large in any consideration of the multimedia sector.

In its early days the Internet was dominated by the research and academic community. Its rapid expansion since the early 1990s has been facilitated by a transition from providing for these groups. In their place have arisen a myriad of companies dedicated to exploiting the commercial potential of the Internet for a much more diverse market encompassing residential consumers, commercial users, government, voluntary and trade union organizations. While many of the more high profile successes in this 'Internet Goldrush' are North American (e.g. Netscape, Yahoo and UUNet), a wide range of firms are also involved in this field across the European Union. Again, while the most publicized actors tend to be large corporations, this activity rests on a much broader range of small and medium-sized companies.

Technological change, the Internet and urban and regional development opportunities

The Internet may still be in its infancy, but some commentators (particularly inside the industry), already talk about the Internet in terms of a 'technological paradigm change', comparable with the transition from mainframe computers to PCs. While there is more than a whiff of glib, self-congratulatory rhetoric about many of these statements, the idea of technological paradigm change as it has evolved within an academic context may offer us some initial insights into the urban and regional development implications of the emerging Internet industry.

Dosi (1983), for instance, proposes a model of technological paradigm change where technological change is directly related to market structure: paradigm 'breaks' are only those occasions when technological change is accompanied and fostered by market discontinuity. As Tim Kelly (1987: 16-18) notes, this can indeed be seen in the context of the computer industry of the late 1970s. The lack of interest shown by the dominant computing firms (e.g. IBM) in the *micro*-computer market allowed for the rise of new entrepreneurs (e.g. Microsoft, Apple) that undermined the existing oligopolistic nature of the industry. For our present concerns, it is important to note that this combination of technological and market change also embodied major changes in the space economy of the computer industry, such as the rise of Seattle as a software centre to rival Silicon Valley.

The beginnings of the micro-computer market, I would argue, are (rightly or wrongly), paramount in the minds of the development community when contemplating the Internet industry. Once again we appear to be witnessing the emergence of major new markets born of technological change, and the industry may, once more, be 'up for grabs'. There are, however, a number of problems with this broadly upbeat scenario, not least of which is: which industry: computing? Telecommunications? Media? Also, after a slow start, established players including online service providers such as CompuServe and AOL, computer software manufacturers (principally Microsoft) and network operators such as the PTOs (Public Telecommunications Operators) and cable companies have all moved into the provision of Internet-dedicated offerings.

Nevertheless, there have been enough signs of market 'discontinuity' to indicate that the commercial and geographical trajectories of the Internet industry are yet to be determined. When this is combined with the possibility that the Internet, as with other telecommunications or 'telematics' networks, might facilitate opportunities for re-evaluating locational attributes (see for instance, Gillespie and Williams 1988), one begins to understand why national governments, regional economic development agencies and local authorities across the world are beginning to see the Internet industry as a 'window of locational opportunity'. The ultimate vision, then, is that the new market opportunities opened up by technological change will result in a far greater geographical spread of activity and employment in the Internet industry than has been the case with previous new growth industries. This stems from the very nature of the technology itself, the ability of the network to overcome the 'friction of distance'

In addition to expectations of direct gains in terms of employment and revenues, a number of perceived indirect benefits make the Internet industry attractive to the development community. First, Internet companies can be useful for a locality in terms of image making and place-marketing strategies as they are commonly associated – deservedly or not – with wholeheartedly positive attributes: high-tech, 'knowledge intensive', creative, 'clean' and other such buzzwords. Second, development agencies hope that the presence of locally-based Internet companies will speed the uptake of the Internet throughout their wider business community, helping to create a critical mass of users and stimulating the development of local online services (see for example, M and I and Partners 1996). These factors and other associated 'learning spillovers' may in turn be successfully translated into a margin of urban or regional competitive advantage in much the same way as has been seen where other telecommunications products and services have been successfully adopted (Capello and Nijkamp 1996).

The location of commercial Internet suppliers may also provide insights into wider trends in the future geographical spread of employment. Although recent studies on the impact of new information and communications technologies (ICTs) on employment agree that the net result will be positive (e.g. Ad-Employ 1995, Freeman and Soete 1994), determining the actual locations that will experience ICT-related employment growth is a more difficult task. A knowledge and understanding of the geographical distribution of the Internet industry may offer early indications of how some places become 'winners' and others 'losers' in an increasingly technologically mediated economy. With the insights gained from such knowledge, it may then be possible to identify strategies for intervention designed to produce more benign outcomes.

Spurred on by a pervasive feeling that the European Union is increasingly lagging behind the US in exploring these opportunities – and indeed in terms of IT provision and adoption more generally (see for example, Smart and

Miller 1997, Kirkpatrick 1997) – much policy rhetoric within the EU has been expounded at all levels on the future importance of the Internet for European societies.[3] It is only in the last eighteen months or so that these high level but insubstantial policy pronouncements have begun to be backed-up with substantive research.

However, despite positive market forecasts outlined in some documents and occasional vague policy exhortations in others to see 'the indigenous development of information-based activities . . . stimulated in the regions' (UK Regional Policy Commission 1996: 184), concrete economic development considerations at the urban and regional scale are largely ignored. Similarly, academic literature, while building up a considerable body of work on regional economic restructuring and telecommunications/telematics in general (e.g. Graham 1992, Dabinett and Graham 1994, Tanner and Gibbs 1997), or on more specific and established telemediated activities (Richardson 1994, Richardson and Gillespie 1996), also has little to say regarding the Internet industry.

The present chapter, then, is intended as an initial contribution to the field that examines the emerging Internet industry and urban and regional development opportunities in one country in the European Union: the Netherlands. For the remainder of the chapter, I will attempt to outline the scale and scope of the Internet industry in the Netherlands, how this is embedded in the geographical economy, and detail a number of contrasting urban and regional development policy responses that, in turn, reflect contrasting experiences of economic restructuring.

The chapter is based upon research undertaken in the Netherlands between October 1996 and April 1997, which consisted of two main components. First was the gathering of data on the actual companies supplying Internet products and services. As accurate official statistics on these companies are, for a variety of reasons, very hard to come by – they straddle standard industrial classification codes, have a high start-up and death rate, grow very quickly, etc. – the primary data used in the study is a self-compiled database drawn from a variety of sources: online directories in the main, used in conjunction with listings and advertisements drawn from offline, trade sources. Spatial analysis of the database has subsequently been used to delineate locational and geographical trends.

The second strand of the research involved extensive field interviewing to identify underlying trends, key players, market dynamics, typical activities and so on. Firm-based interviewees were chosen to represent the range of market entry points and business models as well as the differences in the scale and scope of actors' operations. In addition, interviews were also conducted with development agencies and third party experts. Finally, to provide more detailed data giving a snapshot of the relations between firms and territory, a case study of Rotterdam was undertaken involving semi-structured interviews by telephone and in person with all the companies active in the Internet market. Selected examples from this case study will be used, where appropriate, over the course of the chapter.

Context of the use and adoption of the Internet in the Netherlands

Since measurement of its use began, the Scandinavian countries – and Finland above all – have been shown to be the leaders in the adoption of the Internet within the EU (as measured by the number of Internet hosts per 100 population), but with the Netherlands a close fourth.[4] While they are almost polar opposites in terms of population density, there is one pertinent factor that the Dutch population shares with those of the Scandinavian countries: high levels of English language skills. This seems to have enabled the Dutch to be among the early adopters of the Internet and overcome most of the linguistic barriers that might have been posed by such an Anglophone network (an estimated 75 per cent of all World Wide Web (WWW) content is in English). In addition, the Dutch have played host to a number of important technological and institutional 'milestones' that may well have contributed positively to the development of the Internet in the Netherlands.

EUnet was the first and is now the largest European-wide ISP (Internet Service Provider).[5] It grew from its original incarnation as an organization, established in 1982 by the European UNIX User Group, dedicated to the provision and harmonisation of e-mail services and USENET newsgroups. EUnet's original connections ran between the Netherlands, Denmark, Sweden, and the UK. When deciding upon a base for their headquarters (including the centre of their network operations), they chose Amsterdam. This laid the foundations for Amsterdam to become, arguably, the Internet hub of Europe, a role that was reinforced in 1989 with the location in the city of RIPE (Reseaux IP Européens). This is an administrative and technical organization jointly formed by European ISPs to oversee the operation of the pan-European IP Network.

If we accept that these indicators do point towards the Netherlands being relatively advanced in terms of the adoption of Internet technologies, then it is plausible that there should also be a correspondingly high level of activity in terms of the number of firms supplying Internet products and services. In order to gain a better understanding of what it is that these companies actually do and how they relate to each other, it is worth briefly outlining a general Internet value chain.

The Internet value chain

The first problem that one encounters in any attempt to study the multimedia industry is to identify its essential features in terms of its sectoral structure and representative products. This is a particularly difficult task because the boundaries of the industry (like many other industries in their nascent stages) are extremely fluid and its outputs changing constantly in form and substance.

(Scott 1995: 2)

Allen Scott's remarks regarding the multimedia sector as a whole are perhaps particularly pertinent in relation to the Internet. The speed of technological and market change is such that insiders and observers alike have coined (only half jokingly) the term 'web years' – where one year in real life is equal to seven years on the net – to capture the accelerated pace of development. Nevertheless, it is possible to identify a core of interlinked products, services and firms that operate together as part of an Internet value chain as illustrated in Table 9.1.

At the core of the industry is the supply of access to the Internet either by dial-up modem, ISDN or leased line. For organizations, this is often accompanied by the implementation of intranets (closed user groups), together with systems integration with existing computer networks. The second major area of activity is helping users to establish an Internet 'presence'. In effect, this largely revolves around the building, design and hosting of WWW sites, including the supply of tailored software to support specific applications such as electronic commerce. It should be stated that the 'suppliers' outlined in Table 9.1, such as computer, switch and server manufactures, do not feature in the present research and neither do their distributors. Either the product is too generic (e.g. PCs), or production is very specialized and concentrated outside the Netherlands. For instance, the (highly lucrative) market for Internet routers that control and direct traffic is dominated by US companies and one Californian firm in particular: Cisco Systems, which had an estimated 85 per cent of the global market share in 1996 (*Economist* 7 December 1996).

It should also be noted that many firms now provide Internet products and services in 'bundles', some even claiming to offer 'total Internet solutions' – although, in reality, this is often more akin to 'project management' as a degree of outsourcing may still be required. While there are many start-up companies whose sole business resides in the supply of Internet products and services, an increasing number of firms with roots in other sectors have entered the market since the Internet became established as a viable business medium. These typically include cable television, telecommunications and computer services companies in the market for access provision, multimedia design studios, publishing companies and advertising and market research bureaus for the supply of presence solutions.

That the Internet has not, in fact, arisen fully formed 'out of nowhere' – as much of the lazy 'boosterism' surrounding it would have us believe – can be illustrated with reference to the Rotterdam situation. The first two companies in the city to establish an Internet presence are typical of the sort of backgrounds from which the industry is developing. Both had existing operations in other markets. One firm, established in 1988 as a specialist producer of medical software, began supplying their existing clients with Internet access around March 1993. The other, the second site of a multimedia content production company headquartered in the Dutch Antilles, was founded in 1983 and specialized in CD-ROM publishing and video and computer game design. It too moved into the construction of corporate websites during the first quarter of 1993. Since that time, a further seven companies from the computer services sector have established an Internet offer in the city (thus representing nearly a third of the Rotterdam total). Six are design firms; there are two companies with roots in telecommunications, and one each in publishing, marketing and public sector information services.

One of the few relatively clear distinctions that can be made in the Internet market is the split between services aimed at consumers and those offered for the business market. The two market segments are very different and require comparably distinct organizational and technical resources.

It was estimated that as of 1 July 1996, 12 per cent of Dutch businesses were connected to the Internet, twice as many as at the start of that year. A further 15 per cent of businesses had concrete plans to establish an Internet presence in the year to July 1997.[6] The business market for Internet products and services world-wide is proving to be a lucrative one, and the Netherlands is no exception. The 'killer application' has arguably been the innovation of corporate intranets and extranets, connected with the wider Internet behind security firewalls. Much of the attraction of such services is that by using Internet protocols, companies can perform much the same functions as with a private proprietary network, but at a fraction of the cost. As these services often require a considerable degree of systems integration with existing Local Area Networks (LANs), Wide Area Networks (WANs), internal databases and other systems, this has proved lucrative territory for computer services companies to supply Internet access in conjunction with their existing expertise in computer networking.

The consumer market, in contrast is still waiting for the 'killer application' that will turn it from a niche market into a truly mass medium. Of the twenty-seven Rotterdam companies surveyed, only the city's major ISP (bART) generated the majority of its turnover from domestic subscribers and only four other companies were involved in the consumer market at all.

Estimating the market share for both the business and consumer market is difficult. The business market is perhaps easier to chart as one company, NLnet, has dominated the national market until very recently. In the business to business market, NLnet still had an estimated 43 per cent of market share when measured directly, rising to 63 per cent once their resellers are added in, as of January 1997.[7] This has largely resulted from the fact that NLnet was the first commercial Internet supplier in the Netherlands. The company grew out of SURFnet (the academic network) in 1992, becoming a limited

Table 9.1 Internet value chain

	Connectivity and network solutions		
	Infrastructure provision ⇒	*Telecoms value-added products* ⇒	*IP network management* ⇒

	Fibre
	Leased lines
	SDH
		Traditional
		VPN
		ATM
		Frame relay
		SMDS
		Number
		  translation
		  services
		ISP specific:
		VPOPs
		Bandwidth
		  on demand
			IP backbone
			Routing
			Peering
			
			Services:
			  News servers
			  IP addressing
			  E-mail

Skills/ resources	Capacity	Technical skills Telecom expertise	Technical skills Critical mass Network managment
Typical operators	PTOs	PTOs ISPs	ISPs

Suppliers	Cable
	  manufacturers
	Transmission
	  equipment
	  manufacturers
		Switch
		  manufacturers
		Computer
		  manufacturers
			Central server
			  manufacturers
			Maintenance/
			  operators

Source: adapted from Spectrum 1996

Access and commu-cation solutions ⇒	Customer service and support ⇒	Presence solutions	
		Content enabling ⇒	Content provision ⇄
Dial-up access ISDN access Leased-line access Intranets/extranets Hosting Security Remote local rate access IP applications (e.g. fax to e-mail Voice over packet switched networks IP-based VPN etc.	Customer support Billing Account management	WWW 'store fronts' Platforms for electronic commerce Search and retrieval Integration with other media. etc.	Information Education Entertainment etc.
Understanding user needs Systems integration Software engineering	Branding Customer relationships Customer management	Understanding user needs Creative multimedia production and packaging skills Marketing skills Software engineers Systems integration	Knowledge of target audience
ISPs	ISPs	Multimedia design companies ISPs Advertising and marketing companies	Companies Universities Governments
End-user PC manufacturers Software companies	Computer manufacturers	Software companies Computer manufacturers	

company a year later in order to cater for the burgeoning demand of corporate Internet users. It has subsequently benefitted from being first in the field, as competition in the business market did not begin seriously until two years later, in 1995.

In the consumer market, the estimating of market shares is a more contentious issue. Table 9.2 contains official figures as given by the ISPs themselves.

While this shows the top ten ISPs in the Netherlands by subscriptions, the actual rankings within the ten and the numbers that they are based on have been seriously called into question.[8]

Number and scale of companies

Due to the previously-mentioned difficulties involved in collecting accurate data on companies involved in the industry, the following survey will obviously not have captured every company that is active in the Internet market in the Netherlands. Aside from this proviso, after checking and refining the database, 381 companies with accurate four-digit post codes have been collated. The survey includes companies for whom the Internet is their core and/or sole business, together with the new market entrants from the computer services field, design and marketing companies, and others. An indication of how this group of market entrants swells the ranks of companies offering Internet products and services is provided by a recent market survey conducted by EIM. The survey concentrated solely on Internet-dedicated companies and consequently reported only 145 such companies in the Netherlands (Jonkheer 1998).

A rough typology of companies by activity is given in Table 9.3, mainly

Table 9.2 Top ten Internet Service Providers in the Netherlands by domestic subscribers, February 1997

Provider	Location	Subscribers
World Access	Amersfoort	80,000
Planet Internet	Amersfoort	50,000
CompuServe	Utrecht/Amsterdam	50,000
World Online	Naarden/Hilversum	50,000
TIP (The Internet Plaza)	Almere	29,000
Inter NLnet	Nijmegen	22,000
EuroNet	Amsterdam	16,000
XS4all	Amsterdam	16,000
Trefpunt NL	Zeist	13,000
bART	Rotterdam	10,000

Source: adapted from TelePC at: http://www.bpa.nl/telepc/zweit/ip_abo.htm (15 March 1997)

Table 9.3 Number of companies supplying Internet products and services in the Netherlands, by activity, April 1997

Type	Number of companies	% share
Business services	50	13.1
Connectivity and network solutions	168	44.1
Internet cafés	5	1.3
Presence solutions	158	41.5
Total	381	100

Source: Original survey.

drawn from the information given on their own company websites and supplemented with information derived from trade listings. Those firms in the categories of 'connectivity and network solutions' and 'presence solutions' correspond to the functions listed in Table 9.1.[9] The companies described here under the heading of 'business services' are not directly indicated in Table 9.1 because they do not readily occupy a stable position within the value chain. Most of their activities are based around intermediary functions such as consultancy, training provision and project or 'strategy' management. Such activities may extend right across the value chain or, alternately, be concentrated at one of a number of links in the chain, depending on the particular company and their client(s). Internet cafés form a very small fourth category.[10]

The number of employees in each of the 381 companies is not known, although figures are available for most of the largest ISPs. It is however possible to make a number of remarks about general trends in the size of companies. Firstly, the size varies dramatically according to the services they offer. Companies offering connectivity and networked solutions (CANS) exhibit a much wider diversity in terms of size than do companies involved in providing presence solutions and business services. CANS firstly includes the multinational PTOs (although the number of Internet-dedicated staff in these companies is still low). Also included in this group are the 'headline' success stories of the Dutch ISP market, typically with between forty and 100 full-time employees (FTEs), although some are now larger.[11] Finally, CANS includes a much greater number of very small operators employing only two or three people.

In contrast, companies offering presence solutions exhibit a much narrower range of size. Freelance and home-based workers are quite common, working individually on a subcontracting basis for a range of companies or as part of a 'virtual company' together with (typically) two, three or four other networked professionals. Most other companies have between four and ten FTEs and even the larger companies within this market (e.g. XXLink) rarely reach the fifteen to twenty FTEs bracket, as of April 1997. These trends, identified nationally through interviews, are again borne out by the evidence from the Rotterdam survey.

Map 9.1 shows the spread of Internet-specific employment (measured in equivalent FTEs) in the twenty-seven Rotterdam companies, in direct relation to each company's total employment. It is clear that Internet-specific employment is concentrated in a small number of (relatively) large companies, as can also be seen in Table 9.4. Eleven of the companies employed only one or two Internet-specific equivalent FTEs. The mean average is much higher than this because of the presence of a few large employers, three companies in particular. An important feature to note is that, unlike the biggest of these (bART), the second and third biggest employers are not Internet companies *per se*. For these firms the Internet is just one of their market areas and represents only around a third and a quarter of their total employment respectively. This indicates that the Internet is at the heart of a group of growth-related telematics and multimedia products and services. In fact, while the total of Internet-specific staff has grown from zero in 1993 to a total of 213, outright employment for the twenty-seven companies is more than double this figure at 429 FTEs.

The location of Internet suppliers in the Netherlands

While accepting that the information on each firm is minimal, I would argue that it is already possible to delineate a number of locational trends. As Table 9.5 shows, at the level of municipalities, Amsterdam dominates the sample in numerical terms with seventy-two companies, more than double the number found in any other municipality.

The city also has the two most dense concentrations of Internet suppliers in the country, as measured by four-digit post-code areas: the Amsterdam Science Park (twenty-five companies) and the canal area of the city centre (nine). The municipal level is key to understanding the spatial distribution of the industry. Although activity is geographically dispersed across all twelve provinces, as Map 9.2 illustrates, the companies are concentrated in a small

Table 9.4 Internet-specific employment in Rotterdam, equivalent full-time employees, April 1997

	Numbers	*Percentage share*
Mean per firm	8	n/a
Mode per firm	2	n/a
Total (twenty seven firms)	213	100
Ten biggest employers	178	84
Five biggest employers	137	64

Source: Original survey.

194

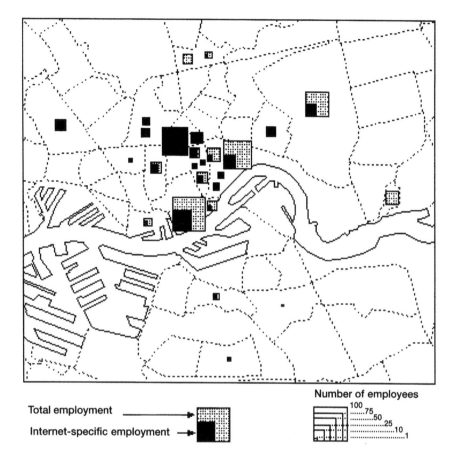

Number of employees

Total employment

Internet-specific employment

Map 9.1 Internet-specific employment in relation to total employment in companies supplying Internet products and services in Rotterdam.
Source: Equivalent FTEs, April 1997

group of urban locations, with the top ten municipalities (by firm numbers) accounting for just over half of the sample. In order to control for the size of municipalities, the number of companies has been supplemented with location quotients based on 1993 employment figures.

As can be seen, all the municipalities with the highest absolute numbers also have a greater representation of companies than would be expected on the basis of employment. There is, however, significant variance in the degree of over-representation between each of the municipalities within this group. Den Haag, for instance, has the lowest figure, of only a 5 per cent greater representation than would be expected on the basis of employment. This contrasts rather unfavourably with the other major metropolitan areas of the Netherlands: Amsterdam (nearly 200 per cent over-representation);

Table 9.5 Top ten municipality locations in the Netherlands for Internet suppliers measured by firm numbers, April 1997

Municipality	Firms	% of the sample	Employment (1993)	Location quotient
1 Amsterdam	72	18.9	401,896	291
2 Rotterdam	33	8.7	325,341	165
3 Utrecht	18	4.7	171,769	170
4 Gravenhage, 's-Den Haag	14	3.7	216,883	105
5 Eindhoven	14	3.7	121,883	186
6 Nijmegen	11	2.9	76,822	233
7 Haarlem	9	2.4	63,110	232
8 Groningen	8	2.1	101,375	128
8 Delft	8	2.1	46,272	281
10 Amersfoort	7	1.8	56,373	202
10 Diemen	7	1.8	14,116	806
Total	201	52.8		

Source: Original survey; employment figures from the Central Bureau of Statistics.

Utrecht (70 per cent over); and Rotterdam (65 per cent over). In contrast to Den Haag's weak performance, perhaps the most striking feature of the table is Diemen's staggering 700 plus percentage points over and above the number of companies that would be expected on the basis of 1993 employment figures.

To place this in context, the municipality of Diemen is actually part of Greater Amsterdam, a small suburb that lies on the city's south eastern edge. The significant Internet cluster that has developed in Diemen has sprung from NLNet's relocation into the municipality. When NLNet's burgeoning space requirements became too big for the Amsterdam Science Park (ASP) in 1995, the company wanted a move that would still keep them in close proximity to the network hub located in two buildings of the Centrum voor Wiskunde en Informatica (CWI), the Maths and Computing University, directly adjacent to the ASP. Diemen fulfilled the requirement, being only two km down the road. Since their move, NLNet have again proved to be a 'hub' firm by attracting a number of other Internet companies to co-locate in Diemen.

Moving up to a greater geographical scale, to the level of provinces as in Table 9.6, a further trend becomes identifiable. Once again, concentration is evident as eight of the twelve provinces (two thirds in total) have a lower representation of companies than would be expected on the basis of employment. It is also worth remarking that, as illustrated in Map 9.3, the top three provinces are all adjacent to each other, forming what might be described as a 'hotspot' of activity where their borders meet.

Other interesting trends to be noted at the province level are the low

196

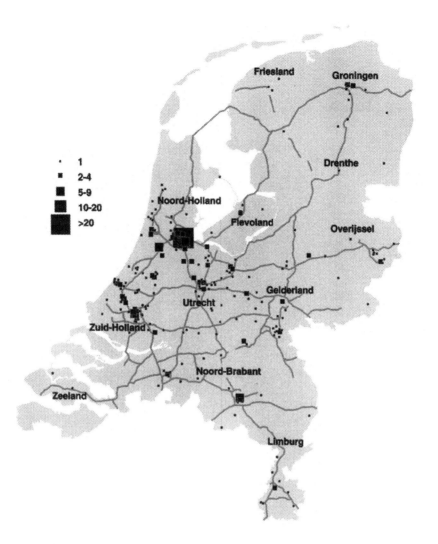

Map 9.2 Distribution of Internet suppliers in the Netherlands, by firm, at the level of four digit post codes, April 1997.

representations of companies both in the rural areas of Friesland and Zeeland, and in the predominantly industrial province of Noord-Brabant where, in particular, one might have expected the presence of Philips in Eindhoven to have stimulated more activity than appears to be the case.

Clearly, then, agglomeration is a feature of the Internet industry in the Netherlands, identifiable at a number of levels. First, Internet suppliers are concentrated in urban areas. This would seem to refute those writers who have suggested that the technological possibilities of new ICTs will overcome

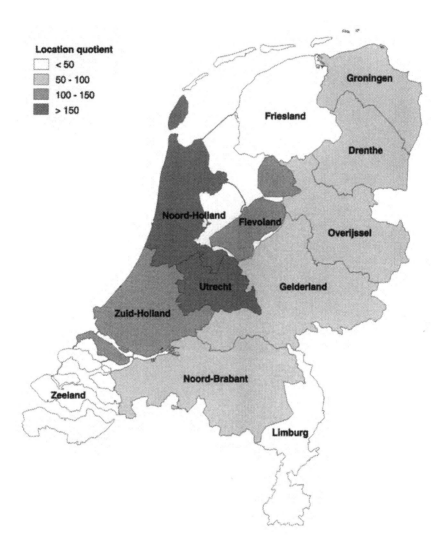

Map 9.3 Province level concentration of Internet suppliers in the Netherlands, by
location quotients, April 1997

the 'tyranny of geography' and support the radical decentralization of activity. Nicholas Negroponte (1995: 6-7), for example, argues that 'the digital
planet will look and feel like the head of a pin', whilst John Naisbitt and
Patricia Aburdene have suggested that 'if cities did not exist, it now would
not be necessary to invent them' (Naisbitt and Aburdene 1991: 329).
Unfortunately for Naisbitt and Aburdene, at least in relation to the development of the Internet industry, this statement would seem to have no validity
whatsoever outside of the realms of intellectual 'make believe'. In addition to

198

Table 9.6 Location of Internet suppliers in the Netherlands measured by location
quotient at province level, April 1997

Province	Firms	Employment (1993)	Location quotient
Noord-Holland	120	1,084,212	180
Utrecht	48	492,596	158
Flevoland	6	71,058	137
Zuid-Holland	92	1,370,223	109
Gelderland	35	710,993	80
Groningen	10	213,500	76
Noord-Brabant	36	915,237	64
Overijssel	13	405,277	52
Drenthe	5	158,797	51
Limburg	10	433,564	37
Friesland	4	207,761	31
Zeeland	2	136,919	23

Source: Original survey, employment figures from Central Bureau of Statistics.

the evidence already presented in Table 9.5, the Rotterdam case is once again instructive. Of the twenty-seven companies, twenty-two are located in the city centre. The only other regularly-occurring location is the home; three companies are home-based, and two of them stated that they would rather be in the city centre, but could not afford to rent there.

The pattern identified, then, seems to be consistent with the work of academic geographers who have argued, with much historical evidence on their side, that the 'information economy' in general is an essentially urban one. It depends very heavily on the agglomeration economies and dense webs of transactions and networks that are seen as underpinning the urbanization process (Wheeler and Mitchelson 1989, Gillespie and Robins 1989 among others).

A second spatial characteristic of the industry is that, although there are important clusters in cities such as Nijmegen and Eindhoven, activity is concentrated in the country's traditional core region of the Randstad ('the Ring'). At a finer level, activity is further concentrated within a very particular area of the Randstad itself, around the top arc of 'the Ring', as illustrated in Map 9.4.

This area's western boundary is marked by Haarlem and Hoofddorp. The main body of the arc runs across Amsterdam and Naarden and down through the affluent area known as Het Gooi en Vechtstreek, an important corridor that links Amsterdam and the (largely) dormitory suburbs of Flevoland in the north with Utrecht in the south. If further confirmation were needed, a quick check on the biggest employers in the industry would reveal that almost all are located within this arc.[12] Notable exceptions include bART (Rotterdam) and InterNLnet (Nijmegen).

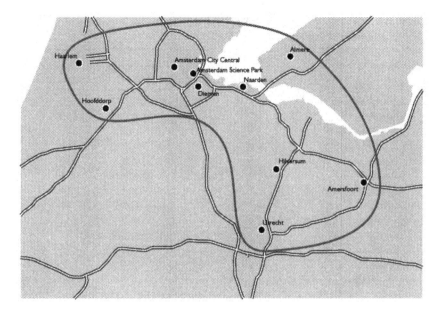

Map 9.4 Concentration of Internet supply activities within the Randstad, April 1997

Possible factors influencing agglomeration

It should be apparent by this stage that, while companies supplying Internet products and services can indeed be found across the length and breadth of the Netherlands, they are more likely to be found in certain places than in others, and this is particularly true for the large firms within the industry. The following discussion outlines some of the more likely contributory factors towards this pattern of geographically uneven development. Firstly, classic factor analysis at the urban/regional scale yields a number of plausible determinants for the spatial and geographical structure of the Internet industry, particularly infrastructure and knowledge resources.

Infrastructure

Infrastructure considerations for Internet suppliers relate primarily to the need for access to the appropriate telecommunications infrastructure, as getting connected to the Internet is one of the first tasks for any company in the industry and Internet charges will be one of its main costs. At the most basic level, there is the question of being situated in a location that has local-call-rate access to the Internet. Although the main access providers now offer this service across almost the whole of the Netherlands, this was most certainly not the case until recently. Provision of the service followed the typical pattern of investment in telecommunications infrastructure for value-added services not covered by universal service obligations (see Gillespie and Robins 1989, Beesley and Laidlaw 1995).[13] The rollout of local-call-rate Internet access concentrated first on select metropolitan 'hot spots' of demand (i.e. Amsterdam and the rest of the Randstad). Although this particular disparity has largely been erased, there is still no uniform platform of services across the country as, in a competitive telecoms environment, there is still a wider range both of providers and of service provision in these areas than in more peripheral regions.

A second, related dimension in which infrastructure-costs vary geographically concerns the distance from the user to the provider. Obtaining the maximum geographical proximity to your access provider is still an issue for Internet suppliers, because the further the distance, the more expensive a leased line becomes. As there are fewer points of presence (PoPs) that are geographically dispersed outside the Randstad, leased line costs for companies located in outer areas are higher than for those firms inside the Randstad.

In addition to these geographical implications, telecommunications infrastructure promotes a particularly noticeable form of spatial clustering at a micro-level. This is shown in the frequent examples of Internet suppliers co-locating in the same building. Typically, this will involve an ISP with a number of smaller multimedia/web design companies. This arrangement results in cost savings all round. The smaller companies benefit from being able to connect to their access provider via an ethernet link rather than a more expensive leased line. In turn, the Web companies represent guaranteed customers for the ISP, providing income to help cover the unavoidable, fixed cost of their own connection as well as being potential collaborators in the marketplace. This characteristically 'symbiotic' relationship was, for instance, one of the main stimuli behind the initial development of the Amsterdam Science Park, as small companies moved in to take advantage of cheap access to NLnet's own fast Internet connection.

Knowledge resources

In terms of knowledge resources, the key factor appears to be higher education institutes. These are important first as sources of Internet firm founders. The close link between NLnet and the academic community has already been documented, but it is by no means unique. The founder of Digicash, currently the largest company in the ASP with around thirty FTEs, was a member of the CWI Maths and Computing Faculty before leaving to move across the road to develop commercial applications from his insights into encryption algorithms. Indeed, the Science Park in its entirety is a dedicated facility for the 'incubation' of university-spin-off start-up companies. Links as occupationally and locationally direct as these are probably not the norm. More representative of the industry as a whole is the more diffuse relationship between higher education and firm formation found in the Rotterdam sample. Nearly a third of the companies (eight out of twenty-seven) had one or more founders who started immediately after leaving the education system, or in a few cases, who founded the company while still in education.

More generally, locally-based knowledge resources are vital to creating and maintaining a skilled labour pool and this is particularly important for the Internet industry where skills and experience are at a premium due to their scarcity. The great majority of companies interviewed have encountered serious difficulties in recruiting well-qualified staff, especially those with technical networking expertise. Proximity to an higher educational establishment, preferably offering appropriate courses – the precise content of which may vary but would seem to focus around IT, multimedia design and marketing – can give companies a lead in tapping this scarce labour pool at an early stage.

A common and cost effective method for a company to undertake this is through placements whereby the company, in effect, gets to select the best personnel and take the *stagiaires* through an induction and in-house training period whilst they are not formally on the pay-roll. This does not only apply to university students, but also to those attending schools of Higher Vocational Education known as HMOs (*Hoger Beroepsonderwijs*). One such school in Den Haag (with a particular specialization in IT), was the seedbed for the corporate access provider Internet Exchange Europe (IXE). The company continues to maintain close links with the HBO and this relationship is facilitated by the fact that the school is situated within one kilometre of IXE's building. The prominence of high levels of formal educational attainment within the Internet industry is also highlighted by the EIM study that found that 68 per cent of all respondents had either a university, technical university or HBO qualification (Jonkheer 1998: 18).

Regional demand factors

One would expect high levels of business activity to have a demand-pull effect on the supply of Internet products and services. Further, one would envisage that certain economic activities entail a greater demand for Internet products and services than others. It is very difficult to obtain figures relating precisely to the quantitative and qualitative dimensions of market demand, but an indicator does present itself as a close approximate. While the two are not commensurate, a plausible index of the demand for Internet services is the level of Internet penetration by sector.

From the surveys that have been carried out, the service sector has the highest rates of Internet penetration in the Dutch economy, 23 per cent as of 1 July 1996. Manufacturing has the lowest at less than half this figure, some 11 per cent.[14] For the existence of 'positive' regional demand factors, then, we would expect the presence both of a certain volume of economic activity, and high representations of services, particularly non-consumer services.

Any such demand is presently not typically satisfied by firms beyond the region. This was shown by interviews at the national level and, more quantifiably, in the Rotterdam case study. 56 per cent of the firms reported a regional, Randstad-based spread of clients and around half specifically referred solely to the local area of Greater Rotterdam.

A positive relationship between supply and demand does suggest itself if we look more closely at the performance of Internet supply activities at the province level. Table 9.7 shows a selective sectoral breakdown for the three 'leading' provinces in terms of the absolute numbers of Internet companies (Noord Holland, Zuid Holland and Utrecht) and Noord Brabant, the third-largest province (as measured by total employment) but 'lagging' in terms of the number of Internet suppliers..[15]

The divergence in the sectoral mix between Noord Brabant and the three leading provinces is striking. Brabant has a significantly lower representation of both financial and business services, while roughly double the proportion of manufacturing employment. Brabant's particular industrial structure, then, possibly indicates weak demand conditions for Internet products and services, that may be a contributory factor in the low level of Internet companies within the province.

Related and supportive sectors

The role of companies in related sectors in terms of their involvement as suppliers, investors, buyers or cooperative partners may also be influential. This might be visible in terms of a number of actors in the Internet industry developing specializations that are related to existing strengths within the local economy and/or are spin-off developments from, or diversification by, particularly dominant actors. In the case of the Internet industry, related and supportive sectors would primarily be computer services, telecommunications, publishing, and the broadcast media.

Fully establishing how these industries influence the geographic structure of the Internet industry is a complex task that is beyond the scope of this chapter. However, I would briefly like to develop two points. First is the way that the related and supportive sectors for the Internet industry are closely aligned with the Internet companies themselves in terms of their geographical distribution. Second, I wish to illustrate more concretely how corporate strategies of firms in related sectors can influence the locational decisions of Internet companies.

The related and supportive sectors for the Internet industry are geographically concentrated across the northern and eastern end of the Randstad, broadly commensurate with the area delineated in Map 9.4 as the locus for Internet supply activities. Although it is difficult to quantify the geographic distribution of employment in telecommunications – PTT Telecom's more than 70 per cent share in most provinces prevents the official statistics being made public – it is still possible to make a number of remarks. PTT has a distributed network of regional business centres across the twelve provinces, with the headquarters of KPN (the state holding company for both PTT Telecom and PTT Post) located in the far north in Groningen. Both of these locational arrangements reflect an earlier, now discarded mode of Dutch regional policy geared, as Oosterhaven (1996: 531) outlines, to the 'spreading' of economic activity.

It is almost inconceivable that the current dispersed pattern of PTT's employment will remain unchanged in the face of (newly arrived) competition. The network of regional centres is likely to face a period of prolonged contraction and consolidation similar to the ongoing experience of British Telecom since liberalization (Sinden 1995). The spatial impacts of PTT's job shedding will be exacerbated by the concentration of the majority of PTT's major and growing competitors in the top arc of the Randstad: Telfort in Amsterdam, Unisource and Global One in Hoofdorp and so on.

In terms of the remaining sectors, publishing is overwhelmingly concentrated in Noord Holland (specifically Greater Amsterdam) as shown in Table 9.7; while computer services – one element of the composite 'business services' classification – again follows the trajectory of the top half of the Randstad. The broadcast media in the Netherlands centre around a purpose-built Media Park in Hilversum, to which the industry relocated in the 1950s.

One concrete example of how the actions of companies in related and supportive sectors influence the development of the Internet industry, including locational decisions, is provided by TROS, the television production company. TROS is one of the four main backers for the major Dutch ISP World Online. From the outset, World Online developed proprietary content for their own website. As the number of subscribers increased, it was decided to hive-off the creative production unit and expand its operations as a third party supplier of multimedia products and services, as of April 1997. An integral element of the re-organization was the re-location of the new company from World Online's site in Naarden, to TROS' own premises in Hilversum. Staff of the new venture work side-by-side with existing TROS personnel. It is hoped that both companies will reap synergistic benefits from the arrangement, in addition to the source of potential clients for the new company that proximity to the broadcast sector offers.

A potential for 'institutional thickness'?

So far, the discussion of factors influencing the commercial and geographical development of the Internet industry in the Netherlands has concentrated on the 'status-oriented' endowments of cities and regions. But, as Fuchs and Wolf (1997: 8) argue, analysis 'has to be supplemented with an approach which treats value chains as a dynamic set of processes which are continuously

Table 9.7 Selective sectoral comparison of the three 'leading' Internet provinces and one 'lagging' province by employment numbers, 1995

Province	Financial services		Business services		Publishing		Manufacturing (exc. publishing)		Total employment	Internet firms	Location quotient
	No.	%	No.	%	No.	%	No.	%	No.	No.	
N. Holland	52,300	5.2	155,800	15.5	11,100	1.1	104,900	10.4	1,004,400	120	180
Z. Holland	47,800	3.8	191,600	15.4	4,400	0.4	139,200	11.2	1,243,400	92	109
Utrecht	24,700	5.4	76,300	16.6	2,100	0.5	44,200	9.6	459,000	48	158
N. Brabant	22,900	2.8	103,700	12.5	2,800	0.3	188,000	22.7	829,100	36	64

Source: Central Bureau of Statistics

changing and which are under the pressure of outward influences'. Since the 1980s, work on industrial districts has added much to these debates, stressing the contribution of the mobilization of social and cultural factors in the drive for economic success. In trying to analyse the 'industrial atmosphere' of innovative milieux, more recent work has concentrated on the importance of local 'institutions'. Included here are not only formal mechanisms for the support of business and research and development, but factors such as high levels of inter-firm interaction and more intangible elements related to commonly held norms and values that produce a 'shared industrial purpose' and help to establish mutual trust between actors. Cities and regions that are able to develop and capitalize upon these factors can be said to possess 'institutional thickness'.

It may indeed be appropriate to analyse the multimedia industry in terms of 'institutional thickness'. At the time of writing, however, the embryonic nature of the Internet industry in the Netherlands is such that it is premature to use the term widely here. It is true that some initial signs seem to give the appearance of an emerging institutional thickness: high levels of firm inter-action, the emergence of new trade organizations, the existence of a very small, dispersed but networked creative community.[16] On the other hand, there are at least as many signs that buck this trend: competitive market dynamics dominating collaborative dynamics, lack of social networks between firms within the same cluster, and trade associations with narrowly defined administrative and technical roles or simply stymied by sectional interest. The state of flux in which the industry currently exists means that these and other outcomes are far from clear and unequivocal.

Policy actions

Despite such uncertainty, I would argue that it is possible to examine one of the more concrete 'outward influences' that has affected the development of the Internet industry in the Netherlands, and that is the action of state development agencies. Unlike the more intangible elements of institutional thickness, such as shared norms and values, that one would expect to sediment in places only over the medium to long term, intervention by state development agencies is often designed as the 'spark' to ignite a burst of activity that will then become self-sustaining. As such, urban and regional development policy aimed at promoting growth sectors tends to have clearly defined goals that are (usually) executable in the short to medium term.

While it would be misleading to suggest that policy development with respect to the Internet industry is widespread throughout the Netherlands, there is now an accumulation of initiatives that bears consideration. I would, then, like to conclude this chapter with a short discussion of three contrast-ing examples of policy approaches in this field. They reflect three equally contrasting experiences of economic restructuring in Amsterdam, Rotterdam and Almere.

At the outset, it is perhaps helpful to outline the generic possibilities that are open to state development agencies seeking to support and promote the development of the Internet industry:

- *Direct involvement in projects*: the commitment of the organization's resources above and beyond the simple provision of funds.
- *Capital:* relocation grants, help with costs of infrastructure, seed capital, training budgets, etc.
- *Brokering:* coordination and promotion of 'innovation'-type networks and projects between other public and private sector actors.

Not surprisingly, the city with the longest standing involvement with the Internet agenda, is Amsterdam. Efforts directed towards the social and community uses of the Internet have included the direct involvement of state development agencies with individual projects, such as the Amsterdam Digital City (see for example, Brants *et al.* 1996). However, there is virtually no project involvement or brokering activity in terms of economic development issues. Instead, policy is very much market-led: provision of basic infrastructure (such as transport), coupled with generic business measures but not with targeted incentives as such. The rationale is that Amsterdam's positive regional factor endowments, coupled with strong demand conditions and the presence of related and supportive sectors, will encourage development efficiently without the need for state intervention.

Cities and regions with rather less favourable status-oriented conditions for the development of Internet companies are more likely to have public policy in this area. Rotterdam Development Company, for instance, is attempting to move away from the city's over-dependence on declining port-related activities.[17] It has pushed telecommunications-related issues up the development agenda over the last three years. A telecoms audit of Rotterdam, commissioned in 1995, led to the production of a Telecoms Business Plan in September 1996, 'Business@Rotterdam', in which the Internet features highly. The key elements of this ambitious plan will not begin to have an impact for a least another year as they are long-term measures aimed at raising the overall level of infrastructure, skills and Internet services in the city.[18]

The Development Company has also accompanied these strategic measures with more piecemeal activity aimed at increasing the rate of adoption of the Internet among the city's business community. An important element within this has been re-location incentives to major companies involved in the supply of Internet and other advanced telecommunications services. The Development Company was instrumental in the relocation in 1996 of bART from Den Haag, through buying stock in the company, and also in the relocation of Orion Telematica from Zoetermeer in the same year (through a more standard financial relocation package). Importantly, these two companies are by far the largest employers of Internet specific equivalent full-time employees in Rotterdam.

A final, contrasting example of direct intervention strategies by state development agencies is provided by Almere City. The city of Almere, even more than Rotterdam perhaps, lacks positive status-oriented advantages in relation to the development of the Internet industry. Far from being an old industrial city needing to restructure its economic base towards a more digital future, Almere faces the challenge of establishing an economic base in the first instance, for the city itself has only been in existence since 1976. Almere New Town (to give the city its proper name), is the urban centre of Flevoland, the newest Dutch province, that was created from land recovered from the Zuider Zee. Despite rapid population growth, Almere – and Flevoland in general – have difficulties encouraging and embedding indigenous economic activity due to the close proximity of Amsterdam and Het Gooi. These concerns formed the background to the City's direct and ambitious intervention in promoting the development of an Internet 'cluster' in Almere.

Almere's strategy has focused around the operations of one company, an ISP called TIP (The Internet Plaza). TIP was started in 1995 by a former television company Director who lives in Almere. The company has since grown rapidly and at the time of writing has over fifty FTEs. By the middle of 1996, it became clear that, due to the increase in personnel, new premises would be required. It would also be necessary to upgrade their Internet connection significantly if they were to continue progressing. Such an upgrade would not prove cost effective if they remained in Almere, in view of the lower connection costs that could be achieved were TIP to relocate to Amsterdam. As social networks already existed between TIP and Almere City and Flevoland province, the dilemma was discussed and an alternative agreement reached.

TIP relocated to new premises in Almere in May 1997, forming the heart of what was christened 'Digital Centre Flevoland'. In return, funds from the city and the province were used to upgrade the Internet connection between Almere and Amsterdam to 34 megabits per second. In addition, all usage charges were to be covered for the first three years. It was hoped that these very low costs, coupled with the attraction of sharing with TIP, would bring in small Internet and multimedia start-up companies. Space was also reserved in the building for hire by private, IT-oriented higher education schools.

Almere City viewed the initiative as an opportunity both to retain a significant local company and to realize the 'image-raising' potential that (as commissioned research had indicated) Internet companies represent. In total, the costs for re-fitting the premises – they had already been built for use as standard office space – and for covering the Internet connection amounted to over a million guilders each for Almere City and the province of Flevoland. The city also planned to formalize the social networks that exist between Almere's Internet community and the development agencies, towards a more explicit 'innovation'-type network. Its first objective was the cloning of the Digital Centre formula for a new building.

The previous discussion has demonstrated the range of responses that the Dutch urban and regional development community are currently exploring in relation to the economic development opportunities associated with Internet companies. It remains to be seen how effective these policies will prove in the long term. However, the direct involvement of public authorities in projects has already given rise to a number of difficulties.

First, the reader should be aware that Amsterdam City's policies towards Internet companies have been formed against the backdrop of an unsuccessful prior involvement in the Amsterdam Science Park. Indeed, the Economic Development Department played a major role in the establishment of the ASP. However, although the City's financial commitment to the project persists and it is a major stakeholder in the venture, it is no longer responsible for the day-to-day running of the facility as it was at the outset. Operational control was relinquished in 1995 when it was acknowledged that the Park was not performing to expectations in terms of fulfilling its function as an 'incubation' centre for small and medium-sized enterprises (SMEs). Subsequently, the contract for managing the facilities was awarded to the Zernike Group, an organization with a proven track record in the commercial exploitation of university spin-offs. It is only under the stewardship of Zernike that the Park has become successful.

Amsterdam City's experience does not, on its own, assume particular significance. But when examined in light of the recent downturn in the fortunes of Almere City concerning Digital Centre Flevoland (DCF), it raises serious doubts about the appropriateness of state development agencies' direct involvement with cluster-based strategies. Over the period of the present research, Almere City have encountered severe difficulties managing and running DCF, so much so that they have curtailed their further active involvement in the project, as of February 1998. The City's lease of the first two floors has been transferred to TIP, who now rent the entire building.

The public authority's problems sprang from a failure to rent the ground floor of the facility, which was initially intended for use by educational institutes. In addition, while the seven purpose-built start-up units were let, the communal café facilities promised by one of the tenants failed to materialize. Around this time, the city also discovered that they had run over budget on the whole project, and as a result the period of subsidy for the Internet connection was reduced from three years to two. With the building's owners pushing for them to rent the ground floor, or face losing the lease for the entire building, the city came to the compromise solution of handing their leasehold over to TIP, who already had a taker for the empty space, one of their own biggest clients. Needless to say, plans for the second building of the DCF complex have been abandoned, while some of the start-up companies already *in situ* are reconsidering their position after finding that their larger neighbour and competitor has now become their landlord, although TIP are contractually bound to maintain the present subsidized rent formula for the next four years.

Above all the city was 'undone' by the commercial pressures that built up around the project in a very short space of time. With the bureaucratic decision-making structures typical of a public authority, the city was ill placed to respond to these pressures with sufficient speed and flexibility. As the former operational manager of the project put it, 'it was a mistake . . . it was too complicated for the city, everything came at once'.[19]

Multimedia growth poles versus 're-orienting core competencies for the digital age'

The experience of Amsterdam and Almere signals a lack of capability of public authorities to operate directly in the (Internet) market. As the Director of Economic Research for the City of Amsterdam put it, 'I just don't see how we can get a handle on it [the Internet industry]'.[20] Their cases also illustrate the high risk of cluster-based multimedia strategies, not least because such strategies are often intimately bound-up with property development dynamics, as other chapters in this volume illustrate in relation to their locations.

More fundamentally, the policies pursued by Almere and Rotterdam constitute a cleavage in thinking about the value of Internet and multimedia companies to the local economy. The qualitative difference concerns the way new ICT-based industries are viewed. On the one hand, they can be seen as a motor for the local economy. In this view, promoting the development of 'growth poles' of multimedia clusters is a major factor. On the other hand, the value of the local presence of such companies is seen to reside more diffusely in an innovative potential on the supply-side. In the latter case, while it is important that there should be *some* supply-side actors within the locality, the focus of policy shifts more towards a form of technology transfer. This can be implemented through a broader variety of policy mechanisms, aimed at the updating and the re-skilling of existing strengths within the local economy. In the case of Rotterdam, the attempt is to re-focus traditional strengths in trade towards new electronic commerce opportunities, to 're-orient core competencies for the digital age'.[21]

When assessing the possible strengths and weaknesses of the two approaches, it is important to state that due to their 'visibility' and more narrowly defined goals, cluster-based strategies are probably easier to monitor and evaluate. In terms of harnessing local Internet capacity as an innovative supply-side instrument, one pitfall to avoid would be the 'blackbox' approach to (multimedia) technologies. The strategy should concentrate rather on the development of user-producer communities (Cawson *et al.* 1995). A second initiative would be to pursue a parallel development in terms of upgrading the more general skill base of the population, through actions involving local educational institutes. Similar attempts regarding skills associated with prior waves of new technology-driven innovation, such as the semi-conductor industry, have been documented in other EU contexts (for example, Pratt and Totterdill 1992), and this is presently one element of Rotterdam's strategy in relation to the Internet and electronic commerce. Interestingly, educational capacity is now Almere City's new priority in terms of supporting ICT-based businesses. The public authority is presently involved in brokering the establishment of an HBO further education college in the city that will specialize in IT and multimedia. Once again, though, the benefits of such strategies will not be apparent for a number of years and will require more sophisticated evaluation mechanisms if they are to be properly identified.

Returning to cluster-based strategies, it probably remains only to re-emphasize the precarious nature of Internet companies in particular, and multimedia companies in general. The death rate for small companies as a whole is high and Internet/multimedia enterprises are predominantly small. Companies engaged in Internet and multimedia content creation, or 'presence solutions' as I have referred to earlier, are particularly susceptible to cyclical fluctuations in the economy. Many of their products and services are heavily dependent upon corporate advertising and training spend, and such expenditure is one of the first areas for cost cutting when companies enter a downturn.

That there is already a high death rate among Dutch Internet companies – even during a period of sustained economic prosperity that is often referred to as the 'Dutch miracle' – is borne out both by the recent EIM market report and the author's own research. EIM initially identified over 190 Internet providers from reliable trade sources, but around forty of the companies could not be included in the survey, not because they chose to not respond, but because they were simply unreachable. Similarly, of the initial thirty-two companies identified in the present Rotterdam case study, five companies could not be reached through any of their stated contacts or re-found by standard search methods. Added to these, two of the market entrants reported that they were curtailing their Internet operations, while a third start-up company closed during the course of the research. This amounted to an exit rate of 25 per cent for the firm population in Rotterdam over the course of the research. What this points to, in particular the market exit by companies in related sectors, is increased competition and rapidly falling profit margins for many areas of Internet business.[22] Behind this, is the progressive move to maturity of the Internet market.

The processes driving this are consolidation and merger, resulting in a major shake out of the industry. This is already well underway in the more advanced US market where, for instance, the number of ISPs has fallen dramatically: from 2,248 in 1996 to 303 in 1997, and an estimated 150 by the end of 1998.[23] So, while content creation is fragile because of its susceptibility to intensified cyclical business fluctuations, it is now apparent that the market for Internet access is scale driven, and therefore will benefit the telcos in the long run. Recent research comparing the cost structure of an independent ISP with a telco has estimated that the latter's costs may be as much as a third less than the ISPs'.[24] Not surprisingly, many of those Dutch ISPs that were not already (in part) owned by a telco have been quick to spot the underlying economics of the market and opt for a degree of vertical integration with them.[25] The prospects, then, for local and regional ISPs, and for national ISPs without 'backwards linkages' to telcos, are not encouraging.

It is tempting to view the development of the Internet industry in terms of a product life-cycle approach that Tether and Storey (1997), for instance, have charted for other new technology-based sectors in Europe. The early 'expansionary' phase sees increases in both the number of business units and the level of employment. After a period of time, Tether and Storey argue, the industry moves into a second phase, 'shakeout', where employment continues to rise, but the number of business units decreases as consolidation takes place. It is reasonable, given the US precedent, to speculate that the Dutch Internet industry would appear to be on the cusp of this initial transition. The likely drop in the number of companies should not adversely effect overall employment levels due to the continued upward demand curve and sustained product innovation. Employees of the smaller ISPs and web designers that find their companies failing, or taken over and merged by their bigger rivals should, in general, be re-absorbed by companies looking to diversify up or down the value chain and/or increase the scale of their operations. But the geographical implications of this process are less benign.

It would represent the 'shutting' of the 'window of locational opportunity' that the Internet industry represents (such as it is). As Tether and Storey write, 'the eventual winners in an industry are likely to be amongst its earliest entrants' (1997: 4). Relating this back to ideas of market 'discontinuity', the market will only take a certain degree of discontinuity before its established actors wise-up and push in; in terms of the Dutch Internet industry, that level would seem to have been reached. In addition to the cost savings reaped by large players in the access market (referred to in relation to telcos and ISPs), the main advantage of established companies would appear to be better access to the limited financial resources available for investment in the industry, resources that are vital if the company is to grow.[26] *Significant* employment growth related to the supply of Internet products and services is, therefore, unlikely to be produced by new firm formation. In turn, this would reduce the number of possible locations that experience job growth as it would increasingly develop in established firms in established locations. So, although the almost certain transfer of jobs between companies in the shake-out will continue to embody net gains, there is likely to be some geographical transfer in the location of these jobs. They will probably move up the urban hierarchy, further re-inforcing the uneven pattern of geographical 'winners and losers' identified in this chapter.

Given what has already been outlined regarding the precariousness of Internet/multimedia companies, should the *majority* of state development agencies be overly concerned regarding the very limited prospects for direct economic benefits associated with cluster development that prevail in most areas? Is it not far better to pursue instead policies that, rather than concentrating on a tiny fraction of their business community, will focus on promoting the benefits of Internet and multimedia technologies throughout their existing industrial base? I hope that the present chapter has, at least, helped to focus attention on these important questions and contribute to the ongoing research task that will help us to draw more informed conclusions.

Notes

This chapter draws on research undertaken in TNO–Inro Delft, The Netherlands, during a seven month stay (October 1996 until May 1997) as a visiting researcher in the European Union Network on Innovation and Territory (EUNIT), funded as part of the European Union's Human Capital Mobility programme.. I would like to thank all my colleagues at TNO–Inro in Delft, the Netherlands, but particularly Stephan Boks for producing the maps, Elwin de Groot and Sivert de Groot for help with the statistics, and Hinne Paul Krolis for all-round support and putting up with me for seven months. Thanks also go to my CURDS colleague James Cornford with whose close collaboration I have developed this ongoing research agenda.

1 For the present study, the term 'Internet' will be used in its widest sense i.e. to include interconnected networks, applications and services that are 'stitched' together using Transmission Control Protocol (TCP) and Internet Protocol (IP), typically used in conjunction and referred to simply as TCP/IP. This is broadly commensurate with the 'official' resolution of the Federal Networking Council in 1995 at http://www.fnc.gov/Internet_res.html (25 August 1997).

2 By the first half of 1997, investment in network capacity aimed at IP traffic was estimated to outstrip that for voice channels by a ratio of 3:1 (*Communications Week International* 14 July 1997).

3 As with many other telematics and multimedia-related subjects, the debate took off in earnest in the wake of the influential 1993 'Bangemann Report', *Europe and Global Information Society*.

4 The 'host' computer count used to quantify the growth of the Internet is carried out for European countries by RIPE, whose web and FTP sites hold figures dating from 1994 (http://www.ripe.net/).

5 The term 'ISP' is not a generic term that refers to any firm engaged in the Internet market, rather, it is an industry category that refers specifically to firms whose core business is the provision of Internet access.

6 Figures from NIPO Business Monitor at, http://www.nipo.nl/result/pers/2737$. htm (17 October 1997).

7 Figures are NLnet's own estimate based on Internet traffic measurement.

8 A parallel survey carried out by the online trade magazine *TelePC*, based solely on measuring the 'active' accounts of each ISP, produced conflicting figures for

many of the companies in Table 9.2. In general, the companies claiming the highest numbers of subscribers diverged more significantly from *TelePC*'s lower estimations, by up to a factor of three. *TelePC* concluded that some ISPs include accounts that were given away free as bulk trial offers, those that were no longer in use and so on, while other ISPs concentrate purely on paying subscribers. The figures should consequently be read with due care and attention.

9 Again, as already stated, there is a high degree of overlap between these categories focusing around the design and hosting of websites. When companies offer these services in combination with access provision, the categorization is derived from an estimation of their core activities.

10 For the present study, only Internet cafés offering a minimum of six networked PCs have been included in the sample.

11 For example, World Access/Planet Internet, the largest Dutch ISP and newly-formed by the merger of the two companies, already had more than 120 by April 1997.

12 At present, the biggest employers are the major consumer ISPs as listed in Table 9.2 (with their locations), plus a handful of ISPs that concentrate exclusively on the business market such as NLnet (Amsterdam) and Orion Telematica (Rotterdam).

13 As in the rest of the EU, universal service obligations in the Netherlands do not yet extend to value-added telecoms and data services, including Internet access.

14 Figures from the NIPO Business Monitor at http://www.nipo.nl/result/pers/ 2737$.htm (17 October 1997).

15 Publishing has been extracted from manufacturing. Its classification as such is somewhat of a misnomer given that employment in manufacturing activity related to print publishing is accounted for under a separate classification ('printing').

16 Here, I am referring to what might be called the 'left field' of web designers: those with particular interests and backgrounds in the potential of the Internet as a digital media art form and/or educational medium. Networking activities among this group do take place and coalesce around social and professional contacts stemming mainly from a few key, non-profit-making organizations such as the V2 Organisatie in Rotterdam and the Netherlands Design Institute in Amsterdam. V2 is particularly active, organizing monthly drop-in sessions (known as 'Wiretaps') on differing aspects of digital media art and communication that provides a regular focus and meet-up point for this constituency within the Netherlands.

17 Rotterdam Development Company was formed by the merger of the Council's Real Estate and SMEs Development departments.

18 The three components of the strategy are: the implementation of a Metropolitan Area Network (MAN) for Rotterdam businesses (a metropolitan wide intranet in effect) that will improve upon the current quality of Internet access and be accompanied by the development of city-based information and content services; the set-up a multimedia 'shop'/demonstration site in the city; and the establishment of an Institute for Electronic Commerce involving all levels of the city's education sector.

19 Jolande Mensink, Management Assistant, Economic Affairs, Almere City, 12 February 1998.

20 Peter Tordoir, Director of Economic Research, City of Amsterdam, 17 December 1996.
21 Kees Machielse, Head of New Initiatives in Economic Deveolopment, Rotterdam Development Corporation 16 December 1996.
22 For example, one company reported that at the start of 1996, the market in the Netherlands for 5MB of web space could support rates of up to fl.330 per month, but by the start of 1997, prices had tumbled such that their company was offering the same amount of web space at just fl.55 per month.
23 Figures from The Yankee Group cited in Kleeman (1997).
24 Advantages of incumbent telcos include the use of the network at marginal cost; shared skills on traffic management; shared costs on customer service; and the local sharing of PoPs (Kleeman 1997).
25 Examples of the former include World Access (part owned by PTT Telecom) and World Online (part owned by NS Telecom). An example of the latter is Euronet who sold 30 per cent of their stock to the cable operator Telekabel in 1996.
26 Once again, the Rotterdam sample indicates the importance of this. Of the ten companies that expected the Internet side of their operations to 'rapidly increase' in scale over the next six months, eight had ready access to investment capital either through a parent company or institutional investors. The rest of the sample (seventeen) were less optimistic and all bar two struggled to fund investment through cash flow or personal equity.

References

AD-EMPLOY (1995) *Employment Trends Related to the Use of Advanced Communications: Synopsis Report*, Report to the Commission of the European Communities by Tele Danmark Consult A/S, PREST and the Institute of Technology Assessment.

Beesley, M. and Laidlaw, B. (1995) 'The development of telecommunications policy', in M. Bishop, J. Kay and C. Mayer (eds) *The Regulatory Challenge,* Oxford: Oxford University Press.

Brants, K., Huizenza, M. and van Meerten, R. (1996) 'The new canals of Amsterdam: an exercise in local electronic democracy', *Media, Culture and Society* 18: 233–47.

Capello, R. and Nijkamp, P. (1996) 'Regional variations in production network externalities', *Regional Studies* 30, 3: 225–37.

Cawson, A., Haddon, L., and Miles, I. (1995) *The Shape of Things to Consume,* Aldershot: Avebury.

Dabinett, G. and Graham, S. (1994) 'Telematics and industrial change in Sheffield', *Regional Studies* 28, 6: 605–17.

Dosi, G. (1983) 'Technological paradigms and technological trajectories', in C. Freeman (ed.) *Long Waves and the World Economy,* London: Butterworths.

Freeman, C. and Soete, L. (1994) *Work for All or Mass Unemployment: Computerised Technical Change into the 21st Century,* London: Pinter.

Fuchs, G. and Wolf, H.-G. (1997) 'Regional rejuvenation with the help of multimedia?' Position Paper for the International Workshop on Regional Economic Restructuring and Multimedia, Stuttgart, Germany, 8–11 October 1997.

Gillespie, A. E. and Robins, K. (1989) 'Geographical inequalities: the spatial bias of communication', *Journal of Communication* 39, 3: 7–18.

Gillespie, A. E. and Williams, H. (1988) 'Telecommunications and the reconstruction of regional comparative advantage', *Environment and Planning A*, 20: 1311–21.

Graham, S. (1992) 'Ringing the changes: telecommunications, local economic restructuring and local policy innovations' in M. Geddes and J. Bennington (eds) *Restructuring the Local Economy*, London: Longman.

Jonkheer, K. (1998) *Bedrijfsleven in beeld: Internet Providers – een profiel van de Access–, Content– en Back Bone Providers*, Zoetermeer: EIM.

Kelly, T. (1987) *The British Computer Industry: Crisis and Development*, Guildford: Croom Helm.

Kirkpatrick, D. (1997) 'Europe's technology gap is getting scary', *Fortune* March 17.

Kleeman, M. (1997) 'Pricing Internet Access', paper presented at 'Internet Service Provision '97', conference organized by First Conferences, 16–18 April 1997, RAI Centre, Amsterdam.

M&I and Partners (1996) *Business@Rotterdam: Business plan voor Rotterdam als kopler voor het zakendoen op de elektronische snelweg*, Rotterdam: M&I and Partners.

Naisbitt, J. and Aburdene, P. (1991) *Megatrends 2000*, London: Sidgwick and Jackson.

Naylor, R. and Cornford, J. (1996) 'Shovel sellers of the Internet Goldrush: Internet–based business in Britain', CURDS Discussion Paper 96/1, University of Newcastle.

Negroponte, N. (1995) *Being Digital*, London: Hodder and Stoughton.

Oosterhaven, J. (1996) 'Dutch regional policy gets spatial', *Regional Studies* 30, 5: 527–32.

Pratt, A. C. and Totterdill, P. (1992) 'Industrial policy in a period of organizational and institutional change: the case of inward investment and the electronics sector', *Environment and Planning C: Government and Policy* 10: 439–50.

Regional Policy Commission (1996) *Renewing the Regions: Strategies for Regional Economic Development*, Sheffield: Sheffield Hallam University Press.

Richardson, R. (1994) 'Back officing front office functions – organizational and locational implications of new telemediated services', in R. Mansell (ed.) *Management of Information and Communication Technologies*, London: Aslib.

Richardson, R. and Gillespie, A. (1996) 'Advanced communications and employment creation in rural and peripheral regions: a case study of the Highlands and Islands of Scotland, *Annals of Regional Science* 30: 91–110.

Scott, A. J. (1995) 'From Silicon Valley to Hollywood: growth and development of the multimedia industry in California', The Lewis Centre for Regional Policy Studies, School of Public Policy and Social Research, University of California, Los Angeles, Working Paper 13.

Screen Digest (1995) 'The Internet', *Screen Digest*, April 1995.

Sinden, A. (1995) 'Telecommunications services: job loss and spatial restructuring in Britain, 1989–1993', *Area* 27, 1: 34–45.

Smart, V. and Miller, J. (1997) 'Lost in Cyberspace', *The European*, 383.

Spectrum (1996) *Development of the Information Society: An International Analysis*, London: HMSO.

Tanner, K. and Gibbs, D. (1997), 'Local economic development strategies and information and communication technologies', in J. Simmie (ed.) *Innovation, Networks and Learning Regions*, London: Jessica Kingsley.

Tether, B. and Storey, D. (1997) 'New technology–based firms in Europe: an overview', paper presented at the 5th Annual International 'High Technology and Small Firms' Conference, Manchester Business School, 29–30 May 1997.

Thompson, V. (1996) 'Europe's Internet infrastructure', *Byte* (International), October: 13–17.

Wheeler, J. O. and Mitchelson, R. L. (1989) 'Information flows among metropolitan areas in the United States', *Annals of The Association of American Geographers,* 79, 4: 523–43.

10

THE SOUTH-EAST ENGLAND HIGH-TECH CORRIDOR

Not quite Silicon Valley yet

Puay Tang

Introduction

Small high-technology firms are regarded by many as the seed corn for the future growth of the UK economy, both regionally and nationally. The UK government, through the Department of Trade and Industry (DTI), has launched several initiatives to foster the development of innovative small firms, particularly in information technology (IT). The most recent programme is the Information Society Initiative which has a budget of £34 million to disburse among existing and start-up companies for the development and use of IT-based applications. For the purposes of this paper, high technology refers to extensively IT-based service applications and products, such as multimedia products, electronic publications in various formats, and web-based (Internet) developments.[1]

This chapter asks whether there are any particular reasons for the growth of the high-tech activity in the Sussex region, an area that purports to hold a concentration of innovative multimedia activity. The findings of the chapter are primarily based on the findings of a project on UK electronic publishing undertaken by the author in 1996 and early 1997, entailing a case study of thirty-one small and medium-sized electronic publishing companies. All thirty-one firms, drawn mainly from the Sussex region, including London, were interviewed for an average of three hours.[2]

The chapter will first provide an overview of the British multimedia sector, which is reputedly the dominant player in the European Union. Against this backdrop, the chapter will then describe the main activities undertaken by local organizations and councils, particularly in the south-east part of the region, comprising the London and Brighton–Hove coastal area which claims to be one of the fastest growing segments of the 'corridor'. Underpinning these activities is the belief that networking and robust working relationships enhance sectoral vitality and development.

218

This will be followed by a discussion of the main entry barriers to the sector and the resources required for sustaining market presence. Here, the chapter argues that in an overall understanding of sectoral development, it is useful to study both the entry barriers and the later requirements firms will have to meet in order to maintain their businesses in a particular sector. This is largely because 'static' factors, such as locational or structural characteristics, provide only one aspect of development. Examining the additional facets of entry barriers and resource requirements could provide a dynamic perspective to growth. For instance, changes in, and demands for, skills and technological capability entail adjustments. This is particularly relevant to multimedia which experiences rapid technological developments. The chapter will also assess whether social networks, formal and informal, are considered to have featured prominently in the development of multimedia firms in the Sussex area. The foregoing analysis provides a basis for appraising any particular or significant reasons that have contributed to the growth of this activity. What is tentatively concluded from the review of the two dimensions is that, regardless of common locational and institutional attributes, certain conditions have to be met cumulatively to help set off a particular form of industrial activity in a region. The chapter concludes with some policy implications for regional development of multimedia activities.

The British multimedia scene

The British multimedia sector concentrates to a large degree on publishing a wide range of databases, entertainment and leisure software, specialized and reference material, and on the production of Internet-based applications. In a study on electronic information services and products commissioned by the UK DTI in 1994, it was found that the UK is the predominant producer and user of electronic products and applications among the Member States of the European Union (Mansell and Tang 1994). The study showed that British firms led in several sub-sectors of the multimedia market. For instance, in 1992, Britain exhibited robust growth in database production capability vis-à-vis the European Union.

Table 10.1 shows the numbers of databases, database producers and gateway services in the European Union and the United Kingdom at the end of 1991. Although Germany and Italy are reputed to be producing more databases than they did in 1992 (there is no currently available specific data), there is little to suggest that the trend has been reversed among the top five producers in the European Union.

Similarly, in 1991–92, the UK registered the greatest percentage increase in the production of CD-ROM titles (see Table 10.2). The CD-ROM market in the United Kingdom was pre-eminent in Europe and continues to experience growth, according to analysts. Data for domestic consumer demand are not available, but data for total demand, at least for 1991–92, show that the

Table 10.1 Online ASCII database production/distribution, European Union (end 1991)

Country	No. of databases	Database producers
United Kingdom	708	341
Germany	256	110
France	245	154
Italy	134	39
Other EU states	273	148
European Union total	1,616	792

Source: Adapted from Gale and Cuadra, *Directory of Online Databases,* 1992, quoted in Mansell and Tang (1994: 7).

United Kingdom has a strong capability in title output. The data also suggest that publishers are confident of a growth in demand, although consumer demand is still tenuous, but clearly increasing in the business sector.

The growth of the multimedia sector can also be portrayed in terms of the increasing technological awareness of the country. The take-up and delivery of Internet-based services in the UK indicates the British response to the latest 'electronic revolution'. According to Roland Perry of Online Services Inc., a consultancy service monitoring UK growth of the Internet, an average of 15,000 users accessed the Internet each month in 1996.[3] The rapid take-up of Internet services suggests both an expanding technological awareness and computer literacy. The decreasing cost of computers and software, and falling telecommunication charges, contribute to the overall increase in the computer penetration of the country. In 1993, the computer penetration per 100 inhabitants was reputed to be 16; in 1995, it had increased to 32 per cent

Table 10.2 CD-ROM title output in selected European countries, Japan and the US (1991–92)

Country	Dec. 1991	Aug. 1992	% increase
World total	2,271	N/A	—
United States	1,267	N/A	—
Europe (total)	698	1,177	—
United Kingdom	186	394	112
Germany	123	169	37
Italy	98	122	24
Netherlands	98	111	13
France	129	169	31
Japan	129	N/A	—

Source: Electronic Publishing Services (1993: 69)

(Tang 1996; Parliamentary Office for Science and Technology 1995). The fostering of digital literacy also can be partly explained in terms of government policies to introduce computers into schools. Although the results are patchy, the national emphasis on the educational use of the Internet and multimedia products has helped to promote innovative entrepreneurship in the multimedia sector.

An associated factor in the comparative 'technology savviness' of British business could be explained by London's position as the financial capital of Europe and the focus for trans-Atlantic and trans-Pacific financial activities. As is well known, financial services were early adopters of IT-based applications on a wide basis as they require constant refreshing of data; thus, the demand they place on electronic information service delivery is considerable. The British online industry is dominated in terms of activity and revenue by real-time financial services and this pattern also applies in the European Union.

The relative importance of real-time and retrospective services in the European Union was roughly in the proportion of 56:44 at the end of 1991. In that year, the ratio for the United Kingdom was 58:42, and 59:41 in 1990 (Mansell and Tang 1994). Despite the paucity of more recent figures for real-time and off-time usage, there is little reason to suspect that there would be a change in the trend. Instead, it is arguable that real-time has increased, given the growing number of such services over the Internet.

There is a lively arts culture in the UK, particularly in London, in terms of performing arts (theatre, music, television, radio etc.) and the film industry. This contributes to the establishment and introduction of new media productions; the benefit of such an environment is well illustrated and explained by Allen J. Scott's chapter in this volume. Associated with this are the innovative British design, fashion and advertising industries. The vigorous cultural environment serves as a vehicle for maintaining and accelerating the diversity of new entrants into resourceful and imaginative undertakings. This point is comprehensively covered by Wolf Heydebrand (this volume). The UK trade press is replete with newcomers into the multimedia sector offering a range of specialized web-based graphics, and 'cyber-related' design, advertising and marketing consultancies, to name a few. The exodus of British software programmers to the US, however, is becoming a cause of concern among multimedia companies.

The Brighton–Hove area is a beneficiary of this arts culture which, locally, has its origins in the eighteenth century when the Prince Regent and his entourage would journey down from London to Brighton for the 'salubrious healing waters' which allegedly cured gout. Another reason for these visits was the amorous activities of the Prince Regent. The seaside, of course, was also an attraction. This epoch saw the construction of Brighton's current landmark, the Royal Pavilion, a splendid gauche building built along the lines of a lavish mosque, replete with Oriental furnishings and art, which was used for theatrical and musical performances. The frequent Royal sojourns were accompanied by members of the aristocracy and the bourgeoisie. Theatres and music halls were built and royal patronage stimulated a buoyant arts culture. Self-contained towns by the sea flourished, each with its own arts centre. Brighton became the 'in place' to be among Londoners, royalty and the aristocracy. The arts tradition exists still today.

An important factor for the development of an innovative high-tech industry is the presence of a sound research base, as explained in part by theorists of the American School of high technology (see Markusen, Hall and Glassmeier 1986). It is arguable whether a sound research base is a *sine qua non* for operating in a high-tech environment, and its 'universal' relevance has been questioned (Storper 1995). None the less, the status of the UK's IT knowledge base is shown, among other examples, by the recent multimillion dollar investment, by Microsoft in the University of Cambridge to establish research facilities there.

The UK research base enjoys a world-wide reputation for creativity; however, it is not as successful as American universities in 'spinning off' companies. In this sense, the American School falls short in its explanatory value with respect to the British system. Of course, in the US, there is a deep culture of business and trading. Right from early schooling days, Americans are imbued with the idea of a 'win-win' situation in which commerce and making money are an important dimension of the American way of life. British academics are more risk averse, although this is slowly changing.

What is happening on a large scale is university collaboration with industry, although mainly with large companies. This impetus partly comes from the need to secure more funding at a time when public research funding is getting scarcer and competition for a share of it is intensifying. Public research councils are also fostering the drive toward university–industry collaboration and in many cases, have made it a condition for receiving public monies. In this way, politics is motivating a change in British academic entrepreneurship.

Technical networks, such as a telecommunication infrastructure, and affordable telephone tariffs are generally agreed to be factors for promoting online multimedia activities (Heydebrand, this volume). The British telecommunication infrastructure, dominated by British Telecom (BT) and supplemented by Cable and Wireless and several cable companies, is reputedly one of the most competitive and technologically-advanced systems in the world. The UK boasts the lowest charges of all the member states of the European Union.

The general reasons for British response to the 'electronic challenge' are summarized by Table 10.3.

Overview of the Sussex multimedia region

In November 1997 Wired Sussex, an organization set up by multimedia companies in the region, was launched to promote joint marketing and further

Table 10.3 Reasons for multimedia activity

Long publishing tradition in the UK
English language
Quality of publishing
A large pool of creative talent
Awareness of technology
UK as an arts centre
Good research base
Good telecommunications infrastructure

Source: Author's research

the development of the 'new media' in Sussex. A primary objective of this new organization is to identify collective needs and design a strategy for helping the region to establish itself as a key player in multimedia, nationally and internationally.

The south-east region, which includes Sussex and the city of London, offers one of the largest clusters of new media companies in the UK, including many with long national track records. These include a wide range of players and practitioners, the majority avowedly committed, in some degree, to the development and production of multimedia. There are, for instance, companies involved in animation; broadcasting; film, video and television production; graphics and design; audio production; copy writing; illustration; hardware development; Internet service provision; photography; publishing; software development; telecommunications; web design; training; and CD-ROM and online publications.

The board members of Wired Sussex represent the Brighton and Hove Council, East Sussex County Council, BT, Mercury Cable Communications, Sussex Enterprise (formerly Sussex Chamber of Commerce), Sussex Rural Community Council, the University of Sussex, and several leading Sussex-based multimedia companies. According to the representatives of the larger regional multimedia firms such as Victoria Real and Epic, an important role for the organization is to encourage closer working relationships among its members and alleviate transaction costs for smaller companies, for instance, through joint direct marketing and shared exhibition space. As well as networking activities the organisation employs other strategies such as harnessing the expertise and experience of entrenched players in the new media industry. It thus hopes to achieve the aim it has set for itself: 'branding' Sussex as a leading actor in multimedia.

Wired Sussex also has a website to showcase its activities, the first of its kind in this region. Supported by the DTI, East Sussex County Council and the University of Sussex, the website also aims to 'educate' and promote the use of new media technologies to businesses and communities throughout the region. A focal point of the website is a database which allows Sussex-based companies and organizations to submit details of their products and services, free of charge, into what is to become the most comprehensive listing of new media contacts in Sussex. In addition, offers of media-related employment and contact details for a multitude of community and business projects, including daily new bulletins, are all intended to make this website a reference point for local opportunities for multimedia activities. The strategic aims of Wired Sussex have prompted Stephen Aitken of the DTI's Innovation Unit to proclaim that Sussex should be 'an example for all other regions to follow'.[4]

The creation of this network of producers, users, politicians, policymakers, academics and so on is professedly based on the belief that such networks provide its members with what they need for information, coordination, adjustment and successful innovation. It is however premature to judge if Wired Sussex will achieve its twin aims of organizational dynamism and fostering multimedia innovation. Later parts of this chapter will assess whether the 'shop floor' in fact accords importance to this form of social network for regional development.

Wired Sussex, however, is not the only organized attempt to bring together multimedia companies in the Sussex region. The Multimedia Development Association (MDA) of Brighton, which started with about fifty multimedia companies in the early 1990s, has seen its membership and activities grow gradually in the last few years. Firms differ, however, in their assessment of the organization's value. Some see it as making a solid contribution to innovation and regional development; many others regard it as tangential to their business. It appears that the benefit derived from such membership depends on the size of the company involved: large companies claim they benefit; smaller ones are less inclined to do so. This thus calls into question the transaction cost argument put forth by Wired Sussex.

Several bigger members of MDA collaborated and successfully received corporate and public monies for the construction of a trial broadband wide area network through which business, education and entertainment services could be trialled. This network – MEDIALAN – was designed to offer specialist integrated communications packages tailored towards small and medium-sized companies in the Brighton–Hove area, including broadband services.

Owing to financial constraints, MEDIALAN has not been realized, and has been superseded by the Brighton and Hove Council's Capital Challenge network which was started in 1996 and completed in late October 1997. This £800,000 infrastructure is aimed at the area's secondary schools which will each be equipped with a 100Mb backbone switch and 650–800 outlets. Each secondary school will be connected via a 2Mb private circuit to the town hall. All schools have been successfully 'wired'. Fifteen libraries also will eventually be connected, the two largest with 2Mb connections and the others with ISDN (Integrated Services Digital Network). An important aim of this network is to conduct distance learning and to offer a model for educational content distribution. The University of Sussex is assisting with the development and experimentation of educational material.

In 1997, East Sussex County Council also intensified its applications for development funds from the European Commission. The East Sussex European Partnership, which comprises the University of Sussex, University of Brighton, East Sussex County Council, Brighton and Hove Unitary Authority and the five district and borough councils of East Sussex, has established an East Sussex Brussels Office in Brussels. The main objective of this Office is to keep abreast of programmes and initiatives that may benefit the economic development and research capability of East Sussex. For instance, the County Council has recently been awarded £17.3 million by the European Commission Single Regeneration Budget to be spent over the next five years by the Brighton and Hove Unitary Authority.

Similarly, the Council has also received funding from the European Commission INTER-REG fund to attract inward investment. Active pursuit of European Commission funding has been applauded by the Brighton–Hove business community, not least by the multimedia sector. It is particularly valued by smaller multimedia firms who generally find applications for European Commission funding for software and telematics development very time-consuming and complex. It is arguable that the availability of such funds has, to some degree, given an impetus to organized collaborative activity for the development of multimedia. It can also be maintained that politically motivated investment can contribute to innovation, particularly among smaller companies, which is an aim of the Structural Funds of the European Commission.

In sum, the organized efforts by local companies to foster the further development of multimedia, and the exploitation of its applications and products by businesses in this region, are illustrative of both the incumbent capacity and the perceived merit of nurturing working relationships. The next section will look more closely at a sample of multimedia companies found in the south-east of Sussex.

Some south-east high-tech firms

The south-east of England comprises the London area, East Sussex, parts of West Sussex and Surrey, and Kent. The 'high-tech corridor' primarily covers the London–Brighton–Hove area of East Sussex and Crawley in West Sussex. Out of approximately 1,100 listed multimedia companies throughout the UK, a total of about 450 are found in the south-east. Most of these are small companies with fewer than fifty employees (using the European Commission definition of small companies). A total of about 110 are found in the Brighton–Hove area, and 170 in the London area.[5] The Brighton–Hove part of the corridor has a population of about 275,000; London supports about seven million.

The south-east high-tech corridor, particularly in the Brighton–Hove area, is a relatively new phenomenon. According to senior economic and development officials of Sussex Enterprise (formerly the Sussex Chamber of Commerce), this area has only witnessed a boom in high-tech activity since 1994, although this area has had a longer history of media activity in fields such as film, audio and video production, design, copywriting and photography. This opinion is collaborated by the age profile of the multimedia companies found in this area; more than 90 per cent of the companies started their activities between 1993 and 1994, including traditional publishers who have recently decided to engage in electronic publishing. London, on the other hand, has had a much longer history of multimedia activity, going back to around 1985.

The majority of the south-east high-tech companies are engaged in the production of a wide range of electronic publications in CD-ROM format, and are moving to provide online delivery of these products and specialized applications. Examples of these publications include games, entertainment and sports, reference and academic material, business and financial information, image and music libraries, and Internet-based specialized indexes. Since 1996, there has been a noticeable trend for companies to offer services in design, construction and maintenance of websites, and the delivery of online services. These include entertainment, education, and financial and business applications, including the development of electronic money and electronic purses.

Most of the firms cater to niche markets, with a particular emphasis on the production of specialized reference material, business and financial information, image and music libraries, and educational material. An underlying rationale for the targeting of niche markets is the perception that small and medium-sized firms cannot compete with the larger players in the consumer market, especially those supplying computer games. The firms claim that developing niche markets is a major means by which small and medium-sized firms can survive on their own. Importantly, however, niche markets are believed to offer a greater opportunity for firms to be innovative and thus distinguish them from the established companies offering multimedia products.

Of the sample of thirty-one interviewed firms who declared their sales revenues from electronic publications for 1995, the figures ranged from £120,000 to £2.5 million for that year. The average was £230,000. All but one is privately owned, with two firms considering flotation. Thirty firms were British-owned, with one financed by foreign (Dutch) capital.[6] Unlike Silicon Valley which has a market value of quoted companies of approximately US$450 billion, the south-east high-tech corridor boasts no such accomplishment, nor does it currently appear to exhibit such potential. Research and development comprised an average of 70 per cent of total gross sales revenues.

As remarked earlier, the robust development of the multimedia sector in the south-east is relatively recent. The flurry of 'electronic activity' by new and established firms was partly catalyzed by the perceived potential of multimedia products, and buttressed, in large part, by the exalted benefits of the 'information superhighway'. Policy makers throughout the advanced industrial world extol the promise of new opportunities for wealth creation and improved quality of life which the superhighway would help to bring about. It is widely argued that the innovative use of IT is an important step toward competitive advantage and new prosperity. Underpinning the realization of these prospects, *inter alia,* is the creation, delivery and wide availability of electronic applications and products.

One could also contend that the large middle class in the London–Brighton–Hove area provides a stimulus to the development of multimedia. The population acts as a conduit of diffusion as it is, for example, relatively well-educated and has the disposable income to purchase multimedia products. A significant number of Brighton–Hove residents commute to London; similarly, a large proportion of the Brighton–Hove workforce are from outside the area. This flow of people serves as a source of ideas by, for instance, improving contact with other suppliers and sources of multimedia products and applications. In a way, the movement of people can be compared to Michael Porter's explanation of how clusters can develop from the interaction between suppliers and customers, thereby generating new business opportunities and ways of competition (Porter 1992). In the same way, the movement of the labour force into and out of Brighton–Hove and London helps to add vitality to the sector.

But what helped to lead the multimedia firms to the south-east of Sussex? To reiterate, the chapter maintains that an analysis of entry barriers and the requirements to sustain growth is useful to an understanding of sectoral development or regional development. Stated differently, an examination of these two aspects could reflect the dynamics entailed in the ability and the accumulation of resources, both of which, arguably, are fundamental to high technology innovations. That is, a distinction could be made between the conditions required for entering a sector and the circumstances for growth, one which could provide an additional insight into regional development.

Entry barriers also will be reviewed in terms of the resources required to enter the multimedia sector. The ability to sustain market presence will be discussed in terms of, first, resources required to remain in multimedia and, second, measurements of success.

What set 'Sussex multimedia' off and sustained its growth?

This section addresses, first, the main entry barriers and, second, requirements for the continuance of business operations. The high correlation between the two sets of conditions reinforces the central notion of skills, common types of knowledge, knowledge creation and technological adjustments that have to be embraced for some form of regional development to occur.

Entry barriers to multimedia

There appears to be widespread agreement that the entry barriers to the multimedia sector are getting lower. This observation is frequently based on the continually falling prices of computing hardware and software: cheaper technology; easier access. In fact such comments misrepresent the reality of getting into the business. The most commonly mentioned entry barrier is 'keeping up with technology' (see Table 10.4). This contradicts the technical assumption that cheap computing technology has significantly lowered an entry barrier to the multimedia sector.

None the less, the progressive reduction of computer prices and the observed increase of enrolment in computing courses have contributed to the development in technological competence.[7] Several small new multimedia start-ups in the Sussex region and London, especially those offering web-based and Internet applications, are headed up by new computer science and media arts graduates. In an informal survey of 186 multimedia companies in the south east by Sussex Enterprise, more than half were found in Brighton and were new entrants formed by recent graduates.

Innovativeness, ranked as the second barrier to entry, is significant because much of the current production is considered by the firms as 'unimaginative' multimedia publications. Interestingly, many firms felt that the UK's

Table 10.4 Entry barriers

Keeping up with technology (technical ability; cost of equipment)	34%
Innovativeness	29%
Lack of financial resources	23%
Marketing	16%
Finding employees with right skills	13%
Uncertainty of payback	13%
Collection and maintenance of data	10%
Establishing brand names and track record	10%
Lack of industry knowledge	10%
Lack of reliability of product/delivery	10%
Entrepreneurial skills	6%
Piracy	6%
Lack of good management	3%
Obtaining easy credit	3%

Source: Author's research
Note: n=31.

successful international publishing industry has not, in their opinion, adequately translated into a wide mix of innovative electronic publications, with the exception perhaps of computer games. Yet, one could conjecture that, despite the apparent 'shortage' of innovative capability, the firms accept the need for 'doing the best one can' under the circumstances with the existing pool of knowledge. This provides sufficient incentive and a basis for them to enter the multimedia business.

The entry barriers listed in Table 10.4 are in descending order of significance. As can be seen, they concentrate on the significance of skills and knowledge building and technological adjustment. Importantly, the entry barriers signal, to a large degree, conditions that have to be met and overcome for development to occur along a certain 'technological trajectory' or pathway, that of multimedia. In a sense, the entry barriers imply choices that have to be made in a time of uncertainty, such as that surrounding the widespread diffusion of multimedia products and applications.

It is noteworthy that access to venture capital was scarcely mentioned. Although 'ability to obtain credit' has been noted as a barrier, albeit minimally, it was seen more in terms of bank loans than in the form of venture capital, and less as an ability to attract venture capital. Unlike Silicon Valley which is reputed to have attracted about US$1 billion venture capital in the second quarter of 1997 and which depends to a large degree on such inflows, the firms interviewed 'shrugged off' the role of venture capital. This attitude is partly explained by the fact that many of these firms are self-financing (family-owned or limited partnerships) or supported by bank loans. More importantly, the concept of venture capital is relatively new to the British and European financial scene. The European Parliament is, however, studying means to attract venture capital for the development of software and multimedia.

Innovativeness was noted as the most important requirement for remaining in business, as shown in Table 10.5. This was closely followed by financial

Table 10.5 Resources required for multimedia

Innovativeness	34%
Financial resources	32%
Management	29%
Keeping up with technology	
(technical ability; cost of equipment)	23%
Distribution channels	13%
Good marketing	13%
Good service	10%
Experience	6%
Risk taking	3%

Source: Author's research.
Note: n=31.

resources, as might be expected for new businesses. However, the emphasis given to management and to keeping up with technology – or, stated differently, technological skills – once again illustrates the importance of intangible assets.

In sum, the entry barriers to, and resources required for, multimedia reflect a set of prerequisites that producers have to meet in a certain way, perhaps generically to begin with. They include the possession of computing skills, knowledge of the industry and the basic inputs, and more specifically the creative and innovative ability to use computer technology to create applications. Stated differently, the entry barriers and required resources represent a catalogue of conditions which have to be satisfied for collective entry into a sector. The number and growth of multimedia companies in the high-tech corridor suggest that there is a 'space' here which provides for some form of regional development (Storper 1995).

Sustaining market presence and 'measuring' success

As noted above, sustaining market presence can partly be explained in terms of perceived difficulties that need to be overcome. Table 10.6 lists the conditions that have to be overcome to remain in the business. They manifest a distinct overlap with those of entry barriers and requisite resources discussed above, particularly in technological adjustment and knowledge development. The discussion so far has implied that technological adjustment and knowledge formation as embedded in entry barriers and resources are 'non-substitutable' and do not reflect an issue of allocational adjustment of resources. Therefore, the three sets of conditions imply sets of *interconnected* and overlapping conditions that need to be satisfied.

Success is naturally perceived by the firms as necessary for sustaining market presence. In this respect, the companies differentiated growth, as a measurement of success, from demand (see Table 10.7). Growth includes

Table 10.6 Difficulties with remaining in electronic publishing

Cost of development	48%
Keeping up with technology	45%
Innovativeness	32%
Business acumen	29%
Distribution	13%
Piracy	13%
Marketing	10%
Bandwidth	6%
Maintaining quality of customer support	6%
Segmented market	6%

Note: n=31.

demand, as reflected in sales, and the increase in the number and 'health' of the employees. Many firms explained that the 'health' of their employees refers to their enthusiasm and commitment to the business; lack of commitment would be deleterious to the growth of the company, even if there is demand for its products. The analogy that was frequently used was that of Silicon Valley which was, to a large degree, built by dedicated and zealous 'tekkies'. Growth was also seen in the number of opportunities seized; conversely, lack of growth was assessed in the number of opportunities missed. For instance, a Brighton company involved in computer training in its early years decided, in early 1996, to offer a specialized service involving customized web design and construction for small local firms. Its business has grown by about 5 per cent, without the need of additional staff. Interestingly, demand, as a separate measurement, was ranked fifth.

Innovativeness differed from quality of product. A good-quality product need not necessarily be innovative; it could instead contain good content, could be well arranged and 'user friendly'. Innovativeness requires special features, such as a high degree of interactivity which, the firms claim, is fundamental to the success of the electronic publishing sector. The firms unambiguously highlighted that the ability to remain in the multimedia business and to be successful was more important than of the ability to enter the sector in the first place.

It is interesting to note that a good telecommunications infrastructure (or the lack thereof) has not been mentioned as a notable entry barrier to, nor as a condition of success for, the sector. This may be because firms took it for granted that there should be a good and widely available communication infrastructure in the region and the country as a whole. Similarly, digital piracy, the 'bogeyman' of the electronic publishing sector, and a prominent cause for world-wide reform of copyright law to protect further multimedia productions from illegal reproduction, provoked scarce comment.

To sum up, the responses captured in Tables 10.4, 10.5, 10.6 and 10.7 show that there is a strong emphasis on intangible assets such as

Table 10.7 Measurement of success

Growth (sales, employees)	68%
Innovativeness	61%
Profitability	48%
Quality of product	23%
Demand	19%
Quality of customer service	19%
Management	13%
Collaborations	6%
Reliable delivery (online services)	6%

Note: n=31.

innovativeness, management, business acumen and entrepreneurial skills, technical and creative capabilities, experience in, and knowledge of the sector and other skills, etc. The evolution of these assets entails 'dynamic processes'; they demand learning, knowledge building and technological adjustment for a sector that is itself undergoing rapid technological development. The challenges that firms face to maintain their activity, and the ability of organizations to respond effectively to market conditions and competition also show the vital role of a flexible knowledge base.

What of social networking?

It is revealing that none of the voluntary responses bring up the role of networking as a necessary condition or factor for the development or maintaining of their multimedia business. When specifically queried on the importance of membership in local trade associations, several firms (about 70 per cent) claimed that they did not gain any material benefit, apart from getting to know what other companies are doing. The cost of membership did not offset the additional information gained. Thus, many of them do not belong to any trade organization, including the Brighton-based MDA. Oddly, this form of networking was not perceived as bestowing a significant contribution to their knowledge development.

Yet it was widely felt that competition in the multimedia sector does not 'smack one in the face'; rather, it creeps up on the players and eats away at market share until the company that is not innovative becomes irrelevant, or ceases to operate. However, those who professed that trade associations are important stated exactly the opposite; that membership confers an important means of knowing what competitors are doing, who the new entrants and potential competitors are, and for exchanging information. This information is also useful in securing new ideas and new contacts, as customers, suppliers or future employees. It is not yet known whether companies in the former group will become members of Wired Sussex, or will be persuaded to the merits of networking and the development of closer working relationships.

Yet when asked, in passing, why the firms 'set up shop' in Brighton–Hove, a common answer given was that there are many multimedia companies in this area, and that this growing density attracts more to it.[8] Though not explicitly spelt out, it was apparent that the stock of skilled and creative employees was an important consideration for locating to this area; in other words, an informal 'labour network.' Moreover, the growing concentration of multimedia companies in this area arguably helps to draw companies involved in similar or related businesses to it in the sense that companies 'feed off' each other. The concentration also lures 'ideas people' and 'tekkies'. In this way competition is sharpened, skills grow and information flows are further enhanced, either formally or informally. It is possible that the firms indifferent to networking perceive it as an organized formal activity, instead of one that can entail informal exchanges of information and communication and, perhaps, sharing a common 'space' of knowledge, skills and interests.

With respect to developing relationships with universities, again, the responses were mixed. As noted above, the American School has argued that an acknowledged reason for the growth of high technology is the presence of several universities and colleges. Acting as 'incubator' innovation centres and a ready source of technical personnel, these universities provide a range of opportunities for companies who are interested in further developing or applying technological innovations. The research base and high-tech activity can also enhance each other as information can flow freely between them. However, the responses do not unequivocally show that proximity to universities is of any particular significance to the development of their business, even in an area like Sussex which boasts good universities and a number of art colleges.

More than half of the thirty-one firms interviewed admit that they have few 'official' ties with universities, and instead have them on a more 'personal' level; a handful have admitted that access to, or direct formalized collaboration with, universities has resulted in new ideas and cost savings. For instance, a firm claimed that its unique method of language instruction, embodied in its language CD-ROMs, was the direct outcome of the firm's collaboration with a university. It is interesting to note how firms differentiate the role of universities in promoting networking activity into 'sources of skilled labour' and 'official ties'.

Inter-firm collaboration is markedly absent. More than 80 per cent of the firms conduct their research and development in-house, with about 15 per cent subcontracting these activities from mainly freelances. A common explanation advanced for this conduct is negative experience from inter-firm collaboration and simply the lack of need for such interaction, but such a business practice may be a symptom of single-minded competition. All the firms, however, maintained that a close customer relationship was vital to their business, and the size of their companies greatly aided a close producer-user relationship. It was also remarked that feedback from users was a significant element in the firm's planning of product lines, and its ability to keep a 'pulse' on the marketplace. In this sense, one could suggest that informal social networks do play a role, even if not clearly recognized as such by the firms interviewed.

Social networks, to sum up, are viewed in different ways by the firms. Some seemingly perceive these networks as formalized activities and exchanges, and do not feel that they matter significantly in the development of the sector. For those who regard these networks as either formal or informal organizations, they are productive and help to draw firms together. Networks such as producer-user interactions, however, were widely regarded as focal to the business.

Wired Sussex aims to act as 'an umbrella for strategic development, inward investment and good business practices' through fostering closer and coordinated working relationships. It remains to be seen if it will succeed in drawing 'network sceptical' companies into its organization, and in further developing Sussex into a greater concentration of multimedia companies. The divergent attitudes shown by companies should, however, serve as a reminder to advocates of formal networking of the importance of informal interaction. Promotion of the latter does merit attention as a parallel measure for sectoral (and regional) development.

It is curious that in the requirements for maintaining market presence, little note was made of the role of the state as a catalyst or source of financial assistance. The following section attempts to draw some policy implications, which are again based upon the responses of the firms interviewed when specifically asked about state contribution.

Policy implications: role of the state

Most firms stated that they had not considered of government help for the development of their businesses. Government assistance was perceived in terms of minimal support and overwhelming bureaucratic obstacles. Firms declared that small companies do not have the time or manpower to understand and fill in the application forms for development funds, but would indeed welcome access to them. More than 80 per cent of the firms were unaware of government programmes for small and medium-sized firms, and the few firms that were aware of these initiatives felt that information on them was vague and unhelpful. Furthermore, government grants are usually a 'one shot deal' and this form of funding was considered inadequate for start-up companies in a rapidly evolving industry. It was argued that businesses that require technological upgrading and adjustment, such as that of multimedia, need a different kind of financial assistance.

Educational multimedia producers, in particular, felt that government should exercise more 'political will' in promoting the use of multimedia products in schools. Many felt that the inconsistency of policy and lack of a coherent strategy (until recently) for the introduction of multimedia products into school curricula have left schools 'uninspired and unmotivated' in their adoption of the electronic medium.

Many also argued that civil servants, especially those of the DTI, do not understand technological development and the needs of smaller multimedia firms. They felt that the DTI's interests are often biased toward large players. Many respondents, however, acknowledged that smaller firms are partly responsible for their lack of input as they are not organized among themselves to present their collective interests to government. Despite this, most of the firms also admitted that they are not members of the main national trade associations as they are dubious of the benefit of these organizations (see page 232).

The role of the state in promoting regional development was not specifically addressed in the interviews. However, responses included: 'the DTI should ensure "fair play" in the industry through competition policy and an equitable regulatory framework' and 'there should be consistency and a coordinated strategy which emphasizes the use of domestically produced multimedia material'. Such perceptions imply that nationally, (or locally) derived rules, expectations, values and public institutions matter for development. One could conclude from them that regional firms do consider that governments should play a role in promoting regional development, since these responses emanate from regional multimedia developers.

Policy suggestions for the role of government in fostering development based on these considerations include:

- Provide *sustained* funding for capital equipment and development.
- Establish a national curriculum that rigorously includes the use of electronic publications and training of teachers.
- Ring fence funds for multimedia development.
- Provide useful information on developments and implications of legislative and regulatory developments in intellectual property, telecommunication tariffs, etc.
- Provide reliable information on the electronic publishing and multimedia industry, world-wide and national.
- Provide clear information on government schemes.
- Reduce the 'red tape' for grant and funds applications.
- Provide more tax incentives for small and medium-sized firms.
- Encourage the formation or availability of venture capital.

Conclusion

The concentration of multimedia sectoral and related activity in the south-east high-tech corridor has resulted from its ability to meet a set of conditions, represented in this chapter by entry barriers and resource requirements for sustaining market presence. The chapter argued that analysis of these conditions shows that development, be it national, regional or local, entails dynamic processes, principally of knowledge and skill building, and technological adjustments. These are particularly evident in rapidly evolving high-tech sectors.

Furthermore, the sample of company responses has shown that entry barriers and resource requirements have a great many features in common. This reinforces the need for compliance with an ensemble of conditions before any sectoral activity can take off, whether locally or regionally. The ability of firms to satisfy the conditions cumulatively creates a 'space' in which further development can proceed.

Recent attempts by the Sussex region to institute formal sectoral networks, such as Wired Sussex, emphasize the perceived contribution of such formal institutions to the vitality of regional development. Yet the chapter has shown that the significance of formal networks is not unanimously agreed by producers. Networks involving direct collaboration with universities are also sporadic. More importance is commonly attributed to informal networks, such as those of labour networks and user-producer relationships. The proximity of several universities and colleges to the region's multimedia producers is regarded as a boon as they are vast repositories of potential skilled labour. Networks such as Wired Sussex could reveal the mutual benefit arising from strategic and collaborative relationships among multimedia producers, and the value of formal networking. At the same time, attention should not be diverted from the utility of informal networks, as evidenced by the successful development of multimedia firms in the south-east region through this form of activity.

The proper role of the state in regional multimedia development is seen in terms of targeted and sustained funding. Firms have commonly charged that the sector is evolving rapidly and requires technological and skills adjustment. It was felt that a one-off financial assistance hardly even begins to address the needs of new entrants to the sector. Firms also asserted that public information on international and national multimedia developments would be useful to their businesses in terms of, for instance, knowledge building.

As a tentative conclusion, there does not appear to be any overwhelming reason or reasons for the growth of multimedia activity in the south-east. Instead, what we have seen is a set of overlapping conditions that need to be meet in order to contribute to regional development. Finally, with regard to the activities of the south-east high-tech corridor, it is reasonable to conclude the companies have a long way to travel to approach the gates of Silicon Valley. But the will and interest in further 'wiring' this area continue to be vibrant. According to Anna Pedroza of Wired Sussex, the Brighton–Hove area can realistically be described as 'silicon beach' for the time being.

Notes:

1 Electronic publications are multimedia products in CD-ROM and online formats, including applications for the Internet. The terms multimedia and electronic publishing will be used interchangeably in this chapter.
2 'Management of intellectual property: the case of UK electronic publishing and biotechnology SMEs' funded by the UK Economic and Social Research Council and the DTI. We wish to clarify that the research was not specifically aimed at investigating reasons for regional development of multimedia.
3 There is, however, no breakdown of the figure into income group and professional groups.
4 See: 'Regions Should Follow Sussex Lead in New Media, says DTI': http://www.wiredsussex.com/news/news43.htm.

5 These numbers are based on 1995–96 figures. Since then, the author is already aware of the establishment of several new multimedia companies in London and the Brighton–Hove area, particularly those offering Internet-based services, such as in web design, instalment and maintenance, and specialized Internet services.

6 This company has recently terminated its multimedia activities.

7 According to recent figures published by the UK Higher Education Funding Council for Education, the number of students who have graduated with computing degrees registered an approximate 40 per cent increase between 1992 and 1996.

8 It is worth repeating that the project for which the above empirical evidence was gathered did not aim to establish the reasons for regional development of multimedia.

References

Electronic Publishing Services (1993) *Publishing in the UK,* London; EPS.

Mansell, R. and Tang, P. (1994) *Electronic Information Services: Competitiveness in the United Kingdom,* London: Department of Trade and Industry.

Markusen, A. R., Hall, P., and Glasmeier, A. (1986) *High Tech America: The What, How, Where and Why of the Sunrise Industries,* Boston: Unwin and Allen.

Parliamentary Office for Science and Technology (1995) *Information 'Superhighways': the UK National Information Infrastructure,* London: POST.

Porter, M. (1992) *The Competitive Advantage of Nations,* Cambridge, Mass.: Harvard University Press.

Storper, M. (1995) 'The resurgence of regional economies, ten years later: the region as a nexus of untraded interdependencies,' *European Urban and Regional Studies* 2, 3: 191–221.

Tang, P. (1996) *Electronic Information Services: The Public as a Client,* Report prepared for the Organization for Economic Cooperation and Development, Paris.

11

THE MULTIMEDIA INDUSTRY IN SWEDEN AND THE EMERGING STOCKHOLM CLUSTER

Åke Sandberg

Introduction

The evolution of new media brings changes not only to the traditional media sector, but also to communications, control and influence in all kinds of organizations and enterprises. It raises fundamental questions of information and communication technologies (ICT), organization and our society and may be a key element in industrial and regional development.

The new media companies see considerable potential for expansion, a view also found in the political sphere, at the regional, national and EU levels. It is the new ICT companies, particularly in their interaction with the media, that will create future employment and help generate a powerful process of renewal. The new media and ICT firms are information-based companies, and a large majority of their employees are highly-educated. They often operate in networks and regional and local clusters. They are modern and they may point the way ahead for other sectors.

This chapter is based on the report from the first comprehensive Swedish study of the multimedia and Internet industry, covering companies that produce CD-ROMs and solutions for the Internet and other networks within and between organizations.[1] It has its background in studies in the field of newspaper production in the 1970s and 1980s and of new forms of company and work organization in which new media now play a central part.[2] It focuses on this emerging new media industry, the challenges and the opportunities in this sector nationally and regionally in Sweden.

New media companies in our Swedish study identify three main impediments to expansion and development: a shortage of qualified staff, a shortage of venture capital and gaps in their customers' knowledge. All three are areas where political decisions about industrial, regional and educational policy can help create favourable conditions.

ICT has brought changes to the work and production of the traditional *media* (the press, radio and TV), including publishing on the Internet and on CD-ROMs. Digitization is a technical prerequisite for this change. The technical advances interact with other basic developments such as internationalization, liberalization, privatization, deregulation and the greater flexibility of production and labour markets. This results in a sectoral shift and the convergence and integration of traditional media industries with parts of the new media industry.

These advances in new media allow substantial changes to be made in *all kinds* of organizations and sectors, and not only in the media industry. They offer new opportunities for presentation and interaction together with 'electronic networks' for communication within and between companies, and between people both as individuals and as citizens. Communication, trust, coordination, control, influence and democracy are all affected by new technology and the new network organization.

There is thus real optimism, although, it seems this does not apply to profit margins, which are causing problems for both the large media corporations' investments in interactive media and the smaller new media companies.

The new media industry in Sweden

The study targeted companies that produce new media: CD-ROMs and Internet solutions. We did not include, for example, suppliers of Internet equipment, hardware and software companies and training companies unless they were also producers in our sense (see Annex, page 249). We identified some 750 companies, roughly 600 of which proved to be active in the sector as 'producers of new media'. Half of these companies answered the questionnaire.

The number 600 is a low estimate of the total of companies in Sweden. Our resources were too limited to build a complete database, and more time and effort would certainly have added more companies to the list. Indeed, a more detailed search for new media companies in the Stockholm region resulted in almost twice as many companies as those we identified.

Sweden and Stockholm appear to have a comparatively large number of companies in this sector. Sweden is also well ahead in mobile telephone ownership, Internet use, computer use and the like (see Teldok report no. 115, on Sweden, Österman and Timander 1997). Their use is not evenly spread across the social spectrum, but various initiatives help to close the information gaps on an access basis. These include the so-called LO-Computer (a bargain-priced package for union members that includes an Internet server subscription), discounted computers made available by employers and the installation of computers in schools.

It is likely that broad knowledge and access to new information and communication technology also creates favourable conditions for the development of the new media sector. As we shall see, the companies in this sector consider the lack of competent personnel and their customers' lack of knowledge to be the most serious impediments to their growth. Infrastructure and telecommunications are not seen as a major impediment. Thanks to its relatively early and on-going deregulation, Sweden finds itself, in fact, in a good position to exploit present and potential market opportunities. This is particularly the case for Stockholm with its municipal fibre cable deployment programme.

Company size and turnover

The new media companies are small, with average annual revenues in 1996 of just over SEK 3 million. However, a rapid growth in turnover is forecast: in 1997 it was estimated at SEK 6 million and the forecast for 1998 is SEK 11 million. In these years the median turnover rose from SEK 1 to 3 and then to 5 million. Thus the forecast is for an exceptional growth rate approaching 100 per cent a year.

In some cases, companies with other activities will also run a new media operation as a small part of their overall business. All in all, the share of new media is only 5 per cent of these companies' 1996 turnover, but is likewise expected to double to 10 per cent by the end of 1998 (see figure 11.1).

Of the more than 200 companies answering the respective question 33 per cent produce solely for the Internet. In 1996 they had a lower turnover in new media than the average for the sector, at just over SEK 2 million in comparison to SEK 3 million for the sector. When the Internet was included as part of the business of companies which had no other areas of activities than new media, such companies had an average total turnover of SEK 5 million in comparison to the sector's average total turnover of SEK 71 million.

The median number of employees in new media companies in 1996 was six. It is estimated at ten for 1998. The corresponding figures for the workforce overall are seventeen and twenty-seven respectively. This includes all employees irrespective of occupation; many companies have a mixed production, which makes it difficult to identify how many people are working on new media. The increase in the number of employees is significantly lower than the rise in turnover, and companies appear to count on an increase in turnover per employee.

Regional distribution

New media companies are very much a big city phenomenon.[3] All in all, 64 per cent of Sweden's new media companies are situated in the three largest cities: 47 per cent in greater Stockholm, 9 per cent in Göteborg, and 8 per

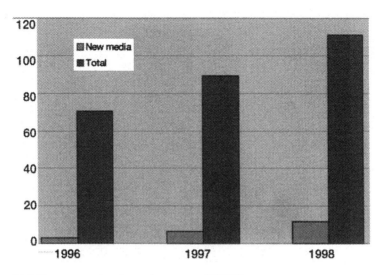

Figure 11.1 Turnover and estimated turnover (MSEK)

cent in Malmö-Lund. Almost 11 per cent of the new media companies are located in the four other university towns of Linköping, Umeå, Uppsala and Luleå. Thus the seven university towns together have a total of 75 per cent of the companies, with the remaining 25 per cent spread around the country (see Figure 11.2).

Although production is in bit format (0s and 1s) which is easy to transmit electronically, we find a particularly high geographic concentration of these companies in the big cities and the university towns. There are other factors that encourage the growth of local and regional clusters of new media companies. These factors include the availability of skills and employees, infrastructure, a creative environment involving other media enterprises in advertising and publishing, companies in related sectors and the location of customers and head offices of larger companies in the vicinity.

Specialized companies, many of them subcontractors to the new media producers studied in this chapter are, and will probably continue to be, more widely dispersed throughout the country.

Stockholm's multimedia cluster

Preconditions for the Stockholm new media cluster

Central Stockholm dominates the picture with as much as 33 per cent of new media companies. Greater Stockholm (central Stockholm and the surrounding suburbs) houses almost half of all those in Sweden (47 per cent). Several factors contribute to the favourable development of the Stockholm new media cluster,

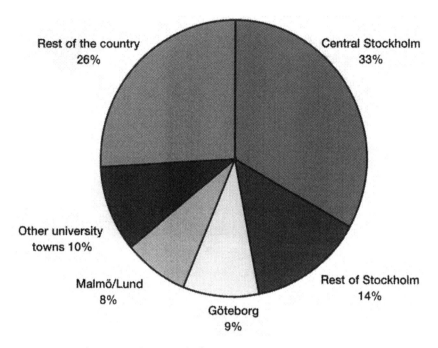

Figure 11.2 The geographic spread of companies

and help to make it one of Europe's leading regions in this new industry.

Stockholm is the business and administrative centre of Sweden, a country which is among the most advanced in Internet use, and the number of cellular phones, computers and modems per capita. Stockholm also contains a domi-nating part of the Swedish media industry including radio and TV, publishing, printing and advertising.

Liberalization and early deregulation of the telecom market (1993) led to tough competition between network operators and low service prices in the telecom market. About twenty foreign telecom operators have established operations in Sweden.

One special feature of Stockholm is the public company Stokab, owned by the City of Stockholm and the Stockholm City Council. Stokab has built a fibre-optic infrastructure, leasing fibre to categories such as telecoms, cable TV, cellular phone operators and others. In this way all operators are given equal and cheap access to the Stockholm telecom market. Fibre-optic cable today reaches city blocks, major suburban centres, all upper secondary schools and so on; within the near future it will be available to all hospitals.[4] Also the state telecom company Telia has a fibre-optic network from which capacity can be leased.

In order to facilitate the development and the use of new media in the Stockholm region, a special ATM 155 mbps service with both 10 mbps

Internet and 10 mbps point-to-point Ethernet is provided by Telenordia (with fibre leased from Stokab) in a service called Media City Net. This service allows new media companies to link to their customers and suppliers with a highspeed capacity for video, sound and data transfer. Big corporations generally have high capacity internal networks. These low-cost broadband services now allow companies to use extranets for efficient cooperation with new media companies. In addition, low-cost broadband allows for effective network-based education and competence development. There are additional examples of broadband services in the Stockholm region. For example MFS Worldcom offers a 2 mbps service to the media industry, and Sonera (formerly Telecom Finland) offers video streaming services.

In a survey of Stockholm companies' opinions about preconditions for production in the region, the most important was telecommunications. This factor was also the one given the highest quality rating: 88 per cent of the companies said telecoms in Stockholm are excellent or good.[5]

Stockholm houses the headquarters and several factories of Ericsson, which has over 100,000 employees world-wide, as well as a major R & D cellular phone research centre run by Nokia. Advanced research in ICT and new media is found at the Royal Institute of Technology, at the research institutes SICS (Swedish Institute of Computer Science Intelligent Systems Lab) and SISU (Swedish Institute for Systems Development), and also in a special interactive media research institute to be located in Stockholm and the southern city of Malmö. Telia, the former state monopoly telecom operator located in Stockholm, has its own new media research division and has cooperated closely with Ericsson in the past.

Stockholm new media companies

If we assume that Stockholm houses 50 per cent of the just over 600 or so companies we have located in Sweden, there are some 300 companies in the capital, at a conservative estimate. In comparison, one of the foremost new media centres, Manhattan in New York, is estimated to have just over 2,200 new media companies, by a very broad definition that encompasses content design and development, marketing, distribution, electronic commerce, software development, and tools for content development as well as the service and support services for new media (see Heydebrand, this volume).[6] It has been estimated that there may be around 700 new media producers out of the 2,200 in Manhattan. Further information from the New York questionnaire survey is that just over 60 per cent of all companies in New York are involved in content design and development, including specialist subcontractors.

Stockholm-based Computer Media Consultants (CMC) estimates that in the autumn of 1997 more than 900 new media related companies were located in the Stockholm region (a somewhat larger area than greater Stockholm, including, for example, the university town of Uppsala). This includes both the core of new media producers as defined in our survey and firms specializing in digital radio, video, animations and so on. A little over 700 of those firms are located in central Stockholm, among them three of the largest in the country: WM-data Education, Spray and Icon Media Lab. The majority of the companies are clustered in the northern part of central Stockholm (Norrmalm, Östermalm and Vasastan) and some are located in the harbour area (Frihamnen) and in southern central Stockholm (on the island of Södermalm). Half of the companies were founded during the last two years.

A rough estimate by CMC is that of the 700 Stockholm companies about 550 are new media producers as we define them and the rest are mainly specialized subcontractors. The difference from our estimate of 300 new media producers may be explained by the fact that the CMC figures are based on a much more detailed and ambitious inventory of companies and new media departments in larger firms. Differences in classification may also be part of the explanation.

New media companies form production networks

Three-quarters of the companies say that they cooperate with other new media companies working on new products. This cooperation is most common with firms specializing in advertising and PR, and over 50 per cent of new media companies have experienced such collaboration. Other partners in cooperation are companies that specialize in video/film, software development and graphic design. 60 per cent of companies that collaborate with other companies usually work only with companies in one or possibly two different categories.

Many of the firms are members of the association Promise (Producers of Interactive Media in Sweden), which organizes courses and seminars and has working groups in areas like education and quality development. It has recently started pub evenings for informal contacts and networking.

Large companies work in close cooperation with specialized subcontractors, and collaboration among small companies enables them to handle large commissions. This applies for example to the Baltic island of Gotland where efforts are being made to develop a regional cluster with companies specializing in different elements of new media production. Gotland in many ways has close links with Stockholm, just half an hour away by air. In further analysing our survey data and case studies our intention is to look more closely into the regional aspects of production networks and the relation of regional networks to hierarchies on a national and global scale (Amin and Thrift 1994).

Collaboration in production and trust between companies are important for the emerging network economy in the network society that Manuel

Castells describes. Cooperation and confidence can be expected to be particularly important in a sector such as new media, where production chains are long and a wide range of skills and actors have to interact under severe pressure of time. Highly-developed cooperation of this kind, despite the competition for contracts, thus appears to characterize regions and successful clusters of companies in the new media sector. Several studies presented at the Stuttgart symposium indicate this.

The products and the type of assignment

Among the types of media, the Internet and intranets (communication networks within companies) constitute an overwhelming majority with nearly 80 per cent of all production in the companies covered by the study. The Internet alone amounts to 72 per cent of the products. CD-ROMs have a share of 16 per cent and disks of 5 per cent.

Calculating the various media's share in turnover may show a different picture. A typical CD-ROM production can cost SEK 500,000, while many Internet products are priced at around SEK 100,000. However, intranet and Extranet products for companies can be costly.

Most products are advertising and company presentations, with the combined share of these two types of production totalling over 50 per cent. Education accounts for as much as 26 per cent, while games and entertainment products make up only 5 per cent (see Figure 11.3).

Companies that produce exclusively for the Internet are almost entirely engaged in advertising and company presentations, which comprise nearly 80 per cent of their production (advertising 46 per cent, company presentations 33 per cent).

The picture of Internet production coincides with the way companies use their home pages. The average figures for home page use in the food, mechanical engineering and electronics industries, transport services and computer consultants show that 88 per cent use home pages to give information about products and services, 70 per cent to provide background information about the company and 22 per cent to give customers the opportunity to order goods and services (electronic commerce). The first two figures are notably higher for the computer consulting companies at 96 and 84 per cent respectively. This is a sector that may be assumed to be similar to the new media sector.

More than half the companies (56 per cent) state that they have other extensive activities in addition to new media productions, and over 60 per cent of them specialize in one of these other activities. ICT consultation is the dominant activity, involving close to 40 per cent of the companies.

Around 20 per cent of the companies operate in advertising, film/video/TV/audiovisual, graphic design and management consultation. Only 10 per cent are involved in publishing, and the same percentage in graphic produc-

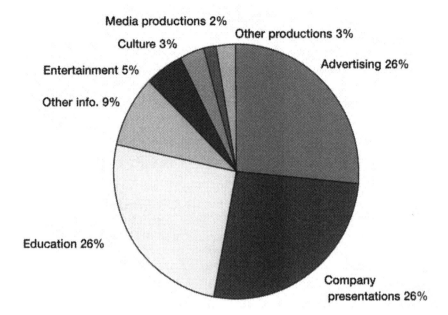

Figure 11.3 Nature of new media production

tion. However, nearly 40 per cent of the companies have substantial opera-tions in quite different, unrelated fields. In emerging innovative sectors, entrepreneurs from quite unrelated sectors frequently see growth potential in a new area (see Figure 11.4).

Some 80 per cent of the products are customer assignments and 20 per cent for the open market. Private companies are in a large majority among cus-tomers, nearly 80 per cent. The public sector and non-profit organizations account for about 10 per cent each. About 45 per cent of commissioned work comes from customer companies with up to 100 employees and 36 per cent from companies with over 500 employees.

Challenges and possibilities for the companies

As Figure 11.5 shows, nearly 30 per cent of the companies identified three factors as major obstacles to their company's development: the shortage of qualified staff, the shortage of venture capital and the customers' lack of knowledge about new media possibilities.

The most widely reported problem is customer knowledge. 80 per cent of the companies feel that insufficient knowledge among customers is a difficulty that obstructs development. Between 65 and 50 per cent of companies identify a shortage of qualified staff and of venture capital, telecommunications and other media technology as a major problem or at

246

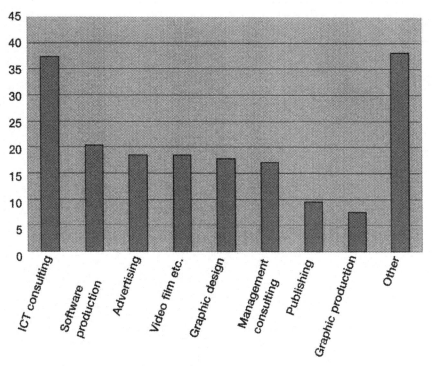

Figure 11.4 Companies' other main business activities

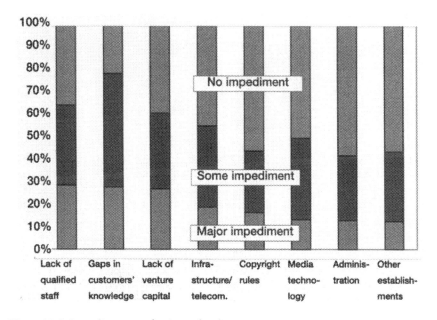

Figure 11.5 Impediments to business development

least as some impediment to expansion. Copyright law, an excessive number of firm foundations in the sector, and the company's own administration are all seen as lesser problems. They are mentioned as impediments by just over 40 per cent of companies. In view of the international discussion in this sector, it is surprising that there are not far more companies that see copyright issues as a problem.

The latest questionnaires distributed in our survey contained more detailed alternative answers to the questions on impediments to company development. This part of the survey produced just over 100 responses. Generally speaking, the companies in this group tend to think that there are not so many 'major impediments'. The greatest problems were again reported to be insufficient knowledge among customers and the lack of qualified personnel and of venture capital. Only 2 per cent of the companies said that their own administration was a significant problem, but we had several alternative answers here which could in part be seen as more detailed descriptions of administrative problems.

Close to 20 per cent gave tax regulations as a major impediment, while 55 per cent say they are no problem at all. Only 6 per cent see labour laws as a major difficulty, 26 per cent see them as presenting some difficulty and close to 70 per cent consider them to be no problem at all. It must be emphasized here that these figures are based on responses from a smaller sample of companies than the total survey.[7]

Conclusions

The aggregate picture is one of a large number of small new media companies and some larger companies that have new media as a minor area of activity. The companies are gathered in clusters in the biggest cities. Stockholm is the leading location with almost half of Sweden's new media companies, and one third of the companies are located in its downtown area. There is considerable optimism about future revenue growth with 50 to 100 per cent cited by several companies. Over half of the products are advertising and company presentations. 80 per cent are commissions from customers and 80 per cent of these customers are private sector companies.

The major difficulties for their development, indicated by almost 30 per cent of the companies, are the shortage of qualified staff and of venture capital, and lack of knowledge in the customer companies. A small segment of the survey shows that tax rules are seen as a major difficulty by 20 per cent of companies and labour laws by only 6 per cent.

One lasting impression, apart from the need for a better supply of capital, is the need for better education, in society generally and in terms of in-depth education for the clients. Most crucial of all is advanced, in-depth training in the different specializations and occupations that, working together, produce advanced interactive and multimedia solutions.

Another lasting impression is the emerging regional clustering of firms, especially the dominance of the Stockholm region.

The considerable confidence about future expansion which the companies express in the survey may, by and large, be justified in the long term. But some individual companies will certainly run into difficulties, and the sector as a whole will have periods of consolidation and self-analysis. This is what may be expected of a young and entrepreneurial sector. We shall be in a position to give a more detailed picture of the changes when the study is repeated, enabling us to make comparisons over time and identify trends.

Annex: the design of the study

The study was carried out in the late spring and autumn of 1997. Our database of new media and Internet companies, contained a total of about 750 companies. About half came from the Promise list of companies in this sector and the other half were taken from a list of Internet companies published by the journal *Dagens Industri* in the spring of 1997.

Promise is a sectoral organization that is part of SINF (The Swedish Association of Industries). It is a non-profit body that seeks to affiliate 'producers of interactive media' who create CD-ROMs and disks or web pages for the Internet, intranets or extranets; that is to say a finished product for a customer or for the market. This product range does not include specialized subcontractors that work exclusively with film or sound, nor hardware suppliers, operators or service companies such as training institutes. Promise seeks to affiliate companies that have such a 'producer operation' irrespective of whether it is an entirely independent company, a subsidiary or a division of a larger company. On this basis, Promise has produced lists of about 400 companies including, for example, new media departments in advertising agencies and publishing houses, but not such departments in newspapers. We have opted to apply the same limitations, but we have added some newspapers to the list.

This means that from the list of 500 'Internet companies' published by *Dagens Industri,* we have included 'producers' of the same kind as are included in the Promise list. The gross list was based on all companies in the Sunet list of Swedish Internet domains, under the Internet heading, under the main heading of companies in the computer sector. This was supplemented with the help of punkt.se's list and *Dagens Industri* also made its own contacts with companies they knew of. All these companies were telephoned, and all those that provided additional details were published in a separate Internet supplement. The list was also made available through the *Dagens Industri* Website, where companies were able to register themselves online, which some ten companies did. Our sample includes most companies that were listed under the headings of 'Consultants' and 'Content providers', quite a number under the heading of 'Retailers of Internet Connections', and a few under 'Operators', 'Internet cafés', and 'Hardware Suppliers'. Our sample was made on the basis of the keywords in the list and the company's product/service.

Future studies may of course review the definition of the sample and consider, for example, specialized subcontractors and service companies for the sector, as well as departments in traditional media companies such as newspapers. Similarly, systematic efforts should be made to identify new media departments in consulting and ICT companies. This would be an important component to a follow-up study.

We combined a number of methods in order to obtain responses to the questionnaire. We sent questionnaires by post, offered an opportunity to 'click' in electronic responses on the Promise Internet homepage, sent out questionnaires by e-mail and carried out telephone interviews. We started with the Promise list and continued with the *Dagens Industri* list. There may therefore be more Internet-oriented companies in the later interviews and more CD-ROM-oriented companies in the early interviews.

Our survey reveals that some of the companies on the Promise and *Dagens Industri* lists were not really 'producers of multimedia/interactive media'. Other companies on the lists cannot be found, and appear to have ceased trading. We estimate the number of companies in the database that were active as producers in the new media sector at the time of the study to be just over 600. We have received a total of 320 responses to the questionnaire, an estimated response frequency of about 50 per cent. This may be considered a relatively high response rate in this new sector with its numerous small companies and one-man businesses and the large proportion of newly-founded companies. However, we have yet to examine how representative our sample is of the sector as a whole. No reliable and complete list of companies is available. However, there is no particular reason to assume that we should have received a systematically distorted selection of respondents.

Because there was only limited time in which to identify companies, it is reasonable to assume, as discussed above, that there were more new media companies in Sweden at the time of our study than the 600 we found.

Notes

Many people have been involved in carrying out the study on which this chapter is based. First I would like to extend my particular thanks to those who, despite the pressures of their work schedules, found the time to answer the questionnaire, and to doctoral student Christofer Edling who skillfully and promptly carried out the data processing and also read and commented on early drafts of the manuscript. On the Stockholm section of this contribution I got valuable suggestions from Ronald Nameth, consultant in Stockholm. The survey was made in co-operation with the sectoral body, Promise (Producers of Interactive Media in Sweden) and the journal *Vision*.

1 The full Swedish original was published in June 1998 as Åke Sandberg: 'Nya medier', Arbetslivsinstitutet, Stockholm, http://www.niwl.se/home/sandberg/. It was also published as Via Teldok 34, http://www.teldok.framfab.se. An English translation of the report has been published.
2 This has been described in books such as Sandberg *et al.* 1992 and Sandberg 1995.
3 The areas were defined by the two first figures of the postal code.
4 www.stokab.se, visited 7 July 1998.
5 Companies with 5–499 employees were surveyed, with a response rate of 80 per cent (USK 1996).
6 *New York New Media Industry Survey* (1997).
7 From the latest interviews we have just over 100 responses to these more detailed alternative answers on impediments to development. It is likely that among these companies there is a greater dominance of Internet productions than in our database as a whole.

References

Amin, A. and Thrift, N. (eds) (1994) *Globalization, Institutions and Regional Development in Europe,* London: Oxford University Press.

Castells, M. (1996) *The Rise of the Network Society,* London: Blackwell.

Nameth, R. (1997) *Stockholm Region New Media Industry Survey,* Computer Media Consultants, Stockholm, <ranameth @oden.se>.

New York City Economic Development Corporation *et al.* (1997) *New York New Media Industry Survey 1997*, New York New Media Association, New York: The New York City Economic Development Corporation.

Sandberg, Å., Broms, G., Grip, A., Steen, J., Sundström, L. and Ullmark, P. (1992) *Technological Change and Co-determination in Sweden,* Philadelphia: Temple University Press.

Sandberg, Å. (ed.) (1995) *Enriching Production,* Ashgate: Avebury.

USK (1996) *Stockholm och företagen, Utrednings- och statistik-kontoret,* Stockholm: Stockholms stad.

Österman, T. and Timander, J. (1997) 'Internetanvändningen i Sveriges befolkning', *Teldok Report* 115, Stockholm.

12

CREATING A MULTIMEDIA CLUSTER IN CARDIFF BAY

Philip Cooke and Gwawr Hughes

Introduction

In this chapter we will explore the evolution of the multimedia industry in Wales (UK) and particularly in Cardiff, the capital city, which is the centre of gravity of the broader print and electronic media, software and creative arts industries serving Wales itself and supplying intermediate users and final consumers in the rest of the UK, Europe and the world.

Multimedia is an important growth sector combining technological advances made during the 1980s that link computing, communication, media and the creative arts. It is a complex industry, ranging from TV, film and video production, animation, software design, computer services, creative arts and multimedia production to specialist insurance, accountancy and legal services geared towards meeting the needs of the industry. Relatively few firms specialize solely in the production of multimedia products, but many are involved in multimedia inputs or final products as an important adjunct to their core competence. This is especially true of the numerous TV, film and video production companies.

Multimedia production companies are highly interdependent and, for reasons to be explained in both theoretical and empirical terms, they tend to operate in geographically concentrated clusters. Companies involved in the multimedia and support industries in Cardiff employ some 2,000 workers with a combined turnover of £90 million. As will be shown, the majority of firms have fewer than six employees and an annual turnover of less than £500,000. Not surprisingly, the industry is young, with most firms having been established after 1981, many as spin-offs of other firms while some are former traders re-established under a new name.

Historically speaking, a relatively large proportion became established as TV, film or video companies at the time when the fourth terrestrial TV channel was established (1982). The UK government's Broadcasting Act of 1990 required broadcasters such as the British Broadcasting Corporation (BBC) to outsource 25 per cent of TV production to independent production companies. These deregulatory actions led to the emergence of a substantial number of independent media, and subsequently multimedia, firms in Wales, as in media cities elsewhere in the UK, notably London.

The industry is thus a text-book example of the emergence of a new mini-agglomeration clustering in a particular area to take advantage of the skills and market-opportunities that were formerly the monopoly of the large public service broadcasting companies. This process has been further stimulated by new quasi-market principles being applied to the BBC, the restructuring of which has produced significant reductions in direct employment. It was further boosted by the new process of franchising commercial TV channels according to market principles, whereby the government licence to supply regional broadcasting was organized by competitive tender, with success going to the highest bidder. This meant that a further round of layoffs and redundancies affected firms such as HTV, the commercial broadcasting company for Wales. Appropriately skilled and qualified producers and technical staff thus formed a further round of new firms to augment the earlier start-ups in the media and multimedia industries.

In what follows, we shall elaborate upon the theoretical and historical dimensions of the processes involved in the emergence of the Cardiff multimedia cluster. In doing so, we will point to some of the classic features of the cluster in terms of 'proximity capital' (Crevoisier 1997), agglomeration dynamics and the importance of tacit knowledge exchange in a sector characterized by high creativity (Malmberg and Maskell 1997, Scott 1998) and the sourcing of highly specialized, firm-specific inputs through cooperation as well as competitive modes of economic coordination (Dei Ottati 1994, 1996). We will draw upon the results of a recent survey of the Cardiff multimedia industry commissioned from us by Cardiff Bay Development Corporation (Hughes 1997). This is a special agency charged by the UK government with waterfront regeneration and the refurbishment of heritage architecture for adaptive re-use. It has played a significant role, indirectly and directly, in shaping Cardiff's multimedia cluster.

Theoretical issues

In general terms, the reasons for small and medium-sized enterprises to cluster in geographical space, first adumbrated by Marshall (1919), are now quite well understood. Marshall pointed to the external economies of scale and scope that could be accessed in industrial districts in terms of three key advantages:

- Specialization by many firms in different aspects of the production of a single product range, with firms engaged in complementary business

activities forming clusters of subcontractors in a localized area and the
same industry.
- Formal and informal communication occurring rapidly and efficiently
  because of the localized 'industrial atmosphere' of common understanding and knowledge existing among firms, workers and the community.
- Skilled labour capable of flexible application being readily available in
  the district because of the dominant industry specialization and familiarity with appropriate technical application.

Among the important developments in theorization of the rationale for
agglomeration, the following are particularly central.

Enterprise support

Sebastiano Brusco (1990) made the key distinction between industrial district models Mark I and Mark II. The former is more organically developed
and was described by Becattini (1979) as a close correlate of the Marshallian
industrial district which, for analytical purposes, should be understood not in
terms of the primacy of the practices of the single firm but rather the cluster
of interconnected firms located in a small area. The main form of interaction
concerns the commissioning and subcontracting of work amongst the firms
and cooperation over accountancy, payroll administration and taxation
returns with a representative artisan's association. Knowledge and information flow informally in a manner cognate to Marshall's concept of 'industrial
atmosphere'.

The Mark II district is more consciously organized, with a recognition of
the need for intervention from the public enterprise support infrastructure in
respect of enhancing the 'absorptive capacity' (Cohen and Levinthal 1990) of
firms and districts towards market and technological innovation. This stage
is marked by the establishment of centres providing real services to district
firms. An example would be the Emilia-Romagna Textiles Innovation Center
(CITER) at Carpi, providing computer-aided design and manufacture services
to firms in the knitwear industry.

Agglomeration dynamics

Recent research by Malmberg and Maskell (1997) throws interesting light
upon evolutionary processes in agglomerations and refers to important features of inclusion and exclusion processes amongst firms concerning tacit
knowledge transmission. On the basis of detailed research at local level in
Scandinavian countries, they show that industry has become more geographically specialized over the past twenty-five years. Thus, investigation of the
widely-observed urban–rural shift of industry also showed that, as industry

expanded away from cities, it also tended to become more sectorally focused in specific, specialized industrial localities. This complements theoretical work by Krugman (1995) whose main thesis regarding spatial development is that under conditions of imperfect competition, uncertain information and increasing returns to scale, firms in specific industrial sectors will tend to specialize their geographical location to gain from external economies of proximity. They further show that this process does not necessarily mean that information and tacit knowledge flow like a free commodity. This is because of asset stock accumulation whereby advanced firms only exchange proprietary know-how with other firms which have equivalent and complementary assets to exchange. In this way, firms in agglomerations protect themselves from rapid imitation of products and processes by newcomers, but bind themselves closely to other firms on a basis of reciprocity, reputation and high trust. Hence, cooperation is not necessarily a ubiquitous feature of agglomerations and there is, even amongst small and medium-sized enterprises (SMEs), something of a hierarchy of dominance and dependence.

Transaction costs

An essential contribution to the analysis of the function of proximity for firms is made by Scott (1996), Storper and Scott (1995) and Storper (1995) in their work on transaction costs. North (1993) estimated that in 1970 transaction costs accounted for 45 per cent of Gross Domestic Product in the USA. He argued that this was one area in which the efficient use of capital was being hampered even though it was a source of growth and employment in the service industries. In this respect he demonstrated ways in which services are parasitical upon manufacturing, though it must also be borne in mind that a substantial portion of such transaction costs occur in trade between service companies themselves.

North identified situations in which transaction costs could be reduced by greater reliance upon conventions which are informal, even tacit, codes by means of which economic actors trust each other, thereby reducing expenditure upon formal contracts. He also identified adherence to 'rules of the game', rather more codified knowledge about acceptable and unacceptable business practices, transgression of which also frequently incurs excessive transaction costs. Both conventions and rules of the game are means of reducing inefficiencies amongst businesses by reducing areas of uncertainty or knowledge imperfection. They thus reduce unwelcome overhead expenditure incurred through transaction costs.

Storper usefully develops these notions in a spatial context by reference to Dosi's (1988) concept of 'untraded interdependencies' whereby firms in close proximity engage in non-monetary exchange such as informal know-how trading, thus gaining advantage from localized economies of externalization.

This leads to the conclusion that, 'The greater the substantive complexity, irregularity, uncertainty, unpredictability and uncodifiability of transactions, the greater their sensitivity to geographical distance' (Scott and Storper 1995).

Learning-intensive contexts often imply close geographical proximity. Such contexts should include highly innovative or creative types of economic activity.

Learning economies

A great deal of research on innovation practices of firms shows that, first, firms learn most of relevance to their business from other firms, notably customers and suppliers (see for example Braczyk *et al.* 1998). However, they increasingly learn also from universities, research institutes and technology centres with which they interact. According to Lundvall and Johnson (1994) this involves interactions among firms and knowledge-centres, including industrial research contracts, personnel exchanges and the funding of scholarships.

Specific kinds of agglomeration can occur, focused spatially upon university settings. Very good examples of these are described for the Nordic countries by authors such as Jones-Evans and Klofsten (1997), Lindholm (1997) and Jussila and Segerståhl (1997). In these cases from, respectively, Linköping and Gothenburg in Sweden and Oulu in Finland it is shown that the learning environment of the university, supported by outreach, industrial liaison and large-firm mentoring attracts large numbers, in some cases well over 300, new start-up firms to local technology parks.

A three-way interaction between laboratories, start-ups, and a large customer firm such as Nokia, Ericsson or Saab, co-located on or near the campus, enables rapid new firm formation and, crucially, sustainable growth during the difficult post-start-up phase. Innovative management support and training for new technology business firms is an integral part of the success of such ventures.

Cooperation and competition

The relationship between cooperation and competition in industrial districts has been shown theoretically by Varaldo and Ferruci (1996) and empirically by Dei Ottati (1996) to be an evolutionary process partly contingent upon the condition of markets. The former authors suggest strongly that, in industrial districts, a high degree of cooperation, based on consensus, reciprocity and high-trust relations leads to cognitive and functional 'lock-in' (see also Grabher 1993). This works satisfactorily during periods of steady growth in demand for products. In periods of stagnation or recession, however, the absence of dissonance in the system tends to stifle innovative responses to crisis on the part of the district as a whole. This may then lead to opportunistic or cut-throat price competition as a panic response by individual firms pursuing individualistic survival strategies.

Dei Ottati (1996) shows how this occurred in the Prato textile district in Tuscany after a period of decline in demand for the woollen fabrics in which the district specialized. Opportunistic firms pressurized subcontractors in terms of price and risk and subcontractors in turn engaged in destructive forms of price-competition as they acquired semi-finished goods at lower prices from outside the district. Hence the incentive to respect cooperative customs was temporarily eroded.

In a short time, however, the perils of what many saw as unfair competition were recognized by the Industrial Association which promoted a new approach to cooperation based on encouraging the formation of groups of firms of a formal or informal nature. These would consist of final firms and stage firms or subcontractors with a refined division of labour among them.

The main reason for this group-based organizational innovation is market-demand which stresses global standards of product diversification and quality. This calls for close coordination of firms and the institutionalization of risk-spreading. The explanation is echoed in Enright's (1996) observation that it is not a question of whether to compete or cooperate for firms in clusters, but rather how, where and when to compete or cooperate, and what is the optional mix of the two under what specific circumstances?

Proximity capital

The degree to which SMEs have access to investment finance has recently been examined by Cooke, Uranga and Etxebarria (1998) as a factor influencing regional or local innovation capacity. It was found that regional enterprise support systems that are blessed with spending and taxation autonomy offer considerable advantage to SMEs. They can provide support indirectly through their intermediary communication capability towards banks and other financial institutions as well as directly through their co-financing competencies.

Crevoisier (1997) has examined aspects of what he terms 'proximity capital' for SMEs in the Swiss Jura Arc agglomeration of SMEs. Proximity capital comprises investment funds deriving from persons (e.g. 'business angels'), companies or institutions that keep sustained relations with firms on financial as well as other managerial matters. Such relations are inevitably personalized and take the form of partnerships or quasi-partnerships. The entrepreneur or his/her representative has to convince, perhaps through force of personality, the investor to invest. This is facilitated where such links are socially, culturally or community-embedded. The capacity for relying upon or building up trust is crucial in this endeavor. Strong endogenous growth of the Jura Arc economy is seen to be intimately connected to the presence of a local bourgeoisie that favours investment into local SMEs and rather disfavours investment in large-scale, global companies.

Hence we have a picture of the robust, localized industrial district, cluster or agglomeration that can attract growth-oriented SMEs. It combines Marshallian externalities such as specialization, communication and skills assets, with modern elaborations of these in the form of institutional and organizational support infrastructures. Foremost among these are: services promoting innovation; mechanisms for facilitating but also controlling tacit knowledge exchange; capacity to lower transaction costs by means of untraded interdependencies; institutional learning and knowledge-exploitation capabilities; judgmental capability to mix cooperation and competition; and the presence of proximity capital.

In the section that follows, we shall provide an account of the emergence of the multimedia industry in Wales, and particularly Cardiff, in recent years.

Historical development of the Cardiff multimedia cluster

We have already noted the effects of deregulation of the TV industry and the creation of a fourth terrestrial TV channel in the early 1980s. These developments provided market opportunities for SME TV and facilities firms to form as independent producers and service suppliers to the main broadcasters or publishing houses, as they refer to themselves, in Wales (BBC, HTV and S4C) and beyond. A study conducted in 1988 showed that at that time these broadcasters employed some 2,500 persons, a total that declined to around 1,750 by 1997. In 1988 independent TV companies had clustered in two key locations, one in Cardiff where the broadcasters are based, the other in Snowdonia, the mountainous stronghold of Welsh language culture in north-west Wales (Cooke and Gahan 1988). Demand for the Welsh fourth channel (S4C) was substantially for Welsh language programming and S4C was established solely as a broadcaster, not a producer of programming. Most of the independents therefore began as producers and suppliers of Welsh language programming, though many subsequently diversified into English and other language programming as well.

In July 1988, Cardiff was home to the three main broadcasters, eighteen production companies and seven facilities houses ranging from editing and post-production to lighting and specialist catering firms. North Wales then had thirteen production companies and four facilities firms. Seven other production firms supplying programming particularly for S4C were located outside Wales, in London and Bristol. The Welsh language demand in Wales (with some English language demand) had given rise to nearly forty independent programme-makers and eleven facilities houses at that relatively early date.

By that time a representative association of independent television compa-nies, whose Welsh acronym is TAC, had been established. TAC negotiates for the sector with trade unions and broadcasters and acts as a conciliation service for local disputes. At the beginning, all companies were highly dependent upon the three main broadcasters for commissions, but were already demon-strating an interest in penetrating foreign markets via co-productions.

Firms covered the following range of programming types: animation, news and current affairs, documentary, drama and light entertainment, religion and sport; some firms specialized in niches, others were more flexible in their programming capability. 60 per cent of the personnel worked full-time and 40 per cent part-time, 80 per cent of employees were in the 21–40 age-range; 63 per cent were professional or technical personnel, 20 per cent craft work-ers and 16 per cent managerial and administrative. 70 per cent of firms were owned by one or two people.

Firms located geographically in places where there were concentrations of programming and support skills, and secure accommodation to protect expensive equipment. Interaction among independents was relatively high, though competitive tendering meant they needed, and still need, to be capa-ble of cooperating in complementary production areas while competing head-to-head for contracts. A hierarchy had developed whereby some 30 per cent of firms were responsible for ten or more hours of programming each per year, 20 per cent for six to ten hours and 50 per cent for less than six hours per year.

Supply of equipment on lease was largely available within Wales and train-ing schemes had been established through an industry company, Cyfle, contracting with local training colleges and universities to ensure an adequate supply of programme-makers and technicians. Thus, despite the relatively precarious dependence of firms upon a few customers, the infrastructural base of the industry was relatively sound and has remained so. Already some firms had begun specializing in a booming corporate video production sector with only occasional forays into TV.

The development of the multimedia industry

Many of the new media companies established in the 1980s were located in and near to a complex of heritage buildings in Cardiff's docklands, once the centre of the world's largest coal exporting port. These included the Coal Exchange and numerous other nineteenth-century offices and warehouse buildings vacated as the coal trade declined. Space in such buildings was ample and capable of flexible use and, crucially, rents were cheap.

However, in 1987 the Thatcher government established a number of Urban Development Corporations in UK cities to hasten the regeneration of such areas, modelled on that set up in London Docklands in 1981. The

Cardiff Bay Development Corporation (CBDC) took over responsibility for Cardiff's docklands regeneration from Cardiff City Council in 1987. One effect of this was to encourage the media independents to vacate the Coal Exchange which was seen as a prime location for attracting large office development. Partnership between CBDC and the private property development sector was expected to attract prestige, large-scale users to an expensively refurbished old building with payback coming in the form of much higher rental values. But although the media SMEs were scattered, the UK property slump of 1990-94 ensured that no property developer was willing to make the necessary investment.

Some media companies found alternative locations in the docklands area near to their former premises. Others, however, moved to two new locations elsewhere in the city. Deregulation and competitive tendering as well as high overhead costs caused two of Wales' three broadcasting companies, HTV and S4C, to vacate part or all of their headquarter buildings. They leased out space to independent firms who were attracted by the media production infrastructure of studio space and specialist equipment in secure premises that such locations offered. Thus, from approximately 1990 onwards, Cardiff possessed three mini-clusters of media firms, some of which were already also moving into multimedia production. This is the current locational pattern of media SMEs in the city.

In 1996, realizing something new was needed to revitalize the heritage area of Cardiff Bay, CBDC announced a policy of developing the Coal Exchange and the Mount Stuart Square areas surrounding it as a Cultural Quarter in which multimedia production and distribution was to be a central feature. In addition, dance, music and the creative arts were to be attracted into the area as part of an integrated policy package. CBDC commissioned Cardiff University's Centre for Advanced Studies to conduct an in-depth survey of the multimedia and related business sector in order to establish the extent of interest among Cardiff's multimedia firms in relocating in the Cultural Quarter. The area was already equipped with a high-grade communications ring linked to a teleport, and would be supplied with customized space, including shared services in Mount Stuart Square and the Coal Exchange (see Map 12.1).

In what follows we provide an account of the industry derived from a survey of 300 firms in multimedia and media, animation, graphics, creative arts and services firms. Forty-eight of these, around 16 per cent, were core multimedia producers (online or offline producers). Of the 145 firms responding to the questionnaire (48 per cent response rate), twenty-eight were core producers (about 19 per cent). Of these firms, seventeen are specifically set up to produce on- and offline products such as CDs composed of film and TV clips for entertainment; CD-interactive musical instrument tutoring; geographical information systems; financial-trading and media business CD databases along with vocational training CDs. A further eleven are providers of Internet

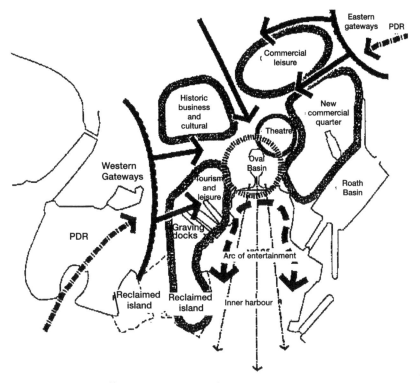

Map 12.1 The Cardiff Bay Development Plan

services or Web page designers. Three of the first group and six of the second are currently located in Cardiff Bay. We have already noted that three-quarters of all 145 firms were established after 1981, 84 per cent of the sample are privately owned, 57 per cent employ one to five persons and 63 per cent have a turnover of less than £500,000.

Firms were asked if they would seriously consider locating in the Cardiff Bay Cultural Quarter. 56 per cent of respondents answered positively, of whom 21 per cent were already located in the area. Of the 145 respondents, thirty-one were thus already there, and of these, nineteen expressed the intent to expand *in situ*. In total, a further fifty-three were seriously interested in relocating to the Cultural Quarter. Given the response rate of 48 per cent, it is not unreasonable to presume that these numbers could, in reality, be substantially higher.

Companies were then asked what were the perceived advantages of a location in the Cardiff Bay area. On a Likert scale of 0 to 5, 48 per cent quoted cheap floorspace, 33 per cent suitable facilities, 30 per cent adequate office space, 23 per cent image and 20 per cent the ability to cooperate with other firms as 'very advantageous' (i.e. Likert-scale ranking of five). Disadvantages were overwhelmingly security problems (45 per cent) and car-parking problems (35 per cent). These results help to put interactive networking among firms in context *vis-à-vis* other, harder, business imperatives concerning the quality and price of property.

We further investigated the issue of the importance of proximity to firms involved in the multimedia industry. Of the 145 respondents, 33 per cent considered it important to be co-located (forty-eight firms) while 67 per cent did not (ninety-five firms). Cross-tabulations revealed that eight categories of firms predominated amongst those for whom proximity is important. These are:

- Visual art
- Craft and design
- Theatre
- Publishing
- Graphic design
- Exhibition organizers
- Printing and copying
- TV, film and video production.

Further analysis showed that 42 per cent of firms desiring a location in the Cultural Quarter also stressed the importance of networking and otherwise interacting with other firms. Qualitative reasons for this included the following:

- Efficient transfer of information.
- Travel costs and time would be less.
- It's important to establish relationships and networking.
- Low communication costs, so less overheads and more competitive prices.
- Easy access to film and media industry to access information and services.
- To cooperate on particular projects and share ideas.
- We could help each other out with contracts.
- For skills and consultations and general exchange of business.
- Producers share ideas and facilities to maximize efficient use of resources.
- Within the TV industry, people like to work with people they know socially, meetings often take place in bars etc., networking and close proximity are essential.
- Working in design-teams, meetings can be called quickly – thus improving service to clients.

Companies were then invited to express an opinion on the idea of a specialist multimedia focus to the Cultural Quarter concept. While thirty-one (21 per cent) thought it was a bad idea, sixty-six (46 per cent) thought it a good idea and twenty-four (17 per cent) an idea worth developing. Those segments of the industry showing the most interest included:

262

- CD-ROM designers
- Computer services
- Web page designers
- Exhibition organizers
- Internet services
- Music/opera/theatre
- Publishing
- TV broadcasting
- TV, film, & video production
- Graphic design
- Visual art
- Specialist advertising and marketing
- Craft and design
- Community arts/arts support.

Some of the reasons given in support of a multimedia centre include the following firm responses:

- We can develop synergy with other service/media companies.
- It will create trade and enhance the sharing of ideas and business.
- Designers could share ideas and overheads could be shared and kept low.
- It's effective to have an area of focus, i.e. similar businesses.
- It will be excellent to network with other firms in a cultural quarter.
- Arts organizations and media find it helpful to cooperate with one another.

Although about half of firms interested in a location in Cardiff Bay also showed interest in being in a multimedia centre, it is worth noting that the 21 per cent who thought it a bad idea commented as follows:

- For my product there would be too much competition for such small customer turnover.
- We would be the only PR company in the quarter.
- It could promote rivalry and under-cutting leading to lower margins and possibly business failure.
- Too much competition – it's better to keep us separate.
- It would be too trendy, too artificial and removed from the audience.

From the survey results we have provided a fairly detailed quantitative and qualitative analysis. It shows the motivations and perceptions of firms in or involved with the multimedia industry on the pros and cons of operating in an industrial-district atmosphere. Four clear points emerge from this analysis. The first of these is that SMEs are primarily concerned that property rentals and space, including such prosaic but important matters as security and parking space, are of suitable quality and availability. Second, multimedia production and distribution are typically conducted by firms for whom it is not the sole activity; only a small minority of firms could be called pure multimedia specialists. The industry tends to operate, as Becattini (1979) notes for Italian industrial districts, more in terms of the primacy of the interactive practices of the various firms in an area rather than in terms of the practices of individual firms themselves. This, of course, will be strengthened if and when the multimedia element of the Cardiff Bay Cultural Quarter becomes a reality.

Third, proximity is particularly important for creative and innovative firms but less so for, say, public relations, legal or insurance firms specializing in multimedia services. This reflects the importance of accessing tacit knowledge in a learning context for the former. The latter probably put more emphasis on legal and other services found in their own industrial districts, which also exist in the city. Fourth, while creative firms welcome proximity for purposes of creative interchange, they also see this as lowering transaction costs relating to time, movement across space, information, communication, project development, contract preparation, skills, facilities and social interaction. But for some, such a hothouse environment threatens their competitive base, especially where they are small, niche firms tied to a limited range of customers. These are firms with their own, limited asset stock accumulation, wary of sharing it with those who possess it in abundance.

Policy support

It should be noted that, in Cardiff and Wales more generally, numerous public support initiatives hover around this industry. The Welsh Development Agency is running a Media Technology Programme. This aims to foster the development of the information technology and multimedia industrial sectors in Wales, through encouraging business to adopt such technologies and the private sector to develop the necessary infrastructures. The eventual objective is for the information technology and related information services sector to represent between 10 and 15 per cent of Wales' gross national product by the start of the new millennium, which would be equivalent to an annual contribution of £2,500 million.

The Welsh Development Agency (WDA), together with Cardiff Bay Development Corporation and Screen Wales, have set up a Multimedia Development Group to bring together public and private sector organizations and individuals with an interest in the development of the industry in Wales. To date the group has some 300 members, and through its carefully planned programme also seeks to encourage businesses take-up of these new technologies.

The Development Corporation in partnership with private interests has also built the Celtic Gateway multimedia and technology business park. It offers multimedia firms the benefits of direct access to a digital satellite system through an on-site ground station. This allows small firms to operate in a global context.

Cardiff has operated its Media City promotional initiative for at least a decade and this assists marketing of multimedia products and expertise as well as those of the media sector more generally. 'Screen Wales' is a joint initiative of the main broadcasters, the city and the WDA. Network Wales and the Wales Information Society projects are led by the WDA to assist the whole range of media and multimedia firms in developing projects to sell content and services, and draw on European Union Information Society programme funding.

At local level, the Cardiff Bay Business Forum and the Multimedia/ Cultural Quarter Users Group both involve CBDC and, in the latter case, the Arts Council of Wales, Cardiff University, the City Council and firms as representatives of the industry. They too are active in problem-solving and promoting the physical development of the multimedia centre. Hence, there is a degree of multilevel governance from grass roots, through the city and regional authorities up to European Union level offering support for the development of the industry.

Therefore, conditions are relatively propitious for the further expansion of the multimedia industry in Cardiff. Until recently the media sector, which largely spawned it, was dependent to a great extent on the regional broadcasters. This is less the case today, as markets have been broadened through global joint-ventures and improved overseas marketing, assisted by the public support infrastructure. The multimedia sector has already diversified into training, corporate, and wider entertainment and information markets. This has been a means by which media firms themselves could become more diversified and somewhat less overwhelmingly linked as suppliers to the dominant broadcasting customers.

While the industry remains relatively small by the global standards of the industry centred in places such as California and London it is, nevertheless, relatively robust. It is creative and dynamic yet largely cooperatively-minded and flexible enough to remain competitive as it seeks to gain further efficiencies from the known external economies of proximity. Proximity capital is not yet a major problem since funding comes through project-based contracts and the public sector continues to supply aspects of overhead through its own project-funding, promotion and marketing services. For the present, the key element of proximity capital for the Cardiff multimedia cluster resides in the intangible capital derived from tacit knowledge exchange and sharing of expertise amongst complementary firms which coalesce and disengage around specific projects as market opportunities evolve.

Conclusions

At the outset of this chapter it was suggested that the multimedia industry, which combines a wide range of different technologies and types of expertise, is a prime candidate for a network-form of evolutionary trajectory. Moreover, the creative and innovative aspects of production suggested that geographical proximity would be important due to the reduction of transaction costs and the need for widespread tacit knowledge exchange characteristic of such an industry, especially where strong involvement by SMEs was the norm.

Building upon the Marshallian analysis of industrial districts, it was shown that six key features of modern industrial districts can usefully be taken into account in understanding where and how such agglomeration economies convey their externality benefits to firms inhabiting them. The first of these is enterprise support to ease certain of the tasks, such as promoting and marketing products, that SMEs sometimes find onerous. The second refers to the evolution of specialization and the nature of trust among expert firms as agglomeration dynamics evolve.

Not all firms are equally able to be free-riders in agglomerations and inclusion in the loop depends upon the ability to transcend barriers to exchange based on difficult-to-imitate asset-specificity. Third, agglomerations can help firms to reduce transaction costs where firms can cooperate. This enhances efficiency markedly and enables project-partners to operate more competitively. Fourth, agglomerations can function as learning economies in which interaction among complementary firms enables the wider diffusion of good practice and access to state-of-the-art knowledge. Fifth, a judicious mix of cooperation and competition is important for the growth of firms in agglomerations. Finally, the presence of proximity capital, itself based on localized high-trust and reputation, is of crucial importance to the ability of firms to function effectively in SME networks.

In discussing the Cardiff case, it was shown to be an industry originating largely, though not entirely, in the media sector in spin-off firms from the broadcasting industry. While these had initially sought to cluster in a single agglomeration, this aim had been countered by the policies of a public governance organization, forcing many to seek mini-clusters elsewhere.

Later, as the multimedia industry developed, Cardiff Bay Development Corporation sought to re-awaken the dream of the earlier media firms to locate in the waterfront district where rents are cheap and the ambiance is appropriate to cultural production. This time, though, the target is multimedia firms which, on the basis of survey evidence, are highly receptive to the idea of inhabiting a customized location such as a multimedia centre in a Cultural Quarter. Reasons for this include enhanced opportunities to reduce overhead and transaction costs, along with the improved possibilities for creative synthesis of complementary assets offered by an agglomeration setting. It is clear that industrial district arrangements are, if they can be found or stimulated, entirely appropriate to creative SMEs in this burgeoning industry, whether in Cardiff or, on a far greater scale, in California.

References

Becattini, G. (1979) 'From the "industrial sector" to the "industrial district"', in *L'Industria. Rivista di economia e politica industriale* 1 (in Italian), reproduced in E. Goodman, J. Bamford and P. Saynor (eds) (1989) *Small Firms and Industrial Districts in Italy*, London: Routledge.

Braczyk, H.-J., Cooke, P. and Heidenreich, M. (eds) (1998) *Regional Innovation Systems*, London: UCL Press.

Brusco, S. (1990) 'The idea of the industrial district: its genesis', in F. Pyke, G. Becattini and W. Sengenberger (eds) *Industrial Districts and Inter-firm Cooperation in Italy*, Geneva: International Institute for Labour Studies.

Cohen, W. and Levinthal, D. (1990) 'Absorptive capacity: a new perspective on learning and innovation', *Administrative Sciences Quarterly* 35: 128–52.

Cooke, P. and Gahan, C. (1988) *The Television Industry in Wales*, Report to Welsh Broadcasters, Cardiff: University of Wales.

Cooke, P., Uranga, M. and Etxebarria, G. (1998) 'Regional systems of innovation: an evolutionary perspective', *Environment and Planning* A, 30: 1563–84.

Crevoisier, O. (1997) 'Financing regional endogenous development: the role of proximity capital in the age of globalization', *European Planning Studies* 5: 407–16.

Dei Ottati, G. (1994) 'Cooperation and competition in the industrial district as an organizational model', *European Planning Studies* 2: 371–92.

—— (1996) 'Economic changes in the district of Prato in the 1980s: towards a more conscious and organized industrial district', *European Planning Studies* 4: 35–52.

Dosi, G. (1988) 'Sources, Procedures and Microeconomic Effects of Innovation', *Journal of Economic Literature* 36: 1126–71.

Enright, M. (1996) 'Regional clusters and economic development: a research agenda', in U. Staber, N. Schaefer and B. Sharma (eds) *Business Networks: Prospects for Regional Development*, Berlin: de Gruyter.

Grabher, G. (1993) 'The weakness of strong ties: the lock-in of regional development in the Ruhr area', in G. Grabher (ed.) *The Embedded Firm: on the Socioeconomics of Industrial Networks*, London: Routledge.

Hughes, G. (1997) *Mount Stuart Square Multimedia Village and Cultural Quarter: Survey Analysis*, Report to Cardiff Bay Development Corporation, Cardiff: University of Wales.

Jones-Evans, D. and Klofsten, M. (1997) 'Universities and local economic development: the case of Linköping', *European Planning Studies* 5: 77–93.

Jussila, H. and Segerståhl, B. (1997) 'Technology centres as business environments in small cities', *European Planning Studies* 5: 371–84.

Krugman, P. (1995) *Development, Geography and Economic Theory*, Cambridge and London: MIT Press.

Lindholm, A. (1997) 'Entrepreneurial spin–off enterprises in Göteborg, Sweden', *European Planning Studies* 5: 659–74.

Lundvall, B. and Johnson, B. (1994) 'The learning economy', *Journal of Industry Studies* 1: 23–41.

Malmberg, A. and Maskell, P. (1997) 'Towards an explanation of regional specialization and industry agglomeration', *European Planning Studies* 5: 25–42.

Marshall, A. (1919) *Industry and Trade,* London: Macmillan.

North, D. (1993) 'Institutions and economic performance', in U. Mäki, B. Gustafsson and C. Knudsen (eds) *Rationality, Institutions and Economic Methodology*, London: Routledge.

Scott, A. (1996) 'Regional motors of the global economy', *Futures* 28: 391–411.

Scott, A. (1998) 'From Silicon Valley to Hollywood: the multimedia industry in California', in H.-J. Braczyk, P. Cooke and M. Heidenreich (eds) *Regional Innovation Systems*, London: UCL Press.

Storper, M. (1995) 'The resurgence of regional economies, ten years after: the region as a nexus of untraded interdependencies', *European Urban and Regional Studies* 2: 191–221.

Storper, M. and Scott, A. (1995) 'The wealth of regions: market forces and policy imperatives in local and global context', *Futures* 27: 505–26.

Varaldo, R. and Ferrucci, L. (1996) 'The evolutionary nature of the firm within industrial districts', *European Planning Studies* 4: 27–34.

13

FROM PURPOSIVENESS TO SUSTAINABILITY IN THE FORMATION OF MULTIMEDIA CLUSTERS

Governance and constituency building in Scotland

Tony Kinder and Alfonso Molina

Introduction

Multimedia is generally related to the emerging fast-growing industrial activities based on new network technologies (e.g., Internet) and new products, processes and services integrating a variety of media (text, graphics, audio, pictures, animation, video, etc.), available in a digitized format that can be accessed interactively. These activities are perceived as the growth industries of the future and affect the concerns of a wide range of players, including network operators (for online multimedia), hardware producers (servers, computers, etc.), the media industry, service providers and content providers (entertainment industry, software producers, etc.). In this realm, new and established firms are active.

Not surprisingly, industrial policymakers from most countries or regions would like to have a strong, dynamic and long-term multimedia industry or capability that contributes centrally to the growth, employment and wealth creation in their countries or regions – in short, a sustainable multimedia capability. Here, sustainability would not be merely an issue of presence, quantity and time. It would also be, fundamentally, an issue of quality and the harmonious integration of the activities which take place in a region. As such, we define sustainability as the ability to shape significantly the content, direction and dynamism of the long-term evolution of multimedia in a given region.

The aim of this chapter is to examine the potential for a sustainable multimedia capability in Scotland, through an understanding and characterization of the depth, breadth, dynamism and purpose of a possible multimedia clustering process. At the basic level the chapter asks whether such a process of clustering exists and whether there are strategic policies guiding its possible development towards sustainability. It defines the *conditions for sustainability* of a globally competitive cluster, and provides a framework to grasp and influence policy processes aimed at fostering cluster formation.

The main part of this chapter is organized in three sections which lay the theoretical foundations for the treatment of the clustering process and analyse the specific situation of Scotland in microelectronics and multimedia. The section on 'Clusters, networking and sociotechnical constituencies' begins by outlining the appeal of clustering as a policy instrument. It argues that knowledge networking is the fundamental characteristic of sustainable clusters. It introduces the sociotechnical constituencies (STC) approach, which assists understanding of how clusters work and how they are shaped in their purposiveness and potential sustainability. The process of cluster formation is here treated as a process of sociotechnical alignment fundamentally influenced and shaped by the governance or 'rules of the game' within which it unfolds.

The next section, 'A Scottish multimedia cluster', looks at the evidence of clustering processes in Scotland. Since multimedia is rather recent and the challenge is more how to stimulate multimedia clustering, this section approaches the problem by integrating insights from the better known electronics clustering process in Scotland, with particular emphasis on identifying governance features of direct relevance to other clustering processes such as multimedia. In the concluding section the chapter looks at policy options for multimedia clustering in Scotland. It argues that the constituency-building focuses policy in a purposeful way, and is necessary for public policy on clustering to achieve more of its desired goals.

Clusters, networking and sociotechnical constituencies

The significance of clustering and networking

In recent years the idea of clustering and its relevance to economic growth has gained acceptance among academics and policymakers. This chapter will refer to various cluster-related policy themes such as spatiality, relationality, partnering and knowledge networking. These themes are all the subject of theoretical debate, and their balanced integration is required for holistic understanding and effective policy application.

Few would now accept a Marshallian view of clustering as resource-driven, or transactional-based 'agglomeration'. Clustering is now generally regarded as a technological and knowledge-based construction. It is not well understood as a construction, particularly in terms of the nature and balance

270

between the various factors governing the emergence and evolution of a cluster. Are clusters market creations, or a result of networking? A central theme of this chapter is that the conscious (and unconscious) direction given by a constituency of players and interests moulds a cluster creation – giving it purpose. It will be argued that cross-institutional networks deepen clustering, and that knowledge networking is the fundamental characteristic of sustainable clusters.

Issues of time and money feature prominently in debates around clustering: how much time, whose money, and at what (social) risk? Commonly, any plan for product or process development will analyse uncertainty and compute risk. Proposals for the investment of public and private funds, and social structures, might well do the same to enhance the chances of achieving a cluster. Policy processes that are founded on shared visions of clusters and invest time and money may play a forceful role in enhancing the prospects for success. However, there are great dangers in 'locking-into' trajectories which are not rewarded by the market, or which will not be sustained for an appropriate period. In this section, we shall demonstrate that the sociotechnical constituency tool helps to clarify the relevant questions.

Networking is an interorganizational perspective cementing the three other building blocks of the clustering concept: spatiality, relationality and knowledge. Network analysis has too often focused on classification of structures rather than on analysis (Kapferer 1993). To be useful, network analysis must also avoid the functional determinism of outcome often found in systems theory. Carefully used, the STC approach we shall discuss below can avoid both these failings.

Commercial networks come in enormous varieties. Knowledge networks are a particularly complex area whose study involves analysis of resources, people and purposes that are dynamic and involve competition both within and between networks (Håkansson 1989). Charles and Howells (1992) argue that cross-institutional linkages may be important at a pre-competitive Research, Development and Design (RD&D) stage of product development, but more spatially diverse global knowledge alliances seem to be more often used at later stages in new product development. Setting the domain of a network, identifying its purpose and dynamics, is a difficult but necessary pre-condition for analysis.

This chapter argues that there is a spectrum of interorganizational relations whose quality is differentiated by the depth of the relationship (that is, how well the knowledge flows and common purposes interrelating organizations are integrated). Table 13.1 and Figure 13.1 provide an illustration of the types of relations in the spectrum: these can involve businesses of different types and sizes, varieties of public agencies, and arrangements of an institutional nature.

At the shallow end of the spectrum are non-value-adding inter-trading relations such as off-the-shelf technology supply, whereas at the deepest end

Table 13.1 Examples of interorganizational relations by type and depth

Non-value-adding supply linkages	Off-the shelf market transaction such as standard screw purchases.
Value-added inter-trading	Improves delivery or information systems but without conscious intent; one-way learning; this may extend to industrial networking, for example local sourcing strategies.
Value-added (relational) inter-trading (partnering)	Two-way learning, but bounded, for example jointly developing a new machined part; 'tactical' rather than 'strategic' partnering.
Advocacy networking (narrow linkages)	No new knowledge generation; seeking to align institutional arrangements to suit a narrow constituency in competition with other constituencies within a spatial boundary.
Knowledge partnering	A strategic, long term and deep relationship, centrally featuring knowledge creation, but bilaterally based, for example 'corner engineering' and improving a sub-assembly or complex part.
Knowledge networking (wider relations)	Strategic multilateral knowledge networking, deepened by trust and previously successful joint knowledge development: a conscious knowledge generation and socialization within a network.
Sustainable cluster	A knowledge network capable of dynamically re-configuring to suit changing patterns of global demand; aligning the local mode of regulation with global regime of accumulation.

are knowledge-partnering and knowledge-networking activities which most clearly characterize the sustainable dynamics of clustering processes. These categorizations are not intended to be exhaustive and should not be seen as having rigid borders. They may certainly be refined or added on but, for our purposes, the selection clearly indicates the existence of different depths in relationships between different organizations. A sustainable cluster is most likely to integrate all forms of relations into a dynamic process that aligns local and global patterns.

The issue for strategists and policymakers is how to approach practical

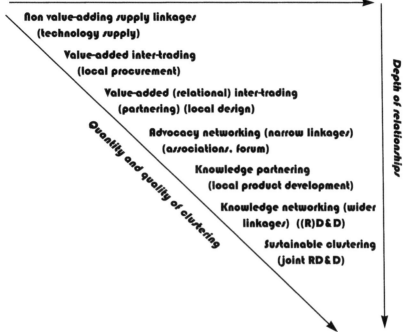

Figure 13.1 Breadth (quantity) and depth (quality) of clustering inter-organizational relations

processes of desired, potential or real cluster formation. It is important to grasp and assess the content and dynamics of these processes with a view to developing consistent policies for influencing and supporting their emergence and development. This is the role of the conceptual instrument provided by the framework of sociotechnical constituencies: it provides the metaphorical spectacles needed to see clearly the multidimensional processes involved in the depth, dynamics and shaping of a cluster.

Sociotechnical constituencies

A rich analytical framework is necessary to analyse networking within a cluster or, more generally, the nature, state of development and dynamism of a cluster. A cluster is a large-scale sociotechnical constituency commonly consisting of broad fronts of sub-processes, involving a variety of specific and interrelated technical, organizational and commercial factors. The latter include, for example, agreements on standards.

In practice, the combination of these sub-processes will not only show a wide range of possible configurations; it will also manifest itself through various levels of operation from intracompany to standard-setting initiatives. The STC approach is an analytical method capable of dealing systematically with this complexity.[1] It is an instrument of interorganizational analysis, a single process of interpenetration of technical, socioeconomic, political and cultural factors, that provides a snapshot of the dynamic creation of a technological artefact or system. It encapsulates relationships between organizations (and key decision-making groups) and varieties of organizations influencing the constituency.

Sociotechnical constituencies may be defined as dynamic ensembles of technical constituents (tools, machines, etc.) and social constituents (people and their values, interest groups, etc.), which interact and shape each other in the course of the creation, production and diffusion (including implementation) of specific technologies.[2]

This approach puts technological processes at the centre of its analytical focus (see Figure 13.2), and the meaning of technology (T) is not confined to a single specific product or process. It can be a product or, as is the concern of this chapter, a cluster. This focus means that STC is necessarily multidisciplinary. It also means that each constituency has a purpose for its members, though purposes may conflict and re-align over time. Indeed, players may take time to identify the hierarchy of goals each brings to the constituency. The types of interaction between different sets of social constituents are critical to the performance of sociotechnical constituencies. At both intra- and inter-institutional constituency-building levels, they may assume many forms (or combinations of forms). These may be, for instance, complementary, collaborative, competitive and so on.

Interactions may involve players of similar or of different types, and again this is valid at both intra- and inter-institutional constituency-building levels. At an intra-institutional level (Figure 13.2, third circle from centre T), for instance, interactions may be among engineers themselves, on the one hand, and among engineers, unskilled labour managers, and other personnel on the other. At an inter-institutional level (fourth circle from centre T), they may be among companies, on the one hand, and among companies and different institutions such as universities or government labs, on the other.

The third and fourth circles also show that the integration of resources inside a constituency building process is effected through the interaction of different intra- and inter-institutional constituents. Since these social constituents control the available resources (directly or indirectly and in varying proportions), they are able to influence the manner in which these resources are integrated. This allows them to shape the development of a given technology in accordance with their own interests, expertise, and generally with their relative weight and power within the constituency. In this respect, each STC entails power relations and, more generally, governance (see below, pages 276–8) informing the relations between constituent actors who contribute towards the unknown but purposive outcome of the STC network.

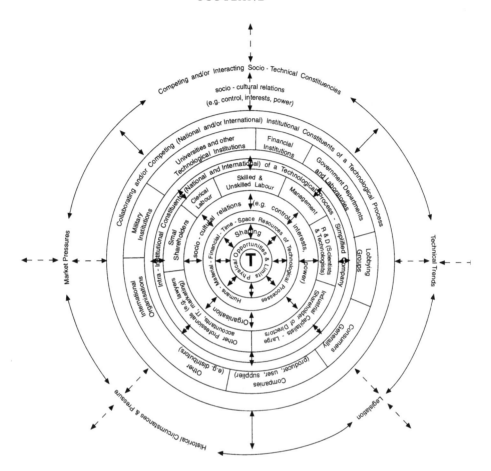

Figure 13.2 Example of a possible sociotechnical constituency
Source: Molina 1994: 6

Formal governance may differ from informal relations. there will be discourse within the constituency over how to achieve the desired outcomes. The knowledge and 'languaging' that junior members of the STC bring to this may give them a degree of intellectual power that allows them to shape outcomes to a greater extent than their physical input would otherwise entail. In this sense, STC easily incorporates specific cultural elements or the wider concept of '*habitus*' into its analytical dimensions.[3]

In the outermost circle, Figure 13.2 highlights the fact that the development of a given technology is not simply the result of an insular, intra-constituency process. It is also the result of that sociotechnical constituency's interaction with other sociotechnical constituencies within its particular historical setting. It is influenced, for example, by legislation, regulation, technical and market standards, and trends; these are themselves the result of interaction between sociotechnical constituencies (i.e. an inter-constituency process). Thus, technical and market standards (trends) are not in fact exogenous to constituencies: sociotechnical constituencies themselves create and alter them according to the extent of their relative strengths, dynamism and growth.

These characteristics of STC enable a systematic integration of the micro- and macro-dimensions of technological processes. Moving from 'inner-to-outer,' or vice-versa, the same framework can be used at all levels of scoping. Thus, the constituency boundaries (key to the use of STC as an analytical device) can be narrowly drawn to understand the shape of particular products, or more broadly defined to understand the nature of a technology cluster or system. As this happens, every higher aggregate level of the constituency always contains or subsumes all previous levels. Thus, a specific product constituency becomes constituent of the broader cluster level and so on. The result is a transformation of context into content and vice-versa.

Finally, it must be noted that despite their perception of benefit, social constituents participating in a constituency do not invariably have a clear idea of where their specific interests lie in relation to a given technology. Nor does the development of this technology necessarily follow the intended path or yield the results expected by the constituents. Purposiveness is not a static well-defined ingredient and unpredictable and possibly unidentifiable factors have consequences which can lead to a change of direction or, indeed, make the difference between success and failure. Uncertainty is inherent in the technological process, particularly where constituents are trying to break completely new technical ground. This uncertainty factor figures prominently in new multimedia technologies, especially as they come to involve the development and integration of a broad front of innovations.

Clustering as intra- and inter-institutional processes of sociotechnical alignment

The emergence of a multimedia cluster can be treated as the intra- and inter-institutional construction of competitive product constituencies through purposive processes of sociotechnical alignment. Sociotechnical alignment is what constituents engage in (however consciously, successfully, partially or imperfectly) when they are promoting the development of specific technologies either intra-organizationally, inter-organizationally, or even as industrial standards. It may be seen as the process of creation, adoption, accommodation (adaptation) and close or loose interaction (interrelation) of technical and social factors and actors which underlies the emergence and development of an identifiable constituency.

Alignment should not be seen as a mere accommodation of static available pieces as if they were parts of a jigsaw puzzle. Nor can it be considered as something complete and permanent, once achieved. For this reason, the term 'alignment' is well supplemented by those of 'mis-alignment' and 're-alignment' which express, on the one hand, situations of tension and disharmony and, on the other, changes or re-accommodations in the life of a constituency. Non-alignment best describes situations in which the parties have not come to each others' attention and in which it is thus less proper to talk of tensions or conflict. Also, alignment between people is not always simply a matter of consensus. 'Consensual alignment' is one possible form it may take, but there might also be, for instance, 'authoritarian' forms enforced by one party over another through sheer use of power.

In alignment the flow of influences is multidirectional. Indeed, as a sociotechnical process, the interrelations involved are not only among people and institutions but, simultaneously, among people, institutions and technical elements. Four types of alignment may be noted here. First, when two or more people or institutions come together (explicitly or implicitly) to pursue a common goal, we may talk of alignment between people or institutions. Second, when developers shape technologies in accordance with the specifications of potential users, we may talk of aligning technology to people. Third, when people have to learn new skills to be able to use a technology, we may talk of aligning people to technology. Finally, when technologies are shaped in accordance with the features of other technologies such as standards, we talk of aligning technology to technology.

In practice, all these elements are likely to be present in the development of a constituency at one time or another. Indeed, mis-alignment and re-alignment must also be included since practical constituency-building strategies may sometimes employ one or other of these alternatives in order, for instance, to generate space within an organization which has a strong competing constituency. The central task of a well-informed strategy is to identify these alternatives and ensure that the most appropriate combinations, emphases and changes are implemented during the life of a constituency.

In this respect, it is important to realize that the four types of alignment just mentioned are not necessarily complementary. Sometimes alignments in certain directions may actually produce mis-alignment in others. For instance, it is not uncommon for people to reach agreement (alignment) on the basis of expectations and specifications which then prove mis-aligned with what is actually feasible with the available resources and technology. This kind of mis-alignment may turn out to be very costly for a constituency and it may well be a major factor in the 'over-spending' that often bedevils technical projects.

When relations of power and authority exist among players, this may guide and even facilitate a process of alignment or decision-making. In large-scale clustering processes, however, no such clear source of decision-making is normally available. Organization, in terms of projects and of formal and informal working arrangements between players, is rather an outcome of the process of alignment: something to be created and shaped in a process of consensus and accommodation.

This task is large and complex. Although alignment may exist on a broad, non-operational goal such as the importance of Scottish capabilities on multimedia technology, the actual process generally starts from a situation of non-alignment or mis-alignment in both perceptions and specific operational goals. In addition, clusters can only start from what existing players bring with them, so the initial 'broad front' may not only be patchy but may also reflect narrower interests than desired. These are all aspects to be aware of as cluster strategies evolve towards long-term constituency-building goals.

It will be mainly the task of 'constituency-builders' and the policy structures embodying the broad clustering processes to provide vision, guidance, encouragement and reality to the integrated constituency-building efforts. Of course, it helps when resources are available to stimulate alignment. In this sense, the fact that multimedia technologies are becoming a major preoccupation of Scottish policy is already a reflection of significant constituency- building. The truly complex part, however, is the gradual build up of constituencies which effectively realize the goal of sustainable Scottish strength and benefits relative to multimedia processes in other parts of the world.

Obviously, given the increasingly global nature of markets, this goal will not be achieved in isolation. Scottish multimedia cluster capabilities must aim for a global presence and this will demand interactions on an equally global scale, with many non-Scottish institutions contributing to, as well as benefiting from, it. The measure of long-term sustainable success, however, will be a cluster relation of knowledge interdependence in which the Scottish voice is strong enough to shape events in the region as well as internationally.

For Scottish multimedia capabilities, this raises the issue of which players come to dominate the constituency-building process and what kind of technical strengths are effectively nurtured in Scotland. One has to take into account that, ultimately, clusters and sociotechnical constituencies only exist by virtue of being rooted in the sociotechnical fabric of specific countries and regions. Their presence and the specific way in which they are realized in given countries (through R&D, production, use, etc.) accounts for the kind of technological capabilities and the role played by these countries in the global development process of a given technology. The implications for Scotland are clear: if the region is to shape and reap the benefits of multimedia technologies with global market scope, it would do well to foster and maintain an influential presence and activity within the respective sociotechnical constituencies.

The diamond of alignment

The complexity of the process of alignment involved in multimedia cluster formation is shown in more detail by the diamond of alignment (see Figure 13.3). The multiple dimensions give detailed substance to the continuum of

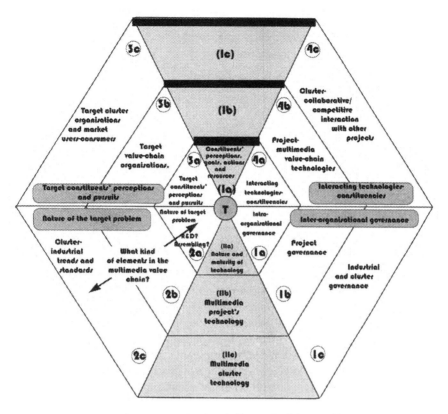

Figure 13.3 Intra- and inter-organizational diamond of cluster alignment

interorganizational relationships in Figure 13.1. The quantity, quality and synergistic integration of these dimensions enables a detailed understanding and characterization of the depth, breadth, dynamism and purpose of any clustering process.

The diamond distinguishes three integrated layers in the clustering process:

- Inner layer (a): intra-organizational layer of companies and other institutions.
- Middle layer (b): inter-organizational layer of projects and programmes that bring together 'value-chain' organizational players in purposive actions.
- Outer layer (c): layer of industrial and market clusters. Synergistic integration of the other two layers at this level is required for global competitive positioning. Collaboration and competition is characteristic of this level.

As said earlier, each of the broader layers contains the inner ones and all of them are cut across by further dimensions.

Dimensions I (a,b,c) and II (a,b,c) characterize the nature and state of development of the sociotechnical constituency and its technology from the intraorganizational to the clustering process.

Dimension I: Constituents' perceptions, goals, actions and resources

This relates to the present state of the sociotechnical constituency: the quantity and type of constituent organizations, people, material and financial resources, knowledge, expertise, experience and reputation. It also embraces other constituent elements such as current perceptions, goals, visions and strategies of the constituency. In short, what the constituency is at a given point in time.

Dimension II: Nature and maturity of the technology

This dimension relates to the importance of the nature and state of development (that is, the maturity) of the technology in the constituency-building process (see second circle in Figure 13.2). The nature of the technologies involved is almost certain to affect the strategic limits and opportunities for its constituency-building process. It is a simple fact that the nature of telecommunications networks is different from that of biscuits or drugs, and a single 'universal' approach will not do. In the case of multimedia, at least three characteristics have critical strategic value: pioneering emerging technology; technologies with indirect network externalities; and consumer product. Pioneering emerging technology stresses innovation and the need to be first to market particular goods or services. This leads to high uncertainty and risk due to lack of precedents. The implication is a much greater need for market-fostering strategies aimed at aligning users with the technology. Indirect network externality stresses the dependence of the use-value of one product on the existence of another. For example, computers are useless without software and vice-versa; content is useless without delivery hardware. Consumer product highlights the fact that the ultimate adjudicators of success or failure are the people in the street.

Dimensions 1 (a,b,c), 2 (a,b,c), 3 (a,b,c) and 4 (a,b,c) characterize the direction, dynamics, and depth of purpose of the process of constituency-building.

Dimension 1 (a,b,c): Governance

This dimension relates to the written and unwritten legislation that governs the behaviour, relations, interactions, calculations, transactions and conflict resolutions between all those involved in intra- and interorganizational constituency-building processes as well as inter-constituencies processes themselves. It includes cultural pre-dispositions and power relations between individual and collective players at intraorganizational, interorganizational and societal levels.

At intra- and interorganizational level, effective constituency-building implies an alignment of the technology with the governance and strategic purpose of the organization, project or cluster. At project and cluster levels, arrangements for interorganizational governance are necessary to express, facilitate, stimulate and guide the alignment between different organizations. Mechanisms of collaboration, for instance, may include business alliances, second-source and market agreements, and many other forms. It is crucial for cluster strategies to acknowledge the existence and quality of these arrangements, either to align with them or to create or modify them to satisfy the needs of the constituency-building process.

Lack of attention to interorganizational governance may be the source of much mis-alignment and conflict. At the same time a careful approach is required to strike the right governance. After all, each institution is likely to have different blends of expertise, perceptions, imperatives and expectations, dictated by its history, current activities, industrial environment and possibly by its ethical stance as well as by idiosyncratic practices. One should stress that the flow of influence is not unidirectional, with the emerging constituency always having to align itself to existing governance. In fact, emerging constituencies may well have to challenge the prevailing governance as they develop, sometimes leading to adaptations, modifications and even major new features.

Dimension 2 (a,b,c): Nature of target problem

This dimension relates to the specific technical purpose and content of the constituency's technological activity (for example, a target activity of assembling rather than R & D and innovation). It thus also relates to the depth of clustering. At intra- and interorganizational level, effective constituency-building implies an alignment between the capabilities of the constituency and the technical demands involved in realizing the use-value of the technology (i.e., target functionality and cost). The literature of technology development is full of examples of failure to deliver what was promised: that is, of mis-alignment between the promise (expectation) and what could eventually be brought to the market. To avoid 'failure', the constituency must simply have the technical capacity to deliver the goods with the resources available at any given time. Capacity and resources, however, are dynamic, mutually influencing, factors and part of the capacity to deliver may imply an ability to expand the resources available.

Dimension 3 (a,b,c): Target constituents' perceptions and pursuits

This dimension relates to the people and organizations the constituency is seeking to enrol behind the purposive process, from intra-organizational constituency-building to market consumers. At intra- and interorganizational level it implies an alignment between the constituents and parties who are potential or target constituents (suppliers, individual consumers, and other relevant organizations such as independent software developers). The aim is for them to become members of the constituency. At cluster level, given the broader context, this alignment does not necessarily mean all parties working together across the board. Often, competing companies are involved (software developers, for example) and mis-alignments at certain levels are an unavoidable part of the constituency's make-up.

In practice, players will be aligned on the broad perception that the technology is worth the investment. At the same time they might be competitors or, indeed, collaborators who may differ on the ways to achieve certain specific aims. The entire process is most likely to involve manifold directions of alignment. These may include perception alignment between suppliers of different technical constituents (for example, hardware and software); alignment between technology suppliers and users; alignment of technology specifications to users preferences and requirements; alignment of users to new technology solutions; and alignment between interacting technologies.

Dimension 4 (a,b,c): Interacting technologies/constituencies

Commonly, a new constituency's technology will emerge in an environment populated by other technologies and constituencies. Some will be required to realize the emerging product (e.g., production technology), others may have a similar and even competing claim for resources. This dimension relates to the type of interaction and relations established with these other constituencies in the purposive process from intraorganizational to market constituency-building.

At intra- and inter-organizational level, effective constituency-building implies an alignment between the products of the emerging constituency and established technical and market trends and standards in the target industrial area (whether for mainstream or niche markets). Included in this alignment is a good understanding of the evolution, present strategies, and likely future actions of actual and potential competing constituencies. Since trends and specific solutions are dynamic mutually influencing factors, part of the capacity of a constituency to deliver may imply an ability to identify and generate new standards in areas not yet covered by existing standards.

At the broader cluster level, the boundaries between collaboration and competition, antagonistic and non-antagonistic relations are much more diffuse. Indeed, as with dimensions 3 (a,b,c) mis-alignments at certain levels are often unavoidable. Technologies may simultaneously collaborate and compete at different levels of the constituency, with the boundaries again very much a matter of players' perceptions, stances and, generally, strategic approaches to constituency-building.

Clearly, the process of constituency-building and sociotechnical alignment implied in product innovation will vary greatly in terms of complexity and conflict. Much will depend on the nature of the technology and its initial relationship to the various dimensions in the diamond of alignment. The diamond of alignment enables a systematic and holistic assessment of the multiple dimensions of constituency-building processes, including significant areas of alignment and mis-alignment at intra- and interorganizational layers (a) (b) (c). It also helps to identify the strength and degree of integration of the different layers, and their competitive performance at the industrial/market level. This knowledge is essential for the formulation of well-informed strategic targeting of future constituency-building actions and pursuits. In the following section, we look at the evidence of clustering processes in Scotland.

A Scottish multimedia cluster?

Scottish Enterprise (SE) – the industrial agency of Scotland – is considering the development of multimedia clustering as one of its strategic lines of action. Since multimedia is rather recent and the challenge is more how to stimulate multimedia clustering, this section approaches the problem by combining:

- Insights from the better known electronics clustering process in Scotland, with particular emphasis on identifying governance features of direct relevance to other clustering processes such as multimedia.
- Insights from the situation specific to the potential process of multimedia clustering in the region.

In electronics, Scottish Enterprise has worked for fifteen years to stimulate the creation of a microelectronics cluster in Scotland, apparently with major success. Financed by both foreign direct investment (FDI) and indigenous companies, electronics in central Scotland has grown at 14 per cent compound during this period, and currently accounts for 42 per cent of Scottish exports, with total annual sales of £6bn.

On closer examination, however, the depth and sustainability of the electronics cluster appears less impressive. In particular, FDI and indigenous manufacturers in the industry occupy separate networks. The indigenous company network benefits little in terms of trade, advocacy, or knowledge flows from the FDI network, and there is a low birth rate of new companies. In limited ways knowledge alliances are more frequent among the SMEs than between them and the foreign investors (FDIs); the latter network mainly with foreign suppliers and within their corporate network. Few companies have important connections with higher education institutions.

Overall, in electronics, it can be said that Scotland has re-shaped itself to the needs of FDIs in the global economy. Nevertheless, FDIs' added value and knowledge generation have largely remained abroad with suppliers, mother plants, or RD&D centres. Indeed, FDIs' spending in Scotland has tended to be upon lower value-added items: services, consumables, machined parts, and metal fabrication, with some turnkey sub-assembly and printed circuit boards (PCBs). This is consistent with an FDIs' strategic approach that has treated Scotland primarily as a lucrative manufacturing platform for the European market.

The result has been a broadly scoped Scottish microelectronics cluster, covering most elements of the value chain, but lacking depth both in its conception and current operation. Figure 13.4 applies the general clustering diagram of Figure 13.1 to the case of Scottish microelectronics.

This demonstrates that inter-firm relations between FDI and indigenous firms have tended to remain at the lower levels of depth – predominantly technology supply (shown in italics) – and far from the deeper levels which would ensure the sustainability of the clustering process.[4] It also draws attention (italics) to the presence of advocacy (cluster-representing) networking, although again this concerns mostly the FDI sector.

This is not to say that the experience has not been valuable. Indeed, this cluster has had considerable impact on employment, capital inflow, and the upgrading of production techniques in the Scottish manufacturing base. But this does not alter the fact that it is a weak cluster with low local product demand, few backward value-adding linkages, exogenous knowledge generation, a limited perspective by public agency actors, a lack of endogenous knowledge networking, and little ability to influence its own development.

The importance of this brief assessment for multimedia is that various of the broad factors operating in the Scottish economy and underpinning the weakness of the electronics cluster are also likely to influence the nature and development of a multimedia clustering process. In the following, we shall integrate these factors in the analysis of multimedia.

Three recent studies have characterized different aspects of the state and dynamism of multimedia in Scotland (Arthur D. Little 1997, Collinson 1997, Danson 1996). These provide a revealing overview of the development of the constituency at three levels:

- Scale of resources and degree and quality of interconnectedness between institutions in the 'value chain' of multimedia clustering. This gives a sense of clustering presence and depth across the three layers of the diamond of alignment (dimension I (a,b,c) in Figure 13.3).
- General Scottish supply and demand infrastructure factors affecting the development of the constituency.
- Governance aspects underlying the dynamism (or lack of it) in the formation of a potential multimedia cluster in Scotland.

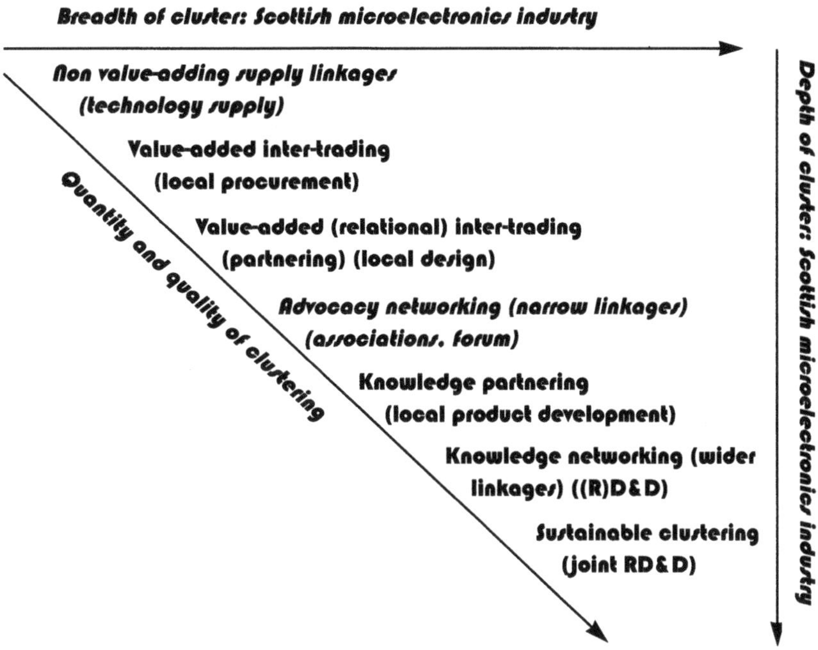

Breadth of cluster: Scottish microelectronics industry

**Non value-adding supply linkages
(technology supply)**

**Value-added inter-trading
(local procurement)**

**Value-added (relational) inter-trading
(partnering) (local design)**

**Advocacy networking (narrow linkages)
(associations, forum)**

**Knowledge partnering
(local product development)**

**Knowledge networking (wider
linkages) ((R)D&D)**

**Sustainable clustering
(joint RD&D)**

Quantity and quality of clustering

Depth of cluster: Scottish microelectronics industry

Figure 13.4 Breadth (quantity) and depth (quality) of clustering in Scottish microelectronics

At the beginning of this chapter a general definition of multimedia
was provided. This stressed the elements of media mixes, interactivity
and networking, including offline multimedia applications (such as CD-
ROM, game stations) and online multimedia applications (including
online services, web publishing, etc.). It was also mentioned that a variety of new and established firms are active in the field. These may be
established firms moving into new business fields (development, production, marketing of new products and services and so on) or new emerging
firms either producing new products and services or using them in a novel
manner (including firms in the field of CD-ROM publications and
Internet services). The latter group is the main concern of this chapter,
since this has so far been the focus of the initial studies carried out in
Scotland.

Thus, the Arthur D. Little (1997) study for Scottish Enterprise
adopted a working definition of the multimedia industry with emphasis
on the provision of interactive content such as corporate communications,
entertainment, education and games (Figure 13.5). This is because interactive content is the element of the multimedia value chain with greatest
value added and is expected to drive multimedia growth.

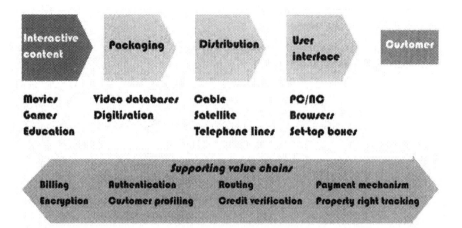

Figure 13.5 The multimedia value chain
Source Arthur .D. Little 1997

Overview of the state of development of the Scottish multimedia constituency

The results of the studies reveal that the Scottish multimedia industry is small, fragmented and only at an early stage of development. Until recently, there was little interaction among established companies. Few links are evident between local companies or between companies at different stages of the value chain. The industry is so small that a company at one stage in the value chain, for example a packager or distributor, has no knowledge of companies at other stages. In addition, there is little informal networking to build relationships between the members of the Scottish multimedia community.

The Arthur D. Little (1997) survey identified sixty-one small multimedia companies in Scotland, employing a total of 550 to 600 people. Most supplied only one or two product lines. These main types of content supply are:

- Animation/games typically for PCs, Sony Playstations, Nintendos and Sega Megadrives;
- Corporate communications;
- Solutions provision, typically interactive training packages;
- Internet consultancy, training and Web page authoring.

Here it is worth noting that, depending on how one defines multimedia, there are other potential players on the scene. For example, Scotland is host to a successful TV production company (STV), several small film producers, colleges of art and design, and software innovation centres. As yet, however, these organizations have not been at the forefront of interactive content production.

The picture of fragmentation gained from the Arthur D. Little survey is tempered somewhat by the existence of two significant groupings, in the areas of content for games and corporate communications. The largest and most substantial group is made up of seven games companies; the group of corporate communications companies has two significant players which have established long-term relationships and partnering across Europe on a small scale. These two groups stand out against the background of other small, sole-ownership multimedia companies and software companies that typically produce CD-ROMs for public agencies.

Business skills and growth-capital

Given the predominant small size and infancy of Scottish multimedia companies, it is not surprising that business skills and capital investment are not well developed. It was found that companies often lacked the management, marketing and finance skills necessary for effective business development.

This is reflected in difficulties in obtaining capital for growth, since venture capitalists want to see strong management teams, and the new companies often find it difficult to demonstrate this strength. This difficulty is compounded by the fact that interactive multimedia has a high-risk image in the UK venture capital market, something which is only reinforced by the characteristics of the small companies. As a result, the survey found that most of the companies had 100 per cent owner equity. The exceptions were the games companies and one corporate communications company.

It is also difficult to gain access to capital through large private sector contracts, simply because of small product ranges and lack of experience in tendering or in business and project management. Public sector projects are not conducive to growth since they tend to be small and very price competitive. Companies have also complained that procurement contracts are often poorly specified and managed, apparently because of a lack of relevant skills on the part of the public sector. Multimedia companies believe that public sector organizations do not understand the multimedia tools and techniques available, or their capabilities and benefits.

On the positive side, Scotland has potential catalysts of multimedia demand and supply in large multimedia projects such as the Millennium Commission-funded Scottish Cultural Resources Access Network (SCRAN).[5] SCRAN aims to digitize Scottish cultural resources and could stimulate demand and encourage networking involving cultural institutions and local companies. The education sector is also looking to use multimedia more extensively in teaching and learning, especially in light of the Blair's government commitment to provide access to the Internet to all schools. As yet, however, this is a possibility waiting to materialize.

Cluster-representing organizations

The small and fragmented state of the Scottish multimedia industry is reflected in the weakness of 'cluster-representing' industrial organizations such as associations or federations. Thus, the Interactive Media Association of Scotland (IMAS) has limited funding and no dedicated premises or administrative support. Board members carry out IMAS activities on a voluntary basis making it difficult to operate efficiently. A business plan is in preparation.

Effective interconnectedness is also affected by the existence of too many trade organizations. For instance, the Scottish Software Federation is planning to set up a multimedia interest group for its members that may overlap with the activities of the principal trade body, IMAS. The Scottish Internet Business Association, representing the distribution element of the value chain, does not appear to have links with IMAS. Other initiatives have little national impact.

Scottish supply-demand infrastructure factors affecting the development of the multimedia constituency

Educational sector supply

The educational system in Scotland is well provided and computer science degree courses at the traditional universities such as Edinburgh, Glasgow and Strathclyde produce high quality graduates. There is concern, however, that the availability of staff with suitable technical skills could be a problem if the multimedia industry develops rapidly. Some graduates leave Scotland while the best of those who stay are absorbed by growth in the software industry and one or two multinational corporations.

In addition, the Scottish system does not compare well in terms of university-industry spin-offs and the commercialization of university-developed technologies. This seems to be a generic situation in Scotland and is also apparent in the workings of the electronics cluster. For instance, FDIs engage in little joint RD&D with Scottish universities, so that there are no significant knowledge flows between the FDIs and the universities.

Role of the Scottish electronics cluster

We have seen that the Scottish electronics industry is dominated by assembly operations and therefore lacks the innovative force that might stimulate synergies with the development and use of multimedia activities. Collinson (1997) also confirms that links and exchanges between incumbent electronics multinational corporations (MNCs) and multimedia SMEs in Scotland are limited. He notes, however, that personnel from MNCs do participate in informal networks, as do technical personnel from the large IT support departments of MNCs, including non-electronics companies (particularly from banks, finance and insurance firms, which have strong IT departments).

At the formal level, however, there are relatively few coincidences of interest between high-tech SMEs and MNCs, while there is a potential conflict of interest due to the overall shortage of software expertise currently affecting Scotland and most other industrial regions. There is a lack of interconnectedness and consequent synergies with the electronics sector in the Scottish multimedia situation. This is a major structural weakness when compared with other places where large and small companies interact through joint R & D initiatives, new product development alliances and frequent exchange of ideas and people in complementary and competing areas of technology.

Telecom infrastructure

Scotland possesses a reasonably well-developed high-bandwidth communications infrastructure for multimedia. In particular, ISDN lines are available in the Central Belt and the Highlands and Islands, and three cable companies operate franchises in the Central Belt and Aberdeen. Also, the Eastman network interconnects most universities with a high capacity fibre optics infrastructure.

Governance in the formation of a Scottish multimedia cluster

Behind the static structural characteristics of multimedia 'cluster' development in Scotland are the governance factors underpinning the dynamics of this development (dimension 1a,b,c in Figure 13.3). Governance factors at the three layers of the diamond of alignment tell us about the likely future of the multimedia cluster formation and about the difficulties of creating missing elements and, generally, overcoming present structural weaknesses. Three types of governance factors have been identified in the case of the Scottish microelectronics clustering process and they are also present in the case of multimedia in Scotland.

General cultural factors

Existing studies have pointed to the presence of a risk-averse culture as an important factor in the low birth-rate of businesses in Scotland (Collinson 1997, Danson 1996). Social and financial rewards do not favour entrepreneurialism and risk taking. Entrepreneurs tend to have a relatively lower status than in the US, and employees are not encouraged to move jobs frequently or aspire to their own businesses. A comparison of new SMEs in Boston and Scotland found that more Scots entrepreneurs saw themselves as 'self-employed' or 'freelance', and more often viewed their attempted ventures as temporary activities in the absence of full-time employment (Collinson 1997). The same study concluded that the Scottish managers were less effective in their networking; they had a narrower range of networks overall and fewer relevant contacts, and were less able to transform these contacts into useful sources of business assistance.

Clearly this situation is far from conducive to the entrepreneurial drive required for cluster sustainability.

Structural positioning in the global economy

Scotland's structural positioning in the global economy (reflected in the predominantly assembling role of FDI in electronics) is also problematic for the establishment of a dynamic sustainable multimedia cluster in Scotland.[6] The driving factors behind the FDI-financed electronics assembling cluster in Scotland are comparatively low wages, government grant incentives, a skilled workforce, English language and fears of European 'fortress' policies. As one FDI company put it: 'We came because we were worried about European barriers and Scotland was a low-cost corner from which to serve Europe effectively.'[7]

Although this combination has helped to attract investment and create jobs, it has clearly failed to create a dynamic of wealth creation and competitiveness based on innovation, rising productivity and high added value. There is a significant flaw in the low-cost free market strategy of Scotland in that although wages may be lower than European or G7 levels, they are not in fact low in global terms. The Scottish cost structure is still significantly higher than that of the low-cost economies of the developing world such as Asia and Latin America. This means that FDI companies – even if they want to embed themselves more fully in the local economy by substantially increasing local sourcing – still face the fact that it is cheaper to buy parts from the global low-cost economies. Furthermore, in multimedia, it is critical to realize that the cost of labour is unlikely to be a determining factor, since the industry is at an emerging stage and demand for creative skills in innovative product and service applications is not easily satisfied. This means that Scotland cannot count on the previous low-cost free market strategy to attract FDI and stimulate an electronic-like clustering process in the area of multimedia.

In this context, the only possibility left at this initial stage is one of long-term positive local strategies and policies to stimulate constituency-building and capability formation, though this may include the role of FDI as one of its aspects. This, however, demands a strong degree of social consensus around a realistic vision and the commitment to persevere, which takes us back to the previous point as well as forward to the social consensus and the role of the policy instruments in Scotland.

Social consensus and policy instruments

The governance factor has a dimension of general influence for clustering processes in Scotland, and also a dimension of more specific validity to the case of multimedia clustering.

The general dimension can be extracted from the experience of the micro-electronics cluster. This has shown that there appears to be little social consensus around a vision of an FDI-led cluster. Society in Scotland has welcomed FDI investment and the employment that accompanies it. It praises manufacturing, easily accepts an export orientation, and approves of skill training and non-conflictual human resource systems. On the other hand, in the context of market ideology, political commentators continually question the value-for-money aspect of FDI subsidy and the opportunity cost of support to innovative SMEs.

In terms of policy instruments Scottish Enterprise is the key player. Its cluster vision, however, has not been informed by a holistic proactive constituency-building perspective. In microelectronics, its activity has primarily concentrated on attracting FDI to Scotland and interacting with the Scottish Electronics Forum (SEF) that largely represents the interests of FDI. Beyond this, Scottish Enterprise's role has been very limited. A number of points have been raised in this connection.

One problem is that Scottish Enterprise is not a single unified body in charge of practical policies for the different regions in Scotland. This local focus is the responsibility of Local Enterprise Companies (LECs), who are related to Scottish Enterprise but have considerable autonomy. It has been noted that this local autonomous focus appears to encourage fragmentation of effort and *ad hoc* initiatives with no common Scottish goal or leadership. Ron Botham of Scottish Enterprise suggests that in this structure the organization sits uneasily with 'functional' and 'local' structures; the problem might be eased if multimedia clusters can work at LEC level, but there are no signs of this happening (personal communication with the author).

Indeed, Botham argues that the organizational structure and mode of operation of Scottish Enterprise (in, for example, resource allocation) is not ideal, and he also points to the following governance elements as problematic:

- Scottish Enterprise's industry partners do not think in strategic clusters.
- Constituency-building is not the normal practice of the organization and is not part of its culture. It stimulates and provides incentives for FDI location in Scotland, but does not engage in mobilizing required players (such as academia) for a clustering process.

This is reinforced by a number of elements which are quite contradictory to the needs of a long-term constituency-building paradigm:

- a predominantly short-term as opposed to long-term thinking
- simple cause and effect thinking as opposed to holistic and systemic thinking
- project-specific evaluation as opposed to strategic evaluation
- free-market flexibility as opposed to a strategy that is also driven by the supply side.

In sum, it is clear that there are deeply rooted cultural, structural and institutional aspects which require substantial changes if the most conducive environment for clustering is to be created. These governance issues must be faced squarely if policy efforts are either to engage in the long-term pursuit of more sustainable cluster dynamics than in the present situation. The alternative is to remain consciously inside the modest confines allowed by the present governance.

As far as the dimensions more specific to multimedia clustering are concerned, the picture is little better. It can be said that, at present, government policy instruments have a significant lack of direction or impact on the establishment of a dynamic process of multimedia cluster formation. This may be about to change with Scottish Enterprise's formation of a widely represented Scottish Multimedia Working Group (SMWG) which will have the purpose of developing and stimulating a coherent strategic approach to multimedia clustering in Scotland. The Arthur D. Little (1997) study on multimedia referred to in this chapter is part of the fact-finding exercise of this incipient process and, as we shall see (pages 293–5), the study argues that there are ways in which government might play an important role in the fostering of a Scottish multimedia industry.

For the time being, however, Scottish Enterprise needs to begin to define its own long-term vision and the practical resource-aligned steps it must take if it seriously hopes to help move the infant industry towards the vision. In this process, the three types of governance factors identified above must be faced squarely, if these visions and actions are to be realistic. Otherwise, the vision is likely to become the centre of 'talking shops' and end in a great deal of disappointment. It seems clear that there are deeply rooted cultural and institutional elements which require substantial changes if the most conducive policy environment for long-term clustering in multimedia is to be created.

Summary discussion

This study has examined the theoretical and practical nature of industrial clusters. It has identified the conditions for sustainability and has provided the sociotechnical constituencies framework to help understand and inform practical processes of cluster formation. Using this framework, it is possible to grasp and assess the content and dynamics (or lack thereof) of such processes, with a view to developing consistent policies for influencing and supporting their emergence and development. In this perspective, a cluster is a large-scale sociotechnical constituency.

The discussion of clustering in Scotland has argued that there is no sustainable cluster in Scottish microelectronics, the most developed cluster process supported by Scottish Enterprise. Scottish Enterprise has helped to create a spatial concentration of microelectronics firms in central Scotland, but this concentration has no knowledge network and therefore little depth. The constituency-building process creating this concentration is narrowly constructed and has focused upon aligning institutional arrangements in Scotland to suit the needs of inwardly investing corporations. On the positive side, aspects of the lean production technological system have enjoyed diffusion by emulation into the indigenous sector, but there is little sign the constituency around microelectronics intends to establish a knowledge network to deepen the cluster. This cluster is stimulated to innovate by RD&D and value-adding suppliers abroad.

The question is whether Scottish Enterprise could have consciously pursued a constituency-building model to improve sustainability. If so, the central aim of clustering microelectronics companies could have been more precisely defined to include and encourage knowledge networks amongst some FDIs and, particularly, with indigenous companies and Higher Education organizations. Such definition would have looked closely at the governance mechanisms at work in the Scottish context and would have faced up to the policy implications. In this respect, the value of a policy framework such as the sociotechnical constituencies model is that it helps to identify key issues and to pose the hard question of how these issues are to be faced by policy strategies. Will this happen with the policies intended to encourage multimedia clustering?

The Arthur D. Little 1997 study has identified some areas of multimedia growth opportunities in Scotland such as Web authoring and Website hosting, network and online gaming, computer animations, and media-integrated call centres. It has also sought to stimulate debate by distinguishing three broad and potentially overlapping visions:

1   Develop a small self-sustaining industry meeting primarily local demand by producing largely bespoke, high quality, products and sourcing skills locally. Developing local demand, principally for multimedia products, will be important in all visions. It could also be stimulated in education. The impetus would come principally from public sector initiatives designed to create demand and develop the industry's competencies through, for example, demonstrator programmes. Practically, stimulating local demand could be the responsibility of a number of organizations. Scottish Enterprise and IMAS, for example, could produce

demonstrator toolkits to show multimedia consumers and suppliers the benefits of state-of-the-art applications, building on the activities of the Department of Trade and Industry's (DTI) Information Society Initiative.

2   Develop global businesses in niche multimedia products such as games; a large niche product cluster would have global players in selected multimedia sub-segments, high quality world-wide brands, and would be a recognized centre of excellence. Games seem to offer Scotland an opportunity to establish such niche clustering. The main intervention needed to support the niche products on a global scale is to provide, or encourage the provision of, risk capital to expand R&D activities and ultimately increase companies' product portfolios. This would make them less vulnerable and less dependent upon packagers and distributors. A self-sustaining and commercially operated Scottish Multimedia Fund (SMF), for example, would provide impetus for this strategy. Various organizations, such as Scottish Enterprise, universities and IMAS, could take responsibility for supporting financing and product development in established companies.

3   Develop a large, world-recognized, multimedia centre producing a complete range of multimedia products. As the cluster became recognized for high quality off-the-shelf products, the cluster would grow both in size and visibility throughout the world and this would encourage global players to locate in Scotland. Regions such as Victoria in Australia are aiming for this goal. The main requirement for this option is to have at least one major FDI multimedia company locating in Scotland. Potential investors could be encouraged through offering financial incentives, and marketing the skilled, flexible and competitively priced workforce, reputable education system and supply of competitively priced land.

The viability of each of these visions is subject to doubts, particularly, in the light of the findings of this study on the nature of clustering in Scotland and the trends towards globalization pervading every industry. There must be doubts, for instance, on the viability of vision one, propounding a small self-sustaining industry meeting primarily local demand. Stimulating local demand is indeed critical, but this does not amount to a vision of sustainability. Likewise, vision three will not automatically follow any possible success in locating FDI multimedia companies in Scotland. The experience of FDI in the microelectronics sector indicates that close attention to the depth of interrelations, including knowledge networking, will be necessary to sustain a multimedia centre producing a complete range of multimedia products.

Vision two can be construed as seeking to stimulate a variety of focused project- or programme-driven constituencies, potentially opening the way for wider cluster-type interrelations. In terms of the diamond of alignment (Figure 13.3), this would imply a great deal of activity starting from the middle-layer (b) and radiating to layers (a) and (c) of the diamond. This would identify and positively engage in focused action on 'value chain' opportunities oriented towards internal and external demand. Here large projects such as SCRAN (Scottish Cultural Resources Access Network) may have the potential to stimulate demand and encourage value-chain networking focused, for instance, on education. Another example may be the new venture Scottish Knowledge with its intended university-networking programme focused on distance-learning exploitation of multimedia training courses.

Of course, the three visions may be combined. Whatever the options, how-ever, the common challenge for all of them, separately or in combination, is to define and implement the practical process of constituency-building. Here the catalytic role is largely in the hands of government institutions who should stimulate the process, remaining within the confines of its own gov-ernance and resources, but with enough openness and innovativeness to question these constraints if this proves necessary and possible.

The support and effectiveness of Scottish Enterprise's Scottish Multimedia Working Group may offer a first test of the depth of commitment to stimu-lating multimedia constituency-building in Scotland. Scottish Enterprise has also recently decided to support the formation of a European Group aimed at enhancing Scottish participation in European information society projects. In principle, there should be substantial synergies between these two actions and others, such as the Scottish dimension of the UK Information Society Initiative (promoted by the UK DTI) supported by the Scottish Office and Scottish Enterprise.

In all instances, this emerging process will require identification of and access to 'value-chain' project opportunities focused on real demands. In this connection, a more precise mapping and assessment of the depth of relations in Scottish clustering processes should prove valuable. This would help iden-tify strategic 'hot points' for implementation of targeted policies for both indigenous growth and sustainable FDI-based developments. It should also help to identify more precisely in which areas of the multimedia value-chain Scotland possesses real or potential competitive advantages for growth (for instance, knowledge creation, knowledge capture, programming, production, sales, servicing, etc.). Conversely, it would reveal weaker areas, in which Scotland might find it necessary or expedient to rely on others, or face the long-term challenge and difficulties of their generation if considered neces-sary and viable.

The gauntlet has been thrown down. Whether Scotland will succeed in gen-erating a multimedia cluster only time will tell. The challenge of multimedia constituency-building is not easy and it is better to face it now, at the early stages of development of the industry. In constituency-building there are no straightforward mechanistic recipes, but a clear understanding of the nature of the complexities, factors, issues and alignment processes involved is a definite strength. This is what this chapter seeks to contribute to the challenge.

Notes

1 Various publications have dealt with the interrelated themes of the 'sociotechnical constituencies' conceptual framework. In particular, see Molina 1990, 1993, 1995, 1996, 1997, Klaes 1997.
2 The phrase sociotechnical constituency provides consistency of language in that constituency is derived from constituent-elements and the complete phrase is designed to encapsulate the evolving ensemble of all constituent-elements playing a part in the creation, production and diffusion of technologies.
3 Regulation theory addresses the agent-structure issue by using Bourdieu's concept of *habitus*, see Bourdieu 1977: 95 and Bourdieu 1971: 200. *Habitus* is a 'matrix of perceptions, appreciations and actions', grounded in material existence but not determined by it, avoiding reductionism by theorising that unmet intentionality or unintended consequences of action provoke a reappraisal of dispositions. See also Robels 1994: 17.
4 This research conclusion confirms that of Oakey 1985.
5 The Millennium Commission funds projects of national interest in the UK out of Lottery money.
6 Many of the points here come from personal communication with Ron Botham from Scottish Enterprise. See also Botham 1997.
7 Quote provided by Ron Botham from Scottish Enterprise. Personal communication.

References

Arthur D. Little (1997) *Multimedia Research Study,* Report to Scottish Enterprise, Glasgow.

Botham, R. (1997) 'Inward Investment and Regional Development. Scotland and the Electronic Industries', Paper for the Regional Science Association (British and Irish Section), Annual Conference, Falmouth, 10–12 September 1997.

Bourdieu, P. (1971) 'Systems of education and systems of thought', in: F. D. Young (ed.) *Knowledge and Control,* London: Collier-Macmillan.

—— (1977) *Outline of a Theory of Practice,* Cambridge: Cambridge University Press.

Charles, D. and Howells, J. (1992) *Technology Transfer in Europe – Public and Private Networks*, London: Belhaven Press.

Collinson, S. (1997) 'Innovation networks in the Scottish multimedia industry', TechMaPP Working Paper Series, TechMaPP, Department of Business Studies, Edinburgh: University of Edinburgh.

Danson, M. W. (ed.) (1996) *Small Firm Formation and Regional Economic Development,* London: Routledge.

Hakansson, H. (1989) *Corporate Technological Behaviour – Co-operation and Networks,* London: Routledge.

Kapferer, B. (1993) 'Social network and conjugal role in urban Zambia', in: J. Boissevain and J. C. Mitchell (eds) *Network Analysis: Studies in Human Interaction,* Paris: Mouton.

Klaes, M. (1997) 'Sociotechnical constituencies, game theory and the diffusion of compact disks. An inter-disciplinary investigation into the market for recorded music', *Research Policy* 25, 1221–34.

Marshall, A. (1965) *Principles of Economics,* London: Macmillan.

Marshall, M. (1987) *Long Waves of Regional Development,* London: Macmillan.

Molina, A. (1990) 'Transputers and transputer-based parallel computers: sociotechnical constituencies and the build up of British–European capabilities in the information technology', *Research Policy* 19, 309–33.

—— (1993) 'In the search of insights into the generation of techno-economic trends: Micro- and macro-constituencies in the mircoprocessor industry', *Research Policy* 22, 479–506.

—— (1994) 'Technology diffusion and RTD programme development: What can be learnt from the analysis of sociotechnical constituencies?', *CEC/DGXII* (XII–378–94), Brussels.

—— (1995) 'Sociotechnical constituencies as a process of alignment: The rise of a large–scale European information technology initiative', *Technology in Society* 17, 4, 385–412.

—— (1996) 'The role of the technical in innovation and technology development: the perspective of sociotechnical constituencies', TechMaPP Working Paper Series, TechMaPP, Dept. of Business Studies, Edinburgh: University of Edinburgh.

—— (1997) 'Insights into the nature of technology diffusion and implementation: the perspective of sociotechnical alignment', *Technovation* 17, 11/12, 601–26.

Oakey, R. (1985) 'High-technology industries and agglomeration economies', in P. Hall and A. Markusen (eds) *Silicon Landscapes,* London: Allen and Unwin.

Robels, A. C. (1994) *French Theories of Regulation and Conceptions of the International Division of Labour,* London: St Martin's Press.

Scottish Council for the Development of Industry (1993) 'SPEED', Glasgow: SCDI.

14

STUTTGART

From the 'car city' to the 'net city'?

Gerhard Fuchs and Hans-Georg Wolf

Introduction

Multimedia, as the most recent source of innovation in information and communications technologies, has the potential to influence greatly the development of regional economies. Major efforts are being made in industrialized countries around the globe to benefit from this potential. As in the cases of earlier technological innovations, the emergence of multimedia industries will have both positive and negative effects on regional economic development and these effects will be distributed unevenly across regional economies. It is important, therefore, to monitor and analyse the different regional paths of development related to multimedia.

This chapter serves this purpose by examining the case of Stuttgart. The region of Stuttgart has achieved its considerable prosperity from a number of traditional, 'mature' industries. The crucial question from this perspective is whether existing industrial strengths are a springboard or a hindrance to multimedia development. We will argue in this chapter that Stuttgart's success in mature industries has impeded the rapid development of a regional multimedia industry. Still, although Stuttgart lags behind other regions, we contend that the prospects for successfully making the transition from a 'car city' to a 'net city' are quite promising.[1]

An important theme that runs through the literature on regional development is that cooperation and 'fuzzy boundaries' among firms contribute greatly to the innovativeness of high-tech regions. California's Silicon Valley is the most obvious example (see Saxenian 1994). The Stuttgart region is host to several big electronics and telecommunications companies such as Alcatel-SEL, Hewlett Packard, IBM, Bosch and Sony. To date, however, the presence of these potentially multimedia-prone companies has not been translated into the development of a significant multimedia cluster. Stuttgart is also renowned for a well-developed network of research facilities, universities, technology transfer institutions and the like. In the case of multimedia, these

298

institutions have yet to stimulate rapid market development in the region. We suggest that there are three reasons for this failure: a lack of cooperation between the main actors, the orientation of traditional network structures towards the old industrial core, and the lack of a dynamic sector of small and medium-sized multimedia firms. As a result of recent efforts in the Stuttgart region, we argue that this picture is beginning to change.

The chapter begins with a brief introduction to Stuttgart's regional economy in the section on 'Stuttgart's tradition: the 'car city'. This is followed by an analysis of the current state of multimedia production in Stuttgart. This section, 'Stuttgart: not the net-city yet', draws on various statistics, a survey of multimedia firms and in-depth interviews. We then discuss how the present state of the multimedia industry relates to the region's previous path of economic development ('Past economic development and multimedia in the Stuttgart region'). The specific problems of stimulating inter-organizational cooperation in the field of multimedia are then illustrated by the case of an ambitious pilot project that took place in Stuttgart between 1994 and 1996 but ultimately failed. In the final section, we look at the most recent efforts by public actors to foster the multimedia industry in Stuttgart.

Stuttgart's tradition: the 'car city'

Stuttgart is the capital city of Baden-Württemberg, the regional state (*Bundesland*) in Germany's southwest. The region of Stuttgart comprises, besides the city itself, five adjacent administrative districts and is home to more than 2.5 million inhabitants. Over one million people, more than a quarter of all employees in Baden-Württemberg, are employed in that area.[2] Although there are other economic centres in the state – above all the regions of Karlsruhe and Mannheim/Heidelberg – the Stuttgart region is the most important.

In many respects, Stuttgart's economy is representative of the state as a whole. For instance, the region features exactly the same comparatively high share of people employed (40.8 per cent) in manufacturing (*Verarbeitendes Gewerbe*) as Baden-Württemberg in total (see Statistisches Landesamt 1996: 232, 234). In spite of the considerable economic diversity one encounters in different parts of Baden-Württemberg, many of the problems and perspectives of the state's economy can be studied by looking at the Stuttgart region.

The region also displays similar sectoral strengths to Baden-Württemberg as a whole. Three sectors are particularly important in Baden-Württemberg: the automotive industry, the mechanical engineering and electronics/electrical engineering. Among these three, the car industry stands out, and it is particularly strong in the region of Stuttgart (see Table 14.1) which contains 'the largest, thickest, and the most powerful auto cluster in Europe' (Morgan 1994: 37) – and is the home of Daimler Benz and Porsche. As this cluster has strongly influenced not only the region's economy but also its institutions and culture, it is no exaggeration to portray Stuttgart as a 'car city'.

Table 14.1 Employment in selected economic sectors of Baden-Württemberg and the region of Stuttgart

	1980 (1,000)		1995 (1,000)		Change (%)	
	Ba.-Wü.	Stgt.	Ba.-Wü.	Stgt.	Ba.-Wü.	Stgt.
Mechanical engineering	249.7	74.0	239.3	62.7	- 4.2	-15.3
Electronics/electrical engineering	253.7	87.5	231.6	75.5	- 8.7	-13.7
Automotive	233.3	106.9	217.6	106.5	- 6.7	- 0.4
Media	242.5	85.9	232.6	79.3	- 4.1	- 7.6
All sectors of economy	3,438.0	987.6	3,737.7	1,040.3	+ 8.7	+ 5.3

Sources: Grammel and Iwer 1998; Fischer *et al.* 1996; own calculations

Building primarily on its highly competitive core sectors, Stuttgart (and Baden-Württemberg as a whole) has long enjoyed economic prosperity and growth and is one of Germany's most prosperous regions. It has one of the lowest levels of unemployment and a comparatively high export ratio. Social scientists interested in explaining the region's economic success have laid emphasis on institutional factors. They characterize the region as coming close to the ideal model of an industrial district (see Sabel 1989, Schmitz 1992, Semlinger 1994, Rehfeld 1995), endowed with a relatively self-contained regional economy and system of governance (Amin and Thrift 1995: 7). They attributed the economic success of the region to a successful partnership among state government, dominant industries, financial institutions, research institutions, and universities (Wallace 1994: 68).

In recent years, however, Stuttgart's (and Baden-Württemberg's) fame as an outstandingly successful region has begun to fade (Richter 1988, Heidenreich and Krauss 1998). Economic growth declined to a low level while Stuttgart's unemployment rate rose. From 1992 to 1996, employment in the Stuttgart region decreased by 110,000 or 9.6 per cent, which is significantly worse than Baden-Württemberg's average (see Statistisches Landesamt 1997).[3] The very key sectors of Stuttgart's economy have contributed significantly to the worsening situation. The automotive and the mechanical engineering industries, along with electronics and electrical engineering, underwent a process of retrenchment. Between 1980 and 1995, employment in mechanical engineering dropped by 15 per cent, and in the electronics and electrical engineering industry the decline amounted to almost 14 per cent of jobs (see Table 14.1). Employment related to the production of electronic data processing systems declined by 10.5 per cent between 1980 and 1996 (see Statistisches Landesamt 1997). Long-term employment prognoses for these sectors remain dim. In 1994 one research institute predicted that between 1991 and 2010, employment would drop by

9 per cent in Baden-Württemberg's electronics and electrical engineering industry, by 15 per cent in the mechanical engineering industry and in the automotive industry by 26 per cent (Saebetzki 1994: 92). Even though there is reason to doubt the validity of such long-term predictions, it is clear that the recipe for regional economic success no longer works as smoothly as it used to in the Stuttgart region.

Many actors in the region now agree that Stuttgart is faced not only with a temporary crisis but with profound structural changes, due to trends towards the globalization of markets, the decline of mature industries, and the rise of highly innovative, knowledge-intensive and service-oriented industries. There is also broad agreement that Stuttgart cannot successfully cope with these changes merely by concentrating on its traditional key industries. Instead, the call for a fundamental restructuring of Stuttgart's regional economy is getting louder.

Multimedia is often seen as a paradigmatic example of the highly innovative industries that will be of increasing importance to regional economic prosperity. It is therefore not surprising that multimedia is also targeted as a crucial sector in strategies for the restructuring of Stuttgart's economy. Few people in the region today would contradict the notion that it is important and desirable to establish a strong multimedia industry. The municipal administration and other regional actors have explicitly supported this aim, describing the desired direction with catchwords such as 'multimedia city' (*multimediale Stadt*), 'intelligent city' or 'net city' Stuttgart.

Thus, one of Stuttgart's goals is to become a multimedia location of importance, possibly even one with a world-wide reputation as a central location for a highly developed media services sector and telecommunications equipment and as the headquarters location of international corporations. On the level of political rhetoric the path appears to be marked out clearly. However, one has to ask: how far has Stuttgart really progressed towards a region significantly influenced by and benefiting from multimedia?

Stuttgart: not the 'net city' yet

In terms of multimedia, experts quote Munich, Hamburg, Berlin and Cologne as important centres in Germany. Stuttgart is hardly mentioned, despite the fact that the technological basis or infrastructure (in terms of technology and human resources) is better developed than in some of the cities mentioned. Let us examine in more detail the state of affairs with regard to multimedia in the Stuttgart region.

Within Baden-Württemberg, Stuttgart commands a dominant position (see Table 14.2). It has a 27.8 per cent share of all employment in the state, and more than a third of all those employed in the media sector work in Stuttgart.

As mentioned earlier, the city shares many characteristics with the overall economy of Baden-Württemberg. In the case of the media economy, things

Table 14.2 Employment in the media sector in Stuttgart (1995) as a percentage of total media sector employment in Baden-Württemberg

Economic Activity	Stuttgart
Data processing, office equipment	36.0
Production of radio and TV equipment	32.8
Electronics/electrical engineering *	32.1
Printing nusiness	32.1
Posts and telecommunications	30.7
Advertising	46.0
Culture, media	33.8
Movie theatre/movie production	42.4
Radio and TV corporations	39.4
Publishing	44.3
Book and magazine publishers	45.6
News agencies	44.1
Total: media economy	34.1
Total: employed persons	27.8

Source: Grammel and Iwer 1998: 25.

Note:: * Subsector only (measuring, controlling and communications technology)

look slightly different. In the state's media sector, as in the whole arena of economic activities, industrial activities loom large. Within Stuttgart's media economy, however, service-oriented activities are much more prominent. Nearly half of all employees active in Baden-Württemberg's publishing business work in Stuttgart; two of the ten biggest German book publishers (Ernst Klett AG, Mairs Geographischer Verlag) are located there. The same holds true for movies and advertising. Employment in these service-oriented activities grew between 1980 and 1995. In the same period, however, there was a significant overall decline in employment in the broadly-defined media sector (see Table 14.3), due mainly to a loss of jobs in hardware-oriented sub-groups such as data processing and office equipment, production of radio and TV equipment, and the printing business.

Nevertheless the hardware sector is structurally dominant. The Stuttgart region hosts the headquarters of Alcatel-SEL, Bosch, the European headquarters of Hewlett Packard and important divisions of IBM and Sony.[4] Just as in Baden-Württemberg in general, the electronics industry is still well positioned in Stuttgart. In the state as a whole, the electronics sector is still more important in terms of employment than car manufacturing. In Stuttgart, however, the automotive industry is the most important employer, and also the sector which saw the smallest decline between 1980 and 1996. The electronics sector, in contrast, declined significantly and much faster than in other parts of the state during this time (see Table 14.1).

Stuttgart's electronics sector is very heterogeneous. It includes, first, a host

Table 14.3 Employment in the media economy of Stuttgart

Economic sector	1980	1995
Data processing, office equipment	13,142	3,443
Production of radio and TV equipment	7,785	4,685
Electronics/electrical engineering *	24,625	25,825
Printing	16,632	14,483
Posts and telecommunications	10,073	10,491
Advertising	2,546	4,927
Culture, media **	4,070	5,000
Publishing ***	7,041	10,473
Total media economy	85,914	79,327

Source: Grammel and Iwer 1998: 13

Notess:

* Subsector only (measuring, controlling and communications technology).

** This includes movie theatres and production (532 in 1980, 586 in 1995) and radio and TV corporations (1,629 in 1980, 2,126 in 1995).

*** Including book and magazine publishing (6,802 in 1980, 10,119 in 1995) and news agencies (145 in 1980, 252 in 1995).

of small and medium-sized enterprises which serve as suppliers for the big electronics firms and companies in the other two leading sectors. In the state as a whole, almost 36 per cent of the output of the electronics and electrical engineering sector is supplied to the automotive and mechanical engineering industries (see Table 14.4). Thus there is a close linkage between the three sectors, with electronics functioning as a support industry for the other two. Those parts of the electronics sector working as suppliers to the car manufacturers have done relatively well over the last few years. This is due mostly to the increasing number of electronic parts that go into new vehicles (see Batz *et al.* 1998: 74).

Second, there is a huge spectrum of very specialized firms working in a wide variety of areas (e.g. Wandel and Goltermann, Diehl) ranging from consumer electronics to electrical tools (e.g. Metabo, Festo).

Third, there are the big electronics companies like the five already mentioned (see page 298). There is little cooperation and few horizontal links between the main actors in the electronics sector. Another characteristic of most of these big hardware firms is that they are not indigenous companies. Alcatel-SEL (specializing in telecommunications equipment for public networks), Hewlett Packard (server technology and laser printers), and IBM (computer hardware and software solutions) are dependent on corporate-wide planning and performance strategies. As a result, the scope of their German subsidiaries for independent action is drastically reduced. This might explain, at least partially, why they have not succeeded in playing a substantial role in establishing a local multimedia cluster – either through developing a specific product portfolio within their companies or with respect to spin-off activities.

Table 14.4 Regional input-output flows between production sectors in Baden-Württemberg 1990*

Output to ➡ Input from ⬇	Electronics/ electrical engineering		Steel, mechanical engineering, data processing		Automotive industry		Total**	
	Mill. DM	%	Mill. DM	%	Mill. DM	%	Mill. DM	%
Electronics/ electrical engineering	3,585	35.7	1,958	19.5	1,638	6.3	10,045	100.0
Steel, mechanical engineering, data processing	555	5.9	5,182	54.9	719	7.6	9,443	100.0
Automotive industry	56	0.5	387	3.2	9,906	81.5	12,148	100.0
Total**	14,062		21,956		26,042		242,666	

Source: Statistisches Landesamt 1995.
Notes:
* More recent data are not available yet.
** Including other sectors not listed here.

One might expect that the employment loss in the electronics sector would have created a significant growth in the number of self-employed people attempting to regain a foothold in the media economy. There are, however, few indicators that this has happened. Furthermore, even though major economic transfers between the electronics sector and the automotive and machine tool industries exist (see Table 14.4), there are few stable cooperative links between the main actors of the electronics sector and the other two sectors. Two exceptions in this respect are Bosch, whose product line is significantly oriented to the automobile industry (electronic ignition systems, electronic scout systems etc.), and IBM, which recently has started some widely publicized cooperative projects with Daimler-Benz.

One of Stuttgart's strengths is a host of important institutions in the field of education and research that make possible a transfer of personnel and knowledge which can assist the development of multimedia. The Polytechnical School for Printing and Media as well as the Polytechnical School for Library Sciences have important concentrations in the field of multimedia. The University of Stuttgart has an outstanding informatics centre, which also works as a hub for European Union activities. The Fraunhofer Institute for Industrial Engineering (IAO) is very active in multimedia-related research. There are also renowned private institutes like the Merz Academy, which provides educational facilities for multimedia productions.

A leading institution in the field of professional training for the movie industry is located in Ludwigsburg, which is part of the region of Stuttgart. These institutional prerequisites would allow for the close cooperation and technology transfer between research and industry which is already so well developed in other parts of the Baden-Württemberg economy. Finally, the state government has created the Medien- und Filmgesellschaft Baden-Württemberg (MFG), a special agency (also located in Stuttgart) formed to coordinate media projects in Baden-Württemberg and to function as a hub for media-related activities.

Stuttgart also benefits from the fact that new multimedia companies (at least in Germany) tend to settle in urban centres. Eckert and Egeln (1997) have demonstrated that multimedia companies in Germany have a strong preference for locating in densely populated areas with relatively wealthy population (measured in a low rate of unemployment) and a high degree of service-oriented activities. These features are again well developed in the region of Stuttgart. Indeed, as Map 14.1 demonstrates, the spatial distribution of multimedia companies in Baden-Württemberg shows a marked concentration in the region of Stuttgart. Other statistics confirm that multimedia corporations are in fact more concentrated in Stuttgart than in other locations of Baden-Württemberg (see Table 14.5).

The authors collected more detailed data on Stuttgart's multimedia firms in a series of oral interviews and a survey (performed at the end of 1997) which used a written, standardized questionnaire (see Fuchs and Wolf 1998). We identified 117 multimedia firms in the Stuttgart region. The forty-seven firms that answered the questionnaire are predominantly young and small. 61 per cent of them were founded after 1993, 32 per cent in 1996–7. Fifty-five per cent had an annual turnover in 1996 of 500,000 Deutsche Mark (DM) at the most and only 21 per cent of more than 2 million DM.[5] On average, the firms had 8.5 regular employees and stable relationships with 5.8 freelance workers. As a few large firms in the sample shifted the mean upwards, the median numbers of employees and freelances were only four and three,

Table 14.5 Multimedia corporations in Baden-Württemberg

	1995 (n=95) per cent	1996 (n=132) per cent	1997 (n=130) per cent
Stuttgart	38	35	35
Karlsruhe	12	13	15
Mannheim/Heidelberg	14	12	14
Other parts of Baden-Württemberg	37	40	36
Total Baden-Württemberg	100	100	100

Source: *Multimedia Jahrbuch* 1996, 1997, 1998; own calculations.

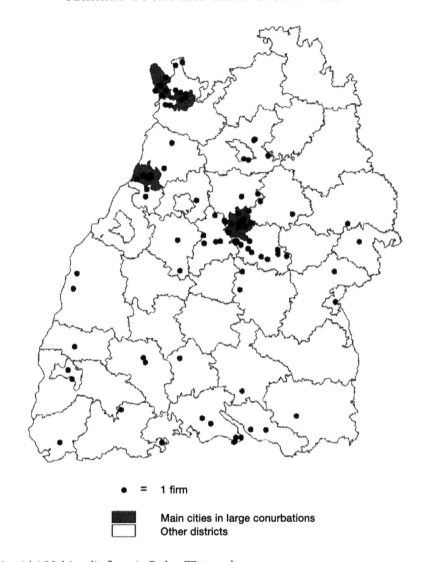

Map 14.1 Multimedia firms in Baden-Württemberg
Source: adapted from Eckert and Egeln 1997

respectively. Most of the firms expect to grow in the coming years: 98 per cent predict a rise in turnover and 74 per cent expect to take on more staff. Thus, Stuttgart's sector of multimedia producers is clearly characterized by a strong dynamic. Clearly too, however, its present contribution to value creation and employment is still very limited.

The firms make the bulk of their turnover (66 per cent) with Internet-related services and products, with CD-ROMs (and CD-I) following in the second position (22 per cent of turnover). Business-to-business services account for 63 per cent of turnover, and most (73 per cent) comprises services and products specifically tailored for one customer (for example, the production of a World Wide Web site for a corporation).

Customers from the Stuttgart region account for more than half (53 per cent) of turnover. Proximity to customers is important for the multimedia companies: in a ranking of fifteen locational factors, proximity to customers turned out to be the fourth most important (after telecommunication costs, labour costs and availability of personnel). Interestingly, banks and insurance companies are the single largest group of customers, while the whole manufacturing sector follows in second place. Considering the extraordinarily strong position of manufacturing industries in the Stuttgart region, one might expect a different ranking. We take this as an indication that the potential demand for Stuttgart's multimedia firms from the dominant industries in this region has not fully come into effect so far. Whether or not this will change could be crucial to the further development of a multimedia cluster in the Stuttgart region.

When asked about the locational factors they deemed in need of improvement, the multimedia firms ranked the high costs of telecommunication services first, followed by the level of taxation. In the third and fourth positions were the costs and availability of personnel. Indeed, the provision of qualified personnel turns out to be an important factor hindering the development of multimedia companies in the Stuttgart region. 44 per cent of the firms stated they found it very difficult to find new staff while only 11 per cent reported no difficulties at all. It is very likely that, but for these difficulties, the companies would envisage faster growth in the years to come.

Although there is certainly a concentration of multimedia firms in Stuttgart, we contend that this does not justify claims for a fully-fledged multimedia cluster in that region. This would require a significantly higher number of companies and employees and much more networking between the companies and the supporting institutions within the regional economy. Thus, in spite of the quite impressive infrastructure described on page 304–5, a significant multimedia industry is only emerging comparatively slowly in Stuttgart. Although most of the relevant elements of a multimedia value chain seem to be present, some other ingredients are obviously missing.

One important weakness in this respect seems to be Stuttgart's cultural environment. In our survey, the firms from Stuttgart pointed to the need to improve the cultural sphere in their region more often than the firms from Karlsruhe and Mannheim/Heidelberg.[6] In our in-depth interviews, multimedia firms voiced significant dissatisfaction with the innovative and supportive environment in Stuttgart. The companies had the impression that neither the official institutions nor the domestic industry are geared towards experimenting with new ideas and spending money on multimedia projects, especially if financial pay-offs cannot be proved. Stuttgart's general image compared to other German cities such as Munich, Berlin and Cologne is rather conventional.

Most of the multimedia companies interviewed have not used the official support agencies and programmes. Many firms voiced the impression that the established networks and support mechanisms did not fulfil their needs and provided few incentives. Correspondingly, in our survey the multimedia firms of Stuttgart named the support and consulting agencies as the least important locational factors. It must be admitted that most of the technology promotion-oriented programmes have been cancelled over recent years due to the state's budgetary problems. But there are still several consulting agencies and technology transfer agencies which could provide valuable support. So far, however, the supporting agencies which seem to be so important in the general success of Baden-Württemberg do not appear to play a relevant part in the case of multimedia. In the following section, we will turn in more detail to the relationship between the regional success story and the state of development with regard to multimedia production.

Past economic development and multimedia in the Stuttgart region

In the preceding section, we argued that the Stuttgart region so far has not succeeded in bringing forth a fully-fledged, self-sustaining multimedia cluster. Given the past success of the region's economy, one might have expected a different development. One might ask, as for instance do Heidenreich and Krauss (1998: 222): since Stuttgart had a well-functioning system of regional governance that was well-suited to an industrial region, why was it not better able to adapt to a technology whose importance for the future of regional economies is so widely accepted? Why was it not possible for the region to transfer what Morgan (1991: 13) called 'its capacity for innovating by networking' to the new growth industries?

Drawing on the general discussion about economic development and industrial policy in Baden-Württemberg, we can trace an answer to this question in the way that past success has become the very reason for the region's comparatively slow orientation towards new industries. Grabher (1993) has aptly described how the Ruhr region became caught in a rut on a once-successful path of development, leading the region into deep economic crisis. According to Morgan (1994: 11), it would be 'surprising' if some of the problems described by Grabher were not applicable to the Baden-Württemberg case. Indeed, Braczyk et al. (1995) identify several of these problems. They point to the slow adaptation of Baden-Württemberg's industry to the 'Japanese challenge' as a case of 'cognitive lock-in' and to the bias of Baden-Württemberg's technology policy towards the core industries as a case of 'political lock-in'. They detect a 'functional lock-in' in Baden-Württemberg's high level of economic integration: the fact that the three industrial core sectors are so closely interwoven makes the whole region particularly vulnerable to economic crises.

In a similar vein, Heidenreich and Krauss (1998: 223) point out that the major companies in Baden-Württemberg's core sectors are quite reluctant to buy in services from external providers. As a result, opportunities for communication and cooperation outside the established trajectories are missed and economic restructuring is hampered by barriers to learning. Heidenreich and Krauss (1998: 229; see also ifo 1995) furthermore show that Baden-Württemberg's system of R&D and technology transfer strongly concentrates on the three industrial core sectors and medium technology rather than on the most advanced technology.

In short, according to this view, the past success of the region's economy now translates into rigidity, placing obstacles on the way to economic restructuring while networks that could further innovative industries remain underdeveloped. Redirecting our focus to the topic of this chapter, we have found some confirmation that this argumentation is valid with regard to the development of Stuttgart's multimedia industry. Regional reorientation towards multimedia indeed seems to be hindered to some extent by a lock-in situation, by the inertia created by the strong dominance of established key sectors. However, to avoid over-simplification we need to consider some aspects in more detail.

On the one hand, the dominance of Stuttgart's three core sectors, *per se,* cannot explain the comparatively slow take-off of a multimedia industry; after all, the electronics and electrical engineering industry, which in principle should be a good starting point for a multimedia industry, is among these core sectors.

As we argued in the preceding section, however, large parts of Stuttgart's electronics and electrical engineering industry still have a rather traditional orientation and were very slow in turning to multimedia. Most of Alcatel's multimedia-related activities are situated in France, and Hewlett Packard does most of its relevant development in the US. Bosch's activities in the Stuttgart region are primarily geared towards car parts, an area with little demand for multimedia. Close interaction between the electronics and electrical engineering industry and the other two core sectors might in principle provide good opportunities for building a regional specialization within multimedia (products and services adapted to the needs of these industries). However, we argued that these opportunities have not yet been taken full advantage of.

As mentioned above, Stuttgart is renowned for its range of book publishing companies. Book publishing without any doubt has a very close affinity to multimedia and one might expect a significant push from this corner as well. Thus, it is not the sectoral structure alone that hampers the development of a multimedia cluster in Stuttgart but also processes within and between the key sectors.

On the other hand, there is indeed some indication that inertia created by the strong presence of mature industries has been hindering the development of multimedia. For instance, only a couple of years ago a member of the Baden-Württemberg government proudly proclaimed that the state would not become a movie state, and ridiculed a potential development towards the services sector (see *Wirtschaftswoche,* 7 March 1996: 10). The intangible, highly creative, often experimental character of multimedia seems to be at odds with the orientation towards the more concrete products of traditional industry, an orientation relevant actors in the region have adhered to for a long time.

This can be considered to be a case of 'cognitive lock-in' closely related to a 'political lock-in': as a consequence of the cognitive dominance of the mature industries, political efforts to support multimedia-related industries were not as strong as they might have been. Among other consequences, specialized support institutions for the (multi)media sector were slow to come into being. The Medien- und Filmgesellschaft Baden-Württemberg (MFG) only became operational in 1996. Another indicator of the way regional political actors neglect (multi)media is the fact that competencies relevant to the sector are dispersed among many ministries of Baden-Württemberg's government (see Fuchs and Wolf 1997a: 54–5). Only in 1996 did the government introduce a steering committee 'Information Society' to coordinate the government's activities.

Many of the multimedia firms we interviewed bemoaned an image and leadership problem. In their view, the public image of Stuttgart is one of negligence towards multimedia. There is a call for political leadership (especially with reference to the examples of Bavaria and North Rhine-Westphalia where leading politicians have made the promotion of multimedia a top priority).[7] There is also a feeling that more 'symbolic politics' are needed to promote Stuttgart as a vibrant centre of activity for multimedia-related affairs.

While the policies of the Land government affect Baden-Württemberg as a whole, Stuttgart as the capital city certainly would receive above-average benefits from a more intense stimulus coming from the Land government.

We do not, however, want to push too far the argument about lock-in and inertia in Stuttgart. During the last three years, there have been remarkable efforts to strengthen the potential for multimedia in the region. We will discuss these efforts in more detail in the following two sections, beginning with an initiative that was central between 1994 and 1996 but ultimately failed. We will then move on to an evaluation of the most recent efforts.

IVSS: a failed attempt to establish an innovation network for multimedia in Stuttgart

It is worth taking a closer look at the most ambitious attempt during the last five years to establish an innovation network for multimedia in the Stuttgart region: the project named 'Interactive Video Services Stuttgart (IVSS)'. The idea was put forward in 1993–4 by the Ministry of Economic Affairs of Baden-Württemberg and aimed to demonstrate in a field trial the new possibilities of interactive television (iTV). The initiators clearly considered the project an important part of their industrial policy. For the ministry, IVSS was a major element of its strategy for economic renewal and a great opportunity for Stuttgart's economic players.

The principal idea behind the project was to induce cooperation between regional actors to develop new iTV-related products and services. This would allow them to achieve an advanced position in the market for this promising new technology, to export their products to other regions and to create new jobs or maintain existing ones. The regional actors particularly addressed by the ministry were a group of big hardware companies represented in the Stuttgart region, namely IBM, Hewlett Packard, Alcatel-SEL and Bosch Telecom. It was in talks with these companies that the idea of the trial was worked out. Along with Deutsche Telekom as the provider of the telecommunications network and the ministry as a general manager and coordinator, the hardware companies constituted the core of the IVSS network (see Figure 14.1).

The partners worked on the plan for the pilot project for almost two years before signing a contract in December 1995. The trial design they agreed upon implied that 2,500 households in the Stuttgart region were to test the new iTV programs and services. The content (e.g. movies) would be stored in digital form in a central server and would be transmitted to the households on demand via fibre and cable television networks.

From the very beginning, the project struggled with technical and organizational problems and the launch was repeatedly delayed. The trial was finally

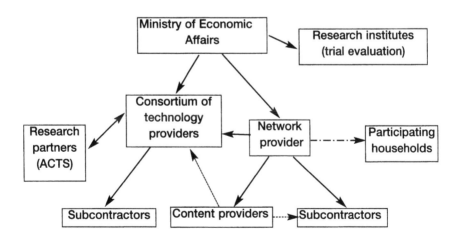

Figure 14.1 The IVSS Organizational Network

set to begin in the Autumn of 1996, but by the end of October 1996 Deutsche Telekom had announced its withdrawal from the project, claiming that the technical system provided by the consortium of hardware suppliers did not function satisfactorily. The company would not accept another extension of the deadline for the provision of equipment but declared the joint project finished. The Ministry of Economic Affairs immediately concurred with Telekom's decision, thereby cancelling the entire IVSS project.

The reasons for the failure of IVSS are complex and cannot be explored in full detail here (see Fuchs and Wolf 1997b for a more complete account). On the one hand, the project was confronted with an extraordinarily high degree of external uncertainty. Significant components of the system to be tested were and still are at the cutting edge of technology. The complexity of the technology for transmitting interactive TV over hybrid fibre-coaxial networks has often been underestimated. Even now, no system for interactive TV with the technical sophistication of IVSS has successfully been implemented with large numbers of participants anywhere in the world.

In addition to the technical difficulties, internal factors relating to the marketability of iTV programmes and services still are hard to predict. Technologies such as digital TV with low-level interactivity or Internet-based services are increasingly considered to be attractive alternatives to iTV in the IVSS version. Inevitably, a momentous decision for a certain technical design had to be made in the early period of the IVSS project and in retrospect one may argue that this decision was less than ideal.

On the other hand, problems related to the setting-up and running of the innovation network added to the uncertainty created by a turbulent and uncertain technological and economic environment. While the project was tightly centred around the large hardware providers, the potential content providers as well as the small and medium-sized multimedia companies in the region were at best loosely coupled to the network. The same holds true for the future users of the iTV services, especially those interested in iTV for business applications (contrary to initial plans, business applications were not developed for the trial).

Cooperation and coordination among the companies participating in IVSS turned out to be difficult and time-consuming. The network members had divergent interests. There were frequent changes of personnel, no clear, unequivocal vision and no central mobilizing actor. All this hindered the efficient development of the IVSS network.

Moreover, while the project was designed to support the aims of regional industrial policy, the participating companies had limited interest in the region. As described above (page 303), major players in Stuttgart included subsidiaries of corporations such as Alcatel–SEL and IBM. They had to align their decisions with the general strategy of their mother companies' headquarters in other parts of the world. At various points changes in the general corporate strategy hampered cooperation within the IVSS project.

It is obvious that multimedia strongly depends on complex interactions among a multitude of heterogeneous actors. On the one hand, the IVSS project shows that important actors in the Stuttgart area are aware of that fact: it was an effort to bring regional forces together in the production of an innovative multimedia application. Thus, it may be regarded as an attempt to transfer what is often considered the region's traditional strength – its well-developed system of interorganizational cooperation – to a new technological field. On the other hand, because of the internal problems described above, IVSS did not succeed in bringing the participating partners into a cooperative relationship that was strong and stable enough to ride out the problems emerging in the project.

Our conclusion from the IVSS experience is that the project headed in the right direction: among other things, it was an attempt to stimulate more cooperation among the big electronics and communications companies in the region, which might be very helpful for the development of a multimedia cluster. Yet the project did not fully meet the demanding requirements for a successful innovation network in the field of iTV.

Unfortunately, from the region's point of view, this big project had the side effect that for more than two years other multimedia-related activities in Baden-Württemberg were stymied. We have already noted that political decision-makers in Baden-Württemberg pay only limited attention to multimedia. The pilot project largely absorbed their limited attention, and the scarce financial resources available, until the end of 1996. More than one year after the end of IVSS, new multimedia-related projects and initiatives in the Stuttgart region are only gradually developing. We turn to these more recent efforts in the following section.

Stuttgart's future: looking for a way to become a 'net city'

As we demonstrated in the previous section, the promotion of the IVSS project aimed at exploiting existing strengths in the Stuttgart region and at addressing the 'global players'. It was expected that they could open up a new window onto the world market for the Stuttgart economy. This attempt was undertaken by the state government of Baden-Württemberg and it 'silenced' possible activities by the regional or city government. Since the failure of the IVSS project new regional activities have begun to develop.

These activities follow a different rationale from the IVSS project, which was based on the idea that innovation is driven by big multinational corporations. The new activities are more directed towards organizing and supporting small and medium-sized enterprises, which are seen – rightly or wrongly – to be the innovative core of a new multimedia economy. Another difference is that the major initiatives are not being undertaken by the old traditional institutions. The 'Wirtschaftsförderungsgesellschaft Region

Stuttgart' (WRS) was set up in August 1995 in order to target new areas and sectors, a task for which the established institutions had shown themselves unfit. Furthermore a new office at the city administration is being formed which also aims to further economic activities in new domains.

The WRS started the 'Medieninitiative Stuttgart' in early 1997. The aim of this initiative is to bring together people interested in multimedia, have them form working groups and develop demands and projects. Working groups dealing with publishing, advertising, multimedia and the movie industry were formed although the big players showed little interest in them. Those involved were predominantly small and medium-sized companies, and individuals trying to become active in multimedia. They raised issues and voiced complaints that are similar to the results of a survey conducted by the Center of Technology Assessment (see Fuchs and Wolf 1998). Nearly all of them expressed dissatisfaction with policies in the field of the media economy, citing a lack of enthusiasm for multimedia among decision makers at all levels. They criticized the inattention of existing promotion and counselling agencies to their needs, and in particular were very pessimistic about the overall cultural climate in Stuttgart, which in their opinion is not conducive to the development of a multimedia cluster (see page 307). The participants in these meetings also had very little knowledge of the market in general and other competitors or people working on similar subjects.

Currently the WRS is advocating the establishment of infrastructural institutions (for example a 'Film Office') which will act in a liaison capacity, relaying requests from the outside world to regional companies, or in a supporting role. An institution to promote small and medium-sized publishing houses is now taking form as an online organization.

Another, even more promising initiative, has been started in the city of Ludwigsburg. A centre for new as well as established media companies has been started close to the Movie Academy. The premises are already fully occupied with occupants who value its proximity to the Academy as well as the possibilities for contact and exchange among the companies there.

Compared to other regions these activities look somewhat belated. The process of defining an objective for regional activities is still incomplete and, moreover, the Medieninitiative Stuttgart is in competition with activities that want to promote Stuttgart as a 'Bio-Region' or as an 'Environmental Technology Region'. As this shows, the process of self-definition is still under way and it is not yet clear whether supporting the creation of a multimedia cluster is actually the way to proceed. All these activities, however, also demonstrate that there is significant potential in Stuttgart and the resources guarantee that there is space for a variety of specializations. Given the need to concentrate scarce (public) financial and personal resources, it might be worthwhile, however, to think about some prioritization. There is a considerable economic potential beyond cars, tool-making and publishing, but to break away from a long-established and familiar path of development creates considerable uncertainty.

314

Conclusion

Drawing on empirical information (provided, *inter alia,* in the chapters of this volume) and theoretical considerations, we suggest that there are two logics or patterns of development allowing for the emergence of regional multimedia clusters. To be sure, these are ideal types, analytical distinctions, which abstract from, rather than exactly depict, empirical cases. In reality, the two patterns tend to co-exist and intermingle.

The first pattern is characterized by the autonomous momentum of development in certain economic sectors. A multimedia cluster emerges in an organic, 'natural' way thanks to the existence of strong predecessor industries. These predecessor industries may be directly related to the *supply* of multimedia products and services (e.g. the sectors of computer software and hardware) or they may be ones that create a strong *demand* for multimedia (e.g. the television or movie industry). Within this pattern, the pre-existing industrial structure in a given region is of crucial importance. As this structure usually developed over long periods of time, a strong element of path-dependency comes in here. If a region is dominated by industries which cannot be considered multimedia predecessors, then path-dependency may make it difficult for this region to bring forth a significant multimedia industry.

While in the first pattern the structural dimension prevails, in the second the dimension of agency is crucial. It is the support for regional development strategies, initiatives and policies that allows a multimedia cluster to develop. Again, this support may address the *supply* side of multimedia (e.g. support for new companies or subsidies to existing ones) as well as the *demand* side (e.g. public procurement of multimedia products and services). This is a counterargument to pure path-dependency: even if the past development and present economic structure of a given region have created unfavourable preconditions for a multimedia industry, efforts to realize a reorientation may be successful.

How do these two logics apply to the case of Stuttgart? Our conclusion is that both patterns of development might help this region to bring about a multimedia cluster but that there is still serious uncertainty and some important questions remain unanswered.

With regard to the first logic, we argued that Stuttgart's pre-existing industrial structure has had a predominantly negative effect on the development of a multimedia industry. We found some evidence of path-dependency and lock-in effects. The dominance of mature industries apparently has not supported a dynamic take-off of multimedia. As Egan and Saxenian (this volume) put it, there are 'untried' industries whose potential for supporting the emergence of a multimedia industry has not been fully explored. Arguably, Stuttgart's key sectors – the automotive and mechanical engineering industries – do possess such a potential. We conclude from our analysis that this has not yet been exploited. Whether this may change in the years to come is difficult to predict and certainly merits further research.

With regard to the second logic, our conclusion is that efforts to establish a multimedia cluster in the Stuttgart region so far have not had a very strong impact. What has often been described as a particular strength of Stuttgart and Baden-Württemberg – the sophisticated forms of cooperation in interorganizational networks – has not turned out to be a strong supportive factor with regard to multimedia as a new growth industry. IVSS, the most ambitious attempt in this context, failed. After its cancellation, a number of new initiatives have been launched. These new initiatives pursue a different approach than the IVSS project. They are broader and more open, less orientated towards the big players, and lay more emphasis on discourse and communication than on large-scale trials. It is too early, however, to evaluate whether they will be able to stimulate the dynamic growth of a multimedia industry in the Stuttgart region. It certainly will take time before the WRS initiative achieve results that enable new forms of multimedia-related cooperation to arise, stabilize and finally translate into the emergence of new firms and employment. The same time-lag has to be taken into account with regard to other institutions such as the MFG which have not been operating long enough to assess their impact on multimedia in the Stuttgart region. There is also the frequent criticism of practitioners that Stuttgart lacks the appropriate cultural climate for multimedia. If this is justified, it is an impeding factor that will at best change very slowly.

Thus, some question marks remain with regard to the future of Stuttgart's multimedia industry. Among other things, competition with other regions in Germany does not improve the prospects for a cluster's emergence. All in all, we conclude that Stuttgart does not contain a fully-fledged multimedia cluster yet but that it has the chance to bring one about. Nonetheless the region has still a long way to go in its drive to transform itself from a model 'car city' to an innovative 'net city'.

Notes

1 We are not implying, however, that it is necessary or obligatory for the economic well-being of the region of Stuttgart to develop a multimedia cluster.

2 The exact figures (as of 31 March 1997) are: 1,020,642 people employed in the Stuttgart region, 3,654,703 in Baden-Württemberg, Stuttgart's share in Baden-Württemberg's employment: 27.8 per cent (the numbers refer to persons officially employed and registered in the social security schemes, see Statistisches Landesamt 1998).

3 It should be mentioned that in a European context, Baden-Württemberg is counted by the European Union among the eight star regions of Europe: fast growing, extremely technology-intensive with a comparatively low unemployment rate. To this extent we are talking about a relative decline (EC 1998: 361).

4 Sony recently announced that it will close its research and development centre in Stuttgart and move to Berlin.

5 In August 1998, one German Mark was equivalent to approximately 0.56 US dollars.

6 This outcome is corroborated by a comparison of soft locational factors in fourteen major German cities published by the German Institute of Urban Affairs
(see Grabow *et al.* 1995: 302). According to this comparison (based upon an
opinion poll of entrepreneurs), Stuttgart is only in the 11th position with regard
to 'high culture' (theatre, concerts, opera etc.) and 12th with regard to 'low culture' (cinema, pubs, entertainment etc.). Only Essen, Leipzig and Nürnberg
figure worse.

7 More generally, practitioners from Baden-Württemberg's media industry frequently complain that the government lacks a single, top-level representative of
(multi)media (see *SuperHighway Journal*, No. 4/1996).

References

Amin, A. and Thrift, N. (1995) 'Living in the global', in A. Amin and N. Thrift,
(eds) *Globalization, Institutions, and Regional Development in Europe*, London:
Oxford University Press.

Batz, U., Grammel, R., Iwer, F., Vogl, G. and Volkert, J. (1998) *Strukturbericht
1997/98 zur wirtschaftlichen und beschäftigungspolitischen Lage in der Region
Stuttgart*, Stuttgart: Industrie-und Handelskammer Region Stuttgart.

Braczyk, H.-J., Schienstock, G., and Steffensen, B. (1995) 'The Region of Baden-
Württemberg: a post Fordist success story?' in E. Dittrich, G. Schmidt, and R.
Whitley (eds) *Industrial Transformation in Europe. Process and Contexts*, London:
Sage.

EC (European Commission) (1998) *Second European Report on S&T Indicators 1997*,
Luxemburg: Office for Official Publications of the European Communities.

Eckert, T., and Egeln, J. (1997) *Multimedia-Anbieter in Westdeutschland: Existieren
Cluster?* Arbeitsbericht Nr. 76, 2nd edition, Stuttgart: Akademie für
Technikfolgenabschätzung, Baden-Württemberg.

Fischer, A., Grammel, R., Iwer, F. *et al.* (1996) *Krise als Normalität. Wirtschafts-und
beschäftigungspolitische Lage der Region Stuttgart. Strukturbericht 1996*. München:
Institut für Medienforschung und Urbanistik.

Fuchs, G. and Wolf, H.-G. (1997a) 'Multimedia-Land Baden-Württemberg?' in M.
Heidenreich (ed.) *Innovationen in Baden-Württemberg*, Baden-Baden: Nomos.

——— (1997b) 'Regional economies, interactive television and interorganizational
networks – a case study of an innovation network in Baden-Württemberg',
European Planning Studies 5: 619–36.

——— (1998) *Multimedia-Unternehmen in Baden-Württemberg. Erfahrungen,
Erfolgsbedingungen und Erwartungen*, Arbeitsbericht Nr. 128, Stuttgart: Akademie
für Technikfolgenabschätzung, Baden-Württemberg.

Grabher, G. (1993) 'The weakness of strong ties. The lock-in of regional development
in the Ruhr area', in G. Grabher (ed.) *The Embedded Firm. On the Socioeconomics of
Industrial Networks*, London and New York: Routledge.

Grabow, B., Henckel, D. and Hollbach-Grömig, B. (1995) *Weiche Standortfaktoren*,
Stuttgart: Kohlhammer and Deutscher Gemeindeverlag.

Grammel, R. and Iwer, F. (1998) *Mögliche Arbeitsplatzeffekte durch Multimedia in ausgewählten Regionen Baden-Württembergs*. Arbeitsbericht Nr. 81, 2nd edition, Stuttgart: Akademie für Technikfolgenabschätzung in Baden-Württemberg).

Heidenreich, M. and Krauss, G. (1998) 'The Baden-Württemberg production and innovation regime. Past successes and new challenges', in H.-J. Braczyk, P. Cooke and M. Heidenreich (eds) *Regional Innovation Systems*, London: UCL Press.

ifo Institut für Wirtschaftsforschung (ed.) (1995) *Der Wirtschafts-und Forschungsstandort Baden-Württemberg*, München: ifo.

Morgan, K. (1991) 'Innovating-by-Networking. New models of corporate and regional development', *Papers in Planning Research No. 125*, Cardiff: University of Wales College of Cardiff.

—— (1994) *Reversing Attrition? The Auto Cluster in Baden-Wuerttemberg*, Arbeitsbericht Nr. 37, Stuttgart: Akademie für Technikfolgenabschätzung in Baden-Württemberg.

Multimedia Jahrbuch (1996) *Multimedia Jahrbuch 1996 mit CD-ROM. Das Jahrbuch der interaktiven Medien. Produzenten und Dienstleister in Deutschland, Österreich und der Schweiz*, München: Hightext Verlag.

Multimedia Jahrbuch (1997) *Multimedia Jahrbuch 1997 mit CD-ROM. Das Jahrbuch der interaktiven Medien. Produzenten und Dienstleister in Deutschland, Österreich und der Schweiz*, München: Hightext Verlag.

Multimedia Jahrbuch (1998) *Multimedia Jahrbuch 1998 mit CD-ROM. Das Jahrbuch der interaktiven Medien. Produzenten und Dienstleister in Deutschland, Österreich und der Schweiz*, München: Hightext Verlag.

Rehfeld, D. (1995) 'Disintegration and reintegration of production clusters in the Ruhr area', in P. Cooke (ed.) *The Rise of the Rustbelt*, New York: St. Martin's.

Richter, G. (1988) *Stuttgart – Problemregion der 90er Jahre?* IMU-Studien 7, München: Institut für Medienforschung und Urbanistik.

Sabel, C. F. (1989) 'Flexible specialization and the re-emergence of regional economies', in P. Hirst and J. Zeitlin (eds) *Reversing Industrial Decline? Industrial Structure and Policy in Britain and her Competitors*, Oxford, New York and Hamburg: Berg.

Saebetzki, A. (1994) 'Perspektiven der Beschäftigung im Maschinenbau, in der Elektrotechnik und im Straßenfahrzeugbau bis zum Jahr 2010', in *ZEW-Wirtschaftsanalysen* 1, 2: 78-95.

Saxenian, A. (1994) *Regional Advantage: Culture and Competition in Silicon Valley and Route 128*, Cambridge, Mass.: Harvard University Press.

Schmitz, H. (1992) 'Industrial districts: model and reality in Baden-Württemberg, Germany', in F. Pyke and W. Sengenberger (eds) *Industrial Districts and Local Economic Regeneration*, Geneva: International Institute for Labour Studies.

Semlinger, K. (1994) *Industrial-district-Politik in Baden-Württemberg. Zwischen Neubesinnung und Neuanfang*, Arbeitsbericht Nr. 39, Stuttgart: Akademie für Technikfolgenabschätzung in Baden-Württemberg.

Statistisches Landesamt Baden-Württemberg (1995) 'Input–Output–Tabellen Baden-Württemberg 1990', unpublished paper, Stuttgart .

—— (1996) *Statistisches Taschenbuch Baden-Württemberg 1996*, Stuttgart: Metzler-Poeschel.

—— (1997) 'Region Stuttgart: Seit 1992 gingen 110000 Arbeitsplätze verloren', *Eildienst Statistisches Landesamt Baden-Württemberg, Nr. 265/1997*, Stuttgart: Statistisches Landesamt.

—— (1998) 'Statistische Berichte Baden-Württemberg, A VI.5/vj 1/97 – Sozialversicherungspflichtig beschäftigte Arbeitnehmer in Baden-Württemberg am 31. März 1997', Stuttgart: Statistisches Landesamt.

Wallace, W. (1994) 'Rescue or retreat? The nation state in Europe, 1945–1993', in *Political Studies* 42: 52–76.

15

FROM SMOKE-STACK INDUSTRIES TO INFORMATION SOCIETY

Multimedia industry in the Tampere region

Gerd Schienstock, Henrik Räsänen and Mika Kautonen

Introduction

Not only old industrial regions, but also some which prospered during the 1970s and 1980s now have to contend with serious economic problems. This development has aroused scientific as well as political interest in processes and strategies of economic transformation. It has become obvious that modernizing existing industries is not sufficient to set many regions onto a new path of economic growth. A successful transformation strategy for regional economies must also include the development of technological innovations as the basis for establishing new industries or industrial clusters.

Multimedia is seen as a new industry with considerable growth potential. Regions all over Europe are now trying to develop a multimedia cluster or – even more ambitiously – to turn themselves into an information society. In Finland, the Tampere Region has declared its aim to transform itself from an old industrial region into the centre of the Finnish information society by developing a multimedia cluster. This chapter will analyse whether the region has the potential to realize this aim.

Our perspective on multimedia takes into account all the relevant actors of the multimedia value chain located in the Tampere Region including hardware and software producers as well as network operators and actual content providers. This is because of the pattern of development in the region, where the earlier layers of productive fabric have created a sound basis for a content industry to emerge. Due to this development, the elements are closely interconnected. The aspects of institutional and regulative environment are also studied.

A theoretical framework

The development of new industries

For quite a long time the controversy between the science/technology push and the demand pull approach has dominated innovation and diffusion research. Nowadays, however, there is widespread agreement that the development and diffusion of technological innovations depend on the demand of potential clients and the scientific and technical knowledge of possible producers. It is more important to analyse how these factors are related to and influence each other than to decide whether supply or demand side factors are more critical for product and process innovations (Nelson and Winter 1977).

Furthermore, the development of new industries based on technological innovations does not depend only on market demand and scientific knowledge; the existing industrial structure also plays an important role. In this respect we should note that learning processes within firms often lead to innovations (Johnson 1992). Firms also play an active role in the diffusion process as they develop new technological applications. It is therefore necessary to analyse the development process of new industries in a region as a process in which accumulated production knowledge and new scientific and technical options interact with each other as well as with new market demand (Lovio 1985). Such a complex approach has been developed in what is often labelled 'evolutionary economics' (Dosi 1988).

It is overwhelmingly the firms which produce and commercialize technologies that influence what products and processes emerge in industry and on markets. Their actions will largely decide whether technological innovations are created on the basis of which new industries in regional economies can develop. As technological change is a cumulative process (Lundvall 1992), the level of technical and production knowledge among the established companies in the region is important here. But the development of production in new technological fields also depends on the intensity of knowledge exchange between the companies located in the region. The more cooperation between them has already been established, the more likely it is that they will work together to develop new technologies and industries. It is also important to consider whether the existing regional production system corresponds with technological innovations in a new field, and whether the new products and processes can be applied in the traditional industries. Such compatibility is an important factor for the success of regional transformation processes. Thus when analysing new evolving industries or industrial clusters we have to take into account how they fit into the established industry structure within the regional economy.

In evolving industries, thresholds are generally quite low, as initially mainly small production series are required. This gives newcomers a good chance to survive. As new firms are often offshoots of research units in universities or established firms, it is important that these organizations support entrepreneurship among their members. Besides this, it very much depends on cultural aspects whether new firms based on technological innovations will be founded, and become the forerunners of a new industrial cluster. A culture of openness to new technologies will support the development of new industries while resistance to technological change may be an obstacle difficult to overcome.

Turning to the demand side it is important to mention that for the establishment of a new industry or industrial cluster the home market is fairly significant. Here the following aspects are of particular importance:

- The need for trust and close cooperation between producers and customers to support collective learning processes.
- A market which is easy to survey and which allows reliable anticipation of future demand.
- Less intensive competition and specific advantages for insiders (Lovio 1985).

In the long run, however, export prospects are of great importance, particularly when the regional or national market is small. Regions that are home to globally oriented firms exporting to different parts of the world have a great advantage. Thus, for the successful development of a new industry or industrial cluster it is crucial to have both a local market capable of absorbing technological innovations and firms integrated into the global market.

The scientific and technological potential of a region to establish new industries depends in the first place on its capacity to produce new knowledge in the relevant scientific fields. Universities play a key role in this; they must provide enough research capacity to support companies with the scientific knowledge needed to develop new products and processes. Here again it is important that the actors in this field trust each other and can cooperate closely to ensure that knowledge transfer takes place.

Nowadays, in a period of rapid technological change, it is not sufficient for companies to have close relationships with regional knowledge providers only. It is equally important to be connected with other knowledge centres all over the world. For firms to develop products in new technological fields, it is necessary to have the research and development capacity to transform abstract scientific knowledge into innovation projects. Technology transfer organizations with close relationships to the main economic actors in the region can also be useful in technological innovation processes.

As has already been stressed, because of the complexity of their innovation activities, companies very seldom innovate in isolation. They interact with other organizations to gain, develop and exchange various kinds of knowledge, information and other resources. Cooperation partners may initially be other firms, including not only customers and supplier firms but also sometimes competitors. They may be universities, technology transfer institutes, private and public research institutes, investment banks, management consultants, training organizations, local or regional governments, economic associations or trade unions. This regional environment, however, is often geared to the traditional production structure and is therefore only mildly reform-conscious or capable of introducing major innovations.

Technology

For various reasons, multimedia is a good example of the development of new industries or industrial clusters in general.

- The development of multimedia is very dependent on local demand.
- Multimedia takes in a range of industries, which makes establishing a new industrial cluster a quite complex process, depending on close cooperation between key actors.
- It has a considerable employment potential. There is some hope that multimedia will stimulate economic growth to such an extent that it can compensate for job losses in traditional industries.

It is not easy to define multimedia, as various industries are integrated; the concept therefore has extremely fluid boundaries (Scott 1998). There is no official designation of the multimedia industry in Finnish economic statistics, nor is there any designation of the multimedia content designers in the labour statistics. Other terms such as telecommunication or information technology very much overlap with multimedia, although they are not congruent. Information technology, for example, can be used in many other ways than in multimedia, as in computer-aided manufacturing, for example.

What is central to multimedia is the process of social interaction on the basis of computer applications in which different types of media – video, audio and print – are integrated. Therefore multimedia is characterized by the following three aspects:

- Different media which can be combined in various ways.
- Interaction or communication among social actors through or with such media.
- Computers and information technology as a technical basis.

As can be seen in Figure 15.1, the technical basis of the multimedia cluster is formed by some machinery and hardware sectors, namely computers, communications systems and an assortment of related components and peripherals. In order to gain access to this hardware base an appropriate software and programming interface is needed. Equipment, channels and tools are an important part of the more widely-defined multimedia cluster.

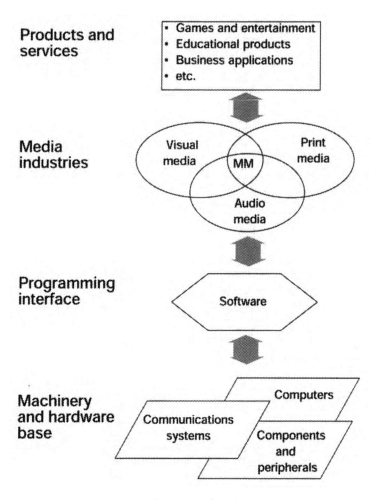

Products and services
- Games and entertainment
- Educational products
- Business applications
- etc.

Media industries

Visual media   Print media   MM   Audio media

Programming interface

Software

Machinery and hardware base

Communications systems   Computers   Components and peripherals

Figure 15.1 Multimedia industry in a functional context
Source: (Scott 1998: 139)

The core of the multimedia cluster, however, is the content industry: the production and compiling of data, information, works of art, video programmes or other performances for dissemination through information networks or electronic media. Content is represented by the three primary media:

- Visual media, in the form of motion pictures, television, graphics and the like.
- Print media, including books, magazines, newspapers, directories and statistical materials.
- Audio media, such as musical recordings, sound effects, radio and so on.

Media products may, of course, assume conventional analogue forms such as celluloid films or books, but they can nowadays also be digitized and stored electronically. This electronic form makes it possible to combine them interactively. The multimedia industry comes into existence at points where the various primary media intersect, and is associated with full digitization. At the turn of the millennium, this convergence will be realized technically. It has been said that the most notable novelty in the ever-faster shift to multimedia is not the mix of the three media but interactivity (Jääskeläinen and Oesch 1995). Interactivity allows users to have an effect on media instead of only being passive consumers.

Some characteristics of the Tampere Region

The Tampere Region (Pirkanmaa) lies inland at the heart of southern Finland, 180 km northwest of Helsinki, the capital. With a population of over 430,000, it contains about one-eighth of Finland's population and is the country's second largest region after Uusimaa, which includes Helsinki and its 1,300,000 inhabitants. The city of Tampere, the centre of the region, is Finland's second largest city with a population of 176,000 inside its city limits.

Tampere and its environs have always played a special role in the Finnish economy. As early as 1840 it was an industrialized city with large-scale enterprises from which the industrialization process of the whole country started. The city's industry was based on the Finlayson cotton mill and on paper mills, and later on engineering. At the turn of the century food processing and the chemical industry also became important for the region.

In the past twenty years, the traditional industries of Tampere have undergone profound changes. The number of employees in industry fell from more than 90,000 in 1975 to 46,000 in 1997, as many plants closed down or restructured their organization to reduce the workforce.

Two-thirds of the population are aged between fifteen and sixty-four, which by European standards is a fairly high figure. The number of employed people was 164,000 in 1997, which means that the region accounts for roughly the same proportion of the Finnish workforce as its total population implies. As in the rest of the country, women account for a large percentage (46 per cent) of the workforce.

As can be seen in Table 15.1, the bulk of employment in the region is in the service sector, which accounts for 59.7 per cent of total employment, although this is below the national average of 66.2 per cent. A total of 97,280 people are employed in services. The proportion of those employed in manufacturing and construction in the region is above the national average: 34.8 per cent as compared to 26.4 per cent for the country as a whole, amounting to a total of 56,691 jobs in the Tampere Region. The manufacturing sector alone employs a total of 46,991 people. It generates FIM 11 billion (2 billion ECU) in exports (Raines and Bachtler 1996: 8, Pirkanmaan Liitto 1996).

Table 15.1 Sectoral distribution of employment 1970–95, per cent

Sector	1970	1975	1980	1985	1990	1993	1995
Agriculture and forestry							
Tampere region	15.3	11.7	9.9	8.3	6.6	6.8	5.5
Finland	20.5	15.2	13.0	10.7	8.7	8.8	7.4
Manufacturing and construction							
Tampere region	45.9	47.0	44.3	39.8	37.2	33.5	34.8
Finland	35.1	36.3	34.1	31.8	29.2	26.3	26.4
Services							
Tampere region	38.8	41.3	45.8	51.9	56.2	59.6	59.7
Finland	44.4	48.5	52.9	57.5	61.6	64.8	66.2

Source: Statistics Finland 1997

The most important industries in the Tampere Region are the pulp and paper industry and mechanical engineering, which together account for over 40 per cent of the total value of industrial production, with the rubber and chemical industries accounting for 14 per cent. The textile and clothing industry, which used to be at the heart of the regional industrial structure, has declined quite dramatically over the past two decades and now represents less than 10 per cent.

There are about 23,000 firms in the region, of which nearly 3,300 are industrial companies. About 660 of them have world-wide operations, and a dozen of them are world market leaders. The majority of firms in Finland are small, a characteristic which the region shares with the country as a whole. Approximately 78 per cent of the firms in the region have four or fewer employees and only 10 per cent have ten or more. The firm formation rate for the region, however, is relatively low.

The Tampere Region has twenty-four companies ranked within the 500 biggest companies in Finland (by turnover). Four of these companies are ranked within the largest 100 companies, earning a combined annual turnover of FIM 6.5 billion (1 billion ECU). These firms are engaged in manufacturing, publishing and printing, forest industry products, and food products. Companies in the electrical products and instrumentation sectors, chemical products, telecommunications and textiles are also important.

The economic crisis that swept across Finland in the early 1990s hit the Tampere Region very badly. Industrial production reached rock bottom during 1991, dropping by some 10 per cent from the record levels reached just a few years earlier. The recession also caused a significant decline in export figures as well as in investment. It also caused an extremely high unemployment rate which peaked at more than 20 per cent of the working population. The unemployment rate in the region is still very high (17 per cent) and is only gradually decreasing even though the economy has begun to boom. It is quite clear that the economic upswing in the traditional industries will not reduce unemployment rates significantly. Therefore great efforts are being made to develop new industries; the multimedia industry is seen as most promising of these.

The multimedia industry in Tampere: an emerging cluster?

Some general remarks

In the following sections, a broader concept of multimedia will be used including information technology as the basis of the multimedia cluster.

In the Tampere Region, a total of 180 companies and over 6,700 people are involved in the multimedia industry in this broader sense. Information technology producers in the region operate in the following areas: data communication, cellular networks, work station software, work group software, databases, integrated systems, instrumentation, sound and picture processing, production control logistics systems. The major producers are ICL Data, Nokia Mobile Phones, Nokia Telecommunication, TPO (a local telecommunication company) and Telecom Finland. We must keep in mind, however, that not all the information technology industry in the region is included in the multimedia sector. There are, for example, firms producing software not connected to multimedia production but designed to monitor manufacturing flows, to handle firms' accounts and so on.

The electronics and telecommunications industry, compared to Finland as a whole, is under-represented in the Tampere Region: its share of total industrial production of electrical equipment in the country is only 4 per cent. This weakness in manufacturing is offset by the region's prominent role in R&D and in services. In addition to numerous firms using information technology in their daily operations, the major single users of information technology are the media trust Aamulehti and the national TV channel TV2. The content producers in the region are small companies generally employing fewer than ten people.

To illustrate the region's strength in information technology R&D, let us take a few examples. About half (about 17 million ECUs) of the national technology multimedia programme will be carried out in the Tampere Region. One of the most interesting new information technology products in the world – the Nokia 9000 Communicator – was developed in Tampere. Nokia developed this hybrid of mobile phone and pocket computer in its R&D unit in Hermia Science Park in close cooperation with Tampere University of Technology. One of the best-selling teamwork PC programs in the world, TeamWare, was also developed in Tampere by ICL Personal Systems Oy.

The content industry as the core of the multimedia sector is still rather small but it is growing very fast. Growth of the industry seems to be limited only by how many educated and suitably qualified persons the education system can produce. In 1995 the whole multimedia sector created 607 new jobs, in 1996 as many as 1,610, and in 1997 the number of new jobs was 1,539. These figures are remarkable considering total employment in the sector. In fact, employment in the whole multimedia sector has more than doubled within four years from about 3,000 jobs to 6,756 in 1997. This increase was mostly due to Nokia Group and its suppliers, but there was also growth in the small firm sector.

The structure of the multimedia industry in the Tampere Region

This section will describe the different industries which together form multimedia. Figure 15.2 gives an overview of companies and other organizations involved in the multimedia industry.

The total number of firms in the hardware industry in 1996 was fifty-five. The most important employers among the producers of hardware information technology are:

* Nokia Telecommunications Oy.
* Nokia Mobile Phones Oy.
* Kyrel Oy (component and system supplier).
* Finnyards Oy (electronics).

These four organizations employ more than 1,200 people. This is nearly a fifth of all employment in the region's multimedia industry sector. The smaller firms in the hardware sector employ about 150 persons altogether. Thus, the firm structure is bipolarized with about fifty firms employing fewer than twenty and four employing more than a hundred people. Altogether about 1,400 people are employed in the sector in the whole region (Räsänen 1996).

According to a survey carried out by the Information Technology Centre of Expertise Programme (Räsänen 1997), the IT hardware sector had a turnover of FIM 1,850 million (320 million ECU). The figure demonstrates that the Tampere Region does not have an important role in the manufacturing side of information technology. Nokia, the dominant company in the region, has its manufacturing plants in a small town near Turku, but many of its new products are developed in Tampere, as was the new Nokia Communicator.

Tampere and its neighbouring municipalities have a strong agglomeration of software houses. These had a total turnover of as much as FIM 2.1 billion (350 million ECU) in 1995. In 1996, growth continued with a resulting total turnover of about FIM 2.6 billion (450 million ECU). The most important

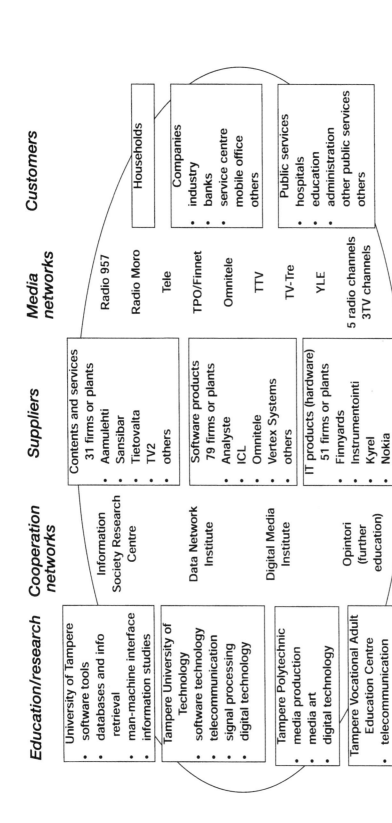

Figure 15.2 Multimedia industry in the Tampere region (Räsänen 1996)
Source: Statistics Finland 1997

single product developed in Tampere is the TeamWare PC program by ICL Personal Systems Oy, which has world-wide markets through its owner company ICL Fujitsu. The Finnish ICL was formerly Nokia Data Oy.

Software producers in the Tampere Region are mostly quite small firms. However, many of them are branch plants or subsidiaries of larger groups and thus may have better marketing channels, resources for R&D etc. than a company of their size usually has. The largest firms in software technology in the Tampere Region are:

- ICL Personal Systems Oy.
- Analyste Oy.
- KT-Tietokeskus-group.
- Omnitele Oy.
- Tampereen Tiedonhallinta Oy.
- Tietonauha-group.
- TT-Tietokonserni.

These companies do not only deal in programming and software products in the multimedia industry. However, they have increasingly dominated it.

Eighty-three firms were engaged in software production in 1996. They employed 3,400 people, compared to about 2,700 in 1995. Most of the companies were situated in the city of Tampere.

The hardware and software sectors of the emerging multimedia cluster are, as was shown before, developing rapidly, with an annual growth rate of turnover of about 25 per cent. However, the newest sector – the content industry – shows a growth rate of more than 80 per cent. Some producers in this field established themselves in Tampere in the late 1980s, but most of the content providers are newcomers founded during the last two or three years. Although the industry is fairly new in the region, the total turnover of the content producers was as much as FIM 100 million (15 million ECU) in 1995 and FIM 140 million (24 million ECU) in 1996, according to the survey carried out by the Centre of Expertise (Räsänen 1997). The demand for the Internet in particular, but also for other kinds of multimedia services, has expanded enormously within the last two or three years.

Thirty-four firms were engaged in multimedia content production in Tampere in 1996. The total employment was about 330 people in 1995 and about 500 in 1996 (Räsänen 1997). Of the thirty-four companies, five have more than ten employees, whereas most of the others employ from one to five people. Larger firms employ about 150 persons altogether and the smaller ones combined about the same number. However, content producers often employ many more people indirectly, using freelancers or sub-producers from other sectors related to multimedia production such as printing, audiovisual or other media producing companies. Table 15.2 indicates the most

Table 15.2 Workforce in selected multimedia-related industries in the Tampere region, 1993.

Sub-sector (included activities mentioned)	Workforce
Performing arts (musicians, actors, entertainers, film directors, radio and TV editors and directors etc.)	743
Visual arts (visual artists, commercial artists)	170
Journalism (newspaper journalists, editors, copy editors and writers etc.)	272
Printing and publishing of books	644
Film/video/animation/photo	232
Total number of employees	2061

Source: Statistics Finland 1995

significant sectors. The number of people employed in selected industries related to multimedia is about 2,000.

The total workforce in the Tampere Region in December 1997 was 198,137 (T&E Keskus 1997). If we compare this figure with the 6,700 jobs in the multimedia industry, this sector employs about 3.5 per cent of the workforce. This is quite a small share of the total in the region, particularly if we take into account that companies in the information technology industry are not always connected with multimedia. On the other hand we have to keep in mind that this calculation ignores the media sectors mentioned in Table 15.2 as well as R&D personnel in the field of multimedia employed in the public sector and users of multimedia products.

Large companies related to multimedia production in Tampere

At this point, it is worth taking a closer look at some of the large companies in the multimedia industry and outlining their main activities in the region. The Aamulehti Group is a mass communications company. Its core businesses are newspaper publishing, printing and the distribution of information by electronic means. In addition to mainstream communications, the group is investing intensively in research and development in electronic media. It also has a division comprising information technology companies. Its consolidated net sales in 1995 were FIM 1,433 million (240 million ECU), approximately 20 per cent of which came from exports. In Finland it has almost forty operating units in twenty-five localities and it employs about 2,600 people. Though its headquarters have recently moved to Helsinki, the most important units are still located in Tampere. A few years ago a large Swedish publishing house Marienberg took over the Aamulehti Group.

Alexpress is the Aamulehti division responsible for digital information distribution, research into new media and development of new products based on it. The division is organized into three business units. Radio Business is responsible for Alexpress' local radio broadcasting activities in Tampere. Multimedia Services produces multimedia network services and is, among other things, also responsible for the Aamulehti Group's CD-ROM products. The responsibility of Network Services includes distribution of the Group's digital media products and its short-message services. Network Services was the first company in the world to introduce a news service distributed directly to GSM mobile phones.

Since 1993 the Aamulehti Group and Alexpress have taken part in the 'News in the Future' project of the Massachusetts Institute of Technology's Media Lab. This project focuses on research into electronic communications and new media. Using results from this project, Aamulehti Group and the Helsinki University of Technology started a networked media experiment called OtaOnline in a closed network in 1994. This experience formed the basis for a digital edition of the Aamulehti newspaper, Verkko-Aamulehti, introduced onto the public Internet in 1996.

Alexpress has also been responsible for implementing the Nääsnetti network multimedia project, a sub-project of the National Multimedia Programme financed by the Technology Development Centre of Finland (Tekes). The public Infoville Information Kiosk Project, run by Alexpress itself, will continue in the form of projects tailored to specific company needs.

The Aamulehti Group and the commercial TV channel MTV have recently merged to become a media giant with a FIM 2.5 billion (400 million ECU) media operation. It is believed that one of the primary reasons behind the merger is to prepare for the emerging battle for the digital market. Another factor is the TV and print media giant Sanoma Osakeyhtiö, which owns Finland's biggest newspaper, Helsingin Sanomat, and its companion Helsinki Media. Aamulehti-MTV hopes for at least one more television station, and a place in the planned multiplex companies which own and control the digital distribution networks of non-satellite television.

Nokia Group is an international telecommunications group which had net sales of FIM 36.8 billion (6.1 billion ECU) in 1995. It has its headquarters in Helsinki and employs about 34,000 people in some forty-five countries. It is organized into the following business groups.

Nokia Telecommunications is a global leader with net sales of FIM 10.3 billion (1.6 billion ECU) and 11,300 personnel. It develops and manufactures infrastructure equipment and systems for cellular and fixed networks. It is a leading supplier of GSM/DCS cellular networks and has delivered them to fifty-six operators in some thirty countries. Nokia has supplied fixed network systems to PTTs, new operators, public utilities and railways throughout Europe and the Asia-Pacific region.

Nokia Mobile Phones is Europe's largest and the world's second largest manufacturer of cellular phones, with markets in more than 120 countries around the world. The company offers a full range of mobile phones for digital and analogue cellular markets. It is a pioneer and a market leader in the fast-growing wireless data business. Due to its pioneer development work in cellular phone products, today Nokia plays an important role in this industry world-wide. This group has net sales of FIM 16.0 billion (2.6 billion ECU) and employs 11,800 people.

Nokia General Communications Products combines Nokia's know-how in image and voice processing and in transmission. It focuses on offering advanced multimedia equipment, interactive digital satellite and cable terminals, PC and workstation monitors as well as accessories and components for mobile phones. The range of products includes programmes and services for education, entertainment, safety and work. The group's net sales are FIM 10.8 billion (1.7 billion ECU) and the number of personnel is about 9,900.

Nokia Research Centre interacts closely with the R&D units of the other Nokia business groups. The centre covers the full range of activities from exploration of new technologies and product or system concepts to their exploitation in actual product development. The Centre also introduces new methodologies into Nokia's business processes. It participates in various international R&D projects in cooperation with universities, research institutes and telecommunications companies. The Centre's technology areas include telecommunications, audio-visual signal processing, software and electronics. Its main areas of interest include GSM enhancement and third-generation cellular systems, broadband communications as well as multimedia.

In 1995 about 1,150 Nokia staff worked in Tampere: 61 per cent were in Nokia Telecommunications, 26 per cent in Nokia Mobile Phones and 13 per cent in Nokia Research Centre. This figure has grown quite significantly in the last two years as, for example, Nokia Research Centre has increased its staff to 500. These people are mainly employed in research and development, whereas there is hardly any production in the Tampere Region. Nokia Telecommunications in Tampere develops GSM network management and private mobile radio systems. The main emphasis in software development is on real time and integrated systems. Nokia Mobile Phones' Cellular Data Unit is also situated in Tampere. The Tampere unit of Nokia Research Centre, including the Video Technologies Laboratory, the Speech Processing Laboratory and the Audio Laboratory, focuses on digital signal processing. In addition to the laboratories mentioned above, Nokia Research Centre has teams in Tampere working on software engineering, electronics and telecommunication systems.

Tampere Telephone Company (TPO), Finland's second largest private telephone company, provides a broad range of telecommunications services, including telephone, leased circuit, wireless and data communication facilities and miscellaneous services. TPO is also the leading organization of the local call area of Häme, of which Tampere Region is a part.

Yleisradio Oy – the Finnish Broadcasting Company – is Finland's national public service broadcasting company. It operates two full service television channels, four national radio channels and twenty-seven regional radio services and provides programmes in Finnish, Swedish and the Sámi language. The Tampere radio and television centre (TV 2) has been profiled as a quality alternative channel: it has been a pioneer in Finland in current affairs programmes and documentary production. TV 2 is also distinctly profiled as a non-Helsinki channel. The channel has a great deal of local production not only in Tampere but also in a number of other localities.

TV Tampere (Channel 6) has broadcast programmes since the beginning of February 1995. At least half are produced in Tampere and the favourite is Pirkanmaan uutiset (local news) which is the only local TV news in Finland. The local radio companies, Radio 957 and Radio Moro, are privately owned. The University of Tampere has its own radio station featuring science, the arts and distance learning programmes. This radio station also provides students of journalism with broadcasting experience.

Content providers in Tampere: some examples

Media Company Sansibar is a producer of digital media. It is one of the pioneers in the field employing fifteen persons in addition to about ten freelances. Sansibar Oy produces CD-ROMs and Websites for Finnish and international publishing houses, business enterprises and television companies. Products are published both for the consumer market and business to business. Furthermore, Sansibar is producing a computer-animated, interactive children's TV program called 'Galilei and the Lost Toys'. 'Galilei' is a part of the Finnish National Multimedia Programme and is co-produced by Sansibar and the Finnish Broadcasting Company (YLE TV2).

Tietovalta Ltd creates multimedia and WWW programmes in five different categories: communications, entertainment, education, sales and Internet. The company has been producing multimedia programmes since 1988. By the end of 1997 Tietovalta's reference list had about 200 designed projects, including short and snappy as well as extensively comprehensive programmes. Tietovalta's customers include: Valmet (producing e.g. paper machines), Finnair (national airline company), The Finnish Post Office, KT-Tietokeskus (a large ADP software producer), ICL (computers and software), Metsä-Serla (a large forest products company), Tekes and Alexpress.

Institutional support structures of the multimedia industry

Seen from the perspective of research and education, Tampere is very strong in multimedia with many institutions, some of the most significant of which we outline here. Among the key institutions in the region are two universities. Both the University of Tampere and Tampere University of Technology (TUT) host a research centre for information society as well as other units concerned with multimedia. The supply of multimedia knowledge from support organizations in the Tampere Region covers a broad variety of different fields from technical (such as ATM and signal processing) to a more social kind of competence (human interface, interactive learning etc.).

Tampere has two science parks, Hermia Science Park and the newly established Finn-Medi Science Park. Hermia Science Park was opened in 1988. It is formed by TUT (1,000 employees), VTT (The Technical Research Centre) (300 employees), the units of Nokia Mobile Phones (about 350 employees) and Nokia Research Centre (about 150 employees), and small firms operating in Hermia (600 employees). Another 500 firms are located within a radius of about one kilometre.

Small operations employing fewer than fifty people account for 80 per cent of the companies at Hermia, but there are also a number of R&D units of larger companies as, for example, the Nokia Research Centre. The fields represented at the Science Park include computer design and programming, information technology, electronics, electrical engineering, instrumentation and automation. More than half of the employees working at Hermia are university graduates, and one-third are graduates of the Tampere University of Technology. It is characteristic of science parks in Finland that they are very closely connected to the universities. In an international comparative study titled World Competitiveness Report, Finland was evaluated as having the best cooperation between universities and companies (Tekes 1996a). The links between Hermia and Tampere University of Technology are especially strong.

The Digital Media Institute (DMI) is a separate research unit of Tampere University of Technology located in Hermia Science Park. The institute was founded in 1985 as the Institute for Research in Information Technology. In 1994 its activities were directed to the area of the digital media and the institute was renamed the Digital Media Institute. The majority of researchers work with digital media technology, but there is also close cooperation with marketing, communication, sociology, information research, mathematics, psychology and educational studies. In these areas, a very important cooperation partner for DMI is the University of Tampere.

The institute, which employs about 120 researchers, is highly decentralized. Research staff are located in the premises of the laboratories involved in the operation of the Digital Media Institute. The institute has about sixty research projects coordinated by the senior staff (professors, associate professors and project managers) of the institute's laboratories. The Academy of Finland has chosen the DMI as a new centre of excellence in research.

The budget for 1996 was over FIM 30 million (5 million ECU). Funding for the projects comes from Finnish industry (41 per cent), the Technology

Development Centre of Finland, Tekes, (17 per cent), the Academy of Finland (18 per cent) and other sources (30 per cent).

The Digital Media Institute has a very international outlook. It currently has researchers from about eighteen different countries and is involved with several EU funded projects. EU finance is increasing rapidly, currently representing about 7 per cent of the funding.

A lack of information network professionals in Tampere Region resulted in the establishment of a new training organization named the Data Network Institute. This institute is an independent unit of the Tampere University of Technology. The two other founding organizations are Telecom Finland and the City of Tampere. The European Social Fund (ESF) has also had an important role in providing funds as most of the training provided meets the requirements of Objectives 3 or 4.[1] The training provided by the Information Network Institute is threefold: learn, practice and apply. Topics have been gathered into modules so that during the lectures, participants learn a certain topic during a two to three week period. Afterwards, the theory is put into practice in an information network laboratory. The laboratory exercises are based on the equipment that the enterprises are currently using. These arrangements make the institute well-equipped to meet the rapidly changing demands in the ICT sector.

The hypermedia laboratory at the University of Tampere was founded in 1992. Its main purpose is to arrange courses, study hypermedia in its different aspects of science and do joint research work with the private and public sectors. The laboratory currently employs eight people. The Information Society Research Centre has recently been established to coordinate the research done in the University related to the information society. In autumn 1996 it received its first larger project finance from the Academy of Finland. The Work Research Centre, established in 1988, is involved in several European research projects on Information Society.

VTT is a key actor in the field of IT knowledge production. VTT is the biggest of some twenty-five state-owned research institutes in the country. The institute is divided into nine research units (electronics, information technology, automation, chemical technology, biotechnology and food, energy, manufacturing, construction and traffic). It has five research units in Tampere, of which one is the unit for information technology (including hospital technology). VTT's main specialty is in applied research, concentrating on the improvement of product and process technology. Most research projects are commissioned by private companies as well as state-owned institutes, particularly Tekes, but the VTT institutes are also engaged in self-initiated research projects.

The Tampere School of Art and Communications was established in 1991, with the first students graduating in December 1994. In 1996 it became a part of the Tampere Polytechnic where it forms the School of Cultural Industries. The main strength of the study programme is that it brings together media production and the visual arts combining traditional and digital technologies for use in the production of both art and media. The curriculum has been developed in cooperation with industry professionals as well as with various educational and cultural institutions operating at the local, national, and international levels.

The Vocational Adult Education Centre's (TAKK) main task is to produce educational services and training according to the needs of the working population in the Tampere Region. In the field of multimedia and information technologies, the Centre's focus is on vocational and technician levels.

Opintori, a further education 'platform' within the Centre, represents a new concept in vocational training. Customized for each adult student, the Opintori courses may vary from some days' training to long extension studies with a vocational degree according to personal needs. The focus areas of teaching are information technologies and business skills. Opintori is partly funded by the European Social Fund. TAKK is also participating in a three-year Erasmus project on computer science and telematics.[2]

Regional strategies and regional participation in national projects

Strategic plans in the region

The key political actors in the Tampere Region agree in principle that 'information society' should become the overall vision on which they orient their strategic planning. This can be demonstrated by the strategic plan of the regional council which in 1996 published a revised version of its first strategic programme (1994–9) for the Tampere Region. In this programme, emphasis is also laid on various activities connected to the development of an information society (Pirkanmaan Liitto 1996):

- To promote the activities of an information society (focus on content industry, access to information highways, the abilities of individuals to use new technologies).
- To improve the use of knowledge and to support innovations (focus on vocational skills, apprenticeships, networking, entrepreneurship, the Centre of Expertise programme).
- To strengthen the basic structures of the region (natural and artificial environment, transportation, tourism).
- To create new jobs (especially in health care services, technology oriented services, content industry of the IT sector).

The total costs of implementing the development plans over the next five years are about FIM 2,000 million (330 million ECU). The main sources of funding are the European structural funds (European Regional Development Fund, European Social Fund), private companies, local municipalities, the Ministry of Labour, the Ministry of Trade and Industry, and the Council of Tampere Region.

The Strategy Programme of the City of Tampere entitled 'Guidelines of Urban Policy for the 21st Century' emphasizes that Tampere should become the leading city of an information society in Finland.

> In Tampere, there is a concentration of different kinds of expertise related to the information society which enables the urban region of Tampere to reach a key position in Finland as a city of the information society, and also a significant European centre of the field. Only after this goal has been achieved, will the restructuration process of the leading industrial city in Finland be complete. Tampere will by then have regained its position as the centre of the main field of production as society has turned from an industrial society into an information society. To reach the goal, it is required that all the actors of the region adopt this development project as their own.
>
> (Tampereen kaupunki 1997)

The City of Tampere refers to a demand-oriented technology policy as it states that the City's own development activities (e.g. education and training, cultural activities, other public services) will be planned in such a way that they strongly support the development of a regionally-based content industry. In the Strategy Programme five main topics have been stressed:

1   Tampere will become both a service and an industrial city in the future.
2   Tampere will develop into a leading city of the information society in Finland.
3   The urban region of Tampere will be consolidated into a European city.
4   Inhabitants will be taken care of throughout their lives from childhood to old age.
5   Tampere will be developed towards an international partner through networking.

The most significant single action carried out by the City of Tampere related to an information society is without doubt the Inforengas project (Info Circle). This network was started up in 1995 to bring together all schools and educational institutes and libraries in Tampere. In 1996, thirty-seven schools and nine libraries already had connections with the Info Circle. Some of the schools have fast ATM connections. The project has had a great impact on the educational system as many curricula have had to be revised. Via the Info Circle net, Internet connections, e-mail, international discussion groups and other facilities can be integrated into teaching activities. The project has been carried out in cooperation between the City of Tampere and the local tele-operator company TPO, which is a part of the large national tele-operator company, Finnet Group.

The multimedia sector has been chosen as one of the three strategic sectors to be supported by the Centre of Expertise Programme. The content industry is particularly emphasized as the future growth area. Compared to the strategic plan for the Tampere Region, the Centre of Expertise Programme is more pragmatic in nature. In 1994, the Finnish government nominated eight national centres of expertise, among them the Tampere Region. The aim of these centres is to bring together enterprises with a high degree of expertise, including research and training institutes and other experts, for purposes of reciprocal cooperation. With the aid of a nationally drawn-up programme, the centres direct public spending allocated to education, research and development. Finance for the programme comes from the central government through the ministries and the regional councils, from the municipalities of the urban regions concerned and from companies as well from the Technology Development Centre of Finland (Tekes) and the EU. Although the programmes are initiated by the central government, it is up to the regions to carry them out and further develop them. The city's two science parks play a very important role in this programme.

Information technology, especially multimedia, has been nominated as one of the three focal areas along with mechanical engineering and process automation as well as health care technology. These areas were assigned to the Centre on the basis of expected synergy effects from cooperation within the fields concerned.

In IT, three strategic target areas have been defined as follows (Tampereen seudun osaamiskeskusohjelma 1996):

1   To enhance cooperation and networking between different actors of the IT sector.
2   To support the development of a content industry, i.e. multimedia.
3   To develop new businesses within the sector.

By the end of 1995, the IT Programme was involved in projects with a total budget of FIM 31.5 million (5 million ECU). In 1996 the annual budget jumped to FIM 48 million (8 million ECU). Projects are funded by different kinds of sources involving companies, research and educational institutions. The budget of the IT Centre of Expertise itself is very small; it acts more as a catalyst or mediator promoting new developments and bringing together different actors. The development projects coordinated by the Centre cover all the factors relevant to business success: technology, sales and marketing, production, education and training, finance and administration.

Participation of regional companies in national projects

The single most important programme on the national level to develop the multimedia sector has been the Finnish Multimedia Programme, which terminated at the end of 1997. This was a co-project started by the leading Finnish media houses, tele-operators and telecommunication companies. The main objective was to improve the Finnish 'information superhighway' with a selection of multimedia services.

Companies involved in the programme represented the most important in the Finnish communication industries: Aamulehti-Yhtymä Oy, Helsinki Media, Helsingin Puhelin Oy, MTV Oy, Oy Nokia Ab, Sanoma Osakeyhtiö, Telecom Finland Oy, TPO and Yleisradio Oy. The programme also involved small firms producing different kinds of information and communication technology products, content and service producers, publishing houses, small multimedia firms as well as universities and research institutes. TUT and its Digital Media Institute played an important role in the programme. The programme was coordinated by Nokia Research Centre located in Hermia Science Park. About a half of this multimedia programme (16 million ECU) was carried out in the Tampere Region, which clearly shows the importance of the region for the emergence of a new cluster.

The common denominator of the projects was digital information technology. The participating companies aimed to create trial systems which would make it possible to offer private consumers and professional and business users new kinds of multimedia-based services needed in everyday life. This meant building fast networks, new terminals and user interfaces for receiving interactive multimedia services containing images, sound, video and text information. The projects included ATM to the Home, Broadband Village, Interactive TV programmes, Media on Demand, Mobile Multimedia Services in Networks, and Networked Multimedia in Mass Communications (Tekes 1996b).

The National Multimedia Programme covered the years 1995–97. The total budget was about FIM 300 million (50 million ECU). Most of the finance came from the private participants in the programme and thus the main goals were commercial. This also guaranteed the participants' commitment to the programme. According to the programme coordinator, the programme was unique world-wide. It has led to many significant technical innovations, but the results in content production are rather poor.

A special multimedia programme has been prepared for the social and health care sector from 1996 to 1998. It involves three ministries: the Ministry of Trade and Industry, the Ministry of Social and Health Affairs and the Ministry of Labour. The main aim is to enhance cost-effectiveness and quality as well as equal access to services of the social and health sector (Tekes 1996b). Other aims include support for the sector's exports with the aid of multimedia products, the development of services based on new technologies, and an increase of cooperation between different actors in the sector with the aid of the nationally strong telecommunications sector.

The focal areas of the programme are services to support independent, home-based performance; telemedicine; telediagnostics; telenursing; developing data and telecommunication platforms to serve and network the sector. The programme is coordinated by DMI and Tekes in Tampere.

Conclusions

The key political and economic actors in the Tampere Region agree in principle that the establishment of a new industrial cluster of 'multimedia' and support for the development of the information society in the region is the most promising way to overcome the severe economic crisis and the high unemployment rate caused by structural changes in the early 1990s. When the multimedia sector began to form about twenty years ago only the technical side of an information society developed quickly, but nowadays the content and service industry is also growing fast. The regional development strategy is in line with the national policy to turn Finland into an information society, so the actors in the region also gain support from national programmes and projects. They are also involved in several EU projects.

The aim of becoming the centre of the Finnish information society and a significant European centre in the field, announced by theRegional Council as well as by the City of Tampere, is ambitious but the plan seems to be based on solid ground. The various industries related to the multimedia sector show very dynamic growth in the region, although growth in the content industry began from a very low level. The region also has a variety of different support organizations which can assist in developing the multimedia cluster. Some large companies, particularly from the information technology industry, have subsidiaries in the Tampere Region and the merger between the Aamulehti Group and the commercial television channel MTV has created a new competitive company in the service sector.

One may still have some doubts whether the Tampere Region will achieve its ambitious goal. In this respect, the shortage of qualified people which currently prevents the sector from growing even more rapidly is only a temporary problem. Here the multimedia industry in the Tampere Region is suffering from the phenomenon that many resources – particularly human resources – are bound to the traditionally dominant industries, hindering the development of new ones. At the same time unemployed people cannot be integrated into the multimedia sector as they tend to be unskilled or have the wrong skills. However, the economic crisis at the beginning of the 1990s and the persistently high unemployment rate during the last few years have caused a change in the views of regional authorities, who now look for a second economic cluster to stand alongside the forest cluster, including the machine industry. The establishment of various support organizations in the field of information technology and multimedia clearly indicates the attempt of regional authorities to break free of path-dependency.

The fact that other leading regions of Finland are also competing to become the centre of information society in Finland is more serious. In particular the Uusimaa Region, including the capital city Helsinki, clearly has some major competitive advantages. The Finnish service industry is mainly concentrated there. With Sanoma Osakeyhtiö, which also publishes Finland's main newspaper, Helsinki hosts the biggest media agglomeration in the country. Even the Aamulehti Group has moved its headquarters to Helsinki, although its stronghold is still in the Tampere Region. Nokia, the dominating company in the Finnish information and telecommunication technology sector, has its headquarters in the capital, as have most of the other important companies in this sector. Last but not least, Helsinki hosts the national government and state administration, which in the future may becomea potential customers for multimedia products.

Although key political as well as economic actors support the idea of the Tampere Region becoming the centre of an information society in Finland, there is, according to outside experts, little cooperation among them. The strategic plan for the Tampere Region, for example, was evaluated by these experts as a package of different kinds of projects put together in strategy form rather than a real strategy with the participants' commitment behind it as a whole (Raines and Bachtler 1996). One can argue that, since regional councils in Finland have only recently acquired a leading role in directing regional policy, strong cooperation has not had enough time to develop. However, one may also question whether the international companies – such as the Nokia Group or the Swedish-owned Aamulehti Group – can have a real long-term interest in the development of a particular region as they continuously search globally for regions which have specific advantages to offer for investment. Despite these shortcomings, the region is – obviously with some success – trying to develop an institutional setting, which in the longer perspective may attract other firms, even from foreign countries.

We have to bear in mind that the future of the Tampere Region concerning the development of a multimedia cluster very much depends on the engagement of the Nokia Group. The company so far has invested quite heavily in R&D but not in production in the region. It is unlikely that Nokia will set up more production sites in Finland in the near future, as the company is currently following the strategy of globalizing its business by concentrating heavily on South-East Asia. On the other hand, it is unlikely that Nokia will withdraw any of its businesses from Finland, and particularly from the Tampere Region, because the wages for research personnel are comparatively low. However, the regional government needs to find new investors in the future, which may become a problem as Nokia recruits most of the engineering graduates there.

The ambitious aim of the Tampere Region concerning the multimedia industry encounters other barriers which are not related to the region in particular, but to Finland as a whole. The country – with its five million inhabitants – is rather small and Finnish is not spoken elsewhere. It is often not profitable to produce multimedia products for such a small market but due to the language problem there is no global market for Finnish multimedia products and services. A recent study of the consequences for the emerging information society in small countries with their own languages concluded that, although English is by far the dominating language in the multimedia industry, less-used languages have a chance of creating niche markets. The report argues that the Scandinavian countries with their specific culture and tradition in education, form a kind of niche market which gives companies in this area a chance to survive even in conditions of increasingly tough competition. However, it is necessary for national governments to support these firms. Finnish companies in the content industry will also have difficulties surviving in such niche markets and need to find partners in other Scandinavian countries.

We conclude that there are serious obstacles to the aim of turning the Tampere Region into the centre of the Finnish information society, and even more into a significant European centre, although most of the key political and economic actors share this vision. The heavy involvement of regional companies in national projects clearly indicates that some key economic actors have committed themselves to this image. The multimedia industry in Tampere no doubt has some growth potential. By providing considerable resources for this sector and by establishing a supportive institutional set-up, political actors have created important preconditions for further growth in this industry. But competition with the Helsinki region, the small number of inhabitants, the language and cultural problems will probably reduce the growth potential of this sector in the region quite significantly. Development potential is surely much greater for the information technology industry than for the content industry, but even here the globalization strategy of Nokia, the dominant company in the industry, may become a factor limiting further growth. Nevertheless, the fact that the region's stronghold in the multimedia sector lies in R&D in the field of information technology leaves some hope that the Tampere Region will become a centre of the European knowledge society.

Notes

1 The cohesion policies of the European Union have led to the creation of four Structural Funds, among them the European Regional Development Fund (ERDF) and the European Social Fund (ESF). The ERDF aims at strengthening

the economic potential of regions, supporting structural adjustment and helping to promote growth and lasting employment. Spain, Italy, Greece, Portugal
and Germany are the largest beneficiaries of the Fund at the moment. The ESF
has the objective of combating long-term unemployment and improving the
employability of young people and of promoting adaptation to industrial
change. Regions to be assisted by these funds are categorized into four
Objectives. Objective One regions are seen as the most worthy of support, since
development there is lagging behind considerably.

2 Erasmus is the name given to the Higher Education section of the European
Community action programme in the field of education. Erasmus provides a
wide range of measures designed to support the European activities of higher
education institutions and to promote the mobility and exchange of their teaching staff, students and administrators.

References

Dosi, G. (1988) 'Sources, procedures, and microeconomic effects of innovation',
Journal of Economic Literature 26: 1120–71.

Jääskeläinen, K. and Oesch, K. (1995) 'Multimedian sisällöntuotantoon erikois-
tuneen pk–teollisuuden kehittäminen', (in English: Development of the SME
sector specialized in multimedia content production), *Kauppa– ja teollisuusminis-
teriön monisteita* 17.

Johnson, B. (1992) 'Institutional learning', in B.-Å. Lundvall (ed.) *National Systems of
Innovation. Towards a Theory of Innovation and Interactive Learning,* New York:
Pinter.

Lovio, R. (1985) 'Emerging industries. Interactions between production, technology
and markets in a small open economy', Technical Research Centre of Finland,
Research Notes 554.

Lundvall, B.–Å. (1992) 'User-producer relationships, national systems of innovation
and internationalisation', in B.–Å. Lundvall (ed.), *National Systems of Innovation.
Towards a Theory of Innovation and Interactive Learning,* New York: Pinter.

Nelson, R. and Winter, S. (1977) 'In search of useful theory on innovation', *Research
Policy* 6: 36–76.

Pirkanmaan Liitto (1996) 'Pirkanmaan menestyksen strategia 2000+', (in English:
Success strategy for the Tampere Region), Julkaisu B:40, Tampere.

Räsänen, H. (1996) 'Pirkanmaan IT–toimialan rakenne', (in English: 'Structure of IT
sector in the Tampere Region'), unpublished report, Tampere: Tampereen
Teknologiakeskus Oy.

—— (1997) 'IT-industry infrastructure of the Tampere Region', unpublished report,
Tampere: Tampereen Teknologiakeskus Oy.

Raines, P. and Bachtler, J. (1996) 'An evaluation of regional development potential
and strategic planning in Tampere Region. Final report of Stage II: strategy
analysis', unpublished report, EPRC, University of Strathclyde, UK.

Scott, A. J. (1998) 'From Silicon Valley to Hollywood: growth and development of
the multimedia industry in California', unpublished paper, Los Angeles: UCLA.

Statistics Finland (1995) *Culture and Media 1995,* Helsinki: Statistics Finland.

—— (1997) *Statistical Yearbook of Finland,* vol. 92, Helsinki: Statistics Finland.

Tampereen kaupunki (1997) *Kaupunkipolitiikan suuntaviivat 2000–luvulle,* (in English: *The City of Tampere. Guidelines of urban policy for the 21st Century*), Strategiaohjelma, Tampereen kaupunginkanslia, suunnitteluryhmä. Tampere: Tampereen kaupunki.

Tampereen seudun osaamiskeskusohjelma (1996) *Toimintakertomus 1995, toimintasuunnitelma 1996–1998,* (in English: *The Centre of Expertise programme of the Tampere Region, Annual Report 1995, Action Plan 1996–1998*), Tampereen Teknologiakeskus Oy, Tampere: Tampereen seudun osaamiskeskusohjelma.

Tekes (1996a) 'Vuosikertomus 1995', (in English: Technology Development Centre of Finland. Annual Report 1995), Teknologian Kehittämiskeskus, Helsinki: Tekes.

—— (1996b) 'Kansallinen multimediaohjelma', (in English: National Multimedia Programme), Internet document, http://www.tekes.fi/ohjelmat/info/dme /kansallinen/, download: August 1996.

T&E Keskus (1997) 'Pirkanmaan työvoimakatsaus 12/1997' (in English: 'Employment overview of the Tampere Region'), Tampere: Employment and Economic Development Centre for Pirkanmaa.

16

NEW MEDIA POLICIES AND REGIONAL DEVELOPMENT IN JAPAN

Rolf Sternberg

Introduction

Since the early eighties, the Japanese central government has created several programmes of regional and innovation policies aiming to achieve regional and national goals. Most of these programmes focus on new and/or high technologies. Since the 'fourth comprehensive national development plan' (which is still effective) was passed into law in 1987, a greater emphasis on information- and new-media-related regional policies has had an impact which cannot be ignored (see National Land Agency 1987). The most ambitious technology policy programme was named 'technopolis'.

The next part of this chapter describes the current regional economic structure and the disparities in Japan. This is necessary in order to understand the reasons for the implementation of the programmes discussed later.

This is followed by a section on the government's promotion of information and new media infrastructures. This gives an overview of recent regional innovation strategies, as far as they are concerned with new media and new communication policies. The focus of this section is both on the role of the regions within new media development and application (endogenous approach) and on the function of regions within new media strategies of the central government ministries (exogenous approach). Spatial sciences place a special emphasis on the effects of new systems of telecommunications on regional development and general locational patterns. However, no clear spatial pattern exists at present with respect to whether diffusion or concentration effects are likely to be prevalent, nor are there definite signs of a reduction of negative externalities associated with mobility (Bertuglia and Occelli 1995). Despite a lack of clear locational trends in general, the Japanese government at least acknowledges the strong need for the development of a strategic scenario (or 'vision', to use a very common term of the Japanese policy making process). A clear strategy is necessary to orient and organize the opportunities made available by new technology, especially new media, information and communication technologies. In addition to the general aims of Japanese information policies, three representative strategies ('teletopia', 'new media community', 'intelligent city') and the 'technopolis' programme are discussed more extensively.

The next section consider the case of the Kyûshû region, a truly peripheral area and the southernmost of the four main islands of the Japanese archipelago. This is investigated in order to assess the impact of 'technopolis' sites located there, as well as possible effects of recent new media programmes on regional development.

The concluding section discusses whether economic disparities can be reduced with the help of new media policies and 'technopolis' zones.

Spatial disparities in Japan and their implications for technology and regional policy of the central government

Unlike most other leading industrialized countries, in Japan there are significant economic and technological disparities between the three core regions of Tokyo, Nagoya and Osaka, on the one hand, and the peripheral parts of the country, especially in the north (Hokkaido, Tohoku) and south (Kyûshû) (see Map 16.1), on the other. These disparities have been typical of Japan for many decades (see Abe 1996, Japan Regional Development Corporation 1996). In the late 1980s, almost half the population and industrial output, 55 per cent of Gross Domestic Product (GDP), about 70 per cent of university students and 80 per cent of the headquarters of large enterprises belonged to the core regions (see Flüchter 1990, Economic Planning Agency 1991, Nishioka 1991).

Since the 1980s an ongoing population shift especially towards the Tokyo Metropolitan Region has been witnessed. This has been particularly marked by the impoverishment of local areas due to slumps in key industries such as mining and fisheries. It is also shown in the concentration of city functions in Tokyo (Sassen 1991) in an effort to meet international integration and globalization and the increased use of sophisticated information technologies. In 1987, the net population inflow into the Tri-Metropolitan Region (Tokyo, Osaka, and Nagoya) reached 158,000 persons. Since then, land prices have soared in the Tokyo Metropolitan area with a consequent increase in costs for industrial location and private housing. This forced a decline in net population inflow and even resulted in an outflow of population in 1993 – for the first time since 1976 (see Japan Regional Development Corporation 1996).

The per capita income in the forty-seven prefectures impressively documents these regional disparities (see Map 16.2). The difference between the Tokyo prefecture (peaking in 1994 with an index of 182, with 100 being the national average) and the Nara prefecture (index 62) has remained nearly constant since the mid-1970s.

347

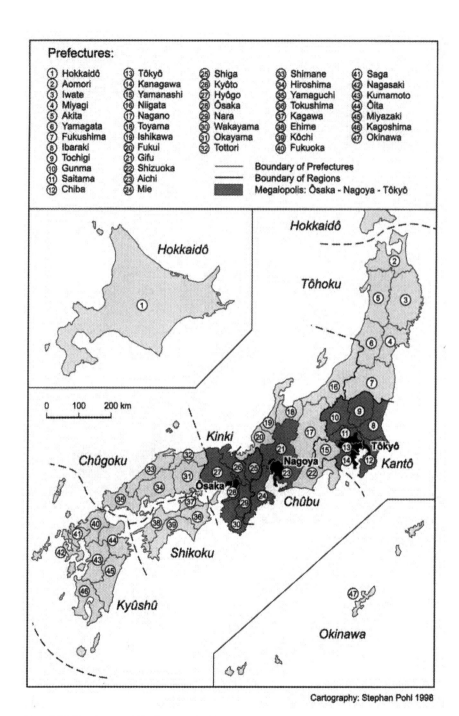

Map 16.1 Regions and Prefectures in Japan
Source: Author.

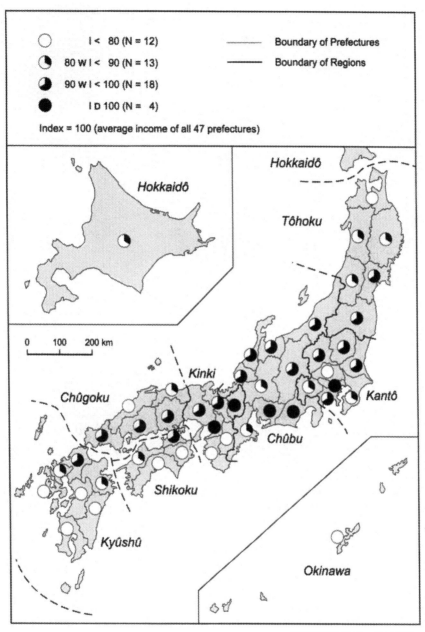

Map 16.2 Index of per capita income of Japanese prefectures 1994
Source: Japan Industrial Location Center 1997

Intra-regional industrial decentralization is leaving its mark on the regions, and the three core areas mentioned above are expanding into the neighboring prefectures. Growth dynamism within the regions' boundaries has become insignificant due to agglomeration disadvantages (including high rents, shortage of space and labour). Therefore, the disparities are especially pronounced between those prefectures close to the metropolitan centres and those which are more remote.

Since the oil crises and their catastrophic effects on the domestic raw material industry, R&D-intensive products and the corresponding high-tech industries have been of crucial importance to Japan. In 1991, eight branches of the Industrial Classification, comprising a total of 40,251 enterprises (4.7 per cent of manufacturing) and 1,836,949 employees (13.0 per cent of manufacturing), officially count among high-tech industries. The regional distribution of high-tech enterprises reveals a pattern that resembles the disparities described above. Both by absolute (number of enterprises) and relative criteria (share of high-tech enterprises among all manufacturing enterprises) the prefectures of the core regions predominate.

This picture can be seen in more relative terms by the corresponding employment figures, because the plants in the periphery are above-average in size. Especially in the prefectures in central and northern Tohoku the share of high-tech enterprises among all manufactures is above the national average (see Sternberg 1998). Nevertheless, the desired decentralization of high-tech industries in favour of peripheral regions only began in the 1980s (Nishioka and Takeuchi 1987).

Spatial division of labour in Japan utilizes the disparities described above and is also observed in high-tech industries (in particular, the semi-conductor industry). The headquarters and the R&D centres remain in the core regions, because of the availability of highly qualified labour, the presence of R&D institutions and the possibility of making the necessary face-to-face contacts. By contrast, simple production stages (for example, those carried out by contract firms, which depend on large enterprises) can be relocated to the periphery, where labour and space of the required quality and quantity and a good airport infrastructure are available.

In accordance with spatial division of labour, the likelihood of decentralization obviously increases as the complexity of manufacturing decreases. However, in recent years changes in the international environment have caused an alternative locational behaviour among several Japanese high-tech industries. It is not the Japanese periphery but the newly industrialized economies in South-East Asia (low-cost countries like Vietnam, Korea and the Philippines) that are now profiting from the decentralization. One consequence could be the 'hollowing-out' of the Japanese economy, especially the manufacturing sector (see Legewie 1997).

The Japanese government's promotion of information and new media infrastructures

General agenda of Japanese information policies

The Japanese government, like other governments in industrialized countries, has recognized the crucial role of new information technologies for the international competitiveness of its country, at both the national and regional levels. Information and communication technologies are not only important determining factors in their own (world-wide) trade. They are also emerging as transformational technologies that influence a broad range of economic activities such as R&D, technological innovation, new business ventures, socio-economic organizations, and distribution (see Steffensen 1996). The attempts of the Japanese government to strengthen information infrastructure ('infostructure') must therefore be evaluated in context of the government's overall goal of increasing international competitiveness.

In terms of the international competitiveness of Japanese information technology, remarkable changes have occurred in the recent past. Throughout the 1980s and 1990s, Japan had a positive trade balance in all four categories into which information technology world trade is commonly divided: telecommunications, computing, consumer electronics and components. Japan clearly held the lead, leaving the US in second position, and Europe well behind with comparative advantages only in telecommunications (see Steffensen 1996). However, since the mid-nineties the situation has changed, with Japan losing its eight-year lead and falling to number three behind the US and Singapore.

Although there are several reasons for this development, most scholars agree that it stems primarily from the growing weakness in information infrastructures together with a complex set of structural problems related to political, managerial, and social-cultural rigidities (see Steffensen 1996, Latzer 1995). Infrastructure planning for the 'multimedia age' is a good example of the problem.[1] Japan's government needs to undertake a major reorganization if it is to satisfy the need to liberalize respective home markets in the near future; consider, for example, the case of the market-dominating telephone company Nippon Telegraph and Telephone (NTT). This attempt is impeded by the rivalries between the Ministry of International Trade and Industry (MITI) and Ministry of Posts and Telecommunications (MPT) in terms of political control over the tele-info industries. Another comparative disadvantage worthy of mention is the lack of coordination of Japanese new media in the past. This gives foreign scholars the impression of a rather chaotic strategy (if one can be recognized at all), albeit with brilliant rhetoric in all respective publications and speeches.

Recent history of new media and information policies, the 'technopolis' programme and the role of the regions

In order to reduce weaknesses in international competitiveness, Japanese ministries have undertaken several initiatives in the recent past. Most of these have a strong explicit or implicit impact on the regions and regional development.

Japanese information society visions had their origins in the 1960s, but did not really mature until the first oil crisis. It was then that the implementation of information technology in selected industries and in selected, often newly industrialized, regions came to be widely perceived as a master tool in the political effort to spur regional and national industrial change. In the early 1980s, the peripheral regions were still lagging further behind the core in terms of information technologies than in any other economic or social indicator (see Cheung 1991). In response to the designation of 1983 as the 'world communication year' by the United Nations, many ministries tried to outdo each other in announcing their individual information concepts. The list of ministries that published such visions includes MITI (New Media Community Concept 1984), the Ministry of Construction (Intelligent City Concept 1986), the Ministry of Agriculture, Forestry and Fishery (Greentopia Concept 1986) and the Ministry of Posts and Telecommunications (Media Terminal Concept and Teletopia Concept 1983) among others. For a more complete overview of these projects and their development in the recent past, compare the data in Cheung (1991) and InfoCom Research, Inc. (1996).

Since the mid-1990s a new generation of information and communication policies has emerged. Steffensen (1996: 10) predicts that this will mark the beginning of 'an epoch-making period in the Japanese information and communications market'. There is clear empirical evidence for this opinion. Personal computer sales rose by 36 and 70 per cent in 1994 and 1995 respectively; the hitherto low level of personal computer communication network subscribers increased by almost 70 per cent between 1992 and 1994.

These developments have been influenced by huge investments in communication infrastructure which will be equally important in the future. Among the most important of these investments is the completion of a national optical fibre network by the year 2005 (originally 2010) which will cover 20 per cent of the population as early as the year 2000 (MPT 1996, Latzer 1995). In 1994, the Ministry of Posts and Telecommunications forecast a Y123,000 million market and 2.4 million new jobs by 2010 (Steffensen 1996). The ministry is engaged in achieving seamless multimedia radio communications with the optical-fibre network and the digitization of broadcasting networks with a coverage of 10-20 per cent of urban Cable TV (CATV) equipment (MPT 1996). One should note that up to now Japan has remained comparatively underdeveloped by international standards measured, for example, in terms of CATV operators and subscribers.

352

All these efforts are extremely costly (as are those of other ministries), and it remains to be seen how the current financial problems of the Japanese economy and government will influence these strategies. Nevertheless it is obvious that Japan will start to develop a next-generation communications network strategy 'within a tight state-business cooperative environment' (Steffensen 1996: 11) that will integrate various players under competitive market forces, rather than leaving it to purely public corporate formations or the NTT. Having this in mind, many indicators support the hypothesis of a Japanese 'multimedia network revolution' beginning in 1996. The dominant actors within this process will be satellite broadcasting operators, CATV companies and the NTT, as well as other common carriers (see MPT 1996 and Steffensen 1996 for a deeper discussion).

Whereas one can only speculate about the regional impacts of the information policies of the mid-1990s, the aims and effects of the 1980s programmes are easier to assess. In that period, Japan's communication policies were heavily oriented towards general technology and industrial policy with the overall goal of economic growth and international competitiveness. Consequently, regional information policies followed, by and large, the prevailing regional development approaches. They can even be interpreted as an integrated element of the Japanese regional policy regime (see Steffensen 1996 and Figure 16.1).

A characteristic example of the regional development approaches is the 'technopolis' strategy, which has to satisfy both national and regional goals. From a national point of view, the growth of existing and emerging technology-intensive industries (including several of the new media and multimedia industries discussed above) is the main goal of this technology policy instrument. From a regional policy standpoint, the objective is to render underdeveloped rural regions more attractive and thus reduce the economic and technological disparities between central and peripheral parts of the country. It is hoped that widespread relevant information projects, distributed all over the country but particularly in peripheral areas, could help to achieve this goal.

The most recent amendment to the skeleton plans of 1991 sets the objective of 'technopolis' as: the improvement of the quality of regional industries and manufacturing establishments, the promotion of the settlement of high-tech businesses, the intensification of linkages between the regions, and the marketing of the comparative advantages of the individual regions and technopolises (Kyûshû Industrial Advancement Centre 1995). Within this context, new media facilities play an important role. As described in detail by the Japan Industrial Location Centre (1990), each technopolis zone has its specific goals in terms of targeting industries, many of which belong to new media industries.

Since the mid-1980s, twenty-six technopolis sites have been developed, mainly in more or less peripheral areas (Map 16.3). They are by no means all

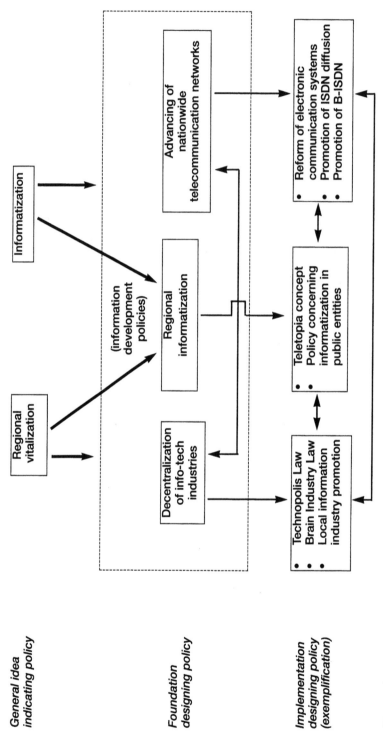

Figure 16.1 Japan's policymaking process with informatization infrastructures with and without regional development goals

Source: Steffensen 1996: 7a (modified)

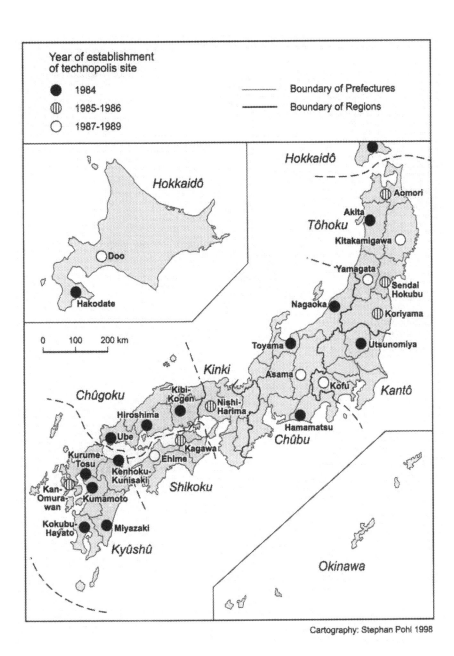

Legend:

Year of establishment
of technopolis site

● 1984
◐ 1985-1986
○ 1987-1989

·········· Boundary of Prefectures
———— Boundary of Regions

Hokkaidô

Hokkaidô

Tôhoku

Kinki

Chûgoku

Kantô

Chûbu

Shikoku

Kyûshû

Okinawa

○ Doo

● Hakodate

0   100   200 km

● Aomori
Akita ●
Kitakamigawa ○
Yamagata ○
◐ Sendai Hokubu
Nagaoka ●
◐ Koriyama
Toyama ●   Utsunomiya ●
Asama ○   ○ Kofu
Kibi-Kogen ○
◐ Nishi-Harima
Hiroshima ●
Ube ●
◐ Kagawa
○ Ehime
Hamamatsu ●
Kurume-Tosu ●
Kenhoku-Kunisaki ●
Kan-Omura-wan ◐
Kumamoto ●
Kokubu-Hayato ●   Miyazaki ●

Cartography: Stephan Pohl 1998

Map 16.3 Location and age of twenty-six technopolis sites in Japan
Source: Sternberg 1998.

situated in the economically underdeveloped regions, although one can discern a certain concentration in Kyûshû and a distinct heterogeneity of area (between 31 and 138 hectares), population (253,000-955,000 as of 1994) and employment (15,400-113,900 as of 1994) are evident.

Although many studies of technopolis have been conducted by regional economists and economic geographers (e.g., Glasmeier 1988; Castells and Hall 1994; Tatsuno 1986; Kawashima and Stöhr 1988), empirical research on the effects of this policy instrument is still hard to find. Summarized very briefly, the existing empirical research (see Stöhr and Pönighaus 1992 and Sternberg 1995, 1997 and 1998 for a fuller discussion) confirms the hypothesis that technopolises close to metropolitan centres are more likely to achieve their goals than the numerous locations on the periphery.

The centrally-favoured zoning policy pursued by the various programmes (including technopolis) achieved a high acceptance among local politicians and resulted in an overabundance of model and/or application areas for most of the programmes (see Table 16.1). However, some of the programmes have had no new designations since the end of the 1980s, although they are, at least officially, still in operation.

Local authorities at prefectural, designated city, city, and town levels started to plan and to develop information networks, to focus on attracting new information industries, or to incubate them using local resources (see Cheung 1991). It is worth noting that local authorities are sometimes pioneers who have started the programme themselves, and then stimulated the recognition of policy formulation and promotion nationwide by the central ministries. Besides installing office automation equipment, local authorities also utilize new media such as Character and Pattern Telephone Access Information Network System (CAPTAIN) service or CATV to provide new services for the community.

In 1981, the public corporation of NTT started the Information Network System (INS) project to establish a new information and communication base. The aim of INS is to digitize the telephone network and integrate transmission of digital signals from telephones, telegraphs, telex, data communication and facsimile into one communication network that can be carried by a single digital cable. Speed and quality of transmission will be improved, and the pricing system will be unified and rationalized to reduce the existing gap between long-distance and short-distance transmissions. Provision of services using optical fibres and satellites at lower costs and with easier access will also be attempted.

This was a time of drastic change in the industrial structure towards high-value products and service industries. Many local and regional economies faced stagnation, and the capital region, Tokyo, had to face the challenge of 'world city' development and adjust itself for further growth in central and financial functions. The 'fourth comprehensive national development plan', adopted in 1987, tries to meet these challenges by proclaiming a new 'multinuclear development of urban agglomerations'. It also promotes regional vitalization through the further stabilization of population movements in local regions, and through increasing opportunities for flows and exchanges. Further infrastructure development for telecommunications and transportation includes building more Shinkansen lines and using commuter planes to shorten the time distance between major nodal cities of the land system into a one-day round-trip.

There are several focal points of local government strategies in the emerging multimedia era. Efforts concentrate on such areas as development and deployment of the next-generation communications network (e.g. optical fibre networks such as the Kansai Cultural and Scientific Research Park) and multimedia information centres (e.g., a specific programme established by MITI with six designations as of 1996 and the clear goal of local residents and enterprises creating and editing multimedia software products). A look at the great variety of info-communications systems adopted by local governments by 1994 shows that 'emergency public alert systems', 'administrative information systems' and 'online administrative service systems' are the most popular regional information programmes of local governments in Japan (InfoCom Research 1996).

Following Cheung (1991), the regional information policies of the 1980s can be classified into three main types with respect to the target for action: 'new media system development', 'specific new media facility development' and 'urban infrastructure development' strategies. The objective of the 'new media system development' strategy is to introduce a new media system to develop or set up various information systems responding to the needs of the local community or city. The programmes include 'teletopia', 'new media community', and 'greentopia'.

The 'specific new media facility' strategy refers to the 'Law to Promote the Participation of the Private Sector in Public-interest Projects', which aims to encourage private sector participation in public work projects in place of, or as a supplement to, national or local government bodies. It aims at promoting the construction or improvement of specified facilities so as to enhance the infrastructure needed for the emerging socio-economic environment, along with technological innovation and the information age. It is a joint approach by five ministries. The list of specific facilities includes ten items, ranging from transport facilities to infrastructure for the information society such as 'research cores', 'telecom research parks' and 'telecom plazas' (see InfoCom Research 1996). The financial incentives provided by this law include tax allowances, subsidies and loans. Finally, we should consider the 'urban infrastructure development' strategies, which include programmes such as 'intelligent city' and 'information-oriented and futuristic city'.

By far the most popular strategies in the regions belong to the 'new media system development' type and to 'urban infrastructure development'. In the following section, three programmes of these two types will be selected for a

Table 16.1 Regional distribution of information-oriented development programmes in Japan as of June 1995

Regions*	First designation	Last designation as of June 1995	Hokkaido	Tohoku	Kanto
Teletopia (MPT, by June 1996)	1985	1995	5	13	41
New media community (MITI)	1984	1994	6	11	19
Greentopia (MAFF)	1986	1988	2	8	5
Construction/improvement of specified new media facilities (MITI, MPT, MOC, MOT, MAFF)***	1986				
Intelligent City (MOC)	1986	1989	1	2	17
Telecom Town Plan (MPT)	1989	1995	2	3	3
Hi-Vision City Plans (MPT)	1988	1994	3	1	5
Plan for the Promotion of Regional Software Development (ML, MITI)	1989	1993	2	4	3
Community Network Project (MHA, as of June 1994)	1991	1993	2	5	8
Plan for Promoting the 'Brain' Industries (MITI)	1989	1994	2	4	4
Information-Oriented and Futuristic City (MITI)	1986		2	3	10
Totals (without specified new media facilities progr.)					
Numbers			27	54	115
In per cent			5.3	10.5	22.5

Source: own calculations on the data basis of InfoCom Research, Inc. 1996, MPT 1996, Chiki Shinkô Seibi Kôdan 1994;

*   Abbreviations for the responsible ministries are MPT (Ministry of Posts and Telecommunications), MITI (Ministry of International Trade and Industry), MAFF (Ministry of Agriculture, Forestry and Fishery), MOT (Ministry of Transportation), MHA (Ministry of Home Affairs), ML (Ministry of Labour) and MOC (Ministry of Construction),

**   The 92 new media Community programmes can be divided into two categories, 21 for Model areas, and 71 for Application Model areas; the location of one area designated in 1994 could not be identified by the sources available, and is not included in the sum of column total.

***   For this type of programme no regional distribution of the 53 programmes and no designation years are given in the sources available; thus, they are not included in the sum of column total.

Chubu	Kinki	Chugoku	Shikoku	Kyûshû	Okinawa	Total
35	15	15	8	16	1	149
17	13	8	6	10	1	92**
10	7	6	5	9	1	53
						(53)
6	10	7	2	7	1	53
4	4	—	—	6	—	22
14	5	3	1	6	1	39
5	1	1	1	3	-	20
5	6	4	3	6	-	39
3	1	3	2	5	2	26
1	2	2	0	0	0	20
100	64	49	28	68	7	512
19.5	12.5	9.6	5.5	13.3	1.3	100.0

more detailed description. The three programmes ('teletopia', 'new media community' and 'intelligent city') are among the best documented with respect to the designated locations' spatial distribution and are among the most popular programmes.

All programmes mentioned are specific development measures with incentives provided by central ministries to local governments in Japan. Most of these programmes match closely with the 'fourth comprehensive national development plan' of 1987 designed by the Nation Land Agency, which emphasizes the consolidation of regional information and communication infrastructures.

However, all these efforts are quite independent of one another, since they are initiatives from various powerful ministries like MITI, Ministry of Posts and Telecommunications or Ministry of Construction (MOC), and supported by different financial incentives.

The regional information projects are part of a strategy to establish nodal points for an infrastructure network of information and communication. It aims to have effects at both the national and regional levels (for the background to the rest of this section, see Cheung 1991). At the beginning of the 1990s, the powerful information field in the Tokyo region (including the neighbouring cities such as Yokohama and Kawasaki) dominated information flows. There was a one-way flow of information from Tokyo to all regions in Japan. At the national level, the strategy aimed to balance this 'one-to-many' flow (Stage A).

The building up of nodal networks for information transmission and communication should gradually transform some major regional nodes in the national network. It will enable them to start two-way communication with Tokyo and, similarly, with cities overseas. Some local nodes are still overwhelmed by the information flow coming from Tokyo, which inhibits their capacity really to generate their own information. However, a stage of some-to-some and/or some-to-many modes (Stage B) is developing. This stage will mature in the near future, if information-oriented strategies are successfully implemented.

The final stage will be represented by the integration of all modes, regional or local, into the national information network. At this stage, every region has its own share of horizontal and vertical functions, on complementary terms with each other. This may be called the stage of many-to-many modes (Stage C).

At the regional level, a study group under the MPT has designed two regional nodal frameworks for local metropolitan areas and for large metropolitan areas. First, the regional INS and value-added network (VAN) will provide network services for economic activities (Local Area Networks, industrial districts for automated factories, databases for agricultural cooperatives, local banks, local resort and leisure areas, regional VAN firms, local industrial databases), community and social services (educational individual-service CATV to schools, local hospitals, clinics offering computer diagnosis, etc.) and personal or household services (e.g. home shopping, home banking, ticket reservation, and other information services). Other features include regional information centres, regional CAPTAIN centres, regional databases, CATV centres, teleports, INS buildings and regional VAN firms, and other facilities. Second, the information network INS/VAN in the large metropolitan areas will have similar features, especially for corporate head offices of large firms, international VAN firms linked with the teleport and large-scale database, and central hospitals.

Overview of selected programmes

Teletopia and neo-teletopia

In 1984, the MPT proclaimed its teletopia concept as a model city for future communication. 'Teletopia' is a word constructed from the combination of 'telecommunication' and 'utopia'. The concept was introduced in 1983, the year designated for international communication. It is an incentive provided by the MPT to a local city, town, or small metropolitan area and aims at resolving problems confronting the various regions and promoting regional information systems as a means of invigorating local communities. Its activities include introducing two-directional CATV, video-text, the CAPTAIN system, INS, data communications, and other new media into certain model regions. Teletopia is by far the most popular of all programmes discussed here with a total of 149 regions designated by the end of June 1996 and 703 systems developed since the programme was initiated in 1985 (MPT 1996).

In the mid-1990s, this concept achieved a new status, when MPT introduced its so-called 'neo-teletopia' programme. It aims is to revive the already existing 'teletopia' concept through other forms of public promotion measures in order to facilitate private investment participation and to increase autonomous and flexible local government involvement (Steffensen 1996). MPT's neo-teletopia concept offers interest-free loans under the teletopia scheme and 'private sector vitality law', subsidies to projects for technical advancement and the reduction of regional disparities, and an industrial investment funding scheme to projects for training and installation of optical fibre networks.

Although there are several teletopia projects in peripheral areas like Kyûshû and Hokkaido, Map 16.4 shows a clear spatial concentration in Tokai, Kinki and especially in Kanto, the core regions of Japan (see Table 16.1). The Hamamatsu area in Shizuoka prefecture (located on the Pacific coast between Kanto and Kinki in Chubu) is both a representative example for this spatial distribution and a model city for MPT's next-generation information infrastructural development schemes. It is not only a teletopia area, but also a 'Telecom Town', a 'High-Vision City', and (since 1994) the first of the official 'Local government network projects' designated by MPT.

New media community

It was in the mid-1980s when the MITI announced its 'new media community' concept as a way for local regions to vitalize or revitalize themselves through new media. The concept is a kind of new media model programme to correct the imbalance between the information status of regions. It aims to develop information systems in regional communities to meet their immediate industrial, social and other needs. The programme aims to develop more vital regional communities through the joint efforts of national and local authorities, and the private sector.

The process of establishing the new media community concept involves various steps beginning with a 'model area', followed by an 'application development area'. The model and application development areas of

361

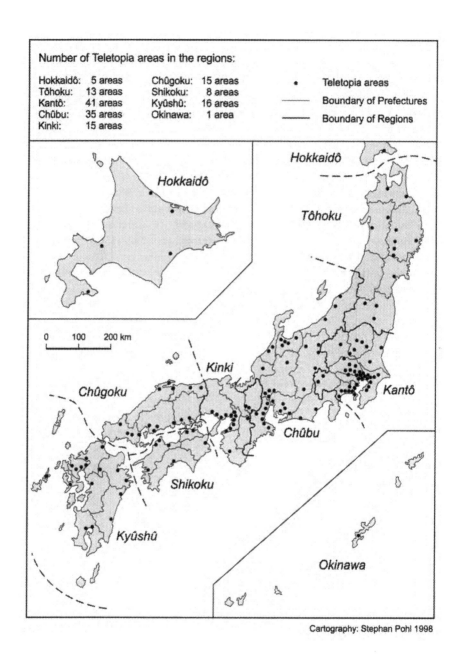

Number of Teletopia areas in the regions:

Hokkaidô:	5 areas	Chûgoku:	15 areas
Tôhoku:	13 areas	Shikoku:	8 areas
Kantô:	41 areas	Kyûshû:	16 areas
Chûbu:	35 areas	Okinawa:	1 area
Kinki:	15 areas		

•   Teletopia areas

----------   Boundary of Prefectures

—————   Boundary of Regions

Hokkaidô

Hokkaidô

Tôhoku

0   100   200 km

Kinki

Chûgoku

Kantô

Chûbu

Shikoku

Kyûshû

Okinawa

Cartography: Stephan Pohl 1998

Map 16.4 Location of designated teletopia areas as of mid-1996
Source: Ministry of Posts and Telecommunications 1996: 16.

information systems are pioneers in the field and will contribute to a further networking of society by forming nodal points in the national information network. By June 1995, twenty-one model areas and seventy-one application areas all over Japan had been designated (Map 16.5). This programme is less concentrated in a spatial sense compared with teletopia, although Kanto again is the region with the highest number of designated areas.

Two case studies, described in Cheung (1991), illustrate the objectives of this programme. The model area in Hiroshima installed a mainframe computer in the District Centre of Commerce and Industry, to develop manpower training systems for small and medium-sized firms and to provide services to firms through online networks. A third-sector organization was set uop in 1988 with the support of Hiroshima City, the prefecture, Hiroshima Wholesale Centre, Hiroshima Industrial System Joint Development, and local financial institutions and firms. Two new media community application areas within the Hiroshima region complete the region's attempt to vitalize local industries with the help of new media infrastructure.

Asahikawa (Hokkaido) belongs to the urban health and medical-care type of new media community programme. Its objectives are to develop a health care system and to strengthen the medical care service. Among the information systems to be developed are health information systems, first-aid information systems, administration systems, and education systems. This new media project is also organized as a third-sector joint venture (university, local government, local business) and is supported by the City, the prefecture, the local Chamber of Industry and Commerce, and the university.

Intelligent city

The 'intelligent city' programme belongs to the 'urban infrastructure development' type of strategy. It has been finalized by the MOC to integrate the development of an advanced information and communication system and urban infrastructure facility (such as optical fibre and CATV network development) into the infrastructure construction process in urban development or redevelopment. Local authorities send their infrastructure development plans to the MOC for recognition. Recognized plans get priority for area development from the ministry, and the incentive of low-interest loans for the construction of 'intelligent buildings'. With the exception of the 'information-oriented and futuristic city' concept, no other programme of those listed in Table 16.1 shows a higher spatial concentration in the core regions of Kanto and Kinki (see Map 16.6). Obviously, it is difficult to achieve considerable progress in reducing spatial disparities with this programme. Since 1989 no new designations have been made.

363

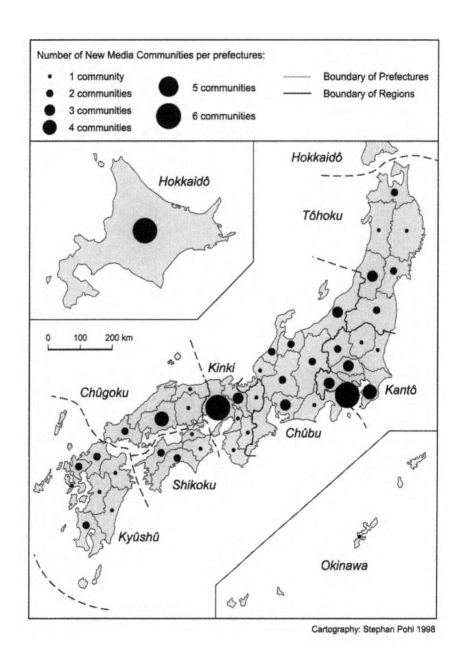

Number of New Media Communities per prefectures:

- • 1 community
- • 2 communities
- • 3 communities
- • 4 communities
- ● 5 communities
- ● 6 communities

Boundary of Prefectures
Boundary of Regions

Hokkaidô

Hokkaidô

Tôhoku

0 100 200 km

Kinki

Chûgoku

Kantô

Chûbu

Shikoku

Kyûshû

Okinawa

Cartography: Stephan Pohl 1998

Map 16.5 Number of designated New Media Community areas per prefecture as of June 1995

Source: InfoCom Research 1996, Chiki Shinkô Seibi Kôdan 1994.

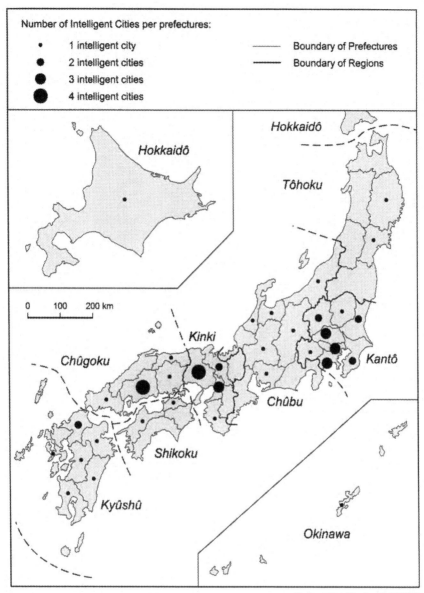

Cartography: Stephan Pohl 1998

Map 16.6 Number of designated 'intelligent city' areas per prefecture as of June 1995
Source: InfoCom Research 1996, Chiki Shinkô Seibi Kôdan 1994.

The case of Kyûshû region

Kyûshû is an appropriate example of a peripheral area within Japan. After a short overview of the regional economic structure, some remarks will be made regarding the existence of multimedia projects and the success of the six 'technopolis' sites. From this, conclusions on respective regional development impacts can be drawn.

Kyûshû, in the 1980s, seemed to have succeeded in advancing from an economically and spatially peripheral region to one sensationally known as 'Silicon Island'. It is, effectively, a 'new industrial place' to use Scott's (1988) term: an industrial region owing its emergence to technology-intensive industries, the majority of which did not settle in the old industrial northern part of the island.

By Japanese standards, however, Kyûshû remains underdeveloped. It is the southernmost of the four main islands of the Japanese archipelago and is often termed the '10 per cent economy'. In 1994, the 13.4 million inhabitants (10.7 per cent of total population) produced approximately 8.6 per cent of GDP. The island – comparable in size to Switzerland – exhibits high percentages of added value in the agricultural and fishing sectors, whereas the manufacturing sector (especially mechanical engineering) is underdeveloped: in 1993, Kyûshû's share of Japan's industrial turnover was only 6.2 per cent (see Kyûshû Industrial Advancement Centre 1994). Seven of the forty-seven Japanese prefectures are located on Kyûshû (Kumamoto, Saga, Fukuoka, Oita, Miyazaki, Kagoshima and Nagasaki); for regional economic analyses they constitute an appropriate administrative level (Map 16.7). Not only the value-added shares but also other economic indicators, such as per capita income, productivity in manufacturing and the relationship between demand for and availability of labour, reveal that Kyûshû is still a peripheral part of the country in terms of location, as well as economy, and lags considerably behind other large industrial regions.

Kyûshû acquired its reputation as the 'Silicon Island' toward the end of the 1970s, when numerous semiconductor businesses began to establish themselves in all prefectures. In 1994, 39.3 per cent of the integrated circuits produced in Japan and 30.6 per cent of the turnover of this industry came from Kyûshû (Kyûshû Industrial Advancement Centre 1994). Taking all eight high-tech branches together, Kyûshû's share of employment in these industries is far above the national average. The high proportion of high-tech employees is mainly due to the semiconductor industry, whereas the remaining seven high-tech industries are strongly under-represented. In 1991, 73.9 per cent of the total of 112,395 high-tech employees and 51.0 per cent of the total of 1,217 high-tech enterprises on Kyûshû belonged to the industrial branch of 'electrical equipment parts', which consists almost exclusively of the semiconductor industry. From this point of view, the term 'Silicon Island' is correct, but the intended association with 'high-tech' is unrealistic and misleading.

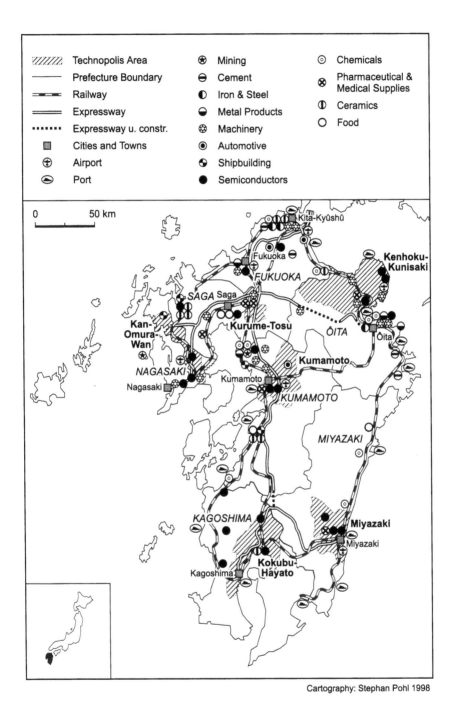

Map 16.7 Economic structure and 'technopolises' on Kyûshû
Source: Kyûshû Industrial Advancement Centre 1994, modified.

Kyûshû's semiconductor industry has undergone continual restructuring. As a reaction to the revaluation of the yen in 1985 and increasing trade restrictions imposed by the Western industrialized countries, many regional semiconductor manufacturers reoriented their production toward value-added-intensive products (custom-made semiconductors and mass production of large-scale integrated circuits with one-megabyte storage capacity) (see Sargent 1987, Matsubara 1992). While the quantity and quality of semiconductors made on Kyûshû was still on the rise in the mid-1990s (after a short setback in 1992, see Kyûshû Yamaguchi Economic Federation, undated), a further increase in employment seems unlikely. In the coming decade, the automotive industry (particularly the production of automobiles) is expected to take the lead leaving the semiconductor industry behind. The automotive industry also exploits the region's comparative advantages, namely, the availability of relatively cheap and flexible labour and fully developed industrial space.

As shown in Table 16.1, Kyûshû's share of the government's new media and information programmes is slightly higher than their share of most other economic indicators cited above. However, the different types of programmes will probably not have the same impact on all regions. Thus there will be a difference between the impact of one programme within different regions and several programmes and projects within one region. Bearing this in mind there are some signs, including public investment and support or popularity among the regions, that in particular the teletopia programme, the new media community programme and eventually the 'brain industries' plan and the futuristic city programme could be the most important ones in terms of long-run regional development.

The share of these various programmes that Kyûshû receives varies, but it is in general lower than its overall proportion of 13.3 per cent. There are no information-oriented and futuristic city projects located on Kyûshû and the share for teletopia and new media community is below 13.3 per cent. However, almost one-fifth of all projects of the plan for promoting 'brain industries' are located on Kyûshû.

Six of the twenty-six technopolis zones are located on Kyûshû (see Map 16.7). They belong to the older zones (founded in 1984 and 1985). For each 'technopolis' there is a skeleton plan giving exact goals in terms of the number of employees, inhabitants, industrial shipments and industrial added value. The specific growth rates of these indicators for each 'technopolis' take account of the basic regional conditions. Of all Japanese districts Kyûshû has overall the most successful technopolis zones. All of the six zones reach above-average percentages for three or four out of the four indicators. In addition, the most successful technopolis site in Japan for each of the four indicators is located in Kyûshû: in terms of population it is Kunisaki (Oita prefecture, 29.3 per cent goal achievement), in terms of employment it is Kurume (Saga and Fukuoka prefecture, 244 per cent), and in terms of both productivity and added value Kumamoto -in the same prefecture – is the most successful of all twenty-six technopolis sites (165 per cent and 134 per cent respectively).

Another method for evaluating the success of the technopolis programme uses the increase in the above-mentioned indices plus the industrial turnover between 1980 and 1994 as a means of identifying growth processes of varying intensity in the technopolises on Kyûshû. (See Table 16.2.) Although not all 'technopolises' are of the same age, the differences between them appear to be rather small. Two significant points emerge. First, the technopolises on Kyûshû (in terms of all five indicators) experienced a more favourable development than the other twenty zones on average. Second, the technopolises of Kumamoto and Miyazaki in terms of all five indicators surpass the average of all Japanese zones and also – unlike the otherwise more dynamic technopolis of Oita – show an above-average population development.

To summarize, the most successful zones are those whose prefectures already had a dense high-tech manufacturing core and employee base before possible technopolis effects had any influence (as in the case of Kumamoto). Moreover, the figures do not indicate that disparities in inter-regional high-tech due to the existence of a technopolis. Relative to all five indicators almost all the technopolises on Kyûshû have undergone a more dynamic development than the other twenty zones, although they started at a very low level. Despite all these positive results, it remains to be seen whether an endogenous, lasting and R&D-oriented economic development, giving qualitative as well as purely quantitative success, will actually be set in motion by the technopolis programme. The growth of the automotive industry – not necessarily a high-tech industry – deeply rooted in the region, does not give any indication to this effect. It seems realistic to assume that those parts of Kyûshû which do not belong to the technopolis zones will be far less successful in their efforts to establish new high-tech businesses.

Reducing economic disparities between regions with the help of new media policies and 'technopolis' zones?

Would it be possible within a reasonable period to reduce inter-regional disparities in Japan by implementing new media projects and technopolis sites in selected parts of the country? Two necessary, but not sufficient, preconditions are that respective projects in peripheral areas must be higher in numbers and more successful than those in core regions.

The analysis has shown that programmes supporting new media and multimedia by the national government's ministries can be found in any of the Japanese regions. In principle, the same is true for technopolis zones, although only half of the prefectures have established such a facility, many of them being dedicated to multimedia. However, significant differences persist between the districts and prefectures in terms of the shares of respective facilities.

Table 16.2 Indices of selected target variables in Kyûshû's 'technopolis' sites 1994 (1980 = 100)

Technopolis name (prefecture)	Employment	Population	Added value	Turnover	Productivity (value-added/employee)
Kurume Tosu (Saga, Fukuoka)	95	108	115	149	120
Kan-Omura-wan (Nagasaki)	105	104	193	238	183
Kenboku Kunisaki (Oita)	148	97	248	387	167
Kumamoto (Kumamoto)	121	116	207	253	172
Miyazaki (Miyazaki)	140	116	204	296	146
Kokubu Hayato (Kagoshima)	100	110	166	166	167
All technopolises in Kyûshû	113	110	174	219	154
All Japanese technopolises	108	108	144	174	134

Source: unpublished data from technopolis administrations

In order to survey the distribution of the regional innovation programmes and projects aiming for information-oriented development, Table 16.1 groups a total of 512 programmes and projects into nine regions, all defined in Map 16.1. The table only gives a rough estimate of the distribution, as it is based only on the number of facilities. A further comparison of the budget and capital outlays of these programmes is necessary, whenever spatially disaggregated data are available.

· The Kanto region comes first with 115 programmes (22.5 per cent of the total) approved and under implementation, followed by the Chubu region with 100 projects (19.5 per cent). The Kyûshû region comes in third with sixty-eight programmes and the Kinki region is fourth with sixty-four programmes. This preliminary analysis shows that information-oriented programmes/projects for the regions are, ironically, rather concentrated in the Kanto region. However, they also allow for active initiatives from local authorities like those from the Kinki, Kyûshû, Chugoku, and Tohoku regions.

Compared with the situation in 1991, this ranking does not differ significantly, although Kyûshû as a peripheral area has surpassed Kinki as one of the economic cores in Japan in terms of the absolute number of projects (for the situation in 1991 see Cheung 1991). For single programmes like the important teletopia and new media community projects, however, the share of core regions like Kanto and Tokai increased. Peripheral areas like Kyûshû stagnated in absolute terms, consequently losing ground in relative terms.

Are the information-oriented policies correctors of imbalance or not? In short, the answer would appear to be 'no'. These policies are not directly geared to places of slow growth, or of a low standard of living. The distribution of the programmes is skewed in favour of the Kanto region and tends to maintain the existing concentration of political, administrative, financial, economic, technological, and international relations functions.

The policies should rather be seen as provisions that improve the capacities of those places where the local initiatives are strongest and most capable of designing and implementing information-oriented programmes (Cheung 1991). The regional distribution of these programmes shows that Kinki, Kyûshû, Chubu, Chugoku and Tohoku are active and they operate more programmes than the rest. We can also observe that key projects such as teletopia (MPT) and information-oriented and futuristic city (MOC) are being concentrated at Tokyo and Osaka. It can be concluded that these policies strengthen the existing hierarchical structure of urban and information nodal places. Those at the periphery are not given special consideration unless they take initiatives themselves.

With the implementation of information and communication innovation programmes in the regions, the geography of Japan is likely to transform into a multi-nuclear formation as Cheung (1991) puts it. Cities with designated or higher status will play the role of nuclei for the emerging networked information society, and help diffuse demonstration and innovation effects to their

regions and other parts of the nation. However, to strengthen the decentralizing effects and further the vitality of the regions, at least one more national
institutional framework needs to be changed: the relationship between
government and prefectures.

The prefectures are too dependent on the central government and ministries and there is no room for them to engage fully in establishing their
management priorities and styles, and generating their own brand of information. At the end of the 1990s, about two-thirds of the income of local
states comes on the Ministry of Finance. This share needs to be adjusted significantly. This redistribution of financial power can be made possible, for
example, by having the local authorities collect the income, profit and property taxes, while the central government collects the consumer tax. Such a
devolution of power to prefectural government and the reinforcement of local
autonomous funds are required to promote regional industrial policy, as Sato
(1994) points out. To achieve the goal, this change must go hand-in-hand
with regional policy and the help of new media industries.

The assessment of technopolis is different, although in the end a very similar conclusion may be appropriate. A major aim of technopolis is to reduce
the disparities between high-tech industries located close to core regions and
those on the periphery. Thus, this instrument constitutes the most comprehensive attempt anywhere in the world to combine regional policy and
technology policy in a large number of locations. Viewing the success factors
determined for the twenty-six zones and the majority of publications on the
subject (e.g., Castells and Hall 1994; Glasmeier 1988; Takeuchi 1996), gives
rise to scepticism.

The technopolis concept is based on the logic of an economy dominated by
large corporations: without their cooperation neither this nor other instrument of regional economic policy could be implemented, even in centralist
Japan (see Broadbent 1990). When technopolis euphoria first began in the
early 1980s, decentralization of high-tech manufacturing into peripheral
parts of the country was welcomed by industry. The soaring demand for high-
tech products and, consequently, for labour and space could not be met by the
central government and gave the domestic periphery comparative locational
advantages in certain stages of production. At that time, the targets set for
the technopolises turnover and population were realistic enough under the
circumstances.

Since the revaluation of the yen in 1986, however, the advantage of sites
on the periphery has drastically diminished. The preferred relocation site of
'simple' manufacturing, especially of the semiconductor industry – the quan-
titatively dominant high-tech industry in Japan – is no longer on the
domestic periphery, but in adjoining South-East Asian states and in the main
overseas markets (USA and Western Europe). This also explains why the
employment increase in the technopolises mainly stems from small and
medium-sized enterprises rather than large ones (see Castells and Hall 1994).

Ever since the mid-1980s, those technopolises close enough to the metropoles to profit from agglomeration advantages, and far enough away to be spared the disadvantages, have had the best chances for success. All things considered, the megalopolis, by intra-regionally decentralizing the industry, contributes to the success of (some of) the (nearby) zones, which then causes the expansion of the core region. The decentralization goal of the technopolis strategy may be reached intra-regionally (within the central region). It cannot, however, be achieved inter-regionally and would therefore miss the target of compensation, which is officially its main objective.

More recent data, however, shows more positive results for peripheral regions and especially for technopolises located there. They show very high degrees of goal achievement for all indicators including productivity, turnover, employment, population and added value. In addition, between 1980 and 1988, prefectures with technopolises experienced more favourable development with regard to goal variables and productivity than those without a technopolis (see Stöhr and Pönighaus 1992). The latter study also proves that the serious disparities between the centre and the periphery with respect to the total number of industrial establishments and the number of high-tech establishments seem to have decreased – at least to some degree – since the implementation of the technopolis programme, which has the support of selected multimedia industries in the agendas of several of the twenty-six zones.

Notes

I would like to thank Dr. Jochen Legewie (German Institute for Japanese Studies, Tokyo) and Dr. Hirotaki Mano (Research Institute for Industrial Location, Tokyo) for their valuable assistance. Additionally, I owe special thanks to Stephan Pohl, who prepared all maps and figures with a high level of quality and promptness, a trait I have appreciated not only in this contribution.

1   The term multimedia here refers to a combination of a variety of media (e.g., text, data, graphics, moving pictures, audio) – available in a digitized format and interactively accessible. Additionally, multimedia is defined as a network technology with several actors within the value network including network operators, hardware producers, the media industry, service providers, content providers, the entertainment industry and software producers.

References

Abe, H. (1996) 'New directions for regional development planning in Japan', in J. Alden and P. Boland (eds) *Regional Development Strategies: A European Perspective,* London and Bristol: Jessica Kingsley.
Bertuglia, C. S. and Occelli, S. (1995) 'Transportation, communications and patterns

of location', in C. S. Bertuglia, M. M. Fischer and G. Preto (eds) *Technological Change, Economic Development and Space*, Berlin and Heidelberg: Springer.

Broadbent, J. (1990) 'Technopoles et aménagement du territoire au Japon. Les technopoles contre la désindustrialization (Technopoles and regional development in Japan)', *Les Annales de la Recherche Urbaine* 46: 57–64.

Castells, M. and Hall, P. (1994) *Technopoles of the World. The Making of 21st Century Industrial Complexes*, London and New York : Routledge.

Cheung, C. (1991) 'Regional innovation strategies and information society: a review of government initiatives in Japan', *Asian Geographer* 10, 1: 39–61.

Chiki Shinkô Seibi Kôdan (1994) *Chikii tôkei yôran 1994 nenban (Data on regional development)*, Tokyo: Chiki Shinkô Seibi Kôdan.

Economic Planning Agency (ed.) (1991) *Overview of Regional Economy*, Tokyo: Economic Planning Agency.

Flüchter, W. (1990) 'Japan. Die Landesentwicklung im Spannungsfeld zwischen Zentralisierung und Dezentralisierung' (Japan: Regional Development between Centralization and Decentralization), *Geographische Rundschau* 42, 4: 182–94.

Glasmeier, A. K. (1988) 'The Japanese technopolis program: high-tech development strategy or industrial policy in disguise?', *International Journal of Urban and Regional Research* 12, 268–83.

InfoCom Research Inc. (1996) 'Information and communications in Japan 1996', Tokyo: InfoCom Research, Inc.

Japan Industrial Location Centre (1990) 'Technopolis policy of Japan', Tokyo: Japan Industrial Location Centre.

Japan Regional Development Corporation (1996) 'Overview of Japan's regional development policies', Tokyo: Japan Regional Development Centre.

Kawashima, T. and Stöhr, W. (1988) 'Decentralized technology policy: the case of Japan', *Environment and Planning C: Government and Policy* 6: 427–39.

Kyûshû Industrial Advancement Centre (1995) 'Encounter Kyûshû. Statistics, facts and figures', Fukuoka: Kyûshû Industrial Advancement Centre.

Kyûshû–Yamaguchi Economic Federation (undated) 'Encounter Kyûshû. crossroads of Asia', Fukuoka: Kyûshû–Yamaguchi Economic Federation.

Latzer, M. (1995) 'Japanese information infrastructure initiatives. A politico–economic approach', *Telecommunications Policy* 19, 7: 515–29.

Legewie, J. (1997) 'Foreign direct investment, trade, and employment: the role of Asia within the discussion of industrial hollowing out in Japan', Working paper 97/1 of Deutsches Institut für Japanstudien, Tokyo: German Institute for Japanese Studies.

Matsubara, H. (1992) 'The Japanese semicon–ductor industry and regional development: the case of "Silicon Island" Kyûshû', *The Economic Review of Seinan Gakuin University* 27, 1: 43–65.

Ministry of Posts and Telecommunication (MPT) (1996) 'Posts and telecommunication in Japan 1996. Annual Report', Tokyo: MPT.

National Land Agency (1987) 'The Fourth Comprehensive National Development Plan', Tokyo: National Land Agency.

Nishioka, H. and Takeuchi, A. (1987) 'The development of high technology industry in Japan', in M. Breheny and R. McQuaid (eds) *The Development of High Technology Industries*, London, New York and Sydney: Croom Helm.

Nishioka, H. (1991) 'Some aspects of Japanese history and economy – the land and people in Japan: Part 2', *Aoyama Journal of Economics* 18, 2: 19–51.

Sargent, J. (1987) 'Industrial location in Japan with special reference to the semiconductor industry', *Geographical Journal* 153, 1: 72–85.

Sassen, S. (1991) *The Global City: New York, London, Tokyo*, Princeton and New York: Princeton University Press.

Sato, K. (1994) 'Regional industrial policy and the role of prefectural government in Japan supporting knowledge-intensive and technology-intensive industries', *Economic Review of the Institute of Economics and Trade*, Kanagawa University, 2: 33–55.

Scott, A. (1988) *New Industrial Spaces. Flexible Production Organization and Regional Development in North America and Western Europe*, London: Pion.

Steffensen, S. (1996) *Time of the Signs. Japanese Promotion of Next Generation Information Infrastructures, Multimedia Network Business, and Informational Economy*, Copenhagen, Working Paper 10–96, Copenhagen Business School.

Sternberg, R. (1995) 'Supporting peripheral economies or industrial policy in favour of national growth? An empirically based analysis of goal achievement of the Japanese "Technopolis" program', *Environment and Planning C: Government and Policy* 13, 4: 425–40.

—— (1997) 'New industrial spaces and national technology policies: the case of Kyûshû and the Japanese "Technopolis strategy"', in J. Simmie (ed.) *Innovation, Networks and Learning Regions*, London and Bristol: Jessica Kingsley.

—— (1998) *Technologiepolitik und High-Tech Regionen – ein internationaler Vergleich (Technology Policy and High-Tech Regions – An International Comparison)* (2nd edn.), Münster and Hamburg: LIT.

Stöhr, W. and Pönighaus R. (1992) 'Towards a data-based evaluation of the Japanese technopolis policy – the effect of new technological and organizational infrastructure on urban and regional development', *Regional Studies* 26, 7: 605–18.

Takeuchi, A. (1996) 'Regional development policy and technopolis in Japan', Tokyo, *Report of Researches Nippon Institute of Technology* 26, 2.

Tatsuno, S. (1986) *The Technopolis Strategy. Japan, High Technology and the Control of the 21st Century*, New York: Prentice Hall.

17

MULTIMEDIA AND INDUSTRIAL RESTRUCTURING IN SINGAPORE

Hing Ai Yun

Introduction

For Western Europe and North America, a protracted crisis of the manufacturing industry dating from the early 1970s has stimulated vigorous debates over the nature of industrial restructuring and its implications for economic and social development path of these advanced capitalist economies (Piore and Sable 1984, Porter 1990, Hirst and Zeitlin 1989). In the case of the East Asian economies, popular myths touting the Asian model of economic growth have only recently been punctured by a widespread series of unsettling news of currency turmoil and looming recession. World markets are currently buzzing with conjectures that the global economic forces that have brought investment and prosperity to countries like Japan and Korea are now threatening to take them elsewhere.

Amid news flashes of strikes, galloping deficits, bad-debt problems, corruption, infrastructure bottlenecks and overheating (*Asian Business* 1997a, 1997b, 1997c, Pollack 1997, *Economist* 1997b), Asia's miracle economies that have grown fat on annual growth rates of more than eight per cent are ill-prepared for leaner times. While Japan continues in slow recovery mode, other Asian economies such as Malaysia and Singapore are restructuring to beat labour shortages and the World Trade Organization deadlines for liberalization. More specifically, concerns over falling growth rates have spurred Singapore to make sweeping changes in work orientation and infrastructures, both soft and hard.

Broadly, this study aims to focus on current restructuring strategies in Singapore as it moves from a newly industrialized (NIE) to a fully developed economy. In particular, attention will centre on the strategic importance of information technology (IT) and its subset, multimedia. Like the rest of the industrially advanced economies, Singapore is targeting IT not only to deliver a healthy recovery but to act as the primary infrastructure and export product for the 21st century. In launching Communicate Asia/Broadcast Asia '96 and Network Asia '96, the Minister of Communications spoke of Singapore One.[1] He emphasized that:

> Rapid technological advances in recent years, coupled with the convergence of the telecommunication computing and broadcasting industries, have resulted in the advent of new leading industries based on high performance multimedia communication. The multimedia industry alone is envisaged to grow and become the leading industry in the 21st century. Singapore must nurture this industry now as it will form the heart of the new industrial structure.
>
> (Tan 1996)

This chapter is divided into four major sections. The first describes the core economic policies supporting Singapore's economic development and aiming to facilitate the positioning of multimedia as a strategy for restructuring. The second section deals in detail with technology as a tool for gaining the competitive edge. It examines the gradual evolution and development of the IT infrastructure in Singapore, a process which culminates in the contemporary development of the National Information Infrastructure. Following this, the chapter goes on to describe the development of the nascent multimedia industry. Finally we show how existing conditions/institutions could support using multimedia successfully as a tool for development.

Key thrusts of restructuring

The past three and a half decades since political independence in 1965 have seen Singapore's economic growth rates advance at more than eight per cent annually from 1960s to 1995. The policy centrepiece driving this growth is the global orientation of Singapore, as expressed in multinational-corporation-based manufacturing using export-orientated industries, combined with a free trade regime and lavish use of immigrant labour at both the high- and low-end skill levels. Ironically this policy, which was forced on Singapore due to resource deficiency and lack of a sizable market during the early years of industrialization, has in hindsight ensured Singapore a competitive edge in an increasingly global economy.

Since the first serious crisis of 1985, which rocked Singapore with a threatening one per cent growth, an array of new goals and strategies have been put on track to shift the economy up the technological scale. To attack rising labour costs and shortages, the state has put together a policy package to help Singapore adapt to the challenge of world competition.

Sectoral transformation

The basic goal of restructuring is to maintain the manufacturing sector at twenty-five per cent of the Gross National Product (GNP) in the medium and long term. Manufacturing is seen as an essential base to support a plethora of other industries such as services. It is also hoped that Singapore will gain new appeal by casting itself as the business services gateway to the region. Realization of this goal can already be seen in a range of developments: the rapid expansion of financial services; the establishment of Singapore as tourism hub; the number of operational headquarters located there; its role as a centre for logistics distribution and media telecommunications hub for the Asia Pacific rim.

In thirty-five years of sparkling growth rates, the Singapore economy faced only one short recessionary spell in 1985 (commonly labelled the 'Oil Crisis'). However, this period sent interesting signals about the underlying structural shift which witnessed the beginning of a process of capital exodus (see Table 17.1).

By 1995, the total cumulative stock of outward FDI amounted to $46.24 billion which is equivalent to 38.1 per cent of GNP. Trying to mitigate this trend, Singapore attempted to keep back as many business activities as possible by providing generous incentives, for example, in R&D. The increasing capital outflow, however, has still not led to a hollowing out of the industrial sector. This could be due to two factors. First, the state actively enters joint ventures with foreign partners to increase the rate of investments in selected industries, including those requiring massive amounts of capital or those requiring long-term investments. Second, the booming Asian market has drawn in a massive flow of FDI. By offering Singapore as a tentative first stop, the state was able to divert selective parts of this flow for its own purpose of shifting the economic landscape to a high-tech one. A third strategy is designed for the uninitiated and smaller investors who do not want to be hassled by dealing with the uncertainties of emerging economies such as China, Vietnam and Burma. Singapore has planned to export its system of governance by building safe industrial parks in these most unpredictable business environments. Investors are thus freed to concentrate on the actual business of production while the park managers work diligently to untangle and diffuse the element of precariousness that operating in such environments entail.

New management orientation

It was envisaged that with the creation of the new industrial economy, the management of human resources will also need to be revamped. The aim is to replace monetary incentives as a motivational force with psychological instruments such as group identification that comes from teamwork and a heightened sense of shared vulnerability.

378

Table 17.1 Outward foreign direct investment by Singapore-based firms, 1976–94

Year	Cumulative stock of direct foreign investment (S$mn)*	As % of GDP	No. of companies which invested abroad
1976	1,427.6	9.8	n.a
1980	2,493.9	10.3	n.a
1990	16,877.9	25.3	2,391
1991	18,607.5	25.2	2,721
1992	22,442.5	27.9	2,954
1993	28,900.4	31.0	3,764
1994	37,319.3	35.6	4,295

Source: Department of Statistics 1996;
Note: * All dollar numbers are Singapore $ (one Singapore $ was equivalent to US$1.708 on 4 September 1998) unless otherwise stated.

The constant portrayal of national vulnerability and insecurity in the mass media has caused anxiety amongst Singapore's population. Both print and electronic media have succeeded in nurturing a sense of national insecurity which in turn provides the motivation for hard work, thrift and a general compliance with particular types of behaviour (Ministry of Trade and Industry 1991) necessary for the enhancement of national competitiveness.

One strategy is to set the country's ranking along internationally-created scales of performance. A regular ranking system was deployed by Business Environment Risk Intelligence (July 1996) which placed Singapore second world-wide in terms of profit opportunity. This ensured a conducive climate and the easy mobilization of human effort in the current restructuring exercise.

Human-resource supply and development

The state, with the help of EDB (Economic Development Board, lead investment agency), works closely with tertiary and training institutions to ensure the development of adequate manpower for the restructuring of the economy. Various specialist manpower programmes have been established to churn out the new skills required by industries targeted for special development. These include:

- Specialist Manpower Programme in Wafer Fabrication, Disk Media and IC Packaging.
- R F Engineers Development Programme.
- Analogue IC Designer Programme.
- Precision Engineering Manpower Programme.
- Specialist Mould Designer Development Programme.
- Broadcasting and Production Training.

Apart from these initiatives, the Board has programmes to assist Singapore-based companies to recruit international talents in order to broaden the local manpower pool. Since 1992, more than eighty private companies and public organizations have benefitted from EDB recruitment facilitation. Finally, an EDB immigration facilitation programme has enabled more than 4,000 foreign professionals and skilled workers annually to take up employment in Singapore (Economic Development Board 1995–6).

The development of manpower in Singapore has been subjected more to overall political considerations rather than to the workings of the market. The main focus of attention and financing was on the education of elites; education policies were conceived within a conservative framework aimed at reproducing a new generation of conforming workers accustomed to strong rule from the top.

It was only in 1997, driven by economic imperatives, that a third university was allowed to be established by the private sector. School and university curricula were revised to ensure a broad-based education so that graduates will be more creative and effective in the now flexible and intensely competitive business environment. Alongside this, to ensure that students learn to love the nation and its leaders, local history was made a mandatory subject for schools and universities. Obviously, government (in the sense of Foucault 1981) needed to ensure both an efficient force of creative surplus producers and, at the same time, docile subjects.

Technologies for competitiveness

Popular expectations aside, it is increasingly recognized that telecommunication technologies are perceived as the 'competitive edge weapons' for advancement into the information age (Gillespie *et al.* 1989, Saunders *et al.* 1983, Knight 1995, *Annals of Regional Science* 1996).

This section examines the leading role of the state in laying the foundations for IT infrastructures. Starting from the 1990s, action in this direction has been transformed to a well-coordinated, concerted and more ambitious drive to build an all-embracing information network to nurture multimedia content industries and a national information infrastructure.

IT infrastructure

Phase 1 (1980)

Science and technology were only seriously expected to take off in the 1990s but the institutional foundations were laid in the 1980s. These early initiatives include the establishment of the *National Computer Board (NCB)* (in 1981), generally to promote computerization and IT industry development. More specifically, NCB's initial role was to spearhead the deployment of IT in the public sector through the Civil Service Computerization Programme thus effectively making the government the lead user of computer technology. Other specific functions of the NCB include the coordination and promotion of computer education and training and the nurturing of a software export industry. The latter task, jointly carried out with the Economic Development Board, was aimed at attracting IT vendors the world over to use Singapore as their business (marketing and technical support) and production/development base.

The 1985 recession had crystallized deep concerns over the need to accelerate transformation of the economy. Singapore from that year onwards witnessed a rapid proliferation of initiatives and institution building to promote technological development. Apart from the *National IT Plan* (National IT Working Committee 1985) which was formulated in mid-1985 under the aegis of NCB to promote IT development in Singapore, a plethora of other institutions were also set-up, including the Technology Institute (1988 for applied R&D), the Information Institute of Singapore (1989 with AT&T Bell Labs to provide postgraduate telecommunications software training), and the Japan–Singapore Artificial Intelligence Centre (1990 for AI technologies). Countless *ad hoc* promotional programmes mushroomed at that time including the Small Enterprise Computerization Programme, the Programme for IT training of office workers, and grants for advanced IT manpower training. Public awareness and mobilization was sustained by annual events such as the National IT Award, National IT Week, and Software competition.

Phase 2 (1990 to year 2000)

The realization that Singapore's competitive position was in grave danger of being eroded by the emergence of regional successes in the 1990s provided added urgency to questions of technological upgrading. This momentum was given a huge push by the 1992 *IT 2000 Report; A Vision of an Intelligent Island* (National Computer Board 1992) which had been in the making under the NCB since January 1991.

IT 2000

Whereas the National IT plan focused on computation, the IT 2000 was more ambitious, extending its goals to include the development of a more advanced all-embracing information network, the nurturing of multimedia content industries and a national information infrastructure. 'The essence of IT 2000 is the synergistic development of a well integrated and extensive national information infrastructure based on advanced information technology' (National Computer Board 1992: 39). This will allow for the storing and

381

sharing of information on a *national* basis. Thus the IT 2000 plan could be perceived as proposing a '3C' dimension of IT: Compute, Conduit and Content (National Computer Board 1992: 39).[2] Efforts at building a national information infrastructure (NII) are centred on conceptualizing and designing an NII backbone and a multimedia broadband network. Projects involving new media technologies such as cable networks and wireless networks are also being explored.

The NII will not be built from a vacuum. The National IT Plan launched in 1986 has created the strategic framework and positive environment for both private and public sectors to collaborate in exploiting IT for enhancing productivity. A first rate telecommunication infrastructure, continuously upgraded, already exists. When the IT 2000 Plan was mooted in 1992, additional services like the Teleview videotex system, narrow-band integrated services, digital networks and cellular phones already existed.

A plethora of electronic data interchange networks was also on offer to the business community. These include Trade Net, Medinet, Lawnet and other sectoral networks. By 1990, the IT industry (excluding hardware manufacturing and telecommunication services) had grown to $2.15 billion. IT R&D capacity was expanded within the public sector by establishing new institutes such as the Information Technology Institute and Institute of System Science, and upgrading facilities at the universities, Singapore Telecom and the Ministry of Defence. Emphasis was also given to IT manpower development and the training of IT specialists. Communication software engineers are educated by the Information Communication Institute of Singapore, knowledge engineers by the Institute of System Sciences and the Japan-Singapore Artificial Intelligence Centre, and computer integrated manufacturing (CIM) engineers by GINTIC Institute of CIM.

The first phase implementing the high-speed network infrastructure involves linking up network providers, data hubs and government networks by the end of 1996. The completion of this phase would facilitate the provision of common services such as e-mail, universal directory and information exchange to the public. In the meantime, the infrastructure for electronic identification (public key) will be implemented to ensure security for transactions in electronic commerce (National Computer Board 1995–6: 27).

Singapore One, total electronic link up

Singapore One constitutes the key component of IT 2000. It is spearheaded by the Multimedia Broadband Network Project and TAS. The NCB is responsible for development of applications on the network. The National Science and Technology Board (NSTB) and its research institutes (such as Institute of

Systems Science and Information Technology Institute), together with the Telecommunication Authority of Singapore, will provide technical leadership in the network architecture and the development of advanced multimedia applications. The project is also supported by the EDB and Singapore Broadcasting Authority. It was launched in 1996 with the aim of transforming Singapore into an intelligent island. This multimedia broadband will possess three elements:

- Digitization to enable the information infrastructures to carry and route a mix of voice, data, graphics and video.
- Abundant network capacity by means of data compression technologies, high capacity fibre-based networks and digitized transmission.
- Personalized services that can be accessed through PCs, personal mobile communications and personalized interactive services such as electronic commerce and video on demand.

The technology deployed will allow the network to be tailored to suit individual bandwidth or speed requirements.

A hybrid fibre-coaxial network, *Singapore One* will provide the telecommunication infrastructure that will enable the whole population to be wired up via a broadband network which will deliver a whole suite of broadband multimedia services. The government will invest $82 million into the system which will allow users to send e-mail, carry out video-conferencing, surf the Internet faster, shop safely online, study, watch movies and even pay their bills. Companies will be able to serve their customers directly in their homes and offices. As of April 1997, seventeen companies have pledged a total of $115 million into the project to develop services and technology for purposes ranging from entertainment to travel and banking (*New Straits Times*, 25 April 1997). Participating companies include Microsoft Corp., IBM, NEC Corp., HP Co., Reuters Holdings PLC, Sun Microsystems Inc. and Yahoo! Inc.

The purpose was to project *Singapore One* as the launching pad for new multimedia contents, hardware and software platforms, and applications and services in the Asia Pacific. It will not only serve as a pilot project site but also as a platform to develop new innovations. This multimedia computer network is to have about one hundred applications, from training and instruction to information services and entertainment.

By February 1997, 40 per cent of all residences in Singapore had been wired (according to K. Toh, Manager, Marketing Communications, Singapore Cable Vision, 19 February 1997). 24,000 homes are provided with cable connections a month as part of a nation wide project costing $50 million. The target completion date is 1998. Satellite links are available in Singapore to all major regional and international satellites such as

Palapa B2P, Apstar 1, Pan Am Sat 4, 2 and the Pas-four whose footprint covers 120 countries. In August 1998, Singapore launched its US$240 million satellite jointly owned with Taiwan.

Telecommunications and the media

Singapore's recent ascent to affluence can surely be attributed to its strategic geographical position combined with excellent infrastructures. This not only allows speedy movement at entry and exit points but also provides an efficient telecommunications system. This was a fact despite the monopoly of Singapore Telecoms (S Tel).

New features are continuously being added to help upgrade existing IT infrastructures. For instance, two high-speed Internet links were recently installed at a cost of $80 million to be spent over three years. The first T3 link was recently installed (2 May 1997) to speed up Internet connections (quadrupling the current speed) and to allow for smoother access to world-wide sites. Each T3 is a forty-five megabits per second (mbps) network connection to the global Internet backbone in the US and can transmit data at 5.6 million characters per second, equivalent to 2,240 A4-sized pages of text. This can be compared to the current 4 million characters per second or 1,600 pages of text. The current connection from Singapore to the US is thirty-one mbps. With the two new links completed, this would increase four-fold to 121 mbps. Singapore is the first country in Asia outside Japan to have such a facility.

Excellent communication infrastructure, however, does not ensure unconstrained free flow of information. The state maintains a tight grip over both the print and media electronic industry. Practically all local dailies are published by the Singapore Press Holdings (SPH) which is closely linked to the state via rules regarding the ownership of paper publishers. The Singapore Broadcasting Corporation (SBC) has a monopoly over terrestrial broadcasting (three TV and radio stations). No public cable TV or satellite broadcast receiving dishes are permitted. Where political dissent and suppression of human rights are seen as synonymous with stability, it is not surprising that IT development is channelled primarily into enhancing training and business goals. Despite these narrow and focused goals for IT development, much care is also taken to prevent the 'liberating' potential of IT to take hold.

Publishing

Booming economies of the Asian region have triggered demand for the commodification of knowledge and information. In business terms this has translated into a vibrant publishing sector expanding at an annual rate of 12 per cent in Singapore. Currently, 100 local and foreign companies (including multinationals like Springer Verlag, Time Life Asia, Hofer, the Viacom group of which Simon Schuster is a member, and specialist publishers such as Reed Elsevier, Pearson, and Imperial College Press) have made their home in Singapore, either for original publishing (in both print and electronic formats) and distribution or as regional headquarters for their newly launched Asian publishing programme (as in the case of Springer Verlag).

Furthermore, led by the increasing emphasis on education, training and higher education in the region, the printing industry is set to experience an unprecedented expansion over the next decade. The publishing and printing industry in Singapore alone is worth $2.5 billion. The Managing Director of International Thompson Publishing Asia (ITP), whose company is involved in the publishing of professional and high technology books and expanding its CD-ROM capability, when interviewed in 1995 said:

> We foresee a rising demand of Asian language books in the region and this is the market niche we are aiming at. Singapore is the ideal location for coordinating all these activities (publishing centre and regional headquarters) and for our business expansion, with its good supporting infrastructure, talented people and high quality colour separation and printing services.
>
> (*Singapore Investment News* 1995: 7)

Mass media and broadcasting hub

Fast becoming the regional satellite broadcasting hub, Singapore is now the regional headquarters of Home Box Office, the largest and oldest pay-TV company in the US. The company is also the cable programming and marketing subsidiary of Time Warner Inc. and the first English movie subscription service in Asia. The move, according to Chairman and CEO M. Fuchs, is designed to grab a slice of the subscription television industry in Asia which is at its nascent stage of development. 'We want to gain entry into the key Asian markets and Singapore will be central to our regional expansion plans' (*Singapore Investment News*, April 1993: 5) which includes establishing a pan-Asia distribution network and the sourcing of locally and regionally produced and orientated programmes, developing additional programmes (especially those in the Chinese language), and introducing subtitling in other Asian languages. The company's service is uplinked from Singapore to the Palapa satellite (whose footprint service area extends to some sixteen Asian countries with a potential reach of 420 million people). Asia Business News. Asia's first business news satellite television channel, is also located here and broadcasts from the Palapa satellite to key South-East Asian countries. It is jointly owned by Singapore-based SIM Ventures Pte Ltd (10 per cent), Dow Jones and Co Inc. (29.5 per cent), Television New Zealand Ltd (29.5 per cent), and Telecommunications Inc. (29.5 per cent)).

Singapore has increasingly been drawing broadcast and media multinationals. ESPN, MTV, Walt Disney Television, Discovery Channel, Sony Entertainment TV, JET TV, Channel KTV and Golden Eagle Communications are amongst the companies which have set up bases here. There are several reasons for this.

First, excellent uplink and downlink satellite communications, global optic-fibre connectivity and international air transport linkages enable programmers to receive incoming programming feeds and material, and to distribute them to the region through their channels with a high level of confidence.

Nikkei Group President and CEO A. Arai, when launching the printing of the Asian edition of its flagship newspaper, *Nihon Keizai Shimbun*, said that Singapore was chosen as the focus of the company's regional expansion because of its developed information services. Managing Director P. Job of Reuters Asia, which has been operating in Singapore since 1868, noted on Reuter's move to relocate their South-East Asian headquarters from Hong Kong: 'we recognize it as a leader in information technology, as a major Asian financial centre, and as the hub for a dynamic and expanding region' *(Singapore Investment News*, December 1990: 5). Reuters was granted OHQ status by the EDB in 1988. It recently moved into its $40 million new quarters at the Science Park which house Asia-wide research and development units, training facilities and administrative staff. M.D. Weetman said, 'Singapore has a growing hub of international fibre circuits essential for the Reuters global networks' *(Singapore Investment News*, December 1995: 6).

Finally, Singapore's multi-ethnic and multicultural population offers companies servicing the region a workforce fluent in a variety of regional languages (such as Mandarin, Malay and Tamil) and English. Moreover, the stress on continuous education has bred workers who are always ready psychologically for upgrading and continuous learning.

Singapore's infant multimedia industry

Information for this section was gathered from personnel of eight multimedia firms involved in multimedia applications for entertainment (games and movies), operational multimedia (databases with multimedia interface), corporate presentations, interactive learning, advertising (virtual shopping) and IT based products and services (client-server solutions, Internet/Intranet solutions, data communication). All of the eight firms studied were less than three years old.

Multimedia is a single neat slogan referring to a more elusive bundle of elements which would rightly belong elsewhere. As it stands, the industry encompasses such a variety of production sectors that it defies definition. The recentness of the industry as it continues to emerge from the computing, media and telecommunications sectors may well account for why the industry has such as nebulous appearance. In Singapore particularly, where the industry is still at the very initial phase of its evolution, it actually straddles the hardware, software and content industries even though the content sector is the most active and generates most business opportunities, along with other supporting companies associated with the production of multimedia products and services.

The manpower situation in multimedia also reflects the diversity of origins that characterizes firms operating in this sector. In Singapore, the industry is characterized by a rather young workforce, with substantial numbers from backgrounds in engineering, information systems and the graphic arts. After all, multimedia is a computing technology capable of processing and delivering a range of existing media such as text, graphics, sound and video as a single experience. Most of the professionals interviewed admitted their training in multimedia was at the practical level and on the job, meaning that they were good enough to pick up these skills as they move from project to project.

The School of Design offered a whole module in multimedia in 1996 whereas previously, multimedia was offered only as a sub-module. Under these circumstances, it can be concluded that state preparation for generating engineering and information system skills has enabled operators to pick up multimedia skills. But since these skills *per se* have yet to be taught widely in academic institutions, there is an urgent need for facilities producing them. This shortage is now only being addressed by the establishment of courses at polytechnics and art schools. However, due to the volatility of the sector (in essence, multimedia has the reputation of becoming anything), even if one were equipped with multimedia skills, one would still require flexibility and innovativeness so as constantly to acquire new tools and improvise new ways of using old applications creatively. As the range of possibilities for manipulation of applications is so wide, it allows and, in fact, encourages behaviour that searches continually for more creative ways of constituting unique products. Moreover, due to the rapid rate of obsolescence of software and hardware in the sector, workers are a self-selected group always eager to experiment and try out new ways of doing things.

For instance, engineer Ng, who is a software analyst, picked up animation design and graphics skills on his first multimedia job. He now owns a multimedia enterprise which specializes in programming interfaces. Another example is graphic designer Yen who only took a sub-module in multimedia at art school. He then went on to perfect these skills while working on more projects. It is commonplace that learning and relearning occurs in every project one is involved in. Much of what is used in everyday practice, according to those interviewed, cannot be taught systematically in schools. Instead, it is picked up and accumulated as one's own collection of integrated skills.

Industry structure

Skill deficiencies and the volatility that is so characteristic of the multimedia sector actually contribute to its inherent structure of thick network relationships that are both formal and informal, contractual and non-contractual. Networks of production groups within firms (including freelances) contribute to a particular project as firms come together out of necessity to complement and supplement the skills and resources needed to customize a product required by the market.

Multimedia production units actually started as departments of large firms in a related business that was discerning enough to seize the growing opportunity when clients requested a related service. Instead of handling these requests in-house or rejecting the client outright, such firms may pass on these business opportunities to another firm and thus earn a commission. Due to the great assortment of skills needed to customize a particular project, it is especially difficult for small firms to handle a whole project on their own. Consequently, firms get tied into all kinds of partnerships with others. Alliance with others also serves the purpose of allowing smaller firms to compete with larger companies when tendering for larger projects. Besides, smaller firms with friendly ties to large firms can ensure their continued existence because of jobs sub-contracted out to them by overloaded larger firms.

Initiation of multimedia firms is very much dependent on networks of friends and relatives. Initial capital for starting a multimedia firm can range from $20,000 to $200,000 depending on the sophistication of equipment and the location of firm. For all the firms questioned, this initial sum was collected substantially from relatives and friends. One father invested $40,000. For all the rhetoric of the state about nurturing this industry, none of the companies received any subsidy at the outset. The reason given was their small size and lack of track record. Neither were loans sourced from banks whose cumulative interest could quickly cripple a new firm just struggling to get on its feet. One production house estimated that a fully-equipped post-production studio would cost around $6 million, a sum only a mature firm could afford. Firms with such facilities are rare at this stage of development of the industry apart from the studios owned by the state. In fact, sophisticated production and editing of films is currently mostly done overseas.

Business is roaring in the multimedia sector, which is expanding rapidly. The multiplication of firms from around twenty (content providers) in 1995 to more than double that figure in 1998 indicates the robust state of the sector. These opportunities for expansion offer clear examples of the significance of social networks in facilitating economic transactions. The expansion of firms has been funded by sale of stocks to friends and to a lesser extent, to kin. Since many friends (old boys/girls) share similar technical backgrounds, they also serve as interested and capable advisors, whereas kin normally only contribute in terms of financial resources. By limiting financial sourcing to selected friendly investors, entrepreneurs try to ensure that control remains in their own hands.

The idea of stock options for workers has been widely bandied about, but with little effect, owing to the need for bosses to keep control in their hands. Giving stock options to workers may lead to awkwardness as stockholders have a right to sit on the Board of Directors. Only one firm interviewed offers shares to workers (who are on the whole also friends of the director). What is so remarkable is that the initial group of employees included like-minded friends who shared the same ideals as the entrepreneurs, including class-mates at college. The entrepreneurs thus felt a sense of obligation to them for helping out when the company was in dire need. For instance, the company could not have employed such workers at market rates. Some worker-friends could not be paid for the first few months because the firm could not yet make enough to meet its cost, yet they have continued work-ing faithfully, hoping for better times to come. Hence the pressure felt by owners to share the fruits with their loyal worker-friends. On the part of the workers, offers of stock options have been turned down because they plan to start their own companies or to leave for greener pastures.

All entrepreneurs interviewed agreed that state activities have indeed stimulated business in this sector. Foucault's description of the power agent actively organizing to constitute its subjects as consumers (e.g. of hospital services) and as political subjects aptly describes the Singapore state, which is an avid consumer of multimedia applications. In fact, hold-ing an account from a state agency in one's portfolio can be considered one measure of a company's size and significance in the multimedia industry. The numerous public campaigns generated each year to encourage cour-tesy, marriage, speaking mandarin etc. are all backed by multimedia spiels.

The billions of dollars of public money poured into the communications infrastructure through institutions such as *Singapore One* and the IT infra-structure for schools and institutions of higher learning have also been greeted with cheers by the multimedia sector. Such moves not only gener-ate demand within the state sector but also have a multiplier effect, triggering the use of multimedia by individuals and companies across the board. In addition, workers trained in multimedia subsidiaries of govern-ment-linked companies have gone on to form their own companies. Simply by playing the conventional state role of providing the infrastructure (partly subsidizing its initial foundation), the state reaps long-term bene-fits such as higher tax revenue and possibilities for more extensive control over its constituents.

The privatization of some state activities such as broadcasting and telecommunications has also created opportunities for new firms in this sector. In fact, one of the production houses interviewed is owned by a for-mer staff member of the SBC. With long years of working experience garnered from work with the SBC, he was able to start (albeit on a very humble scale) a production house which today has grown enough for him to think of applying for a state subsidy which is normally given to firms

389

with a credible and successful track record. The progress of such firms has been held back by a lack of capital to purchase sophisticated post-production machinery such as the non-linear digital editing equipment.

Social design of technology

This section aims to provide a non-technical social orientation to the understanding of IT strategy in Singapore's restructuring. The analysis will primarily be based on the early ideas of Habermas (1971) that considered how the dynamics of capitalism were interrelated and explored the ideological function of science and technology in reducing political normative questions to simple technical problems which can be solved by specialists. This makes it possible to distinguish between the basic structure of modern technology as such and the specific way in which this basic structure is actualized under capitalist conditions, in other words, how it is directed by economic and political pressures and subjected to the imperatives of the capitalist accumulation process.

In the next section we review how existing institutions are largely responsible for shaping the process of IT infrastructure development in Singapore and thus its impact on society.

Institutional shaping of IT

More specifically, borrowing the idea of 'institutional tissues' from Hudson (1994: 197), one can clearly relate the implementation of IT in Singapore to the authoritarian structure of Singapore politics. IT in Singapore is chiefly state-led (hierarchy) rather than market oriented, despite the current liberalization of telecommunications by the WTO (*Economist* 1997a). Superficially, it would appear that the Singapore government, like governments of other countries, will try to separate the regulatory and operational functions of state monopoly telecommunication providers. In theory, it will oversee regulation as a government function but privatize operations, and bring in other providers to compete with the former monopolies. In fact, however, the market dominated by state monopolies has been transformed to one resembling more that of an oligopoly.

Singapore Telecoms (S Tel), the national PTT, was privatized in 1993. Although several new companies were allowed to operate, they include some of the largest GLCs (government-linked companies with significant state-owned shares) such as the Singapore Technology Group, Sembawang Group, Keppel Group and Singapore Press Holdings. In effect, this has raised the question whether with this mode of privatization, the monopoly previously held by S Tel is being replaced by an oligopoly involving a few telecommunications and media giants that control production and distribution of content and conduit.

A good example is the provision of Internet services. The state decided to allocate licences to three large domestic firms (GLCs): S Tel, Sembawang Corporation (by the transfer of a government-developed scientific network) and Singapore Press Holdings. AT&T, the foreign competitor, lost the bid even though its bid was the lowest. The inefficiency of this oligopoly was recently highlighted by letters to the press (*New Straits Times*, 3 March 1998).

Another suggestive indication of the influence of the authoritarian political structures can be found by looking at the choice of products offered to Singapore consumers. Direct satellite broadcast reception dishes continue to be banned for general households although business corporations are allowed access for data communications. In addition, even though cable TV was reluctantly introduced, its availability was only reluctantly accelerated to pre-empt demand for satellite broadcasting as neighbouring countries such as Indonesia and Malaysia announced the provision of these pleasures to their residents. Perhaps the state believed it could exercise greater control over the content of cable TV rather than satellite broadcasting.

The area of implementation is also affected by political considerations. The Internet and the World Wide Web have unexpectedly opened up immense possibilities for user-to-user distribution instead of the conventional distribution mode from provider to user. In reality, however, the model of NII (National Information Infrastructure) is that of interactive TV and commercial online services, such as Pacific Net (a privatized Internet service provided by a consortium of GLC subsidiaries including Sembawang Corp., Sembawang Media, Singapore Technologies, ST Computer Systems and SIM) and Singnet provided by S Tel. These are based on the gateway-model, with control over content and distribution resting with the service providers who bundle content and distribute it through their own conduit. Despite wishful thinking by optimists like Toffler that the new technology of IT could heighten the trend towards democratization, the model of NII that most countries have adopted is that of the gateway, where providers could in theory put an end to lovely fantasies promised by liberalization of pleasures.

Under the guise of restructuring, GLCs have quickly seized the opportunities offered for feverish expansion. More GLCs have also been spawned to cope with the implementation of IT 2000. For instance, the national broadcasting corporation, Singapore Broadcasting Corporation, was privatized in October 1994. In its place, a holding company Singapore International Media (SIM) was born with four subsidiaries:

- *Television Corporation of Singapore (TCS)* allotted two public broadcast channels.
- *TV Twelve* also allotted two channels.
- *Radio Corporation (RCS)* responsible for existing radio stations of SBC.
- *SIM Communications* tasked for Cable TV and Multimedia.

Singapore Cable Vision (SCV), a joint venture between SBC and SIM, offers three subscription TV channels via free-to-air broadcasting. In July 1994, a new consortium with $500 million to invest, (comprising SIM, two GLCs – Singapore Technologies and Singapore Press Holdings – and US-based Continental Cablevision Inc.) was established to provide cable TV access to all Singapore homes in 1998. SCV then contracted to connect its to-the-home coaxial cables with S Tel's optical fibre networks to the curb. SCV also holds the future option to apply for a licence to provide interactive multimedia services to the home via PC or TV.

The common-carrier peer-to-peer model as illustrated by the Internet in the USA and Minitel in France was rejected as unsuitable. Yet, after an initial fright when users began extending the boundaries of the permissible, both subjects and authorities found that total control of the Internet was never plausible.

Finally, the speed of implementation of the NII could be attributed to the penetrative presence of the state in the economy and society. More than 80 per cent of the population live in state-organized housing under the governance of the state-regulated Housing Development Board (HDB). This huge reservoir of households was therefore easily made available for fibre-optic wiring to access the cable. 20,000 HDB homes could be wired per month. The first point put in was also subsidized by the HDB. On the other hand, private houses could only be wired at a rate of 4,000 per month.

Future trends

The innovative nature of multimedia jobs and the quirky requirements of clients catering to ever changing post-modernist tastebuds of consumers tend to translate into a premium on improvisation skills and creativity. The question frequently asked is whether the politics of Singapore will now give way to the economic imperative to restructure with multimedia?

Democracy and inclusiveness

As part of its goal of shifting Singapore to a more cultivated and mature society, state-initiated political discourse has recently even included the radical idea of public participation:

> We must change the mind set that only a few leaders at the top of the system need to think and take responsibility for social and national issues, while the rest of society can simply mind their own business and go about their daily lives.
>
> (Prime Minister C.T. Goh, quoted in
> New Straits Times, 20 July 1997)

There could be some degree of decentralization as a result of IT implementation. For instance, 18,053 out of 22,000 teachers now have Internet accounts. Teachers can now access the Teacher-On-Online facility to bring their queries or comments directly to the Ministry of Education, instead of having to go through their respective principals. This can be said to be an advance, because a study has identified bosses as the second most stressful element in their working lives after heavy work loads (Ko 1997). Principals now no longer have the monopoly over information emanating from or flowing to policy makers. In this way, both teachers and principals can be made more accountable for their actions. More important, however, is how feedback is used to improve the system. The rapid rise in the salaries of teachers shows that dissatisfaction and the problem of a high turnover have yet to be addressed. Instead of allowing more room for decision making, monetary incentives continue to be used to quell dissension, a line of action much in tune with general developmental trends in Singapore society.

On the other hand, the fact that IT is being implemented not to enhance the intrinsic social nature of the human species but for commercial reasons has triggered a clash between the intrinsic inclusive quality of IT and the exclusive nature of commercial markets. There is no doubt that the cost of information and its technologies have been in constant decline. Yet, artificial barriers have been erected and reinforced by the state to exclude from the market those possessing few resources. The role of the state enforcing legal mechanisms for the private appropriation of value – copyright and patents – points to tensions between private property and democratic communication.

Film piracy in the Asia Pacific region costs the industry more than US$530 million annually (a quarter of world-wide losses), according to the Motion Picture Association (MPA) and Singapore has the worst incidence of film piracy in this region. Street operators in Singapore are selling pirated VCDs, usually for $15 a piece. MPA Vice-President and director of anti-piracy operations in the region, L. Strong, had alleged that since VCDs and DVDs are small and easy to conceal and there are enormous profits to be made, it is virtually impossible to stamp out the trade totally. While appearing to enforce the law (operators caught can be charged in Court), enforcement is not always stringent as the losses incurred do not fall on the state. Moreover, the low median wage of the workforce ($1,625 June 1996) would totally exclude them from the multimedia market if these copyright rules were strictly imposed. So, as Strong concedes, the piracy problem in Singapore is manageable. Such an equilibrium satisfies both political constituents and foreign investors.

Production of consumption

WTO agreements threatened to prise open the markets which had been in the grip of state monopolies, thus leading to privatization of these high-tech monopolies. One obvious effect has been the multiplication of media alliances (with foreign providers) that enhance even further the capacity of domestic elites to intensify hedonistic consumption. The multimedia corridor thus formed constitutes a rich matrix for consumers to live out their lifestyle dreams, while design and marketing agents manoeuvre to construct and project goods into ethereal images and ministers move to maximize their own ambitions.

In reality the low level of median income prevents consumers from playing out their indulgences. Teenagers who want more may work long hours at fast food restaurants to accumulate their store of Versace jeans or turn to crime to access designer goods. For adults, the state had to act to regulate an over-rapid expansion of credit card use and rising debts. In expanding the virtual market, the state had thus to contend with issues of higher wage demands and growing numbers of bankruptcy cases. This is not to say that IT has not also been deployed to legitimize the existing system.

Production of consent

Singapore's problem with the potential subversive influence of IT is not peculiar to this island nation. It is experienced by other authoritarian governments in the region whose path to capitalist industrialization has not been accompanied by rationalization of other areas of life. Yet, as emerging Asian economies struggle to restructure their failing economies, they all need to develop IT, both as a tool and a product to survive the global onslaught brought on by WTO agreements. In launching JET TV (the first Japanese broadcaster based in Singapore), Yeo, the Minister of Information and the Arts, gave the assurance: 'We must always remain pro-business. Whatever censorship is necessary must be carried out sensitively and selectively, and with a light touch' (*Straits Times,* 23 October 1997: 3).

He took the growing number of media companies to indicate that Singapore has achieved a good balance between laissez-faire and regulation. In reality, the government's 'light touch' saw the ban of the July 1997 issue of *Vogue* (UK) because it contained an article condoning and promoting drug use. The month before, the publication permit of *IS*, a fortnightly entertainment magazine, was not renewed because it exploited sex to raise its circulation and encouraged undesirable lifestyles. However the permit was renewed on appeal in July because *IS* agreed to drop their columns of personal advertisements. Around July 1997 too, *Asiaweek* (Hong Kong) was allowed to raise its circulation from 15,000 to 18,000 copies (The publication previously had a restricted circulation, only 500 copies in October 1987, because it was deemed to have interfered with domestic politics). At the same time, the *Far Eastern Economic Review* (Hong Kong), another restricted publication, had its circulation increased from 6,000 to 8,000 copies as of 1 July, 1997.

Apart from such clumsy and costly attempts at keeping its subjects docile, Singapore is also making efforts at the global level to expand its capacity for government action. Singapore International Television (SITV) was launched through Indonesia's Palapa B2P satellite to viewers from Surabaya (Indonesia) to Shanghai, Port Moresby to the Maldives. The aim is to provide a window an Singapore for non-Singaporean viewers. To Singaporeans abroad, SITV aims to help 'maintain links with their country' (*Singapore Investment News*, April 1994: 8).

Though multimedia firms could live with censorship of pornographic and political content, this is an inhibiting factor that could cramp both style and flair. On the other hand, the current development of hardware and the emphasis on engineering skills and education and training have served to channel multimedia production from entertainment products towards more technical and neutral contents such as interactive learning and engineering software where higher profits maybe made.

Notes

1 A multimedia broadband network, ONE stands for Singapore One Network for Everyone which will link up the nation so that every person can electronically retrieve information and communicate with each other quickly, easily, safely and inexpensively across time and space.
2 Conduit refers to the physical pipelines that carry information (voice and date lines, broadcast and cellular transmission). Content refers to information (eg. multimedia course, entertainment programme, government database records and payment instruction) that flow through the conduit. Compute refers to the processing of content in the NII (e.g. user authentication, billing and processing of permit documents.

References

Annals of Regional Science (1996) Special Issue 'Information and Communications Networks in Space', *Annals of Regional Science* 30: 1.
Asian Business (1997a) 'Season of Uncertainty', *Asian Business* 33: 44–50.
—— (1997b) 'Thailand's test of faith', *Asian Business* 33: 38–43.
—— (1997c) 'Overheating in Korea', *Asian Business* 33: 32–7.
Department of Statistics (1996) *Statistical Highlights,* Singapore: Department of Statistics.
Economic Development Board (vars. dates) *Singapore Investment News*, various issues, Singapore: Economic Development Board.
Economic Development Board (1995/96) *Yearbook 1995/96*, Singapore: Economic Development Board.
Economist (1997a) 'Not quite magic', *Economist,* 22 February 1997.
—— (1997b) 'Asia's precarious miracle', *Economist,* 1 March 1997.

Foucault, M. (1981) 'Omnes et singulation: towards a criticism of "political reason"', in *The Tanner Lectures on Human Values II*, Salt Lake City: University of Utah Press.

Gillespie, A., Goddard, J., Hepworth, M. and Williams, H. (1989) 'Information and communications technology and regional development: an information economy perspective', *STI Review* 5, 85–111.

Habermas, J. (1971) 'Technology and science as ideology', in J. Habermas, *Toward a Rational Society*, London: Heinemann.

—— (1989) *On Society and Politics*, Boston: Beacon.

Hirst, P. and Zeitlin, J. (1989) *Reversing Manufacturing Decline*, Oxford: Berger.

Hudson, R. A. (1994) 'Institutional change, cultural transformation and economic regeneration', in A. Amin and N. Thrift (eds) *Globalization, Institutions and Regional Development in Europe*, Oxford: Oxford University Press.

Knight, R. (1995) 'Knowledge–based development', *Urban Studies* 32, 2: 225–60.

Ko, Y. C. (1997) 'Stress of teachers in Singapore', unpublished paper.

Ministry of Trade and Industry (1991) *The Strategic Economic Plan 1991*, Singapore: The Ministry of Trade and Industry.

National Computer Board (NCB) (1990) *Report on Usage of IT in Singapore*, Singapore: National Computer Board.

—— (1992) *The IT 2000 Report: A Vision of an Intelligent Singapore Island*, Singapore: National Computer Board.

—— (1995–6) *Year Book 1995–96*, Singapore: National Computer Board.

National IT Working Committee (1985) *National IT Plan 1985*, Singapore: The National IT Working Committee.

National Science and Technology Board (1991) *National Technology Plan*, Singapore: National Computer Board.

Paolucci, G. (1996) 'The changing dynamics of working time', *Time and Society* 5, 2: 145–67.

Piore, M. and Sabel, C. (1984) *The Second Industrial Divide*, New York: Basic Books.

Pollack, A. (1997) 'Korean strike: it's the economy', *International Herald Tribune*, January 18–19: 1.

Porter, M. (1990) *The Competitive Advantage of Nations*, London: Macmillan.

Saunders, J., Warford, R. and Wellenius, B. (1983) *Telecommunications and Economic Development*, Baltimore, Md.: Johns Hopkins University Press.

Tan, M. B. (1996) 'Singapore ONE: building a nation-wide multimedia broadband infrastructure', *Speech* 20, 3: 77–82.

18

CONCLUSION

Diversity and uniformity in the development of multimedia production

*Hans-Joachim Braczyk, Gerhard Fuchs
and Hans-Georg Wolf*

As set out in the introductory chapter, globalization implies a growing uniformity between regions as well as a new emphasis on and exploitation of regional diversity. This volume has explored this complex interrelation with respect to one specific segment of the emerging global information society: multimedia production. In this chapter, we will summarize what the contributions to this volume (and some additional research) add to an understanding of the relationship between diversity and uniformity.

The geography of multimedia production

Multimedia production clusters do exist: a concentration of production in certain regions is manifest. In this respect, the standard expectations why industry would localize in the same region still seem valid. The Marshallian tradition (see Krugman 1991) claims that industry concentrates:

- Because concentration in the same region provides a pooled market for workers with specialized skills.
- Because an industrial district allows for the provision of a greater variety of inputs by specialized suppliers.
- Inter-firm information flows are enhanced by physical proximity. By concentrating within an industrial district, firms can more easily take advantage of technological spill-overs.

The contributions to this volume have clearly shown that, typically, multimedia clusters develop in metropolitan regions with service-oriented economies.[1] For example, 36 per cent of Canadian multimedia corporations are to be found in Toronto, while 47 per cent of all Swedish firms are concentrated in Stockholm. In peripheral and/or less favoured regions, there is usually only a low density of multimedia production. The typical locational pattern *within* regions can be observed as concentrations within urban centres or even specific streets, housing complexes or buildings (facilitated by a low need for office space and the locational preferences of the creative key personnel). A good example for this phenomenon is the concentration of New York firms: 1,106 out of 4,881 firms are concentrated in one small area of Manhattan ('Silicon Alley') (see Map 5.1 in Pavlik's chapter). This bespeaks the persistence of agglomeration effects (the concentration of multimedia production attracts even more firms and staff). It seems very likely then regional disparities will persist or even increase in importance.

The authors share the view that there is no 'death of distance' with regard to multimedia production (see Cairncross 1997, Beck 1998). Multimedia firms value spatial proximity to other multimedia firms, customers and project partners; computer-mediated communication is no substitute for face-to-face communication. The emerging forms of industrial organization in this sector are far from being completely 'virtual'. At least, this holds true as far as the core activities of the numerous small and medium-sized multimedia producers are concerned. So far, virtual organization in this field remains limited. The following reasons for both limited virtual organization of production and local concentration within the core of metropolitan areas can be generalized from the contributions to this volume.

First, the chapter by Egan and Saxenian conveys the crucial role of standardized mass hardware and software products in the information industry as a whole. This leads to the consideration that, on an aggregate sector level, the industrial organization of multimedia production comprises two very different elements, though they are interdependent and connected with one another.

On the one hand, there are a few – mostly – large and globally-operating-corporations. They produce standardized elements and components (integrated circuits, central processing units, network technologies, browsers, authoring software and equipment for developers, programming languages) on a very large scale. One can argue that these general products function as enabling technologies for multimedia producers. To this extent, these large corporations are forming the first sub-sector.

On the other hand, there are numerous – mostly small and very small – enterprises specializing in different segments of multimedia production. They creatively use these enabling technologies in order to satisfy their customers' needs for customized electronic products and services. As the firms of this sub-sector drive and widen the business of specialized and tailored products for individual corporate applications, they indirectly contribute to a steady and even growing demand for standardized mass products.

Therefore the actual role of virtual organization in multimedia production is much more limited than one might expect. Given the assumption that standard components of a complex workflow are best suited for electronic communication with distant actors and collaborators, this is a potential for virtualization which multimedia producers can only use to a limited extent. They buy most standard 'ingredients' for processing as well as for products from the mass market dominated by large and very large corporations. The situation in the multimedia industry is the reverse of what we know about industrial organization in the automotive industry. The big mass producers play the part of the suppliers, and the flexible specialists of small multimedia firms play the part of final producers.

From the point of view of the second sub-sector, the virtue of virtual organization in terms of electronically-mediated cooperation among distant actors is largely outweighed by the fact that the firms involved are predominantly buying standard products as tools etc. for their own production processes. Given this sector organization, there are only a few segments of the overall multimedia production where virtual organization is a relevant factor. This may partly explain why multimedia producers have until now been markedly reluctant to deploy forms of virtual organization extensively. The other factor that helps explain this – at first sight – counter-intuitive phenomenon relates to the properties of the multimedia core production, the related market, and to characteristics of local multimedia labour markets as well.

The industry in general – irrespective of remarkable regional differences in maturity – is still in its pre-mature phase. The actors involved may experiment with different forms of organization, including electronic tele-cooperation, but so far they apparently prefer face-to-face communication where their core production is concerned. Within the framework of a conventional but very flexible in-house organization, the firms practice cross-organizational collaboration with changing partners who, again, prefer to maintain and to rely heavily on direct communication. There is some evidence that the multimedia core production is functionally dependent on in-depth discussions among those people who participate in developing and producing multimedia products. The need for close discoursive relations with customers from the beginning of a project until the product is implemented in the customer's environs adds to this preference.

As we have seen, multimedia producers are exposed to a tight labour market. They need experts and specialists, who prefer to live and work in the centres of metropolitan cities. To this extent, the present shape of the multimedia labour market serves as a force which attracts firms and new entrepreneurs to such locales. Eventually, the core production of multimedia not only aims at tailoring products according to individual customers' needs but also processes content which is predominantly culturally coined. Thus, production in this second sub-sector is embedded in and part of a given local understanding, signification and interpretation of 'the world' which obviously favours face-to-face communication.

One can even assume a specific property of the multimedia industry as a whole, as a result of which the industry will not operate without a minimum of local diversity. We state that parts of the multimedia core production in the second sub-sector will inevitably value and exploit regionally-bound cultural assets.

These arguments confirm a more general impression from innovation research which suggests that knowledge-intensive businesses are not as footloose as it is often thought. An important argument relates to so-called 'tacit' knowledge. It has been suggested that in addition to formalized, well-documented and tradeable knowledge, 'tacit' knowledge plays an important role in innovative activities. Such knowledge is based on practical experience with certain technologies. It has also been characterized as 'implicit', 'idiosyncratic' or 'uncodified' knowledge. It is not available in textbooks or training courses, but it may be transferred from person to person (see Polanyi 1962, Dosi 1988, Storper 1996). These properties of 'tacitness' have a number of implications for firm behaviour: most importantly, firms that depend on tacit knowledge require personal contact and physical proximity.

While its *direct* contribution to job creation (see page 405) and economic welfare is limited, the 'strategic' importance of multimedia production for the regional economy as a whole is much greater. Multimedia producers have the potential to improve the performance and competitiveness of various sectors (manufacturing, services and trade) by providing them with customer-tailored multimedia solutions. The multimedia sector can thus have a catalyzing function, allowing the more established industries to expand or intensify their activities and to organize and coordinate their business processes more effectively. We conclude from the research presented here that this supporting function of a multimedia production sector depends to a certain extent on direct interactions which are enabled by spatial proximity between multimedia specialists and their potential customers from the more established industries.

Thus, regions are right to attach a high strategic value to the development of a multimedia cluster in order to promote the emergence of a relatively new but small business sector and to contribute to their main industries' competitiveness. Further, regional actors should be interested in maintaining and developing their multimedia production clusters to promote agile and innovative local problem solutions for the established main industries in the region. This would help to limit the ongoing attempts of the large corporations to expand their business of standardized mass products. The more these corporations are able to customize their standard products as closely as possible to the different needs of customers, the less chance a local multimedia production industry has to grow, or even survive.

Sources and limits of diversity in multimedia production

The contributions to this volume make it clear that the regions under investigation differ in respect of the maturity of multimedia production. There is a small number of pioneers and top manufacturers (notably in the US, see Chapters Two to Five of this volume), a growing number of routine producers (see Chapters Six to Eleven) and there are attempts in virtually all other regions to catch-up (see later chapters).

Across all three types of regions a different breadth and specialization of multimedia can be detected. Most multimedia clusters specialize in specific types of products (CD-ROM production for cultural institutions, for instance, or services for the advertising industry) and derive from a very specific background (for example the emphasis on the traditional telecommunications or hardware sectors as in the cases of Scotland, Ireland or Finland).

How can this diversity be explained? And what countervailing factors, leading to more uniformity, are most prevalent?

Sources of diversity

Multimedia production builds on diverse sectoral, cultural and social backgrounds ('precursor' industries, industries buying multimedia products and services, etc.). The different strengths in these various sectors and societal segments have consequences for the quantity and quality of multimedia production in the respective regions (even among the leading locations in the USA). Important sectoral backgrounds for the multimedia industry include the publishing sector (e.g. New York), the film industry (e.g. Hollywood), the telecommunications industry (e.g. Tampere), the broadcasting sector (e.g. Wales and Cologne) but also, as in Singapore, the state as a buyer of advanced multimedia products and services. This sectoral background plays a decisive role in the shaping and specialization of regional multimedia production. Correspondingly, Egan and Saxenian (see Chapter Two, Table 2.1) have noted that most of the leading multimedia regions in the USA have concentrated on one or two segments of multimedia production (only the San Francisco Bay Area boasts a leading position in the whole range of multimedia production).

Regional institutions for education and training (universities etc.) are another important background of multimedia production. It is claimed, for example, that half of Silicon Valley's revenues come from University of Stanford spin-off companies. This experience, however, may not be generalizable. In most of the cases examined in this book, the connection between universities and multimedia firms is not very well established. One reason for this may be that multimedia qualifications in the narrow sense were hardly taught at the important educational institutions at the time the analyses were made.

Obviously there are other factors that play an important role, including a region's profile of 'soft' factors, such as regional 'image', cultural atmosphere and, more generally, its ability to attract creative personnel from outside the region. The attraction of San Francisco and a place like Brighton seems to be based on cultural qualities. San Francisco lures artistically-oriented people into the city and the Brighton area seems to benefit from its specific intellectual climate.

The supply of personnel is generally considered a crucial variable. Lack of personnel is identified as an important obstacle for potential future growth across the different regions. In almost all of them, a mismatch between the skills available on the labour market and the skills needed most urgently by the multimedia producers is an acute or potential problem.

This makes it all the more important to be able to lure people to the important multimedia locations, a factor of major importance for regions like California (which attracts significant numbers of workers from outside the state), Toronto, New York, Stockholm and Munich. In view of the present tightness of the multimedia labour market, one should take into consideration that even the most attractive places to live and work in will, as it were, compete with one another for the best qualified workers. In that respect, again, the distinct local profile of a place is very important for the further development of regional multimedia clusters.

Another important source of diversity is the availability of venture capital. There are major differences between, and even within, countries. California still seems to be the place where venture capital and funding is easiest to come by. In other locations, Baden-Württemberg for instance, venture capital does not play any significant role. Munich, also in Germany, has the most venture-capital-friendly climate in the country. This undoubtedly affects the orientation and strategies of multimedia corporations.

The role of state agencies in supporting multimedia production differs very much between regions and thus contributes to regional diversity. In general, however, policies have only very recently targeted multimedia production. A final evaluation of such measures was therefore beyond the framework of this volume. Nevertheless the case studies show that the development of a cluster can be supported by a variety of mechanisms and in fact we find a wide range of different attempts to do this. At one end of the scale is the creation of a benevolent macroregulatory environment, as in Toronto. Other mechanisms range from the support activities of some key promoters (e.g. Düsseldorf, see Belzer and Michel 1998) up to large-scale state intervention in favour of the new industry, seen in the South-East Asian 'tigers'' (see Chapter Seventeen) and Ireland (see Fuchs and Wolf, forthcoming).

Theoretically, three different forms of coordination can be distinguished here (Braczyk and Heidenreich 1998, Fuchs and Wolf 1997): 'market-driven and informal coordination', 'network governance' and 'coordination from the centre'. The relative weight of each of these forms of coordination differs

402

significantly between the regions. In principle, each may support the emergence and growth of multimedia production. For instance, coordination from the centre has been the dominant mode in the development of Singapore's multimedia sector. However, we conclude from the research presented in this volume that this hierarchical mode of coordination is not typical of the world's most advanced multimedia clusters. Instead, the strength of the Californian regions and New York in multimedia production seems to build mainly on the 'market-driven and informal' pattern, on a coincidence of very favourable conditions on the supply and demand side of multimedia markets.

This is not to deny that coordination from the centre has played an important part in these cases, too, if considered in a longitudinal perspective. In fact, as Harrison (1994: 117–22; see also Castells 1996: 40–65) demonstrates in the case of Silicon Valley, public policy, and military procurement more specifically, was deeply involved in the earlier growth record of this industrial region. The positive effect on multimedia production of these centrally-coordinated measures, however, only materialized after a long period. Thus, what we find in this two-step-pattern of state support is more an example of successful failure than of intentional coordination aimed at the development of a new industry.

Interestingly, we found that in many of the most advanced multimedia regions, the call for 'network governance' and for some degree of central coordination has been getting louder recently (see the chapters on New York, Munich and Cologne in this volume, and Fuchs and Wolf, forthcoming, on the case of California). Obviously, in these regions many actors feel that greater efforts for strategic networking and more coordinated action are now required to secure the leading position the regions have achieved in multimedia production. Thus, in the most successful multimedia regions, the typical role of public policy might turn out to be that of a stabilizer rather than an incubator, at least in the short term. More generally, most case studies agree that specific measures to promote multimedia have been belated and merely follow the development of relevant activities rather than acting as a proactive element. It should be added that the cases where state intervention has apparently been most successful build on very specific conditions (see the case of Ireland) and, moreover, often imply severe political restrictions (which, as in the case of the Asian 'tigers', are very much in conflict with the democratic ideals of the 'information society').

The research presented in this volume has also demonstrated that the more successful multimedia regions feature a high degree of cooperation between producing companies. This has been observed in California, New York, Toronto, Cardiff, Stockholm and Cologne. In the less developed regions, the lack of cooperation is often named as a significant impediment to further growth (e.g. Stuttgart and Scotland).

If one considers all the different sources of diversity, it becomes apparent that a region's earlier economic history plays a prominent role in determining the specific path of multimedia development. In most cases, multimedia has been built on regional strengths already existing in the respective regions. Conversely, there are examples which show that an existing industrial structure can be an impediment for further multimedia development. In the cases of Stuttgart, Scotland and Tampere it was argued that significant lock-in effects prevent the regions from developing a more visible multimedia sector.

Finally, the examples of Scotland and Stuttgart show that some of the classical factor endowments such as labour costs and infrastructure may be relatively unimportant. Scotland has been attractive for IT-companies because of relatively low labour costs and a good telecommunications infrastructure. In spite of various efforts this has not led to a significant concentration of multimedia companies. Similarly in Stuttgart the technical and institutional infrastructure is in fact very well developed, but Stuttgart is not yet a widely acknowledged multimedia capital.

There is no guarantee that hitherto 'model' or 'success regions' can realize a swift and frictionless development in the new growth and future-oriented sectors. These regions often concentrate their innovative potentials (research, development, engineers, scientists) on the optimization of already well-established economic sectors. This is very well illustrated by the case of Stuttgart.

Limits of diversity: influences towards uniformity

As we have shown, there are marked differences among regions in industrialized countries around the world in terms of the maturity, competitiveness, density and specialization of their multimedia production sectors. Clearly, then, geography still makes a difference. This, however, is only half of the picture. The other half is the remarkable degree of similarity in the development of multimedia production all over the globe. In many respects, multimedia production seems to be organized in much the same way in America, Europe or Asia. So while we find diversity on the one hand, we find uniformity and isomorphism on the other. What are the factors that support trends towards universal structures in multimedia production?

The broad availability of standardized software tools for multimedia production, driven by the market expansion strategies of some multinational key players (see page 398), is the first important factor. As a consequence, there is comparatively little variance in the technological base or the production processes used by multimedia producers in different regions. In general, the capital requirements for launching an enterprise and running a multimedia production are comparatively low (at least when compared to other high-tech sectors such as biotechnology). This makes for low barriers to market entry and a high level of new firms. Of course, low entry barriers do not guarantee good survival prospects. In fact, a comparatively high rate of firm mortality is also typical of the multimedia industry in many regions. Thus, the average size of

Table 18.1: Staff size of multimedia-producing companies

Region	Average number of employees	
Scotland	9.4	
North East of England	10.0	
Stockholm	10.0	*
Stuttgart	10.5	
Dusseldorf	12.0	
Toronto	13.0	**
Tampere	14.7	
New York	21.6	***
San Francisco	44% have fewer than 10 employees	

Source: workshop contribution; chapter of present volume
Notes: * median.
　　　　** excluding one very large firm in the sample.
　　　　*** including freelances.

multimedia firms is small (see table 18.1), their average age is young (see table 18.2), and in both respects there are only minor inter-regional differences.

Given the small average size of the companies in the core sector of multimedia production, the extent of job creation in this core sector is comparatively small. It is not sufficient to solve the labour market problems caused by a general process of economic restructuring and the loss of jobs in manufacturing. This holds true for even the most advanced multimedia clusters.

In virtually all regions, not only the companies but also the firm founders themselves and their employees are very young.[2] This seems to be partly due to the specific image of multimedia (a technology most popular among the young) but also to the specific qualification requirements. Multimedia entrepreneurs and their employees all over the world are highly qualified and skilled. Many firm founders start their businesses immediately after graduation from university and the percentage of academically-trained personnel is remarkably high.

As multimedia is a very fast-changing technology, the employees must be able and willing to constantly adapt and learn. On average, these employees are highly motivated, ready to work many hours during the week and at 'unusual' times during day and night, and to accept flexible forms of work organization as well as occupational patterns. From the place where they work they expect, among other things, a vivid and varied cultural scene. This is part of the explanation for the locational preferences of multimedia firms that we described above. Moreover, the rapidly changing qualification requirements make it difficult for the education and training institutions to keep pace, and stable training schemes are hard to establish in multimedia production.

Table 18.2: Age of multimedia-producing companies

Region	Year of foundation
Toronto	40% founded after 1993
Stuttgart	61% founded after 1993
San Francisco	64% founded after 1993
*Saarland**	most companies founded after 1995
Stockholm	50% founded after 1996

Source: Chapter 2, 6, 11, 14 of this volume.
Note:: * see Matthäi and Schmidt (1998: 16).

Multimedia products (CD-ROMs or WWW presentations) are complex, integrating different media and combining programming know-how with artistic, didactic and design skills. Few multimedia firms, especially given their small average size, can afford to have all these necessary skills in-house. As a consequence, as mentioned above, we found a comparatively high level of inter-firm cooperation and of free-lance employment in the multimedia industry.[3]

Another factor which puts a limit to diversity is the dominance of the English language in the world of Internet and multimedia. This is not to say that non-English languages are unimportant in the development of regional multimedia clusters. The examples of Wales and Finland demonstrate that regional multimedia producers may occupy a niche for products in the respective language and adapted to the respective cultural environment. Within these niches, the multimedia companies may develop and grow. However, the size of their market will remain limited unless they are also able to produce in English. English language skills thus are of paramount importance to the long-term development perspectives of regional multimedia industries. In fact, the examples of Ireland, the Netherlands and the Scandinavian countries show how a high level of English skills favours the development of multimedia production.

It seems very likely that the tendency towards uniformity will be amplified by the spread of IT-applications in electronic commerce and related fields. Electronic commerce is expected to grow very rapidly in the short and medium term. In fact, 'e-commerce' has become the new buzzword which even outshines 'multimedia' (although the subject-matter denoted by both words overlaps to a large extent). Most observers agree that a set of norms, standards and mass products (e.g. standardized software for encryption and electronic payment) are necessary for electronically-based economic transactions. If so, then the growth of electronic commerce will go along with a trend towards more uniformity. This, in turn, may further restrict the scope – and the market – for the individual multimedia solutions that most specialized multimedia companies focus on today. Increasingly, these companies may have to specialize in add-ons to the standardized products offered by key producers.

Thus, to sum up the argument of this section, many important aspects of the multimedia industry are shaped less by national or regional differences than by factors that affect the whole sector and are not bound to any geographical area. From the perspective of theories of industrial governance, this is a very interesting finding. There has been a long-standing debate (see, for example, Hollingsworth and Streeck 1994) about whether the organization of an industry depends chiefly on the national economic and institutional framework (and therefore varies between different countries and regions) or on properties of the respective sector (and is therefore similar irrespective of the country or region). Our analysis gives some support for the latter hypothesis and can thus be seen as confirming the theoretical position (perhaps best elaborated in Kitschelt 1991) that sectoral, basically technological, properties are crucial in sector organization. This holds true for two dimensions of sector organization at least: division of labour and intra-sectoral cooperation. Whether it is also true for other dimensions, such as the organized representation of sectoral interests or the linkages between the political system and the industry, cannot be elaborated here but would merit further research.

Consequences of diversity and uniformity for the development of regional economies

Diversity and uniformity are closely intertwined in the development of mul-timedia production around the world. From the viewpoint of policy makers, perhaps the most crucial consequence is that they must concentrate on tun-ing their policy to the particular conditions of their region. The diversity of regional sectoral strengths offers a variety of options for the further develop-ment of multimedia production. The task for policy makers is to identify these strengths, to increase awareness of them and to adapt their strategies very carefully to them. Attempts at equalizing inter-regional differences and at pursuing the same strategy in every region, however, will probably not be successful as, among other things, Sternberg's chapter on Japan indicates.

The viability of regional strategies hinges on the complementarity between multimedia elements that are globally standardized and culturally-coined aspects that are more specific to a particular region. The world's most successful multimedia clusters are characterized by their simultaneous strength in both sub-sectors. Those clusters include the headquarters of global multimedia players as well as a vivid scene of small, specialized mul-timedia producers, both sub-sectors cross-fertilizing each other.

For many regions, it will be difficult or even impossible to build up this double strength, if only because there are self-reinforcing trends in the leading clusters which permanently reproduce their comparative advantage. In Ireland a policy attracting global players was also, to some extent, successful in stimulating the sector of local, specialized producers, but this is a very special case. The combination of favourable factors in Ireland (attractive conditions for foreign direct investment, the availability of qualified, English-speaking staff, the country's strategic advantage as an entry point into the European market, and so on) cannot be easily reproduced in other places.

Although this double strength is difficult to achieve, we assume that the long-term sustainability and growth of multimedia industries will depend on the close interplay between a dynamic sub-sector of locally-oriented, specialized companies and a sub-sector of export-oriented companies able to cater for global markets. Given the strategic significance of multimedia, the question whether regions will be successful in holding their own in multimedia production is also crucial with regard to their further economic development in general.

Notes

1 Various research has shown that, due to knowledge spill-overs, agglomerated regions in highly developed countries are better 'breeding places' for innovation than rural areas (see e.g. Feldman 1994). Considering this locational bias of multimedia production towards *urban* places, it becomes apparent that the popular metaphor of the 'global *village*' (MacLuhan and Powers 1989) is misleading with respect to this aspect of the emerging information society.
2 Cornford (1997: 9) cites the example of a company in North East England: 'The firm has 14 full time employees (two have just been taken on); . . . the oldest employee is 45, the next oldest is 35 and almost all others are in their 20s.' In a sample of multimedia firms in Silicon Alley analysed by Heydebrand (this volume), the average age of the CEO is thirty-two.
3 For instance, in the case of Stockholm, 'three quarters of the companies say that they cooperate with other new media companies working on new productions' (Sandberg, this volume).

References

Beck, U. (ed.) (1998) *Perspektiven der Weltgesellschaft,* Frankfurt am Main: Suhrkamp Verlag.

Belzer, V. and Michel, L. P. (1998) *Der Multimedia–Standort Düsseldorf. Arbeitsbericht Nr. 98,* Stuttgart: Akademie für Technikfolgenabschätzung in Baden-Württemberg.

Braczyk, H.-J. and Heidenreich, M. (1998) 'Regional governance structures in a globalized world', in: H. -J. Braczyk, P. Cooke and M. Heidenreich (eds) *Regional Innovation Systems. The Role of Governances in a Globalized World,* London: UCL Press.

Cairncross, F. (1997) *The Death of Distance. How the Communications Revolution will*

Change our Lives, Boston: Harvard Business School Press.

Castells, M. (1996) *The Information Age: Economy, Society and Culture, Volume I, The Rise of the Network Society,* Malden, Mass.: Blackwell.

Cornford, J. (1997): 'The myth of "the" multimedia industry: evidence from the North East of England (and beyond)', draft paper, Newcastle upon Tyne: unpublished.

Dosi, G. (1988) 'Sources, procedures and microeconomic effects of innovation', *Journal of Economic Literature* 26: 1120–71.

Feldman, M. P. (1994) *The Geography of Innovation,* Dordrecht, Boston and London: Kluwer.

Fuchs, G. and Wolf, H.-G. (1997) *Regionale Erneuerung durch Multimedia? Projektbericht und Workshopdokumentation. Arbeitsbericht Nr. 74,* Stuttgart: Akademie für Technikfolgenabschätzung in Baden-Württemberg.

—— (forthcoming) 'The emergence of industrial clusters for multimedia. A comparison of California, Ireland, and Baden-Württemberg', *Current Politics and Economics of Europe.*

Harrison, B. (1994) *Lean and Mean. The Changing Landscape of Corporate Power in the Age of Flexibility,* New York: Basic Books.

Hollingsworth, J. R. and Streeck, W. (1994) 'Countries and sectors: concluding remarks on performance, convergence, and competitiveness', in: J. R. Hollingsworth, P. C. Schmitter, and W. Streeck (eds) *Governing Capitalist Economies. Performance and Control of Economic Sectors*, New York: Oxford University Press.

Kitschelt, H. (1991) 'Industrial governance structures, innovation strategies, and the case of Japan: sectoral or cross-national comparative analysis?' *International Organization* 45: 453–93.

Krugman, P. (1991) *Geography and Trade,* Cambridge, Mass.: MIT Press.

MacLuhan, M. and Powers, B. R. (1989) *The Global Village: Transformations in World Life and Media in the 21st Century*, New York: Oxford University Press.

Matthäi, I. and Schmidt, G. (1998) *Multimedia–Anbieter im Saarland. Arbeitsbericht Nr. 114,* Stuttgart: Akademie für Technikfolgenabschätzung in Baden-Württemberg.

Polanyi, M. (1962) *Personal Knowledge: Towards a Post–Critical Philosophy,* 2nd impr., London: Routledge and Kegan Paul.

Storper, M. (1996) 'Innovation as collective action: conventions, products and technologies', *Industrial and Corporate Change* 5: 761–90.

INDEX

For Product Safety Concerns and Information please contact our EU
representative GPSR@taylorandfrancis.com
Taylor & Francis Verlag GmbH, Kaufingerstraße 24, 80331 München, Germany

www.ingramcontent.com/pod-product-compliance
Ingram Content Group UK Ltd.
Pitfield, Milton Keynes, MK11 3LW, UK
UKHW021836240425
457818UK00006B/210